# The Guru and Disciple Book

**Kripamoya Das**

"Two birds of beautiful plumage, inseparable friends, perch in the same tree. One of them eats the fruit, the other looks on without eating." (*Mundaka Upanishad 3.1.1*)

Readers interested in the subject matter of this book
are invited to correspond with the author at kmdasa@gmail.com.
Or visit https://deshika.wordpress.com/

Published by Deshika Books

Printed in England, UK, by Berforts Information Press

Set in Stempel Garamond LT Std 11pt / 13.2

Kripamoya Das (Michael Harrison) has asserted his right to be identified as the author of this work in accordance with the Copyright, Designs and Patents Act, 1988.

All rights reserved. No part of this publication may be reproduced in any form or by any means without the written permission of the publishers.

A CIP catalogue record for this book is available from the British Library.

ISBN 978-1-910693-41-4

Extracts from the books, writings and lectures of His Divine Grace A.C. Bhaktivedanta Swami Prabhupada courtesy of Bhaktivedanta Book Trust International.

Extracts from The Guru Question, The Perils and Rewards of choosing a Spiritual Teacher by Mariana Caplan PhD by permission of the author.

# *Dedication*

To my parents, John and Doris Harrison, my first gurus;

To the preceptor and guiding light of my life;

His Divine Grace A.C. Bhaktivedanta Swami Prabhupada,

And to all the future gurus of the Vaishnava community.

# Acknowledgements

Many wise, thoughtful and kind people helped me to write this book and bring it to print. May God bless them for their generous contributions and enlightening conversation.

## Learned Vaishnavas

Amara Prabhu Das, Anuttama Das, B.P. Puri Goswami, Badrinarayana Goswami, Bhakticaru Swami, Bhaktimarga Swami, Bhaktividyapurna Swami, Bhaktivikash Swami, Bhaktivijnana Goswami, Bir Krishna Swami, Chandrasekharendra Swami, Gaura Keshava Das, Gopiparanadhana Das, Hrdayananda Das Goswami, Jayadwaita Swami, Jayapataka Swami, Kesidamana Das, Krishna Dharma Das, Krishna Kshetra Swami, Narayani Dasi, Prahladananda Swami, Ravindra Swarupa Das, Rupa Vilasa Das, Shaunaka Rishi Das, Shubhananda Das, Sivarama Swami, Shri Rama Ramanuja Achari, Srutidharma Das, Suhotra Swami, Swami B.G.Narasinga, Swami B.R.Sridhara, Swami B.V. Madhava, Swami Tripurari, Tamala Krishna Goswami, Urmila Dasi, Yadunandana Swami.

## Academics

Dr. Ferdinando Sardella, Dr. Keith Ward, Dr. Kenneth Valpey, Dr. Mans Broo, Dr. M. Narasimhachary, Dr. Mariana Caplan, Dr. Steven Paul Hopkins, Rabbi Dr. Jonathan Sacks.

## Editorial Team

Abishek Singh, Govinda Das, Ganga Devi Dasi, Jahnavi Harrison, Maha Laxmi Dasi, Namamali Harrison, Pranabandhu Das, Prasanatma Das, Radha Govinda Das, Srutidharma Das, Sutapa Das, Yogendra Sahu.

## Encouragement

Guru Carana Padma Dasi, Tony Staveacre, Nick Williams, Seema Ariel.

## Special Thanks

Dr. Sanjiv Agarwal and his team.

# Contents

## Part One: First things first

1. **You are here** – Why our home-made map of life may require updating. .................................................................... 30

2. **Five tales** – Classic tales from the Upanishads suggest that a change of perspective may be necessary before spiritual life can begin. ........................................................................ 38

3. **Understanding the Vedas** – There are two classical ways of gathering knowledge; only one is good enough for spiritual transmission between the guru and the disciple. ............... 46

4. **What are the Vedas?** – A look at the numerous components of a vast library of wisdom. .................................................. 52

5. **The Vedas and other religions** – Ultimate reality is one, perceived differently only due to the consciousness of the seers. .......... 62

6. **Understanding the sources** – The nature, characteristics and roles of the guru and disciple are explained in certain key texts. ........ 75

7. **Commentary and revelation** – Original texts, commentaries, mystical revelation and how to avoid fuzzy thinking ............. 78

8. **Postmodern views** – Postmodernism affects everything– even the guru-disciple relationship. ........................................... 87

9. **The need for a guru** – Why other ways of gaining higher knowledge are incomplete. ................................................ 92

## Part Two: The ancient culture of learning

10. **A is for *Acharya*** – The meaning of the word and the ancient culture of how acharyas lived and taught. ........................ 104

11. **Shiksha, diksha, and sliding definitions** – More meanings of words and how they've gradually changed. ....................... 112

12. **Diksha** – The history of giving mantras or *diksha*; what happens at the *diksha* ceremony; and what has changed over time. ....... 120

13. **Qualities of the guru and the disciple** – A classical description from the *Nyasa Vimsati*, the lifetime experience of the mediaeval Vaishnava saint Vedanta Deshika. ............... 130

14. **What does a guru teach?** – Guru means 'teacher,' but what is he supposed to teach you, and how often? How do you know if he is teaching you correctly? ............... 133

15. **How does a guru teach?** – The guru teaches his disciples the Vedas – but the manner of his teaching is unique. ............ 139

16. **Teaching techniques of the gurus** – Gurus employ a diverse range of time-tested techniques in order to help their disciples on their spiritual journey. ............... 143

17. **The reprehensible delusions of guruship** – Four ways the guru should not think about himself – or his disciple. Wisdom from the ancient sage Pillai Lokacharya. ............... 147

18. **Where can you find a guru?** – Lord Krishna told Arjuna to 'approach' a guru. But where can you find one? Here is what Krishna said years later, as recorded in the eleventh canto of the Srimad Bhagavatam ............... 153

19. **Within you, without you** – How God manifests as the guru, both inside and out. ............... 160

20. **Little ants on a leaping lion** – Who is more important for the disciple – the physically manifest guru or the historical *acharya*? The discussion continues after 900 years. ............... 165

21. **The *parampara* family tree** – How the sweetest fruit is gently carried down through the branches of the tree. ............ 172

22. **A very different diksha** – Misconceptions and movements. How the grandfathers of contemporary Vaishnavism tackled 'mission drift.' ............... 185

# Part Three: Creating and sustaining community

23. **The guru spreads his arms** – His ashrams, *sanghas*, missions and movements ............... 194

24. **Not everybody likes organisations** – Why we don't like 'organised religion,' and prefer small groups to big ones.......... 207

25. **Sustainability through governance** – Why hierarchy and 'due diligence' are essential – even in spiritual movements. .............. 216

26. **Are you church or chapel?** – Religious groups constantly divide and splinter, but by keeping a tradition spiritually dynamic, we can avoid the temptation of separation. ....................................... 226

# Part Four: Shades of saffron

27. **Sannyasa dharma** – Ancient rules for renunciation, or *sannyasa*, and the ten vows a *sannyasi*, a renunciate, must make. ............. 232

28. **Sannyasa - the real and the false** – Real *sannyasa* is internal, and goes beyond the wearing of saffron robes. So why was it important for Srila Bhaktisiddhanta Thakur? ........................... 239

29. **Undercurrents** – The Gaudiya Mission was enormously successful, yet beneath the surface there were already swirling currents. ................................................................................. 246

30. **White skin, orange cloth** – The many challenges in setting up a western *sannyasa* order from 1967 to 1977. ............................. 251

31. **GBC** – Balancing the demands of preaching and governance .. 258

32. **Saffron cardinals** – An order of renunciates as ecclesiastics, and the phenomenon of 'clergy burnout.' .......................................... 264

33. **Reflections and reforms** – Sannyasis who became gurus share their private thoughts. ............................................................. 275

# Part Five: Gurus, scandals and issues

34. **Why become a guru?** – Discussing why, and how, the decision is made to accept disciples. ............................................................. 286

35. **Gurus of the future** – Srila Prabhupada speaks clearly on how he wants his disciples to become gurus after him. ......................... 301

36. **The July 9th letter** – In the 1980s certain members of ISKCON raised this one letter to the level of a religious text. ..................... 301

37. **So what went wrong?** – The turbulent years after the passing of the founder-*acharya* threatened to wrench his movement apart. What mistakes were made? ............................................................ 307

38. **Their father's shoes** – Some of the complications of being a young guru in an even younger spiritual movement. ............................ 319

39. **Diksha lite** – In a bid to attract followers, some gurus offer initiation without training. ............................................................ 326

40. **Diksha and drugs** – In the name of 'compassion,' some gurus try to have disciples without discipline. ............................................ 331

41. **Guru and disciple in therapy** – In which we subject the guru-disciple relationship to an hour on the therapist's couch. ........ 334

42. **When the wise become weak** – It does happen, sadly, so what should be our response? How can it be avoided? ..................... 346

43. **Loyal disciple...or a mouse?** – The guru repeats what he's heard or loses his power. ........................................................................... 353

44. **Leaving a guru** – Can you ever leave? What are the legitimate reasons? ....................................................................................... 357

# Part Six: Becoming a disciple today

45. **Steps towards the big step** – Spiritual life is a journey of a thousand steps. Where is initiation on that journey, and how do we prepare for it? ......................................................................... 368

46. **Are you ready for a guru?** – What should you look for within yourself before initiation? What doubts and myths about the guru have to be dissolved first? ............................................................ 383

47. **Serious to find a guru** – Srila Prabhupada and his own guru write on how to find one. ...................................................................... 393

48. **Testing the guru** – No-one should blindly accept a guru. The candidate is first meant to test the guru. But how is that done, exactly, and for how long? ........................................................... 396

49. **The path to initiation** - How to become initiated in ISKCON today. Stages in the procedure and the support you need to have in place ............................................................................................. 404

**Disciple**
*Old English **discipul**, from Latin **discipulus** pupil, from **discere** to learn, from Proto-Indo-European **dek**, to take, to accept.*

# About this book

*Our Lord and the Twelve Disciples* **was the title of a Victorian print hanging on the wall of my childhood Sunday school in Cornwall.** I can still see it now. In different attentive postures, the twelve are gathered around their Master, whose right hand is held in benediction. They are in awe at his divine words, and their closeness to the Son of God indicates their status not merely as followers, but as The Twelve Disciples. That picture had a lasting effect on me. Throughout my childhood, the word disciple always meant those twelve – and only them.

Fast forward a few years and I was in Africa speaking to a large group of Ethiopians. It was from them that I first heard the term *nefshabbas*, the local term for spiritual teacher or guide. The *nefshabbas* was 'the soul-father' and he guided you on your earthly journey towards God. As a disciple, or *daqa* of such a spiritual helper one would offer reverence and service in exchange for teaching and guidance. Gradually, I learned that every branch of Christianity had versions of this relationship between master and disciple. In Russian Orthodoxy the guide was the *starets* and his disciple the *uchenik*, while in Greece the spiritual elder was the *geron*. In early Ireland he was the *anamchara*, or 'soul friend.' But it didn't end there.

I discovered that every spiritual path, every religion, had such a master-disciple relationship for compassionate and friendly instruction. For the Sufi Muslims the *murshid* or *pir* was the spiritual guide and the *murid* his acolyte; while in China the teacher was the *shifu* and over in Japan he was the *roshi*. European Jews spoke of the *mashpiya* as the learned guide, and the *tzadik* as the saintly master. Discipleship, it seems, is a universal approach to spiritual learning and grace, and knows no geographical or cultural boundaries. The twelve disciples did not have the monopoly on discipleship, after all.

India has embodied the master-disciple relationship in millions of spiritual friendships over thousands of years. Although the ancient Sanskrit language is used to describe it – *guru* and *sishya* – India gives us the archetypal form of that vital connection which is familiar to all religious or spiritual traditions. No other country has had such a full and rich history of spirituality taught by such a time-tested method. The very history of that land is made up of gurus and their disciples and the detailed science of spiritual transmission has been preserved intact.

For the path of yoga, the *guru* and *sishya* relationship was the only way to effect inner transformation. Becoming a disciple was not an easy life, but for someone who wanted to learn both transcendental knowledge and meditation techniques, and to reap the ample rewards of practising both under the guidance of an expert, it was the singular choice to make. It still is today.

But it's a way of life that has all but disappeared. The ancient ways are now challenged by our modern poverty of trust, and of our aversion to holding anyone in high regard. We would much prefer that no-one was our guide for longer than a week, and we hold that asking spiritual questions is much more important than getting spiritual answers. We like to be seen with spiritual figures, but we may not like to follow their path. We'd prefer to have gurus and *lamas* as fashionable friends. Yet the more we demand that the spiritual teacher remains as a mere spiritual friend, or guides us only as long as convenient or comfortable for us, or until we find someone else, the more the age-old tradition weakens. There are still genuine spiritual masters to be found, but their guidance becomes available only to the extent that we agree to become a disciple. That may not always be agreeable, but it will always be beneficial.

# Transformation

So this book is about such traditional spiritual teachers and their students, or gurus and sishyas, and how they work together for each other's mutual benefit. It's also a practical book for those considering following that path themselves. It's about you as a spiritual traveller, and how an external teacher can help your internal transformation, and why it works better that way. These pages explain the long history of the guru in India, how the tradition is now being taken everywhere else, and how that's still a work in progress. This book is about real gurus who can help

## About this book

you, and how to find one - and how to detect a false guru. The chapters also describe how to become a modern-day disciple. They also explain that you may have to give up some things you like if you want to get something better. Disciple implies discipline, after all, and there's talk of rules and principles, early mornings and commitment to spiritual practise, and words like trust, service and surrender. The Guru and Disciple Book is uncomfortable reading at times, and the adjustments required in becoming a disciple may appear daunting, but the rewards are immense and immediate.

I wrote this book after ten years of teaching something called *The Guru and Disciple Course*. Some friends and I wanted to better inform and prepare candidates before they took their vows as disciples, so we came up with a course that was a balanced mixture of theology, history and down-to-earth practicality. We didn't pull any punches, and probably de-mystified some cherished beliefs about the guru along the way. The course proved quite popular and several hundred took it. The students asked searching questions and the conversation was always lively, particularly so because the guru-disciple relationship was already beginning to become so central to their lives.

Yet everyone had their opinions and needed to be heard. My students had done their own research beforehand and came with sincere curiosity tempered by justifiable scepticism. The acceptance of a guru was culturally unfamiliar to most of them, they'd heard rumours of bad gurus, and everyone had a good reason to be cautious. Besides, we don't live in the most favourable times for having a guru, even the notion of taking spiritual advice from another person runs against the grain of contemporary thinking; it's largely regarded as an uninformed choice made by the gullible in a more religious - and therefore more superstitious - part of the world, and time in history.

But people also like the idea of linking up with a perceptive, non-institutional life guide and receiving wise words of direction. On social media many thousands hang on such words of guidance every day. There's also a never-ending fascination with the deeper ideas behind yoga and the other authentic traditions of India. Could those be brought together to form a new, viable guru-disciple culture for today? The people on my course obviously thought so.

Taking the step towards becoming affiliated with one particular spiritual teacher represents a testing time in the life of the candidate. It is a life-changing period. New philosophical ideas conflict with deeply-held personal convictions. There is a need to search out the limits of personal beliefs, cautious scrutiny of the prospective guru, and gradually learning to place faith in his guidance. All these issues deserve as much attention and discussion time as needed.

In my capacity as the speaker on the course, I had to be a good listener – and a good student myself. I read widely and talked to many people with vastly different views. In my own search for answers to lingering questions on the tradition – as much concerning its practical implementation as the theology of it - I came across material that would be helpful for others. Often it was something that my own guru, Srila Prabhupada, had said or written that I'd not come across before. Then there were disciples from other lineages. They highlighted similar questions within their respective traditions and directed me to the writings of historic preceptors in their line, which proved rewarding. I also found several contemporary writers whose experience of the past few decades shed light on the transplant of an eastern cultural pattern to the west. Further writing on pastoral care, chiefly from Christian and Jewish contemporaries, helped to reveal hidden dynamics in the guru-disciple relationship that were not often discussed in our own circles. I wrote short essays based on the material and, when I shared them, readers said they found them helpful. I posted some on my Vaishnava Voice website and readers liked them. So this book is a compilation of that material, plus course notes, relevant essays and answers to frequent questions.

# Perspective

*The Guru & Disciple Book* begins with a questioning of our predominantly self-serving perspective on all things eastern or ancient, and a respectful suggestion that we try to understand the guru-disciple culture as it was, before we try to re-invent it according to our postmodern preferences. The views of reality presented by India's ancient spiritual texts, the Vedas, Upanishads, Puranas and the Agamas, are a perspective radically different from that of the modern intellectual. In their early attempts to understand them, it is quite common for newcomers to the Vedas to bring some preconceptions with them, unwittingly derived from our hyper-individualist culture. Fashionable

## About this book

ideas such as 'neo-atheism,' springing as they have from a justifiable desire to rid the world of religious extremism, can colour our judgement of the Vedic literature. It is easy to be prejudiced and to try to understand classical concepts by processing them through a modern intellectual filter. So there is a need for a gradual orientation and an impartial approach.

What exactly are the Vedas, and why are they different from other sacred books? The term Vedas may be used without knowing the full extent of the literature, their non-sectarian standing or the importance of the Vedic preceptor mentioned within them. So I've included a brief overview of the source of the Vedas, their contents, how they are traditionally taught, and how they are transcendent to what we now call 'religion' yet the fullest expression of it. After that are some chapters on Sanskrit word definitions. Sanskrit is the language of the Vedas and it helps to have a more precise usage of some terms - a conversation on the subject of guru-disciple can become very confusing when words are used incorrectly.

There are then descriptions of the essential characteristics of the guru, his teachings, the qualifications of the disciple, and how to locate a guru. Next, there's a section on what happens when the guru has lots of followers. None of us seem to have anything good to say about 'organised religion,' so what do we call it when the numerous followers of a guru organise themselves? I felt the need to spend some pages discussing the groupings of the guru's followers and the circumstances related to their success or failure.

The last fifty years has revealed that it is not so easy to establish a traditional, spiritual culture in a world that is often pulling in the opposite direction. Gurus and their disciples – in many cases coming from non-Indian backgrounds - have shown that even a brave attempt is sometimes temporarily weakened by philosophical confusion or moral failure. There have been disappointments and spiritual scandals. Is this to be a perennial feature of the contemporary guru-disciple culture or merely a teething stage lasting until it is more established? What needs to change?

The essential feature of the guru-disciple tradition is that the teacher-student links are repeated down through successive decades, with disciples becoming the gurus for the next generation of disciples. This principle of succession – disciplic succession - is another feature that has attracted more than its fair share of heated discussion. The subject was worth more than a few pages. Finding a guru doesn't mean locating a particular species of human being, a charismatic individual with powers of persuasion, public speaking skills or showmanship, or a member of a particular religious order or institution. It means finding an enlightened teacher who is learned, realised, capable and willing to give us mantras and philosophical teaching, and to train, guide and inspire us. But not everyone who knows a mantra is a guru, so how are we meant to scrutinise someone and what are the symptoms to look for? Someone may be a guru for many others, but they may not be our guru – what do we do then?

What about the prospective disciple? What is involved in becoming a disciple, and how does someone know when they're ready? What happens if they change their mind? The text concludes with some step-by-step practical guidance on selecting a guru after a period of testing, some discussion on the various psychological issues that may arise within the relationship, and the stages involved in becoming an initiated disciple.

I've discussed some relevant and important issues in these pages, and I hope that this contributes to a broader perspective and productive discussions in the future. You can read this book in any order, but the chapters are better read in sequence. *The Guru & Disciple Book* was written for the interested newcomer, the experienced practitioner, the aspiring disciple, the guide, the disciple, and the guru. Everyone will find something of interest within these pages.

**Kripamoya Das**

Narasimha Chaturdasi, 2015.

# Foreword

***The Guru & Disciple Book* is dealing with a very important, and to a certain extent controversial, subject matter.** The subject of spiritual guidance is complex and complicated. In the Vedic tradition it is said that *guru-tattva,* or the principle of spiritual guidance, and the nature of the spiritual guide, the *guru*, is inconceivable and cannot be entirely understood from the logical point of view.

This book begins by answering a very important and pertinent question: why do we need a guru at all? The assumption that we need a guide is often questioned by contemporary spiritual seekers who fear losing their independence. Sometimes these doubts become institutionalized, and as a result, we now have religions which reject the spiritual experience of the predecessors and the need of the intermediate link between us and God. Of course, there are a number of serious and legitimate reasons for this, and the most important one is corruption.

Although the culture of *gurus* is well-established in India, and is now firmly here in the West, it has been corrupted by the influence of time, and the misuse of spiritual power is quite rampant. One of the fascinating features of this book is that the author not only gives us a history of the guru institution in the context of the Vedic tradition, but he also touches on other religious traditions, showing similar dynamics at work in them. This educative book deals with different aspects of spiritual guidance including the possible misuse of the *guru* position.

Over the years of my own practice of Krishna-bhakti, or Krishna consciousness, I have realized that even though the practice is externally simple, not requiring much sophistication or excellence of technique, it is extremely difficult internally. On the path there are many hidden pitfalls, and Kripamoya Das warns us about them. His words will hopefully help many seekers to traverse this spiritual path successfully.

Another feature of this book is that it is written on the basis of personal experience. Kripamoya Das is not only a spiritual practitioner himself, but also a very careful and introspective observer who has the ability to learn by other's mistakes. The history of Krishna consciousness in the West certainly provides ample examples of such mistakes in this delicate and sensitive area. The book discusses this subject matter very openly, but at the same time in a very balanced and mature way, strengthening in the reader the conviction of the need for personal spiritual guidance.

*The Guru and Disciple book* comprises forty-nine chapters divided into six parts. In the first part, the author gives a short yet comprehensive overview of the history of the guru tradition. The last chapter of the first part of the book gives a very detailed and logical answer of why accepting a *guru* is a vital necessity for any spiritual seeker.

I personally found the second part of the book particularly fascinating, because it gives an overview of the traditional concepts of the qualities of the guru and disciple, and the traditional warnings of how to avoid the pitfalls on the spiritual path for both of them. The beautiful chapters of this section: *Qualities of the Guru, Qualities of the Disciple* and *The Reprehensible Delusions of Guruship*, give a lot of insight. In this part of the book there is also a beautiful metaphor of a leaping lion, which clearly shows that in other spiritual traditions there is a similar understanding to that which lies at the foundation of ISKCON; that Srila Prabhupada, as the founder-*acharya*, is the main saviour of all the members of the institution. The other gurus, although necessary as living spiritual guides and living examples of spiritual ideals, are remaining as the servants of the founder-*acharya* by helping the disciples to be connected with his teachings and example.

Part three deals with the very relevant subject of the *guru's* community and the phenomenon of the spiritual organisation, and its advantages and perils. This chapter is particularly necessary for people who are by nature somewhat anarchistic and who try to make a sharp distinction between spirituality and religion, implying that membership of a spiritual organisation robs the members of the former and transforms them into the latter.

Part four of the book describes in detail the history of the ancient order of renounced monks, or sannyasis; their *dharma*, and how they became the natural guides for other members of society.

Part five is extremely interesting because in a very tactful, but at the same time open way, it deals with many important issues, many of which are largely unresolved in the circles of the Krishna consciousness movement.

## Foreword

Why do we need a living guru? Is it not enough to have Srila Prabhupada as the guru for all? How do we distinguish the real guru, and what are the psychological problems which may underlie certain unhealthy guru-disciple relationships? It is a very important chapter for everyone who wants very realistic and at the same time deep understanding of the dynamics of the *guru-sishya* relationship. I can only praise the author for an amazing blend of openness, tactfulness and loyalty to spiritual tradition, a tradition that emphasizes the need of the *guru*. He gives a very insightful and thoughtful understanding of the problems of applying this theory in real life.

Finally, the last part of the book gives very practical suggestions for an aspiring disciple. There is a list of meditations and points for introspection to determine one's readiness to accept a guru. One beautiful quote in this section summarises the essence of the book and defines the audience for whom it was written. Srila Prabhupada asks the question: "Does everyone need a guru?" The disciples gathered around him answer him very enthusiastically: "Yes, Srila Prabhupada!" His answer was somewhat unexpected. He said, "No, only those who are really serious to put an end to all material sufferings need a guru. Guru is not a fashion."

In short, this is a very helpful and beautiful book. I wholeheartedly recommend it to any spiritual seeker, to anyone who offers spiritual guidance as a service to others, and especially to those spiritual seekers and guides who are treading the path of Krishna consciousness.

**Bhakti Vijnana Goswami**

Moscow, April, 2015

# *Introduction*

*When I was nine years old I told my mother that I wanted to be a Buddhist monk when I grew up. "...with a shaved head and orange robes." "That's nice," she said, inwardly hoping that in a few months I'd want to be something normal like a policeman, a fireman, or an astronaut.*

**I never did become an astronaut, and neither did I quite make it to Buddhism, although the desire to become a monk remained.** When I was 14, I still had a lingering desire to backpack overland to Tibet. I'd heard that everyone there was a monk, and that you could become one even if you were 14. The monks there all lived a long time, practised martial arts, and attained mystical enlightenment rather quickly. And Tibet had the best views in the world. So I was determined to go.

But by 17 I'd only got as far as Berkshire. It was 1974, and what remained of England's flower people had camped up in Windsor Great Park, audaciously setting up a hippy village in direct view of Windsor Castle. I wasn't so much interested in free love and chemical highs, although I did think they were a necessary part of a young man's education, but I was interested in alternative forms of living where people put philosophy first. And so I arrived there, determined to explore the possibilities for myself.

The Krishna devotees had their own camp where they were staging theatre, handing out free food, and inviting everyone to join in their hypnotic chanting. In a decade when all men wore their hair long, including me, just to see men with shaved heads was quite exotic and somehow challenging. Add to that the smell of incense, the orange robes, and the curious way the devotees spoke – a blend of old-fashioned English interspersed with ancient Sanskrit words - and the total effect was quite other-worldly.

Here were people who, although westerners, had decided to live their lives in a most authentic, traditional eastern way. For me it was by far the most captivating thing going on. I'd already seen the Krishnas at another music festival, and at that time had stood rooted to the spot in the pouring rain while four of them danced ankle-deep in mud. This time I had a fresh opportunity to discuss their life with them. By the middle of the week, when 500 policemen arrived to uproot the happy hippies, I had already been spirited away to the Krishna temple in the nearby Hertfordshire countryside. That was more than 40 years ago.

I became a saffron-robed celibate monk and remained happily so for eight years, travelling the British Isles, wherever there was interest in the Krishna teachings. I lived in a Ford Transit van, normally crammed in with three other monks, woke up in the early morning darkness, meditated deeply before sunrise, surrounded by the sounds and smells of the open countryside, and cooked vegetables picked fresh from the field. We swam in rivers, slept under trees, and sold books about Krishna to interested people. There was no town in England, Wales, Ireland or Scotland, large or small, that we didn't visit at some point. Those years were a never-ending adventure, always driving toward the horizon, and never failing to meet people who told us 'this is just what I'm looking for right now.' We were encouraged by the knowledge that a report of our efforts was being given, every week, to our spiritual master, Srila Prabhupada, who occasionally visited England and personally thanked us.

I was then sent to live in tropical Africa as part of a small mission for two years. I went from a chilly Ford Transit and selling books in Bradford on a wet Tuesday morning to a sun-kissed, white sand beach fringed with coconut palms gently hissing in the jasmine-scented breeze. I ate mangoes and other exotic fruits every day, learned how to cook and perform temple worship, and discovered that the world and the wonders in it were bigger than I had ever imagined. Now I practised my meditation sitting on heavenly beaches or on the shores of the hippopotamus-filled Lake Victoria. Later, I went to India many times, travelling to the mountainous north, the deepest, hottest south, and to the Bengali east and the Gujarati west, visiting countless sacred places and talking with Vaishnavas who lived there.

Things went well and I watched the Hare Krishna movement grow in popularity. It was an exciting time. We published and sold more books, recorded popular music albums, bought buildings, started a restaurant, and opened a school. We even said goodbye to the cold Ford Transits and bought a 'travelling temple,' a converted single-decker bus. A mail-order service kept in touch with thousands of members all over the country, answered their questions and supplied them with everything they needed to be devotees of Krishna in their own homes. The growth did not stop even with the passing away of Srila Prabhupada in 1977. There was a great sense of loss, but we knew he'd given us everything we needed to prosper, and we knew what he wanted us to do. So 1978, 1979, 1980, 1981 all passed by in a blur of successful expansion; many more people became members, and we projected great achievements in the years ahead. We were flying.

# Turbulence

In the spring of 1982 I flew to India with fifteen fellow *brahmachari* monks; our destination was Mayapur, Bengal, where we were going to attend the annual Gaura Purnima festival. We first stopped off in Bombay, where we saw the magnificent ISKCON temple and guest house in the Juhu district. The following morning we loaded up several taxis and asked to be taken to the airport. Once at the international airport, we discovered that our flight to Calcutta was, in fact, leaving from the smaller, domestic airport. It was too late, and we missed our flight. So we decided to take a train - all the way to Calcutta. India is such a vast size, and the train moved at such a moderate pace, stopping in what seemed to be every station along the way, that the journey from the far west of the country to the extreme east took 50 hours. After two entire days and nights on a train, we then had another two-hour train journey from Calcutta to Navadwipa, and then a boat ride across the choppy river Ganges in the dark. Finally, late at night, a little the worse for wear, we arrived by bicycle rickshaw at the gates of the Mayapur temple compound.

After being welcomed, we were ushered upstairs to a large conference room so that some of the movement's leaders could speak to us. This was a little odd considering the time of night, and things seemed a little tense, and for good reason. We were informed that Jayatirtha Das, our spiritual guide and leader in Britain, the brilliant mind who had contributed so much to the movement's fortunes and the guru of many of the devotees there, had just the previous day resigned his position and was now stationed across the river in an ashram in Navadwipa, asking all his disciples to join him. Some had already done so, feeling their loyalty was to their guru and not to the movement; some were in two minds and still weighing up their options; and some dozen more, slightly bewildered, had just arrived by rickshaw.

When it was all over, and, once back in England, we were able to count everyone missing in action, we found that eighty members had chosen to leave. Although some eventually returned, it was at great cost; their faith was now shattered and they felt unable to trust anyone as they had before. Besides the loss of a leader, the loss of faith and the subsequent spiritual weakening of an entire community, those eighty disciples represented hundreds of thousands of hours of outreach activity, philosophical teaching, careful training, and guidance in devotional practise. It was as if the results of five years of our movement's dedicated work had been erased at one swipe.

Only four years later, it was to happen again. This time the devotees did not physically leave, at least immediately, but they drifted away over the next year or two. Cynical and bitter about their experiences, it was almost impossible, as before, for them to trust any figure of spiritual authority. We could all understand and sympathise with their predicament, but it did not help the situation.

In 1977 the natural charisma of Srila Prabhupada had been institutionalised and seamlessly transferred to those we understood to be the next generation of gurus. The spiritual chasm left by Srila Prabhupada's passing away had been filled with persons in whom we invested great expectation. But the absolute power of a spiritually gifted figure cannot be merely legitimised into the *persona* of others by an ecclesiastical body, no matter that the body is composed of faithful and dedicated followers and the leaders concerned are the best of their kind.

The power of the guru in ISKCON persisted for many more years, chiefly because, after Srila Prabhupada, it was the only model of *gurutva* or 'guruship' the devotees knew. Once in the role of guru, and being surrounded by a few dozen disciples, the mistaken notion was that the guru was no longer subject to the governance of the institution. The only occasion when the guru was chastened by organisational authority was when he had already blatantly deviated from orthodox spiritual practise or teaching. And by that time it was far too late.

England was still recovering from the disappointment of two departed leaders in the late 1980s and early 1990s when intrepid devotees began to open small centres in three or four large cities. With great personal effort, and an immense investment of time, new people began to join these small centres. Yet three or four times, after they'd been initiated, those newest members were instructed by their gurus to leave the small centre and move elsewhere. Or they were requested to remain in those cities but to instead raise funds for the guru's own project, normally somewhere else in the world, closer to where he was living. In another instance, one guru, resident in England, chose to divert large sums of money away from local development to several other charitable initiatives overseas. No doubt the recipients of this display of generosity were extremely grateful, but the loss of funds led to strategic weaknesses locally.

The removal of strategic members from our movement's newest and least developed centres, and the commandeering and whimsical disbursement of precious resources, was generally regarded as an unwelcome but legitimate use of the guru's power. The guru, it was argued, was the ultimate authority for the disciple and always acted in the disciple's best interest. The individual devotee was a disciple first, and a member of his local centre second. So the priority was always to accede to the guru's requests, even when that was in conflict with the running of the local branch.

The young disciples didn't lose their faith as a consequence, that is true, and the gurus didn't leave, but it made the movement almost ungovernable and the spirit of the young city pioneers suffered tremendously. They'd given years of their life to teach on behalf of the ISKCON movement and their reward was to see their small operations stripped of manpower, sometimes losing five or six people at a time. The tensions between the local preachers and the gurus – and the effects of those tensions - were to continue, unabated, for another twenty years. The cumulative effect of all this was that what should have been the mighty oak tree of ISKCON England was rendered into a *bonsai* version: perfectly formed and genuinely oak, but much too small to give shelter.

While all this was happening, we learned that our circumstances in England were not unique. Stories reached us of one hundred disciples being removed from several large ISKCON centres in Canada and northern USA, simply on the imperious demands of their guru. Tales continued of guru's abandoning their role, or neglecting their disciples, or in some other way behaving badly. With this challenge to the noble ideals of the movement, it wasn't long before disappointed members began making their feelings heard, and with the birth of the internet every disappointed member could be an international broadcaster.

# Taking a fresh look

This was not supposed to happen. The movement of Chaitanya Mahaprabhu was meant to be the one movement to give spiritual vitality to everyone. Something was not quite right – but we couldn't identify the problem. There were different opinions. Doctrinal differences and succession issues began to arise, provoking small schisms which occasionally led to the formation of splinter groups. Many of my old friends left the movement in dismay. Some of my peers began circulating publications of a conspiratorial nature, insinuating that the movement's leadership had been usurped, and that the theology of *guru-tattva* was entirely wrong. Some of my old friends had already left to find their answers at the feet of other gurus in the Gaudiya line, disciples of Srila Prabhupada's peers. Because of this we were ultimately to lose another 164 members decades later. (Yes, I counted them)

Although I was convinced about the teachings of Srila Prabhupada, and though I remained optimistic about the future of the movement, I thought it was time for me to take a fresh look at things and assess my understanding of the beliefs and the movement generally. I'd been a mere boy of 17 when I first shaved my head, put on saffron robes and banged a drum down Portobello Road; I wanted to be sure that I'd be able to continue to be dedicated in the years ahead. Now I was married with two children. The reasons I joined and the reasons I'd stay would be different.

So at thirty-three I began to retrace my steps. I decided that my subjective analysis of my faith was not quite adequate, so I read books by psychologists, sociologists, religious historians, and critics outside the movement as well as sceptics within. I talked to 'anti-cult' specialists, Catholic priests, Jewish academics, scholars of new religious movements and Hindus of various persuasions. I sat with those devotees who felt bitter about their experiences with ISKCON, the ones who felt they'd been cheated, and the ones who were just confused. I also talked to ex-members of other spiritual movements who'd been through similar experiences and still others that had joined alternative Vaishnava communities and then, perhaps after four years, I'd decided I'd come full-circle.

## Introduction

Full-circle in my mind, that is. Physically I had not moved away from the temple where I was based, and I'd remained committed in all other ways. I'd kept up all my daily *sadhana* practises and continued with my travelling out to teach and encourage others in Krishna consciousness. My journey had been an internal journey. I'd felt the need to re-examine my own motives and compare and contrast my faith community, its organisation and leadership, with similar new religious movements and other old faiths that had weathered their own storms over centuries. I had completed my first circle of introspection, was contented with what I'd discovered and it felt good. Now I could move on. I moved on but with freshly-opened eyes. And over the coming years I kept half an eye always open for helpful perspectives. I was going to need it, for there was to be many more stretches of turbulence.

The worldwide community of Vaishnavas has now grown in numbers and diversity, but ISKCON brings together so many shades of intelligent thinkers that we do make it difficult for each other at times. There are considerable differences of opinion – especially on the nature and identity of the guru, and who is fit to take that role. Our animated conversations on gurus, initiation, disciples and related issues and controversies has never abated in the last thirty years, and all the Sanskrit quotes and counter-quotes, the party political broadcasts in the form of tracts, booklets, magazines and vigorous keyboard-tapping of website comments; the arm-waving and earnest voices, have all generated a great amount of heat.

Certainly the guru-disciple relationship is one of the main elements in our movement's spiritual culture. When it is done correctly, we grow in confidence, inspiration and in numbers. When it is faulty or concocted, not based on the voices of our distant preceptors who lived it, we become despondent, lose hope, and are faced with dwindling membership. So getting it right would seem to be the key to our successful future.

Nevertheless, despite our mistakes, the movement continues to grow in many surprising ways. Several splinter movements and fifty years on, the small following first created by Srila Prabhupada in New York, Los Angeles, Hamburg and London has expanded across the world to become a surprisingly large international phenomenon. It is a remarkable achievement for an increasingly sceptical world, and quite a credit to the innate spirituality revealed by the Vaishnava path that, with around ninety languages, dozens of cultures and ethnic communities, our one religious movement is still as united as it is. It continues to be an embodiment of Srila Prabhupada's grace, wisdom and ingenuity. He gave so much of his life's energy to support and direct its growth, and the legacy of his clear moral and spiritual instructions have preserved it now, guaranteeing its continued presence in the world.

Now the challenge is to learn more about our own tradition, particularly the theology and culture surrounding the guru and disciple relationship, and what kept it sustained for thousands of years. Only by learning lessons from the past – both ancient and recent – can we all play our part in preserving a genuine Vaishnava movement for the future and the gurus and disciples who are yet to come.

# Part One

# First Things First

# 1

# You are here

*After many years of driving all over England, and stubbornly refusing to give up my old paper road maps, I have now surrendered to modernity and there's a satellite navigation device in my car. It's been a revelation. I no longer get lost at night driving down long country roads. Having a guru, it seems to me, is a lot like that.*

**Many years ago, during a period of fund-raising for my local temple, I found myself in the offices of a shipping company, one of many I'd visited that day.** While waiting for the manager to arrive I studied a large and colourful map of the world displayed on the opposite wall. Something about it was wrong, but I couldn't work out what. Then, after one minute, I realised what it was. Instead of the normal projection, with the Americas to the left-hand side and Russia and Asia to the right, this map showed Japan at the direct centre – in the space where the United Kingdom belonged. As I was wondering who would bother to create such an unhelpful map of the world, the manager arrived. Smiling, he introduced himself as Mr. Yamato. I was in a Japanese shipping company and hadn't noticed. It was not the map of the world that was wrong – it was me.

That visit taught me an important lesson: that people see the world according to where they consider to be the most important. Japan was vitally important to that shipping company because it was their home, and the port of Kobe, in southern Japan, was the main dock for their ships. So there it was - right in the middle of the world. In Hereford Cathedral there is another map of the world dating from the 14th century. Jerusalem is right in the middle of this map because the mediaeval mapmakers were Christian monks and the 'Holy Land' was the spiritual centre of Christianity.

## The middle of the world

In 1773, an Englishman named John Harrison produced the first timepiece that would display the accurate time on a rocking ship. Over long sea journeys, it enabled longitude to be correctly calculated and, for the first time, seafarers knew exactly where they were. It saved the lives of many sailors. By 1851 two thirds of shipping around the world was using it. The Royal Observatory in Greenwich, built in 1675, had commissioned John Harrison. Not surprisingly, longitude was calculated from Greenwich, which became the starting point of all future longitude calculation. In 1884 their standard was adopted by other countries as the international norm. Greenwich – at 0 degrees - thus became the middle of the world, and the 'Middle east' and the 'Far East' were named accordingly.

It's not long ago that Britain was a colonial power and Johnny Foreigner had to be introduced to civilised Christian life and subjugated. Trade, territory and theology all went hand-in-hand in those days, with the church and the Gospel following closely in the footsteps of the explorers and the military. All religious practises in Hindustan – which the British termed 'Hinduism' – were subjected to a Christian biblical assessment, and found desperately wanting. Indian temple worship, already well-established centuries before the birth of Christ, was regarded as 'heathen,' and any imagery of the Divinity not resembling Michelangelo's anthropomorphic 'God' was considered the product of a primitive imagination and nothing more.

Only in the past few decades have 'eastern religions' come out of Asia and been investigated by us inquisitive Brits. It took some time for us to set aside our Christian conditioning just long enough to realise that spiritual wisdom cannot be so easily compartmentalised into east and west, and that religions should perhaps not be categorised into those which originated on the European side of Jerusalem (trustworthy) and those from beyond it (suspect). Without even being aware of it, us British had been looking at so-called 'other religions' and judging them pretty much as our forefathers did. We're getting over that gradually, but the Judaeo-Christian bias lingers on in Europe and pervades many aspects of education and the political establishment.

# Not enough English words

There's also a problem in language. Our hybrid tongue of Greek-Latin-Anglo-Saxon-Nordic roots known as English doesn't have all the words needed to adequately convey many of the concepts expressed so precisely in philosophical and theological Sanskrit. So when we try to translate terminology for meditative states of consciousness in English we grasp for non-existent words. And if there's no English word for a concept, it's easy to conclude that the concept itself has no substance. The alternative is to use words from the Christian theological lexicon, or from the vocabulary of the psychologist. But then eastern religion becomes subject to the classification of western intellectual disciplines, further compounding any existing bias.

Take the word *avatar*, for instance. The word actually means 'one who descends,' and refers to the visible descent of God into the world. But clumsily rendered into English without the Vedic theology, the word *avatar* becomes 'incarnation,' a term which is derived from the Latin, meaning 'embodied in flesh.' But that is the very opposite of the actual meaning. The notion of a formless spirit coming into flesh and blood in order to become visible to human beings is a Christian concept based upon an earlier Roman idea. Sanskrit terminology processed through the Latin language and Christian theology has reversed the actual meaning of an important word. This process, repeated hundreds of times with other words, has resulted in a poor comprehension of a great spiritual tradition.

I was raised as a Methodist in a part of England where Methodism is in the majority. Our place of worship was a simple, Victorian whitewashed chapel, and it took me quite some years to understand the precise function of the other religious building in our village: an imposing, grey stone Norman Church dating back to the 12th century. I discovered that Methodism was actually comparatively small in relation to the established Church of England from which it had broken away. It then took me another few years to comprehend that the English Church was not the sum total expression of Christian faith and practise; that there was something called the Catholic Church which was, to my great surprise, composed not of a 'few Italians and Polish people,' as my mother had told me, but of 1.2 billion people all over the world. Some years later, I discovered that there was even something called the Orthodox Church, and that not all Russians were atheist communists. Indeed, there were 300 million in that Church. It then took me until I was 30 to understand that even in India, 52 million people are church-going Christians, and that Christianity has existed there for more than a thousand years. So my life has been a gradual process of peeling off many layers of ignorance and misconception.

## Historical bias

But Eurocentric views of the world and a Judaeo-Christian orientation are not the only factors in shaping our notions of what constitutes an acceptable source of spiritual direction. History, too, plays its part in fashioning our perception. Just as we artificially divide the planet into east and west, we also divide the history of the world into periods based on our modern understanding of the evolving human race and its linear journey through time, with scientific, social and political reformations as our indicators of progress. Since the European Enlightenment, the past is usually portrayed as undeveloped, quaint, primitive, dark and misguided; the present is not perfect, but it's as good as it can possibly be, and since we are just on the verge of astonishing breakthroughs, the future will be even better.

No doubt the Romans, at the height of their immense empire, also thought as we do. They looked back at a primitive past and considered themselves to be at the very cutting edge of human civilisation. But history tells us a different story: their demise was imminent – even as they reached their peak. Civilisations have always thought of themselves as progressive, enlightened and virtuous; and they've been confident of their sustainability into the far future. Yet so many of them have succumbed to forces beyond their control – some external, some internal – and they have disappeared from the world. The names of some of them, such as Egyptian, Greek, Etruscan, Roman, are well known, while even the names of others have faded from general knowledge. Do we really think that the ravages of time will treat any of our contemporary empires with any special affection? Cultural chauvinism can be just as unhelpful as any other variety.

## Scientific sceptics

The rise of scientific reasoning is regarded as one of the great intellectual achievements of the last three hundred years. It is much prized as a social liberator as much as an intellectual one because it helped European civilization break free from the restraints put in place by the church. This separation of religion and science and the accentuation of the hard differences between them is something that did not occur in India. The word *vidya* is a Sanskrit term that can be equally translated as either 'science' or 'religion' since those terms are not regarded as mutually antagonistic. The great mathematician Aryabhatta was as equally enthused by the pure science of arithmetic as he was the science of divinity. Even today in India, largely because of this absence of hard division, one will find many scientists who profess some form of religious faith. They do this without any sense of contradiction.

European education places Science as the king, to which all other strands of knowledge must ultimately be subject. Theology, Philosophy, the Arts and Politics – all of them must present themselves as logically admissible and scientifically verifiable in order to preserve their status. The problem with this is that when we use the expression 'scientific proof,' we refer to evidence that can be verified through empirical means. If something can be examined by the physical senses – or with microscopes and telescopes that extend the senses – and if an experiment can be verified through repetition, this is considered to be scientific. What this actually means is that the process of determining truth is subject not to Science per se, but to the prevailing theories and the physical limitations of the observer. This proves unhelpful in studies of consciousness, a field where the very phenomenon which is to be examined is beyond the range of even the most diligent observer. Not only that, but it is an area where the observer is most at risk of misconstruing the evidence that arises.

So when we approach so-called eastern religion and its spiritual practises, we do so with our natural curiosity overlaid with the spirit of the scientific enquirer. We ask ourselves whether it can be accepted before it has proven itself as scientifically verifiable; and we decline to experiment with it until it has proven itself trustworthy. This methodology is counter-productive. Although the foundational philosophical explanations actually do take us on a journey of inscrutable logic, there comes an intellectual departure point, a point in our intellectual journey beyond which we must depend on pure spiritual experimentation – with ourselves as the laboratory.

Part One | You are here

# Fear of the big idea

The Russian revolution was brought about - at least in part - by the disparity between the luxury life of the Tsar and his poverty-stricken citizens. Communism was seen as the antidote to the inequities of a failing and oppressive system. But years later, Communism itself was to prove no less an oppressive system, a system that once more had to be replaced by a better idea. After the Second World War, there was universal shock at what human beings had done under the influence of Nazism, yet another totalitarian regime. The Declaration of Human Rights was written to ensure that subjugation to dictators and their sweeping idealism would not happen again. But mere decades later, the world reels from many different conflicts in which thousands of innocents die as a result of Islamist extremism.

And I haven't even mentioned the cults, sects, movements, groups and organizations teaching psychological techniques, therapies, and new strains of religious belief. Behind them: a host of spiritual leaders, counsellors, psychoanalysts, lamas, masters and gurus. Many of them are genuine, but many of them are plainly confused, only partially-realised or downright deceptive. It all adds up to a contemporary environment where the average man or woman is very suspicious of anyone claiming to have a big idea that can help us find the truth.

In the early twenty-first century it has resulted in a natural and healthy scepticism towards any meta-narrative that might cloud our judgement, engulf us and take away our right to self-determination. We feel threatened by belief systems and any person for whom such systems are more important than their own unique individuality. Indeed the very idea of the fully empowered individual, free from obligations to any overarching social or political absolutes has become the new Big Idea.

So we prefer being by ourselves and even look down – just a little bit - upon those whose prized individuality has become compromised by others. We pride ourselves as intelligent free-thinkers if we can avoid joining churches, clubs, teams, co-operatives, movements or similar groupings; we even find the obligations of marriage repugnant and families almost impossible, for they involve our individuality being compromised. But triumphant in our individuality and splendid in our loneliness, we then join 'virtual' communities and social networks in order to satisfy our social longings. Fear of joining things and suspicion of relationships and what they might demand has served to make us lonelier, and society more fractured.

All of the above attitudes, misconceptions and reservations contribute to our starting point in examining the path of *bhakti-yoga*. Whether we have justified preconceptions based on personal experiences; scientific or cultural perspectives or plain old suspicions of 'organised religion'; social expectations or political persuasions; they all play a part in our conditioning. The guru-disciple relationship will be seen, not for what it actually is, but through a filter of existing preconceptions. While some of these may actually serve to protect us from being exploited at the hands of bogus gurus, they may also act to prevent us from understanding when we have met a true teacher. Like certain items of excess baggage on an important journey, they need to be jettisoned before we even embark. An awareness of what can be taken on the journey and what must be left behind is required. Only then can we approach the guru in the spirit described in the Bhagavad-gita.

And even when we have approached an authentic guru, examined him and found him acceptable; and much later, after having been initiated by him, the same self-examination must be regularly practised. The guru will help our self-analysis by giving us his own estimation of exactly where we are on the path, but we must always look within to free ourselves from lingering attachments. Without that introspection, we won't be able to take the guru's advice to heart. Such self-examination must be fearless and rigorously honest, and because that is difficult, we may then tend to become evasive.

Fear of taking the next step in spiritual life is common, and often creates doubts which become articulated as arguments against the guru's patient directions. While the firm but gentle voice of a satellite-navigation system will never become forceful or confrontational, the guru is under no such restriction. He will always tell us, and sometimes quite bluntly, "You are here." When we hear from him about our precise location in relation to the destination, but are reluctant to accept his opinion, there follows an internal struggle – should we use our old trusty map that we've been carrying around for so long, or should we trust in his authority?

Setting aside at least some of our old notions, and mustering up a willingness to trust in the guru's direction, will eventually result in spiritual clarity, a breakthrough of conscious realisation, and a renewed commitment to the road ahead.

# 2

# Five tales

*Since my days at the village Sunday school I've loved allegorical tales. I can still remember the parables of Jesus all these years later. When I was a bit older I began to read traditional tales of the East such as stories of the Japanese Zen masters, or the Sufi Tales of Nasruddin Hodja. The stories helped me to understand many ideas that were new to me. They also acclimatised me to the idea of a saintly teacher, or a guru figure. Here's a few tales I still tell.*

## The true value of wood

**Once, a long time ago in India, there was a poor man who lived with his wife in a small cottage deep in a forest.** Every day the man would pick up sticks from the forest floor, make them up into bundles then stack them carefully in a circle. Covering them over with earth he would burn them slowly until the wood had charred black. The result was charcoal – a fuel that was very light to carry but excellent for cooking. He made very little money from this trade but was satisfied with what he had. Not many visitors came into the forest because it was filled with wild animals, so sometimes the man and his wife felt lonely, but the forest was peaceful and they were happy.

One afternoon a stranger arrived at the door of the cottage. He was visibly exhausted and his brow was damp with sweat. "Can you help me please?" he asked the man, "I was out hunting and my horse galloped off - I've been walking for miles and I'm lost." The charcoal-maker immediately gave the stranger a place to rest and some water to drink. His wife set about cooking a meal and the stranger began to feel at home, so much so that he fell asleep and spent the night as the guest of the man and his wife.

Part One | Five tales

The next morning the stranger asked to be escorted to the edge of the forest. It was quite a distance to walk, but the charcoal-maker happily obliged. As the dense forest gave way to a path, the stranger revealed his identity. "What I did not tell you, my friend, is that I am actually the king of this region. I could see that you didn't recognise me, and that all the kind hospitality you offered was from your heart. I am very grateful and I would like to offer you a gift. Please walk another mile with me."

Walking on, they came to a forest from which came a wonderful fragrance. "This is my sandal-wood grove," explained the king, "fifty of the oldest and finest trees – and I want you to have it." The charcoal-maker was astonished that his guest had been the king, and even more surprised that he was being given his own personal wood. He thanked the king profusely and they parted company.

One year later, the king visited the sandalwood grove and discovered, much to his surprise, that all the trees had gone. Not one tree was left standing. Curious, he went deep inside the forest to visit the charcoal-maker. "So I see that you have made good use of the sandal-wood?" he asked the man. "Oh yes," replied the man, "I made all of the fifty trees into charcoal."

"But did you not realise," exclaimed the king, quite aghast, "that just one twig of a single sandal-wood tree can be sold for the price of a hundred bags of charcoal? That the fragrant oil inside the tree is worth much more than the wood that contains it?" "No," replied the man, crestfallen, "I'm a simple charcoal-maker..."

**Moral:** In ordinary consciousness we attribute a greater value to the body than the soul within. Not even knowing the value of the soul, we use our body as fuel and burn through it in seventy years, never capitalising on the sweet fragrance that could have been ours. The guru is the teacher who explains the difference between body and soul; then shows us how to obtain the real value of life.

# The forgetful son

Once upon a time there was a child, a young prince, who went out with his father, the king, on horseback. Returning home through a deep forest, there was a skirmish with some local bandits and the child became separated from his father. He was taken in by some kindly pig farmers who lived in the forest and the child grew up to become a pig farmer himself. He completely forgot who he was and every day thought: "I am a pig farmer." When he was grown he one day happened to meet the king's minister who recognized him. "You are not a pig farmer," he told him, "you are the beloved son of the king." Thereupon, the young man gave up the idea that he was a pig farmer and accepted his royal identity.

This tale is told to illustrate the predicament of the consciousness, which is originally pure but falls into accepting a lower identity because of identification with the physical organism in which it is currently embodied. The prince is the *atma*, or pure spiritual consciousness, and the minister is the guru, who restores his true identity.

In classical Western philosophy there is a simple duality between the self (body and mind) and matter (everything else). In contrast, Yoga philosophy categorizes the mind as belonging to matter. That means that the mind is part of 'everything else' and not part of 'self.' All thoughts, feelings, emotions and memories are matter - as material as a stone. It is subtle rather than gross matter, but matter nonetheless. The self, or pure consciousness, is distinct from matter, but identifies itself with matter.

Yoga philosophy goes even further. It describes several layers and functions of what Western philosophy calls the mind and the mechanics of how they work together to condition the pure self. The Sanskrit word *ahamkara* means 'I-maker' and it limits the range of the self's awareness to fit within, and identify with, the contours of the psycho-physical organism within which it finds itself. When the self is embodied, the ahamkara, or ego, conditions it to individualise itself according to the limits of the organism. When in the body of a spider the self therefore thinks: "I am a spider," and when in the body of a dog thinks: "I am a dog." And when in human form thinks: "I am a human. I am a man, woman, rich, poor, young, old, pretty, ugly." Just as our prince was never at any time a pig farmer, but thought he was, so the self identifies with an organism, a tribe, race or nation due to proximity and repeated interaction.

The faculty of intelligence, or *buddhi*, is another layer and is above the ego or ahamkara. Its function is ascertainment, discrimination; judgement, will, virtue and detachment. When not polluted it allows the self to be peaceful, happy, tranquil, and to properly discriminate. When this stage is reached the person is said to be a *buddha*. This is relatively rare. In most cases the *buddhi* is polluted by the primordial forces of the *gunas*, which create intense desires. These desires push the living being into action, and this is followed by disappointment. In this condition the self is bewildered and cannot come to a sense of how to make progress on the path of spiritual freedom.

**Moral:** The guru proposes a path towards the ultimate state of peace, tranquility and happiness. Sharing his knowledge with the disciple he speaks to remove his forgetfulness, and to reawaken his true identity as the beloved of God.

# The man from Gandhara

Here's a story from the *Chandogya Upanishad*. There was a man from the city of Gandhara (modern day Kandahar, Afghanistan) who was captured by robbers and taken to a remote place in the desert. He awoke to find himself blindfolded, with his hands tightly bound. "Where am I?" he thought, "and how shall I now find my way home?"

"To the south or the north of me there might be wild animals and I may be set upon and killed. To the east and west of me there may be more desert, or deep canyons into which I may fall. How shall I find my way back home?" Thinking in this way he despaired and wept. Then there came to that place a traveller who, filled with compassion at the poor man's plight, and being equipped with a sharp knife, cut the blindfold and freed the man's hands. The traveller then gave him directions, and the man rejoiced and made his way back home, to the beautiful city of Gandhara.

In this story, the blindfolded and bound man is the spirit, temporarily housed in the body; the compassionate traveller is the guru who sets him free; and returning home to Gandhara is the soul finding its way home to the final destination. In ancient wisdom texts, the metaphor of the bound up man is common. Sometimes the robbers who set upon the man are given names, and they are six in number: *Kama* (Lust), *Krodha* (Anger), *Lobha* (Greed), *Moha* (Delusion), *Mada* (Pride), and *Matsarya* (Jealousy). The cumulative effect of these six robbers that the poor man becomes first robbed, then blindfolded, bound-up with ropes, completely lost, and completely anxious of moving in any direction.

In the story, the man is set upon by robbers who surround him and overpower him externally; in real life all six robbers live within us. They also travel with us from life to life. We can't escape them. The guru protects us on our journey home, helping us to arrest the six robbers lurking within and get rid of them once and for all, a task that only we can perform.

**Moral:** The soul has been blindfolded and tied up for a very long time, and the guru's words are like a knife that can cut his disciple's bonds and free him.

# Two birds in a tree

In both the *Mundaka Upanishad* and the *Swetashvatara Upanishad* we find the narration of 'The Two Birds in a Tree.' It is a metaphor for our relationship with God.

It goes like this: There are two golden birds in a fruit tree. The first bird is eating the fruit without looking, and the second bird is looking without eating. He simply witnesses the first bird. They are inseparable companions but the first bird doesn't know this. The first bird is sometimes eating sweet fruit and sometimes bitter fruit, but the second bird is hoping that his friend will turn around and look at him, so that he can take him to a tree that is all sweet.

The first bird is the *atma*, or 'self'. The *atma* is the soul of the body. The other bird is the *Paramatma*, the 'Over self,' or 'Super soul.' The *Paramatma* is the soul of the universe. Just as the individual body has a soul, so the universe has a soul. The individual *atma* is related to the *Paramatma* but doesn't know this, and fails to turn around to see him. Life after life, the *atma* eats the bitter and sweet fruits generated by his karma, always remaining in the same tree of material existence. Sometimes he is happy, sometimes sad, but he can never escape.

Freedom comes when the *atma* stops his incessant activity just long enough to pause for thought; to consider whether there is any alternative to this endless search for happiness. At this time, the *Paramatma* manifests before the physical senses of the *atma* in the form a messenger – another *atma* who is fully awakened to the existence of the *Paramatma*. This messenger is the guru, and he points the way to the *Paramatma* and to freedom. We cannot see *Paramatma*, or experience directly His compassion for us, but when He manifests before our external senses in the form of the messenger, the guru, then we can begin our journey.

**Moral:** Our personal search for God, and God's simultaneous reaching out to us, is the cause of the appearance of the guru in our life. Only when we pause for thought will the guru's presence in our life become a reality.

# Dangerous kite flying

Every year on January 14th comes the Spring Equinox. Known in India as *Makara Sankranti*, it is a holiday that is often accompanied by windy weather. One on occasion, a young prince was on the flat roof of his palace, hoping to take advantage of the strong breeze. In his hands was a brightly-coloured kite made of bamboo and paper. After a few attempts to launch it, the kite lifted into the sky, dipped a few times, then soared and twisted, edging slowly upwards. The young prince smiled with joy, and his gaze held fast to his kite, lifting higher and higher into the sky as he tugged on the string.

The roof of the palace was several floors up, and the prince was not looking around him as he moved, step by step, towards the edge of the roof. Despite being warned never to go up to the roof he had managed to escape the watchful eye of his nanny, and was there all by himself. Down in the street, a man passing by happened to hear the squeals of delight and looked upwards. Alarmed, he saw that the child, although enjoying himself, was only looking upwards to the kite and was about to walk off the edge. Surely he would now fall to his death?

Without thinking whether it was correct for him to raise his voice to a prince, the man shouted out a warning. At that very same moment, the palace nanny came onto the roof, looking towards the young prince, who was still laughing with joy. She was so absorbed in the prince's laughter, she too could not see the imminent danger he was in. Hearing the loud shout from the street, yet not knowing the reason, she called back in response: "Hey you! Who are you to shout at this child? Do you not know that he is a prince? Know your place!"

**Moral:** The young prince is the materialistic enjoyer, looking up to the source of his pleasure yet unaware of the danger; the nanny is the religionist, protective yet interested in preserving the status quo of mundane happiness; and the man in the street is the guru. The guru sees the actual situation and, though he speaks strongly, he does so with the best intention. Both the materialist and the religionist may not thank him, but his message is the best.

* * *

While writing this chapter I thought of another 'tale,' that was even more memorable because it happened to me. Since it conveniently illustrates another important principle of the guru-disciple relationship I hope you won't mind if I include it here.

# To Whom Her Majesty chooses

In 1998 I was invited by Her Majesty's Lord Chancellor to a summer garden party at Buckingham Palace. The Queen, Prince Philip and Prince Charles would all be in attendance. Seeing as it was the kind of invitation that comes only once in a lifetime, I made my arrangements to attend. I was looking forward to meeting the royal family, and even rehearsed what I was going to say when Her Majesty asked me questions. Wearing my traditional Vaishnava garb, complete with *tilak*, I arrived in good time, confidently waved my invitation to the doorman, and was welcomed by the Buckingham Palace staff. Walking in the sunshine across the inner courtyard, I was immediately impressed at the size and sumptuousness of the surroundings. But coming out onto the expansive green lawn skirted by a well-tended garden and large mature trees, I was slightly disappointed to discover that I was not the only one who'd been invited to the tea party that day. There must have been in excess of 1200 others. Not quite the intimate affair I'd somehow expected. Never mind, I was sure that Her Majesty would easily spot me wearing my white *dhoti* and *kurta*.

I mingled for fifteen minutes, chatting to people who, like me, were all long-serving members of organisations that did good for others. On seeing me for the first time, many did a double-take, at first wondering who on earth I was, and puzzled that I wasn't attired in the customary English formal clothing, but then smiling in the knowledge that I'd been invited just like them. Suddenly there was a buzz in the air and all eyes turned to the top of the steps leading down to the lawn. She had arrived. All fell silent and stood just a little taller as the band struck up the national anthem. No-one sang in the presence of the Queen in her home, as per protocol. She stood quietly, dressed in canary yellow, and then moved slowly down the steps, followed at some distance by other members of the family.

She didn't ask me any questions that day. Actually, she didn't even look at me. In fact, I'm not sure if she knew I was there at all. As she moved slowly across the lawn, a number of people were presented to her – around a hundred it seemed – and I later learned that they'd all been especially noteworthy members of voluntary organisations. Some had even been the early founders of national groups, starting their now large organisations on a shoestring; and some had selflessly served the public for over 40 years. So I didn't begrudge them their moment of special recognition. They certainly deserved it. I later learned that they'd all been hand-picked to meet Her Majesty, months in advance of the event. Those who closely serve the Queen create these occasions, as they do the opportunities for deserving people to meet her. Meeting the Queen, it seems, has a lot to do with first meeting those who are closely connected to her.

What has this to do with the guru-disciple relationship? Well, the same principle of meeting an important person in this world also holds true on the spiritual path. The guru is a person who is closely connected with the Divine, who is a person. Due to the strength of his spiritual connection, achieved through austerity, cultivation of knowledge, rigorous and determined practise, and transcendental awakening, he can act as a representative of the Divine. We can be 'introduced' if we first go through him.

**Moral**: The Supreme Source reserves the right to reveal Himself to those He chooses. The guru is someone who has already been 'chosen' And can therefore become our connection to the ultimate Monarch.

# 3

# Understanding the Vedas

*There are many religions in the world today, and each of them has an original founder. The teachings are regarded as a revelation from God and the written or printed form of these teachings are now venerated as holy texts by contemporary followers. These 'revealed texts' are believed to contain ultimate instructions showing the path to self-betterment and final salvation. The Torah and Talmud of the Jews, the Christian Bible, the Parsee Zend Avesta, the Muslim Qur'an, the Buddhist Dhammapada and the Sikh Guru Granth Sahib are some that are revered by millions. In all these cases the authors of the sacred texts, and the date of their composition, can be identified.*

**For those who follow the sacred texts known as the Vedas, there is no single book and no single author.** More than this, the authorship of the Vedas is not attributed to human beings at all. The Vedas are referred to as *anadi* or 'without beginning' and *apaurusheya* or 'not made by men.' How can this be accepted? A book has necessarily to have an author – at least one. So likewise, the Vedas must also have an author. To say that a body of written teachings has 'no beginning' militates against common sense. The scientific mind is compelled to look for a cause and a date for any historical event. Concepts like 'always existent' are taboo for any scientific researchers; they do not permit the application of contemporary disciplines such as mathematics, archaeology or linguistics for their further development or study.

Although it is true that various parts of the Vedas are associated with the names of great sages known as *rishis*, or 'viewers,' they are not acknowledged as 'authors' and there is no claim by them as such. Rather, they are described as mantra-*drashta* or 'mantra-seers,' and not mantra-*karta*, or 'mantra-writers.' The concept is that perception of the Vedas and the illumination they provide the seer, does not depend on the eyes or the ears. The Vedas, it is said, are available within the physical universe but do not originate within it. The universe extends far beyond space and time yet 'space' and 'time' are the two basic devices used by all of us to measure any phenomenon. Without determining the 'when', or the 'from where' or 'from whom' the Vedas do not easily fit within our conceptual grasp.

The soul is a locus of individual consciousness which, under certain conditions, can gain access to the 'sounds' available at a higher level of reality. The method is known as *tapas* or 'austerity,' and *yoga* or 'union,' and involves the nullification of all desire and aversion through sensory restraint, breath control (*pranayama*), a 'turning inwards' (*pratyaksha*) and deep meditation (*dhyana*) over greatly extended periods. Primordial sounds are then 'revealed' to the *rishi* as vibrations within the heart and are subsequently articulated by him as audible sounds. These liberating sounds, in the form of metric chants, bundled together as *suktas* and *mandalas*, are then recited to his disciples along with strict codes of *shiksha*, or pronunciation, for their error-free reproduction through chanting.

If God is the Sun, it is said, then the Vedas are the sunshine, and they eternally co-exist. Thus the Vedas are not created by God but, like Him, exist always. The Vedas thus describe themselves as the breath of God. In the *Brihadaranyaka Upanishad* (2.4.10) it is described that the sounds of the Vedas are *nishvasitam* or 'the breathing of *Ishvara*.' The *Bhagavata-purana* begins by describing the revelation of these sounds to the first created being, Brahma. The transmission is not auditory but within the heart of Brahma after his intense austerity and meditation: *tene brahma hridaye*. It is described as *sputa*, a sudden manifestation of something already existing.

The Vedas are known as *sruti* or 'that which is heard,' and the physical ear is known in Sanskrit as *srotra*. The Vedas were not written down because some sounds do not lend themselves to being accurately reproduced phonetically. They fall in between two syllables and these are consequently best transmitted orally. The sounds of the Vedic mantras are meant to be reproduced accurately using the breath, vocal chords, palette, tongue and lips. Yet just as a slight change in radio tuning will produce another frequency – and a loss of quality of sound - so inaccurate pronunciation of Vedic mantra can result in an opposite outcome. Elaborate methods are therefore used to check the pronunciation and oral transmission of the sounds.

# Preservation

Yet as time passes and diminishes the human capacity to recite from memory, it becomes an urgent need to preserve the Vedas by writing them down in 'the language spoken in the cities of the gods' or *devanagari*. Since the dawn of the universe, the Vedas are transmitted through voice repetition, and only much, much later, around fifty centuries ago, compiled by the *rishi* Srila Vyasadeva into written form, divided, and redistributed to disciples for future preservation. Major portions of the Vedas have thus been preserved, both in written and oral forms, up until the present day.

The Vedas describe two ways in which knowledge – material or spiritual – can be obtained. The first is the 'ascending path' or *aroha-pantha*, and the second, superior 'descending path' or *avaroha-pantha*. The notion that one can obtain knowledge not only by sensory exploration, but by transcending the limits of the senses and receiving the knowledge as it descends from a higher source, naturally flies in the face of the modern scientific method. The claim that accurate knowledge can 'descend,' either through a process of revelation, or by learning at the feet of a realised mystic, is simply unknown.

The Vedas state that knowledge revealed by this 'descending process' is that which is free from limitation. Yet the modern mind seeks to investigate these claims by using the 'ascending process.' And, since it cannot be logically proved that the Vedas are of divine origin using this process it is essential, for the contemporary seeker, to begin the investigations using an element of preliminary trust.

While many in the east accept the axiomatic truth that the Vedas are divine in origin, one cannot accept the Vedas as divine if one doesn't accept that there is any divine at all. But in order to even experiment with the Vedas – and the processes of yoga they describe – it is required to at least hold as a theoretical possibility that transcendental communion and mystic experience may be attained as a result of chanting authentic Vedic mantras.

There are others who, already convinced of the authenticity and efficacy of the Vedas, attempt to convince others, seeking to use the Vedas as philosophical proof of the existence of a divine source. In the process of their attempts, they inevitably introduce the circular logic that there must be a Divine Being because the Vedas, being of divine origin, say that there is. Thus in both investigating the Vedas and in communicating their contents to others, there is need for initial faith and an understanding that there will always be a logical gap without it. The Vedas do not conform to common sense or ordinary reasoning.

Although some may scoff at this demand for prerequisite faith, even before investigation begins, there is much in modern science that is also 'descending.' The number of scientists allowed to work at a particle accelerator buried deep in a mountain is strictly limited. Only a privileged few are allowed access. The rest of us must have faith that their research has produced trustworthy results. Similarly, the number of *rishis* on the tops of Himalayan mountains is somewhat limited, and we also are asked to trust their research.

The *sine qua non* of the Vedas is personal communion with the celestial and experience of the transcendent. Ultimately, the Vedas describe the conclusion of all dharma – to become awakened to the reality of one's spiritual nature and to become united with God. The Vedas do not exist so much as philosophical treatises for intellectual persuasion, but rather as very practical guidebooks for attaining wholeness and transcendence. There is an authority and urgency about the Vedas which make them more demanding than any other source of information. The reader is consequently required to study them with humility first, in order to gain access to them.

But the Vedas have already impressed many scholars over the past few centuries. Whether they were practising humility or not, they found that the 46 letters of the Sanskrit alphabet were a thoroughly logical, and quite brilliant, use of phonetic symbolism. The discovery of Sanskrit by early English and German scholars visiting India in the 1700s led directly to the discipline of linguistics we have today. The investigation of Vedic mathematics has also raised the eyebrows of many a scholar. Our mistakenly named 'Arabic numerals' of 0 – 10 came from the Vedas. 'Pythagoras' Theorem' was discovered independently – and much earlier – by Indian mathematicians. Geometry is contained as part of the *Upaveda* on architecture, and the measurements of periods of time mentioned in the Vedas are famous as being on a par with that of modern astronomy.

In Vedic calculation of time, 1/11 of a second is known as a *lava*; 24 minutes is known as a *danda*; and 48 minutes a *muhurta*. But the periods of time keep going until they reach truly astronomical proportions. The length of the 'four seasons' of universal time are all almost incomprehensively long. The golden age of *Satya Yuga* is 1,728,000 of our years, and the next, *Treta Yuga* is 1,296,000. After this comes Dvapara which lasts for 864,000 years, and then comes the final age, *Kali Yuga*, which endures for 432,000 years. All of these taken together form one cycle of *yugas*, and endures for a grand total of 4,320,000 years. There are 1000 *yuga* cycles in the 'Day of Brahma' and a similar number during 'Brahma's Night.' So for just 24 hours of the creator-god's life, we here on this small blue planet transit through 8,640,000 of our years. Brahma lives for one hundred of his own years and, after that long life, the creation he brings about comes to an end. But there is no need to worry about the end of the world as we know it. The life of Brahma is made up of some 72 million of these *yuga*-cycles - all of 311 trillion, 40 billion years.

The language, mathematics and astronomical conceptions of the Vedas left the early European scholars bewildered. The Indologists were Christians and the Vedas were written by 'Pagans'. It did not make sense. How could such an ancient, primitive culture produce something so sublime and apparently scientific? Unfortunately, the cultural chauvinism of the scholars, and their paymasters, meant that the usefulness of the Vedas had to be downplayed and their origins brought closer to Europe. Using early linguistic palaeontology, the theory of language and how language changes, the scholars produced theories of how the Vedas originated in central Europe. Those theories persisted until very recently.

The age of the Vedas had them puzzled. European history traced the origins of civilization to the Romans and Greeks, and perhaps a little beyond them to the Mesopotamians and Sumerians. Christians held that the world was created in 4000 BC and that anything culturally and religiously significant happened after the time of Moses and during the ministry of Jesus Christ. In India, the people told them that their own civilization was already very old in 4000 BC. But at this time in the history of the world, the spread of Western culture through trade, exploration and the well-funded influence of the Christian missionary groups was already advanced, and the story of world history became a decidedly western one.

Part One | Understanding the Vedas

The Vedas are available for accessing, and the rewards are immense and enduring. But it requires the setting aside of one's cultural and scientific mindset and opening oneself up to new possibilities, in the company of a teacher, to get the best of them.

# 4

# What are the Vedas?

*On October 6th, 1969, in London, Srila Prabhupada gave a lecture about the Vedas. He began as follows: "Ladies and gentlemen, today's subject matter is the teachings of the Vedas. What are the Vedas? The Sanskrit verbal root of Veda can be interpreted variously, but the purport is finally one. Veda means knowledge. Any knowledge you accept is Veda, for the teachings of the Vedas are the original knowledge..."*

**The Vedas are one body of knowledge divided into four, the *Rig*, *Yajur*, *Sama* and *Atharva Veda*.** Each of the four Vedas has several, slightly variant recensions known as *sakhas*. In each of those *sakhas* there are three portions: the *Samhita*, *Brahmana*, and the *Aranyaka*.

The *Rig Veda* contains many Sanskrit hymns of praise directed to many *devas* or gods, in truth many aspects of the one, single divine. What in later ages became known as *slokas*, or metrical verses, were originally known as *rigs*. Each *rig* is a mantra and a number of such *rigs* or mantras make up a poem known as a *sukta*. The *Samhita* portion of the *Rig Veda* contains more than ten thousand rigs (10,170 to be precise) grouped into 1028 poems or *suktas*.

The word *Yajur* is derived from the word Yaj or worship. The word Yajna, meaning sacrificial worship, is also derived from this stem. The *Yajur Veda* spells out the ritualistic procedural details of worship whereby all the rigs of the *Rig Veda* can be employed.

The word *Sama* means to 'make peaceful' and the *Sama Veda* contains music to make the gods peaceful and pleased with the worshipper. In order to attain the grace of the gods who are being propitiated, the priest sings the *rig* mantras to the seven notes of the musical scale rather than the strict upward and downward notes of the *Rig Veda* chanting.

The *Atharva Veda* draws its name from the *rishi* named *Atharva* who revealed it. The mantras in this Veda are for protection.

## Samhita, Brahmana and Aranyaka

*Samhita* means 'that which has been collected and arranged.' A *samhita* brings out the meaning of the particular Veda in the shape of mantras systematically arranged. In addition to the *samhita* portion, each Veda has a part known as a *brahmana* and another section called an *aranyaka*.

The *brahmana* portion lists what rituals are to be performed and exactly how they are to be done. When the mantras contained in a *samhita* are converted into a ritual action called *yajna*, the *brahmanas* serve the purpose of a guidebook or a handy manual explaining how each word should be understood.

The word *aranya* means 'forest' and the *aranyakas* are texts for 'forest dwellers,' those who have renounced sensory pleasures and now live in the tranquil forest of contemplation. These texts are meant to explain the inner meaning, the doctrine or philosophy contained in the *samhita* as mantras, and in the *brahmanas* as *yajnas*. According to the *aranyakas* it is important to understand the reasons why *yajnas* are required to be done, and not merely their actual performance.

## Upanishads

The Upanishads come towards the end of the *aranyakas*. Their main theme is philosophical enquiry and an urgent recommendation to rise above the mental states that keep the soul within the cycle of repeated reincarnation. This message is in contrast to other sections of the Vedas which tend to attract the soul to celestial enjoyments or power and beauty within this world and the next. Because of these two, somewhat contradictory, messages the Vedas are considered to have two portions. The first is the portion dealing with 'actions' or 'ritual' and is known as the *Karma Kanda*. The second portion deals with 'higher knowledge of the self' and is consequently known as the *Jnana Kanda*. These are also referred to, respectively, as the *Purva Mimamsa* and the *Uttara Mimamsa*.

It may appear to be a paradox that the *deva* worship recommended in the beginning of the Vedas is negated by it in the later sections. Certainly it is strange for the western reader who may, rightly, expect to notice consistency within the same holy text. But there is a central commandment running through the Vedas: so long as we wish to enjoy the world we must worship the *devas* and perform karma; and as soon as we understand the temporary nature of material happiness and the transience of our short lifetime we must take to cultivating knowledge of the self, or *jnana*.

The word *upa-ni-shat* means to 'sit by the side' and refers to the student of the Vedas who is called forward to receive higher instruction. In the Upanishads we find that the very same gods who are the objects of obligatory worship in one portion of the Vedas are described as themselves being either students or teachers of a higher knowledge. Indeed, even in the *Vyakaran* section of the Vedas, a dictionary of Sanskrit terminology, the word *devanampriya* or 'beloved of the gods' is synonymous for 'fool.' In the *Taittiriya Upanishad* (2.5) and in the *Brihad Aranyaka Upanishad* (2.3.33) there is a stinging comparison of the bliss attainable by the soul who has become free from material entrapment compared to the soul who enjoys celestial happiness in the heavenly realms. After a progressive analysis – which reads like a multiplication table - we learn that the happiness of a young man in the prime of life here on earth is surpassed by the bliss of the self-realised soul by 100 to the power of 10. But when men learn of the paltry 'bliss' attainable in this world, and they try to practise yoga, they tend to fall out of favour with the gods themselves. The *Brihad-Aranyaka Upanishad* (1.4.10) says that the gods do not like men who try to realise their inner self and often choose to send temptations and distractions their way. Many are the aspirant yogis who have become confounded by the intrigues of the gods.

The Upanishads are so important to the philosophical and theological strength of the Vedic path, that the religion itself was often known as Upanishad Dharma. Although the number of the Upanishads is variously calculated, most schools of the Vedas count at least ten to thirteen as being of great importance. Accordingly, these are studied the most.

The list of the principal Upanishads and where in the Vedas they are found is as follows:

1. **Isha** – in the Sukla Yajur Veda Samhita – 18 verses
2. **Kena** – in the Talavakara Brahmana of the Jaimini Sakha of Sama Veda – 35 verses
3. **Katha** – in the Kathaka Sakha of the Krishna Yajur Veda – 119 verses
4. **Prashna** – Atharva Veda – 65 verses
5. **Mundaka** – Atharva Veda – 65 verses
6. **Mandukya** – Atharva Veda – 12 verses
7. **Taittireya** – 52 verses
8. **Aitareya** – Aitareya Aranyaka – 33 verses
9. **Brihad-Aranyaka** – forms entire Aranyaka of Sukla Yajur Veda Samhita – 438 verses
10. **Chandogya** – Sama Veda – 600 verses
11. **Svetasvatara** – Krishna Yajur Veda – 113 verses
12. **Maitrayaniya** – Krishna Yajur Veda
13. **Kaushitaki** – Rig Veda

Many of the conversations, stories and aphorisms found in the Upanishads have found their way into common language of millions of people around the world. The conversation between Death and Naciketas in the *Katha Upanishad* includes phrases repeated by Krishna as he spoke to Arjuna on the battlefield; while the *Mundaka Upanishad* gives us the classic 'two birds in a tree' image signifying the *atma* and *Paramatma* as well as *satyam eva jayate* or 'Truth Alone Will Prevail,' the motto of modern India. The *Chandogya Upanishad* provides the stories of the legendary honesty of Satyakama who did not know who his father was, and the illuminating conversation between Uddalaka and Svetaketu, a wise father and an inquisitive son; and the teachings to Narada Muni by Sanat Kumar, the son of Brahma. Meanwhile the *Brihad-Aranyaka Upanishad* begins with the prayer spoken by millions: *Lead me from the perishable to the imperishable, from darkness to light, from death to immortality...*

# The Brahma Sutra or Vedanta Sutra

The Sanskrit word *sutra* means a 'summarized code' and in the *Skanda Purana* and *Vayu Purana* the definition is given: 'when a thesis is presented in few words, but with great volumes of meaning and, when understood, is very beautiful.'

*Vedanta* means 'the end of knowledge' and is meant to be the ultimate Vedic text in the matter of exploring the nature or 'perfect being' of *Brahman* (spirit) and its relationship to matter. The *Vedanta Sutra* covers the nature of the infinitesimal, individual being and the infinite being. Since describing the relationship between them must include analysing how the individual living being falls into ignorance and suffers, the nature of forgetfulness and illusion is examined.

The *Vedanta Sutra* was composed by Srila Vyasadeva as an exegesis of all the Upanishads and is compromised of 555 *sutras* divided into 192 *adhikaranas*, or Vedic syllogisms, each of which consist of five parts:

1. *Vishaya* (thesis or statement)
2. *Samshaya* (doubt in the tenability of the statement)
3. *Purvapaksha* (presentation of a view opposing the original statement)
4. *Siddhanta* (determination of the 'final conclusion,' by quotation from Vedic texts)
5. *Sanga*ti (confirmation of the final conclusion by quotation from Vedic texts.

All schools of thought in India have their own commentary on the *Vedanta Sutra* written by the original preceptor of their lineage.

# The Vedangas, Upangas and Upavedas

The *Vedangas* are the various 'limbs' of the Vedas and include texts on pronunciation of the mantras (*Shiksha*) texts on grammar and poetic metre (*Vyakaran* and *Chanda*) as well as a dictionary (*Nirukti*). Since Vedic yajnas or rituals have to be performed in exactly constructed arenas and according to the phases of the moon and stars there are also handbooks for mathematics, astrology and ritual detail (*Jyotish* and *Kalpa*)

The *Upangas* are the 'subsidiary limbs' and consist of texts that support the performance of ritual and the comprehension of their importance and intrinsic philosophical basis. They include *Mimamsa*, the 'deep analysis of a subject worthy of reverence,' *Nyaya*, the system of logical deduction and analysis of evidence; histories or *Puranas*, and the *Dharma Shastras*, codes of living for civilised people.

The *Dharma Shastras* describe household duties, personal work, cleanliness, eating, and ceremonies related to life-cycle events such as weddings and funerals. There are eighteen such texts, known as *smritis*, written by eighteen *rishis* such as Manu, Yajnavalkya and Parasara, and the *smritis* all bear their names.

The *Upavedas* are texts dealing with corollary subjects important for organizing the various features and essential elements of civilized human society. *Ayur Veda* explains an elaborate system of medicine; the *Artha Shastra* describes polity and economics; the *Dhanur Veda* focuses on ethical warfare and the *Gandharva Veda* teaches music.

# The Puranas

It is said that Vedic injunctions are made large by the Puranas, or histories, since within these texts we can learn of how the Vedas have been implemented historically in the lives of humans, gods, sages and kings. By reading of the interplay of Vedic lore in the lives of real people we can be inspired to follow their example, and be warned of the consequences of acting in a manner contrary to Vedic dharma. Also written in the Puranas are descriptions of the compassionate, knowledge-giving actions of the many avatars of Shri Vishnu and the appearance of the Supreme Godhead, Shri Krishna. The Puranas present selected events rather than a strict chronology. There are eighteen Puranas, notionally divided into three sections according to the predominating influence in the mind of the reader. The Puranas for those largely predominated by the influence of *sattvika guna*, or the 'mode of goodness,' for instance, will focus on Vishnu (Narayana), his incarnations and his devotees. Other Puranas may focus on god Shiva or goddess Shakti.

Traditionally, there are five subjects of a Purana:

1. *Sarga* or 'Creation'
2. *Prati-Sarga* or 'Secondary Creation,'
3. *Vamsha* or 'Family Trees,'
4. *Manvantara* or the 'History of the Manus' the creative gods, and finally
5. *Vamsha-anu-charitra*, the details of the dynasties of kings and saints.

The *Bhagavata-purana* or Srimad Bhagavatam contains 18,000 verses, a third of which describe the activities and speeches of Krishna.

# The Itihasas

The Sanskrit word *Itihasa* means 'It happened thus' and the texts are histories, normally written by an author who was contemporary with the events. The *Mahabharata* was written by Srila Vysadeva who witnessed many of the events described therein; and the *Ramayana* was composed by Shri Valmiki who was a contemporary of Shri Ramachandra. The *Itihasas* do not have to follow the structure of the Puranas, but they may also contain elements of the five subjects nonetheless. The *Chandogya Upanishad* (7.1.4) mentions the Puranas and *Itihasas* as the fifth Veda. The *Bhagavata-purana* (1.4.20) also states, "The four divisions of the original sources of knowledge [the Vedas] were made separately. But the historical facts and authentic stories mentioned in the Puranas are called the fifth Veda."Madhvacharya, commenting on the *Vedanta-sutras* (2.1.6), quotes the *Bhavisya Purana*, which states, "The *Rig Veda, Yajur Veda, Sama Veda, Atharva Veda, Mahabharata, Pancharatra*, and the original *Ramayana* are all considered Vedic literature. The Vaishnava supplements, the Puranas, are also Vedic literature."

The Bhagavad-gita is a dialogue contained in the *Shanti-Parva* section of the *Mahabharata*, but the nature of the conversation ranges from Upanishadic verses through to the highest devotional theology. For this reason it is much loved and commonly known as *Gita-Upanishad* or *Gitopanishad*.

Since the times of Adi Shankaracharya in the early mediaeval period, it has been common for all schools of thought to establish their systems of philosophy on three texts, the Upanishads, the *Vedanta Sutra* and the Bhagavad-gita, collectively known as *prasthana-trayi* or the 'three foundations'.

## The Pancharatra Agamas

Additional to the philosophical, historical and theological texts are handbooks specifically focused on the theory and techniques of temple construction, consecration of sacred images, ritual, worship and use of mantras. The literature is very vast and its antiquity is referred to in the *Shanti Parva* section of the *Mahabharata*. The total number of works – generally known as samhitas 'compilations' or tantras - exceeds 200 and, like the Puranas, are divided into those for worshippers of Shiva, Shakti and Vishnu. The Vaishnava *Agamas* include the *Ahirbudhnya Samhita*, the *Lakshmi Tantra* and the *Narada Pancharatra*.

The Vaishnava texts detail the identity of Vishnu as being the *Paratattva* or 'highest reality,' identical with the supreme *Brahman* of the Upanishads. The *Paratattva* is the substratum and support of the universe. He is beyond the *gunas*, or 'binding ropes' of the material energy, but is fully conscious of all that happens within them. He is omniscient, omnipotent, and both immanent and transcendent. Although He is too subtle for the senses to apprehend, He agrees to become accessible to those who dedicate themselves to Him. Whereas the mystic yogi holds the supreme *Brahman* in his consciousness by strenuous personal effort, the dedicated devotee of Vishnu is the recipient of divine grace, which effortlessly draws his consciousness to Him.

The *Pancharatra* texts are also distinctive in that they explain the five features of the *Paratattva*:

1. *Para* – 'The Highest' – Vishnu in his ultimate form in the spiritual sky, or Vaikuntha.
2. *Vyuha* – 'The Emanations' – Projections of Vishnu as four forms: Vasudeva, Sankarshan, Aniruddha and Pradyumna.
3. *Vibhava* – 'The Incarnations' – Vishnu's avataras as the Dwarf-Boy, Man-Lion etc.

4. *Antaryami* – 'The Indweller' - Vishnu as the *Paramatma*, the Lord in the Heart.

5. *Archa* – 'The Sacred Image' – The Deity in the temple or the home.

Also found within the *Pancharatra* texts, specifically the *Lakshmi Tantra*, are the 'Six Aspects of Surrender.' Since the focus of *bhakti* is the cultivation of a relationship of loving service to the Supreme, these are known and remembered by all Vaishnavas and form part of their theology and practise.

1. *Anukulya-niscaya* – Acting in ways that are favourable to the service of Vishnu.

2. *Pratikulya-vivarjana* – Refraining from acts that are opposed to his service.

3. *Raksisyate vishvas* – Having great faith in his protection.

4. *Goptrtve-varanam* – Selecting him as one's sole maintainer.

5. *Atma-nikshepa* – Placing oneself completely in his care.

6. *Karpanya* – Humility.

# Revelations

The Vedas co-exist eternally with the Supreme Person but that does not mean that He remains distant and does not speak to the surrendered souls. Through the speeches of many avatars; through the Deities in the temples; through the heart; and through visions and dreams, the revelations continue to come. What is important is that when divine revelations are made, they are usually in conformity with what has been spoken before. There would be no meaning to the eternal and unchanging message of the Vedas if they changed each time. The changes that are evident are the adjustments to the recommended processes of dharma as the universal cycle of ages slowly move forward. *Satya Yuga* is followed by *Treta*, *Dvapara* and finally *Kali Yuga*.

Each age is progressively different and the appropriate methods of self-realisation are highlighted at the relevant times. Thus mystic meditation gives way to fire sacrifices, temple worship, and eventually the chanting of the names of God as the prime method of spiritual awakening, although all four practises remain relevant throughout the entire cycle.

Accordingly, what is revered as a principal holy text – although it will certainly be within the Vedic canon – revolves as the cycle of ages revolves. The principal text will also be selected according to the consciousness of the worshipper. For some, the satisfaction of the *devas* will be their prime concern, and they will revere the appropriate portion of the Vedas. For others, only the logical analysis of the Upanishads and *Vedanta Sutra* will satisfy their hankering for liberation. For the Vaishnavas however, the *Prasthana Trayi*, the *Pancharatra Agamas*, and the *sattvik* Puranas will be most revered.

For some Vaishnavas the devotional outpourings and mystic utterances of the early saints known as the Alwars form a collection of 4,000 verses known as the *Nalayira Divya Prabandham*. These are held in great reverence and sung and recited daily. The commentaries on *Vedanta Sutra* by great mediaeval Vaishnava acharyas such as Madhva and Ramanuja are given ultimate respect and understood by followers to be on the level of holy scripture.

Shri Chaitanya Mahaprabhu is revered as an incarnation of Radha-Krishna and the writings of his followers who took his dictations are honoured as the words of an *avatar*. Thus the words of the Goswamis of Vrindavan such as Rupa, Sanatana and Jiva are equally held to be 'revelation.'

# The guru

A guru is one who teaches the Vedas. He teaches either a particular recension of one portion of the Vedas or he teaches the Upanishads or he teaches from a Purana. A guru may only teach ethical warfare or botany or mathematics or medicine. But he teaches the Vedas, and he understands them and follows them. Guru is a Sanskrit word that comes from the Vedas; it is a word which belongs to the Vedas, and the Vedas state repeatedly that they are to be taught by a guru. A guru must not deviate from the Vedas and must be able to support his particular teaching by quoting the relevant chapter and verse. Hence there can be no such person as a guru who manufactures his own technique; and there can be no portion of the Vedas that can be fully understood without a guru.

# 5

# The Vedas and 'other religions'

*My life changed a few years ago when I had a life-threatening illness. On my regular trips to hospital for tests, surgery, post-surgical treatment and further check-ups, I was able to witness a complex system of medical care based on the individual needs of the patient. Sitting in waiting rooms on numerous occasions, I found myself thinking about how the Vedas themselves address the spiritual health needs of each and every human being. So while I was sitting there, I picked up my notebook and wrote about it.*

**A doctor writes a prescription based on the individual symptoms presented by the patient.** The prescription is given to alleviate pain or disease, to prevent infection and to bring the patient back to a state of balanced health. Similarly, the Vedas give many prescriptions for spiritual health based on the condition of the soul. According to the Upanishads, the soul is covered by layers of matter and gradually evolves by transferring its focus of pleasure-seeking from a lower *kosha* or 'sheath' to a higher one. From trying to enjoy the physical senses the soul moves upwards to enjoying happiness from the intellectual platform and then the transcendent. This is accompanied by an incremental elevation from self-serving actions to those where happiness is gained by service to others. The progression culminates in various forms of union with the ultimate reality, or *Brahman*. There are many sections of the Vedas and, according to the stage of spiritual development of the individual; many different prescriptions can be correspondingly given.

One who is interested in material enjoyment in the present life and in the life hereafter is encouraged to attain communion with celestials who can provide such things. The first principle, of course, is that such a person should be made aware of the factual presence of *devas* and what they can do for him; and the second principle is to do something to please them. Someone who, on the other hand, is relatively materially exhausted and

Part One | The Vedas and 'other religions'

seeks release or *moksha* from the cycle of birth and death will be advised accordingly. And the Vedas seem to contain a pathway for everyone, with all paths leading upwards.

Every pure spiritual soul is covered by layers of material energy that is composed of the three *gunas* or 'modes'- *sattva* (goodness) *raja* (passion) and *tama* (ignorance). According to the accumulated reactions from all previous lifetimes, the soul will be subjected to a combined influence of these three *gunas*, and will think and act accordingly. Levels of perception and subsequent modes of behaviour, including socialised religious tendencies, also spring from this unique conditioning.

Perhaps an extended analogy will help here. The original consciousness of the soul is like crystal-clear water. On contact with the material world it becomes 'coloured' by the three modes of nature: goodness, passion and ignorance. For the sake of our analogy, let's consider the primary colours, yellow, red and blue, to be the colours of that pure water when touched by the modes. The yellow water is goodness, red is passion, and blue is ignorance. The material bodies are like empty bottles made of clear glass.

Now let us begin pouring the coloured waters into the bottles. When the coloured water is poured into them they change colour. The glass assumes a certain colour – and the coloured water assumes a certain shape. The water is the consciousness – now coloured, and the bottle is the container of that consciousness. Although the water remains water, the colouring will now cause anything viewed through it to assume the same colour. All objects viewed through the red water will appear to be red.

Rather like the bottles in an old fashioned chemist's window, our glass bottles are now filled with the coloured water. Some are of just one colour and others of mixtures. Three bottles are filled with just one colour each, red, yellow and blue. Another is filled with a mixture of blue and red, making a purple bottle. Yet another bottle is filled with half blue and half yellow, making a green bottle. The last bottle has a good mixture of red and yellow, making a bright orange bottle. I hope you're getting a colourful image in your mind.

The Vedas say that those three primary colours – the three *gunas* - are first combined with each other in nine ways, producing that many different ways in which the pure consciousness is 'coloured.' In our example, that would be like having nine identical bottles, each containing a different colour of water. As each combination of *gunas* / coloured waters produces different tendencies, so the soul conditioned in a particular way will have different conceptions of life and therefore different ways of expressing his highest aspirations. This leads to as many different 'religions' as there are combinations.

# Do all paths lead to the truth?

The Vedas urge a moral and ethical life, understanding one's place in the universe, becoming free from bad deeds and increasing one's good deeds, cultivating morality and virtue, understanding one's relationship with gods and goddesses, ancestors and great sages, acting accordingly, developing detachment from temporary pleasure, escaping from the cycle of repeated birth and death, and attaining ultimate union with Godhead.

Since there are so many paths included within the scope of Vedic recommendation, it would seem to suggest that the Vedas support the 'all paths lead to the truth' conception. Although this is a popular idea, and even though the Vedas are sometimes invoked to substantiate this notion, it is quite incorrect. It would be wrong to assume that whatever spiritual path one adopts, conceives or manufactures somehow fits within the many recommendations of the Vedas.

For instance, there are some paths almost entirely dedicated to fulfilment of the basic animal urges such as eating, sex and increase of wealth. There are some paths in which the highest aspiration is to obtain a birth in a heavenly realm. Other paths allow the individual the freedom and power to attain varieties of preliminary mystical experiences. Still others provide for temporary emancipation from birth and death. Logic demands that all paths cannot be the same if the ends of those paths are different. Then there are religious paths where the guidance is drawn partially from the Vedas and partially from human inventiveness. Although the resulting forms of religious practise may be sincerely conceived and executed with respect for the divine, the successive generations of followers, free from exclusive dependence on Vedic authority, drift further and further from the source texts. They can then unwittingly fall prey to influences of the heavier modes of material nature and develop darker aspects of behaviour.

Religions in which the sacred principles of austerity, purity, mercy and truth are challenged, contravened or totally absent,; in which there is a lack of compassion or charity; in which knowledge of rebirth is absent or denied; and in which there is a preponderance of greed, material attachment, lust and violence – are all regarded as occupying a place that can be described as sub-Vedic.

The Bhagavad-gita is quite analytical in its examination of different types of religious activity. The analysis is founded entirely on three elements: the *gunas*, or 'colours,' otherwise translated as 'ropes.' The entirety of material nature consists of the modes – goodness, passion and ignorance – and when the eternal living entity comes in contact with the modes it becomes conditioned by them. The influence of each of the three modes vacillates in proportion to the others, one becoming predominant, then another, at different periods and times. All activity, whether mental or physical, is influenced by the increasing and decreasing *gunas*, and when a religious element is introduced to the activity the spiritual conceptions or religious actions will be proportionately influenced.

In the Bhagavad-gita, Krishna begins his explanation of the *gunas* by describing their indomitable and pervasive power and influence on all that we think and do.

> *"Material nature consists of the three modes--goodness, passion and ignorance. When the living entity comes in contact with nature, he becomes conditioned by these modes."* - (Bhagavad-gita 14.5)

According to the modes, he says, there are 'three kinds of knowledge, action and performer of action.' When there is an increase in the mode of goodness, he explains, all the senses are illuminated, and the individual has a strong tendency to engage in pure, pious actions. Knowledge develops as does a feeling of happiness. The individual predominantly affected by *sattva guna* has an inner sense of morality and easily understands what is right and wrong. Such a person finds determination in spiritual practise relatively easy. This person controls the mind and senses, and is therefore able to do things which are of great spiritual benefit, even though they may feel like 'poison' in the beginning. Such a person would be easily identified by their being peaceful, controlled, tolerant and honest – sometimes in challenging circumstances. The *sattva guna* person experiences increasing happiness, becomes free from the karmic reactions to previous bad deeds, and grows in knowledge of higher truth. At the end of life, the heavens await, and the soul attains the higher planets of the great sages. In exceptional circumstances, often after 'many births and deaths,' such an individual, dominated by the *sattva guna*, comes to the conclusion that there is more to existence and gravitates to other paths of spiritual emancipation, concluding in *bhakti-yoga*.

# Short-term

In contrast, the person predominantly influenced by *raja guna*, or the passion-inducing element of material nature, is conditioned to making intense endeavour for short-term benefits, accompanied by almost uncontrollable desires, always hankering for things but never satisfied when achieving them. Such a soul, explains Krishna, cannot distinguish between true and false religion, and doesn't understand what to do and what not. He or she is determined in religion, but only to the short-term benefits that religion may provide. Their sense of happiness in life is entirely focused around owning, controlling and enjoying things or people, and they tend to want to experience pleasure almost immediately, not comprehending the inviolable law of the world that disappointment will surely follow.

They can be quite determined, even heroic or courageous, and sometimes very generous, but it's usually all about them, their family, community or tribe, and their determination is much more self-centred than that of the person in *sattva guna*. Because of their unlimited desires and longings, they do things whereby they become easily bound up in the karmic reactions of the material energy. The results of their frustrated attempts at enjoyment are just more greed, and ultimately misery. After this short life they take their re-birth on Earth among people who are even busier for ordinary enjoyment. However, even those situated in *raja guna* are slightly better off than those affected strongly by *tama guna*.

The *tama guna* person's ability to actually experience the reality of the world around them is shut down, and they often can't see or understand things as others can. Whereas the person in *raja guna* has unlimited desires and strivings for enjoyment and tends to see opportunities, those in the mode of ignorance often suffer from lack of desire or ambition. They are more inclined to accept their environment and be led by others rather than make changes or grand plans. They become prone to feelings of hopelessness, depression and inertia. They tend towards poor mental health and become confused at what to do in life. When it comes to religion they often consider real religion to be something bad, and they're easily fooled by religious leaders who are, in fact, cheating them into immoral actions. They can also work hard, just like the person in passion, but they strive always in the wrong direction and many of their plans fail as a result. They become most happy when they are escaping from the harsh reality of life either by being lazy or under the influence of various kinds of entertainments or intoxication. If they're not extremely careful, as they move through life they become prone to making foolish mistakes and the end of their life comes with troubles such as panic attacks, depression or dementia. Since the soul may move down, as well as up, the hierarchy of physical bodies, the soul influenced strongly by *tama guna* may slip down into a non-human body in the next life.

It is not only individuals that think and behave according to the modes of nature. When individuals choose to think and work together in any kind of grouping, their choice of friends and colleagues, religious leaders and fellow believers, and the manner in which they subsequently work together, is also dominated by the modes of nature they have in common. Consequently families, communities, religions and even entire countries, also exhibit the symptoms of mixtures of *gunas*, thinking and acting in ways that ensure a collective outcome for their group.

In the field of religion it can be seen how the *gunas* occlude purely spiritual conceptions by mundane considerations; how immoral or thoughtless behaviour is often considered to be good; how violence and cruelty is justified in the name of God; and imaginative theologies lure innocent people away from genuine, life-enhancing spirituality. Krishna explains what we know and how we behave as we do things for the benefit or our eternal soul:

> *"That knowledge by which one undivided spiritual nature is seen in all living entities, though they are divided into innumerable forms, you should understand to be in the mode of goodness. That by which one sees that in every different body there is a different type of living entity you should understand to be in the mode of passion; and that by which one is attached to one kind of work as all in all, without knowledge of the truth, and which is very meagre, is knowledge in darkness."* - (Bhagavad-gita 18.20 -22)

# Anthropocentric

One symptom of the illuminated person is that he can see the same spiritual soul present in a man, an elephant, a dog, a bird or a tree. But a person situated strongly in *raja guna* sees only the external bodies and classifies them differently. Because of this, many religious people hold the anthropocentric view that everything on Earth is for their service, that animals have no souls, and that the function of animals is simply to provide food for humans. Krishna teaches that it is a mistake to consider that the soul in the body of an animal is actually an 'animal soul' and that of a human body is a 'human soul.' But the nature of passion is that it precludes a person from seeing the reality. Consequently humans governed by *raja guna* view one animal as 'meat' and another as 'pet' and direct their emotions and subsequent actions accordingly.

This selective vision also occurs when so-called religious people consider a different soul to be present in those of different religions, imagining that there is one group of souls that is more pure than others, or closer to God simply by their choice of sacred text or chosen messenger of God. Because those in *raja guna* become very attached to their clan and country, the land related to their sacred text or messenger becomes 'holy' and therefore superior by dint of its apparent physical connection. The reality, of course, is that the entire planet Earth is 'the holy land'. Because of their external viewpoint, members of these religions also tend to be very attached to human power structures, and will often misunderstand affiliation to the community of practitioners to be on an equal level to affiliation to their sacred text and its teachings.

Religions affected by *raja guna* tend towards the sole idea of promotion to a heavenly world where the followers will enjoy eternally. They will consider that they have an exclusive preserve on this heavenly future, and imagine, quite wrongly, that it belongs to them and no others. They therefore regard themselves as exclusive or specially privileged, having been given a superior revelation from God, and they scorn others as either being in ignorance of this revelation, or in rebellion against it. They will then adjust their language towards others to reflect their belief in their own superiority. In this way, they project their territorial or tribal conceptions onto the eternal and transcendent, a state which is beyond such human sectarianism, and they then project their resulting prejudices onto others.

Part One | The Vedas and 'other religions'

Those religious practitioners in the lower modes of nature tend to be concerned with asking God for his divine grace merely to enjoy the happiness of eating well, having a productive life and enjoying peace, free from enemies. It is not that the Vedas do not provide for this also – they do - but ultimately the same Vedas explain that there is more. Any religious system that does not also provide directions towards mystical experiences for those qualified to have them, is a system in which certain aspects of Vedic knowledge have disappeared, and a religion that has become somewhat stuck. And where there is a complete absence of spiritual knowledge, that entire system is stuck in *tama guna*.

Those religious paths that advocate (and actually practise) regulation, sense control, attempts to become free from selfish desires and egotism, determination in the face of difficulty, internal and social morality, and tolerance, compassion and charity towards others – that religion is mostly in *sattva guna*. On the other hand, those religions that try to use the power of God for becoming materially rich or powerful; which encourage the followers to make great efforts to work hard and enjoy one life only, ultimately steering them towards greediness and envy; and where the members are intensely moved by alternating joy and sorrow – those are in *raja guna*.

Religion in the mode of ignorance is characterised by almost complete disregard of Vedic scriptural injunctions, even when those injunctions are known; is performed with scant regard for future karmic bondage; and is often done in ways that give distress or actual violence to others. Members of that religion will have lives that fly in the face of the Vedas, and will tend to be obstinate about changing anything they do. They will have a tendency to procrastinate, even after being given good advice, and they will be expert at insulting the members of other religions. The followers of such a religion will often be misguided by their leaders, who may invoke fear of God in them, rather than stimulating their love for God and a sense of universal fellowship. The followers may concoct religious systems that involve the worship of disembodied entities or imaginary beings, or they may engage in *vama-marga* or 'black magic,' invoking the power of evil spirits to be directed against their enemies.

# A time before 'World Religions'

Bhagavad-gita therefore provides a useful system of classification, and we may use this to analyse types of spirituality and human religious endeavour even today. The fact that some of the symptoms described seem to resemble character traits visible in contemporary religions is, of course, coincidental. The Gita is a dialogue from 3000 BC, a time before most of the 'world religions' had even begun. When Krishna, in his final summing up, encourages Arjuna to 'abandon all varieties of religion' he is not asking his friend to repudiate his lingering affection for the Torah, the New Testament or the Qur'an, for they were all more than a thousand years hence. He wanted him to abandon all dharma in *raja* and *tama guna*, and all in *sattva guna* except the highest, selfless devotion to God, *bhakti-yoga*.

It cannot be said, therefore, that the Vedas condemn any other religion. The Vedas, like God himself, are entirely non-sectarian. But they do require all human beings to become free from the grip of the three modes of nature. That may, understandably, take some time. But however long it takes, there is a graduated plan of incremental emancipation, and a corresponding prescription.

Because the Bhagavad-gita is *Upanishadic* in nature, we find within it a condemnation of worship of the *devas*, the half-gods who fulfil human desires if humans worship them. Krishna is quite categorical about this. After describing, quite early on, the process of *yajna* (sacrifice), and how it is the plan for humans since the creation of the world, he later describes that those who only worship the gods are those 'whose intelligence has been stolen.' Krishna describes them as *avipascitah* or 'men of small knowledge,' and explains that their problem is that they are too attached to *pushpitam vacam* 'the flowery words of the Vedas.' He further states that it is he himself, Krishna, as the indwelling *Paramatma*, who makes the living being's faith in the gods strong. Even more, it is he who actually bestows the benefits upon the living being, the gods being mere agents.

## The best religion

According to Krishna, the best religion is that way of life which gives one complete and lasting happiness, a sense of complete freedom, and allows one to re-establish one's dormant relationship with God. Immediately this transcendental state is achieved, one is peaceful and happy in all circumstances and one 'can enjoy nectar, even in this life.'

# Part One | The Vedas and 'other religions'

This fortunate person still experiences the ups and downs of life when the results of previous *karmas* are delivered through the agency of the three *gunas*, but he doesn't hanker for the ups of life, and doesn't hate the downs. Rather, he is unwavering and undisturbed, always remaining neutral whatever his fortune might be. He looks upon a stone or a lump of pure gold as being identical, and regards so-called 'happiness' and 'unhappiness' as being the same. If someone praises him or blames him, he receives it the same, and likewise honour and dishonour, and the attentions of 'friends' and 'enemies.' If he engages in *bhakti-yoga*, the union of all activity in service to the Supreme, he transcends the modes of nature, Krishna says, 'and comes to the level of *Brahman*.'

> *"One whose happiness is within, who is active and rejoices within, and whose aim is inward is actually the perfect mystic. He is liberated in the Supreme (brahma-bhuta) and ultimately he attains the Supreme (brahma-nirvana) - (Bhagavad-gita 5.24)*

It may be reasonably argued that any religious path today in which there is an increase of *sattva guna*, moral behaviour, the cessation of bad karma or 'sin', the glorification of God and the revelation of genuine divine knowledge – a knowledge that conforms to the Vedas – is 'Vedic' in a sense. For instance, one might encounter a moral, self-realised Christian, Muslim or Jew who lives utterly in *sattva guna*. On the other hand, one might encounter an immoral ritualist who pays lip-service to the Vedas but lives almost entirely in *tama guna*. Both are possibilities, and it is often seen that saints appear outside the purview of Vedic culture, and that those who apparently know the Vedas follow them the least.

Transcendence is not limited – it is by definition transcendental to geographical, ethnic and doctrinal boundaries. Transcendentalists can be found in any form of authentic, *sattvic* religion. Yet without the other attributes necessary for Vedic knowledge to be preserved – the Vedic texts, the guidance of a guru and the *sangha*, and the spiritually enlivened fellowship, the transcendent experiences, although genuine, may be short-lived and unrepeatable. With no language for explaining the experiences and no system of teaching it, the knowledge contained in that individual's revelation may be left untaught, or severely compromised by the *raja guna* followers, so much that it all but disappears in one or two generations.

Many are the saints, of every religious and cultural origin, who lived completely blameless lives, steeped in some level of love of God. But equally common is the saint who found it almost impossible to articulate how he or she actually got to be a saint. Why should this be? The Vedas explain that 'saintliness' is something that is carried over from life to life. After several lifetimes of piety, a person is born who naturally, almost unconsciously, gravitates towards purity, austerity, devotion to the divine, and so on. Their internal illumination is manifested externally, and they attract followers who wish to be like them. But the saints cannot explain exactly how they arrived at such a level of consciousness because, of course, it pre-dates their current life time. In their present lifetime they may have had no scriptural education at all; as a consequence they may struggle to put their mystical experiences into words for their followers - as profound and real as those experiences are.

The consequence of this is that the self-realised saint is often survived by a community of people who loved the saint but, due to their poor education in the science of *brahma-nirvana*, can neither articulate his teachings adequately nor practise the saintly life themselves. Although the community continues to expand as the generations pass, because most followers tend to operate in *raja* and *tama guna*, the followers gravitate toward one or other of the saint's teachings, and then fight each other about what he really had to say.

# The Vedas and Hinduism

The word Hindu is not mentioned anywhere in the Vedas. It is a relatively recent term introduced by invading armies when they wanted to describe the peoples of the lands beyond the Indus River. By extension, those lands became known as *Hindustan*. It remained for the British to add the suffix 'ism' to finally create the term *Hinduism*. That all the hundreds of religions of the Vedic tradition could ever be grouped together under one imprecise, and ultimately geographical term, was always going to create problems. But after a thousand years the term has become part of the common parlance of the people of India, and is a convenient handle for academics, politicians and writers of books on world religions.

Still, despite the emotional and intellectual investment in it, the word factually means nothing. Meaning has certainly been invested in it, and a billion people have their own understanding of it, but the actual word

## Part One | The Vedas and 'other religions'

Hinduism indicates nothing more than 'the religions of India.' What that word actually does – by confining the Veda to India – is to reduce the stature of the original divine knowledge to being the mere human product of one tract of land. And that is not correct. Neither is it a knowledge that can, ultimately, be fully embraced by the world. People are genuinely looking for a spirituality that is beyond all 'isms,' something beyond human ingenuity and geographical boundaries; a spirituality that is truly universal.

The image of Hinduism, and what that term means to the world, has been reconstructed over several centuries by Indians themselves as various accommodations were made to Islamic thought, the European enlightenment or Christian theological ideas. Sometimes the intellectuals of India, educated at the best British schools in Calcutta and Delhi, and consequently those most affected by their colonial masters, were keen to reject their indigenous traditions, particularly those not in keeping with more modern ideas. Attempts at harmonising distinct and conflicting cultures often gave rise to hybrid religions. Sikhism was born in the west of the country as an attempted compromise between Hinduism and Islam. The Arya Samaj and Brahma Samaj movements, with their wholesale rejection of temple worship, were fashioned as a response to the perceived intellectual superiority of British Christianity.

The followers of the Vedas are not 'Hindus' and there is no such religion as 'Hinduism' promulgated by the Vedas. Only by their making a radical and ongoing separation of the Vedas from historic human inventiveness will those who refer to themselves as Hindus have a chance of re-discovering the original wisdom and enjoying its benefits.

All religions that have existed in the past, that exist now, and that will be created in the future are in actuality a combination of the modes of material nature as they affect the soul's highest aspiration. Whatever the language and nomenclature used to describe them; whatever the literature, rituals and ceremonies employed, and whatever the stated goals – all can be estimated and categorized according to the simple system described in the Bhagavad-gita. Whatever the religious system, its ultimate worth can be analysed according to the degree it tallies with the Vedas. And, since all souls are ultimately on a long and convoluted journey of spiritual evolution, the 'best religion' described in Vedic texts is the restoration of the soul to complete awareness of the original and supreme person, Shri Krishna. As Lord Krishna comes in every age to restore the forgotten

Vedas, he states quite directly that he is both the knower of the Vedas and the goal of the Vedas, and that to the degree the souls choose to exchange their earthly or heavenly prospects for their eternal destiny, he will reveal himself to them:

> "I am the father of this universe, the mother, the support and the grandsire. I am the object of knowledge, the purifier and the syllable Om. I am also the Rig, the Sama and the Yajur Vedas. I am the goal, the sustainer, the master, the witness, the abode, the refuge, and the most dear friend. I am the creation and the annihilation, the basis of everything, the resting place and the eternal seed. By all the Vedas, I am to be known. Indeed, I am the compiler of Vedanta, and I am the knower of the Vedas."

> "Whenever and wherever there is a decline in religious practice, O descendant of Bharata, and a predominant rise of irreligion — at that time I descend myself. To deliver the pious and to annihilate the miscreants, as well as to re-establish the principles of religion, I myself appear millennium after millennium."

> "One who knows the transcendental nature of my appearance and activities does not, upon leaving the body, take his birth again in this material world, but attains my eternal abode, O Arjuna. Being freed from attachment, fear and anger, being fully absorbed in me and taking refuge in me, many, many persons in the past became purified by knowledge of me - and thus they all attained transcendental love for me."

> "All of them - as they surrender unto me - I reward accordingly. Everyone follows my path in all respects, O son of Pritha. One can understand me only by devotional service. And when one is in full consciousness of me by such devotion, he can enter into the kingdom of God. Abandon all varieties of religion, and just surrender unto me."

*(Bhagavad-gita 9.17 - 18, 15.15, 4.7 - 11 and 18.55 and 18.66)*

# 6

# Understanding the sources

*The subject of guru and disciple is well presented in the Vedic literature, and has been thoroughly discussed and lived for centuries. Confined for most of history to one subcontinent, it has now travelled the world. Over the past fifty years, newcomers to the tradition have been learning what is, and what is not 'Vedic' and they have been trying to implement the guru and disciple culture in contemporary life – with mixed results. Looking at the source texts that explain the details of the guru-disciple tradition may help us, but we should also be aware of events in history that have served to cloud the way we interpret the texts themselves.*

**The guru is the source of all education in the Vedic tradition.**
He teaches the ceremonials and sacrifices of the four Vedas and the professional skills of the *Upa Vedas*, the philosophy of the Upanishads and *Vedanta Sutra*; the temple worship and ritual of the *Pancharatra*, and the theology and narratives of the Puranas. He gives mantras to his students and educates them in their pronunciation and the disciplines supportive of their recitation. The guru teaches the moral principles of the Dharma *shastra*s, and is himself a living personification of what he teaches.

So intrinsically linked are the guru and the Vedas that it is impossible to have one without the other. The authentic guru is always speaking the Vedas, and the Vedas are always declaring the importance of the guru. What this means is that the guru is mentioned throughout the entirety of Vedic literature and as a result there are many relevant texts that can be used as source material. The great sages Agastya, Gautama, Manu and the Yogendras have all spoken about the guru, and the characteristics of guru and disciple and their respective duties are also detailed in various Upanishads. Lord Shiva speaks about the guru in the *Agama* literature, and the guru is described throughout the Puranas. Krishna Himself speaks about the necessity for a guru and the qualities of guru and disciple in both the Bhagavad-gita and the 11th canto of the *Bhagavata-purana*. So the challenge is not locating material but in deciding what are the essential texts.

Fortunately, five hundred years ago, Shri Chaitanya Mahaprabhu requested Sanatana Goswami to take up the task and the result was a book known as the *Hari Bhakti Vilasa*. Shri Chaitanya asked his disciple to write a manual of Vaishnava behaviour and the handbook contains twenty substantial chapters. He told him:

> *"In the beginning, describe how one must take shelter of a bona fide spiritual master. Your book should describe the characteristics of the bona fide guru and the bona fide disciple. Then, before accepting a spiritual master, one can be assured of the spiritual master's position. Similarly, the spiritual master can also be assured of the disciple's position." (Chaitanya Charitamrita, Madhya 24.324 - 345)*

The first two chapters of the *Hari Bhakti Vilasa* thus describe the necessity for a guru, the qualities of a guru and disciple and their respective duties, and the process of initiation. The book incorporates quotations from more than two hundred previous works, both from *sruti* and *smriti* sources and many of these would have been well known to all the other schools of philosophy of the day. At the time of writing, in 1534, the Gaudiya school, or *sampradaya*, had only just begun, so the book was designed to have a wide readership, pertinent to all the other Vaishnava communities of the day, while at the same time establishing the pre-eminent position of Shri Krishna. The book was the first major work dealing with the subject of Vaishnava behaviour, ritual and worship produced by the followers of Chaitanya Mahaprabhu.

Other works dealing with the subject of guru-disciple, such as the *Bhakti Rasamrita Sindhu* by Srila Rupa Goswami (completed in 1542), the *Sat Sandarbha* by Srila Jiva Goswami (written before 1608) and the *Chaitanya Charitamrita* by Srila Krishnadas Kaviraja Goswami (completed in 1616), were all yet to come. The *Hari Bhakti Vilasa* thus became the first inter-school collection of authoritative texts on the qualities and characteristics of a guru and disciple. Later on, the specific theological conclusions concerning the guru, written about by the Goswamis of Vrindavan, became incorporated into successive works, refining the understanding of the guru's role for the following generations of Chaitanya Vaishnavas.

Part One | Understanding the sources

The source material for understanding the guru-disciple relationship must be approached carefully, being aware of when it was compiled and the situation of the times. For instance, reference is made by some authorities to social considerations within the strict Varna-ashram society which still existed in mediaeval India. In the Mantra-Muktavali it is mentioned that the authentic guru 'adheres to duties compliant with his occupational and social status,' or that the guru will be one born in a brahmana (scholar-priest) family. It is also stipulated that should the guru be of a kshatriya (warrior-administrator) family, he must never initiate a disciple who was born in a brahmana family.

Whilst these social differentiations are important, they are much less relevant now, and it would certainly be difficult to implement them in a largely democratic society. The other consideration is that Vaishnavism, in general, tends not to focus on the family or social background of a person, but rather the intrinsic qualities the person has developed as a result of their devotion to Vishnu. Therefore 'even one born in the family of people who cook and eat dogs' can become a guru if he is a pure devotee of the Supreme.

Other physical disqualifications are also listed, warning the prospective disciple not to consider someone as a possible guru if they have 'too little hair, or too much hair, or if they have blackened teeth.' Yet these forms of edict are cancelled by the higher injunction that the disciple should not consider the appearance of the guru if he excels in other good characteristics. Just as the Ganges River sometimes contains sticks, foam and mud but always remains pure, so the guru's physical appearance should not be considered if he has superlative spiritual qualities.

There are ritualistic considerations also. The disciple is commanded to 'live with the guru for one year,' but this has proved almost impossible now for all but the young and single with some months of their life to spare. In the case of women and a prospective guru who is a sannyasi monk, it is forbidden. Yet the spirit of the edict remains, and it is important to try to fulfil it in current times. All of this makes it essential to read the Vedas with the guidance of an accomplished scholar, and who better than the historical acaryas, who leave their guiding words in the form of their explanatory commentaries on the Vedas. And how we understand their commentaries is the subject of the next chapter.

# 7

# Commentary and revelation

*Vedic tradition holds for written commentary on an existing text in order to bring out its meaning. The original Vedic text, together with the commentary, will then appear on the palm-leaf page together. The commentary, in order to be accepted as unadulterated and free from personal speculation, must be in conformity with the original text. It may elucidate the meaning but may never obscure it.*

**The original Vedic texts are known as *shastra* and many portions require further elucidation in order to be completely understood.** This is done in the form of commentaries known as *bhasyas*. Successive writers who wish to render the subject more intelligible for a different audience may write a commentary on the *bhasya* known as a *tika*. The *tika* may then be commented upon using further quotations gathered from different places, with stories and metaphors, and this new literature is then known as a *tipani*. But in all cases the original literature remains the same and is fully respected by successive commentators. There is no question of altering the Vedic literature to make it more appealing, or to compose a fresh 'Veda' for modern times. But through skilful use of commentary the Vedas may be freshly presented for new students. In this way the Vedas remain the constant, unchanging revelation from the Supreme, the pole star around which all commentaries must revolve.

There is also room for revelatory accounts by those who have received the grace of God. Since the Supreme can, and does, reveal Himself to His devotees – and says as much in the Upanishads and Puranas – it is quite permissible for a saintly person to write of his or her mystical revelations. These may have occurred in a dream or in a daytime vision. They may be personally dictated during a personally witnessed visitation from a divine messenger, or heard from an invisible voice. Or they may simply be theological truths revealed after a period of intense scholarship and meditation. Whatever the origin of these super-sensory occurrences of divine knowledge and awakening, they remain secondary in nature and must conform in their basic content, if not their details, to the original Vedas.

The divine songs and poetry of the saints collectively known as the Alwars, for instance, were outpourings of divine love. Some poems were overheard by a follower while the saint was in deep meditation, while others were dictated or composed after a period of devotional ecstasy. The collection of four thousand poems, known as the *Nalayira Divya Prabandham*, is regarded as 'the Tamil Veda' by the faithful followers of the Alwars, but it is understood by them that these revelations must be strictly in concert with the Vedas. The argument may even be offered that because these poems were uttered in a vernacular tongue, the southern Indian Tamil language, and because many more people would then understand them, the grace of God is much more present in a common language. Many people, it might be argued, do not speak Sanskrit, and if God speaks to them in a manner more suitable for their understanding - is this not even more 'Veda?' Because of this argument, some sects of Vaishnavas hold that when God, in His infinite compassion, reveals Himself through the mouth of a saint, in the local language, it is even more important than the Vedas and should be accorded even more respect. "That may be so," say others, "but let us not forget the Lord's original and ultimate instructions that are found within the Vedic texts descending down to us from Srila Vyasadeva and the other sages."

In balance, the revelations of the Alwars were indeed all in keeping with the original Vedas, but sometimes those who gave greater prominence to the Vedas felt they had to reiterate their importance in order that revelation not be seen as a substitute for the Vedas. If it was, they reasoned, the Vedas would be easily forgotten and could even be lost, all in the name of 'more merciful' revelations. In Bengal and Uttar Pradesh, during the early 18th century, the debate of the relative merits of Vedic Sanskrit and the vernacular language of Bengali became strongly polarised, even resulting in a call for certain religious literature written in Bengali to be banned. The saint Vishvanatha Chakravarti Thakur had composed his handbooks for divine contemplation in the common Bengali language so that the followers of Chaitanya Mahaprabhu from those regions would be strongly situated in their devotional practise. There was sharp criticism and even some physical threats from highly irritated pedants but the saint escaped harm.

The same arguments – about which language God could reveal Himself in – also took place in Europe, and Protestants welcomed the relatively new idea that one could learn about God from the Holy Bible translated into English. Sometime later, over to the extreme south-east of Europe, the dictation of the Qu'ran decreed that God indeed spoke to the world in Arabic. God, of course, speaks all languages, chief of which is the language of the heart. The inner revelation of 'the Lord in the Heart' or *Antaryami*, is described throughout the Vedas. But because we may still not be able to distinguish, sometimes, between genuine revelation and the drifting of the mind, the one fixed point must be the Vedas.

# Absolute and relative truth

As Shri Chaitanya Mahaprabhu is understood to be an appearance of Lord Krishna, the Supreme Godhead appearing as His own *bhakta*, so the immediate associates of Chaitanya are also held to be descents of liberated souls, coming from the eternal, spiritual world down into this temporary world. The tradition of ascribing a divine counterpart identity to one's great saints had already been practised by Vaishnavas in historical communities, who identified the south Indian Alwars as being incarnations of Lord Narayana's various weapons and attributes. Even Vedanta Deshika, a later southern teacher, had been identified with 'the bell of Vishnu.' In keeping their divine identities, their speeches, songs and transcribed discussions as well as their written theological compositions were all equated with Vedic revelation.

However, from the mid-1500s it became so important for the guru to have an 'eternal identity' that it became customary for him to be ascribed one by his followers. Either that or he would 'reveal' his inner identity at a later stage. For those Chaitanya Vaishnava gurus who actually had such an identity that was all well and good, but as the centuries progressed there came many imposters who claimed an identity they had no hope in substantiating - yet there were always those who would believe them and follow their every word.

There is a pertinent latter-day story in this regard from the Victorian era. The story concerns a guru known as Bishakishena, who made the audacious claim that he was none other than Mahavishnu, and that his two associates were Brahma and Shiva. Bishakishena was a yogi with considerable power. He could make sparks appear in his long, matted hair, and could lean into a fire without being burned. Using this display and his powerful voice he had managed to convince the nearby king of Puri that his claim had sufficient validity for the king to supply him with a bevy of young women. In the dead of night the guru unashamedly performed circle dancing with the girls, followed by other immoral acts.

While the local British government took this as yet another manifestation of heathen debauchery so typical of the 'god-men of the Hindoos,' and simply tolerated it, they balked some weeks later when Bishakishena began publishing seditious pamphlets challenging Queen Victoria's right to rule India. This was a step too far for the British, and they ordered their local deputy magistrate, one Kedaranatha Datta, to put a stop to the yogi's new career as an *agent provocateur*. The story concludes with the arrest, trial, detention and ultimate demise of Bishakishena – but he was only one of thousands of such persons in India at that time. How had the position of the guru been so radically degenerated?

# Historical waves

The course of any culture almost never runs smoothly, and there are many ecological, financial, theological and political reasons why something as delicate as the guru-disciple tradition may waver with the passage of time. For thousands of years the guru-disciple tradition was well understood and practised throughout India and even beyond. The general principles of the guru-disciple relationship, founded as they were on Vedic texts, were held in common by all theological communities. Yet there were historical waves that would serve to force incremental changes in the details of the tradition, even while the essence was carefully preserved.

The birth of Buddhism and Jainism took place in around the same period of history, six centuries BC. They helped to bring about changes in the physical location of the guru, bringing him from the secluded forest into the built up towns and cities. Both the Buddhists and the Jains were heterodox, meaning they took their followers away from the Vedas as the prime authority, and both had a powerful yet temporary influence on popular religious thinking and the guru-disciple tradition. Their focus on ascetic life and the de-emphasis of the Vedas brought about a new type of renounced guru, the monk or sannyasi, who had neither wife nor fire sacrifice, and who spoke only the teachings of Buddha or Mahavira.

During the ascendancy of those two religions, the popular image of the guru was either the saffron-wearing Buddhist monastic or the semi-nude Jain holy man, both of whom did not teach the Vedas. This trend of the ascetic guru was to be ultimately exemplified by Adi Shankara Acharya in the ninth century, a monumental figure who brought a fresh perspective of the Vedas, thereby giving the Vedic tradition a new life, albeit with his own philosophical slant.

Later, the patronage of wealthy Vaishnava kings and the spiritual leadership of great teachers in southern India helped to develop important towns as centres of Vishnu. Along with the outstanding scholarship and dedication of figures such as Shri Ramanuja Acharya and, a hundred years later, Shri Madhva Acharya , there came a resurgence of Vaishnava architecture, art, music and literature. It meant that Vaishnavism flourished once again. However, the delicate relationship between the *brahmana* intellectuals and royalty was sorely tested, and particularly so during the era of the Persian conquerors. For many years the Vaishnava temples were destroyed and Islamic houses of worship built using the stones. *Brahmanas* were subjected to political repression under *sharia* law and the guru-disciple relationship was even financially penalized.

Then, after many centuries, the Muslim grip on India began to diminish. Absolute monarchy in over five hundred independent kingdoms began to weaken, and in some places there was no proper government for many decades. While the absence of a bad overlord can spell religious freedom, the lack of any social control at all can often spell religious chaos. Without any interference from political masters the Vaishnava religion was free to prosper, but it was also free to grow unchecked – sometimes in immoral and bizarre forms. Hundreds of years of repression had the effect of creating new types of thinking, novel theologies not found in the scriptures. So new 'scriptures' were written to justify new religions. It was a time of experiment and syncretism.

By the middle of the reign of Empress Victoria, while the British were enjoying the late afternoon tea of their two hundred year-long colonial day, the Vaishnavism of northern India was distinctly confused, messy and immoral. New religious cults and hundreds of self-styled 'gurus' and magic men covered the land, and great damage was being done to the spiritual aspirations of many thousands of innocent followers.

Part One | Commentary and revelation

In this period there was a great need to delineate, sometimes forcefully, what was a genuine guru and what was simply a charlatan or madman. The local deputy magistrate of Puri, Kedaranatha Datta, was also known as Srila Bhaktivinode Thakur, and he and his son Bhaktisiddhanta Saraswati gave many speeches and wrote works in which they attempted to restore the Vaishnava teachings of the Six Goswamis of Vrindavan to their original state. Sometimes they had to write books and pamphlets that were highly polemical and condemning in nature.

They saw gurus whose purity and neutrality had been compromised by their encumbered householder disciples, and so they wrote about it. They saw the weaknesses inherent in 'hereditary guruship,' – where the father chooses his son to succeed him in the post of guru – whether the son was eligible or not - and they wrote about that. The sanctity of the guru-disciple relationship had been polluted by greedy gurus exploiting their hereditary disciples. They wrote about it. The giving of a mantra for a monetary fee without a shred of personal instruction in the philosophy had reduced Vaishnavism to a mundane religion of sentimental baptisms, so they wrote about it. The highest theology of Radha and Krishna had been hijacked by lewd individuals and their immoral, sexualised teachings and practises – so they wrote about that, too.

# Standards

Added to this state of affairs was an appalling drop in the standards of even the more orthodox lines of Gaudiya Vaishnavism. In the holiest place of the Vaishnavas, the Lake of Radha in Vrindavan, Radha Kunda, the gurus had previously requested their students to daily recite a minimum of sixty-four 'rounds' of the Hare Krishna mantra on their wooden meditation beads, a feat which took some eight hours per day. After a statutory period of twenty-one years of this intense practise, their disciples would then be given additional esoteric teachings and practises. By the early part of the 20th century that standard had all but vanished and disciples were given the same teachings after a comparatively meagre level of spiritual discipline and a few months of effort. This ensured popularity for the guru and an increasing number of followers who would then fund him, but it devastated the tradition.

The depletion of spiritual potency in the *sampradaya* of Chaitanya Mahaprabhu was a disaster that could not be allowed to continue, and both Bhaktivinode Thakur and Bhaktisiddhanta Saraswati - father and son - directly attributed the sad state of affairs to 'gurus who cheat their disciples.' So they put pen to paper in order to highlight the prevalence of concocted teachings, unorthodox practises, and *bhakti-yoga* that was severely compromised by sensual indulgence and other deviations. Their writings echo the polemical arguments of Vaishnavas such as the Madhva sannyasi Vadiraja Tirtha (1480-1600) whose words, it was said, came out of his mouth like a hammer.

In his turn, and not surprisingly, the founder-*acharya* of the worldwide Hare Krishna movement, Srila A. C. Bhaktivedanta Swami Prabhupada, also spoke and wrote strongly about 'bogus gurus,' deceptive disciples, and the 'hodge-podge' that Indian religion had become. Although his American and European disciples knew little of India, Srila Prabhupada was relentless in his condemnation of fraudulent gurus and '*bhogi*-yogis.' Although he was careful to not mention them by name, he nevertheless pointed out the errors of their teaching, and their refusal to teach the original Vedas, and made sure his disciples understood him. He was uncompromising because he wanted to establish his Society, ISKCON, on the firm grounds of a new paradigm.

He wanted to bring the guru-disciple culture back to its original format and make it fit for purpose for a new century and a global implementation. As it turned out, he had only a very short time in which to do it. Considering that he was attempting to transpose an ancient religious culture from its home in India to a modern industrialised world of city dwellers he did remarkably well. To introduce a tradition with qualities of humility, obedience and personal service to a preceptor as its foundation – to people deeply frustrated with organised religion and priestly corruption – was a proposal that would have been naively idealistic had it not been so successful.

At the same time as he was writing about *sahajiyas*, 'nonsense rascals' and other false spiritualists, people he described as misleaders of the innocent public who deserved to be 'kicked on face with boot,' Srila Prabhupada was also describing the superlatively saintly qualities of the pure Vaishnava, the exalted soul who had reached the perfection of devotional surrender to God. Although he knew that his disciples sometimes became confused and acted in ways that ran contrary to the way of the pure devotees, he nonetheless had a high regard for them and was grateful for their help.

## Part One | Commentary and revelation

In the essays and booklets on the subject of guru-disciple written by a minority of contemporary authors in recent years, the predominant claims have been somewhat combative. Some current followers have used the more affectionate quotations from Srila A.C. Bhaktivedanta Swami Prabhupada to establish the bona fides of their respective preceptors. Others have used his more critical writings – and those of the three acharyas before him – to castigate the contemporary gurus as being all 'unauthorised' and even 'completely bogus.'

The present day preceptors of ISKCON and other Gaudiya institutions are, on the whole, doing a remarkable service to the world in conveying the teachings and example of Chaitanya Mahaprabhu to many thousands of people. That in itself is a remarkable achievement given that many of them are converts, not born into the tradition, and that a predominant portion of the world's population has only marginal interest in the efforts required for spiritual life. Some preceptors may have practised *bhakti* for several lifetimes and be naturally gifted or charismatic. Some are exceptionally elevated in their spirituality. But none of their followers should make public claims of their divinity for them; such private thoughts are not intended to become objective declarations. At the same time, some contemporary preceptors fail in their vows and become prone to weakness and temptation. They are sincere practitioners but have become temporarily delayed in their ultimate purpose. Their critics, and they will have many, should refrain from using the invective of the predecessor acharyas to castigate them. Those hammer-like words were written for a completely different type of incorrigible 'guru.'

It is a great temptation on our part to research the Vedas – and the commentaries and revealed insights of the acharyas – in order to selectively extract quotes to substantiate our particular point of view. Those who are quick to use Vaishnava literature to support their own conceptions can easily find passages to suit their respective purposes. But the Vedas and the writings of the Vaishnavas are actually intended for the pure in heart, the humble and compassionate. They are not meant to be used as foundational arguments for pre-existing persuasions born of the emotions. The Vedas are meant to be honoured and respected and through meditation their deeper meanings will be revealed.

In reading the Vedas, Puranas, and other such literature from any era, particularly when we try to discover more about the guru-disciple tradition, we must treat each passage as being equally relevant. Only if we allow God to speak to us will the true benefit of the printed word become manifest. If we listen to the Vedas with our mind and intellect, we may find them telling us exactly what we want, but if we hear their messages with our awakened heart, we may just hear what we need at this point in our life.

# 8

# Postmodern views

*Despite the success of Vaishnavism as a worldwide phenomenon, there are yet some persistent difficulties faced by converts in understanding and implementing the guru-disciple tradition. Partial understandings of source texts combined with highly selective use of quotes has only served to exacerbate the divisions of thought. The scriptures are often employed in substantiating previously held convictions rather than studied for enlightenment of the mind. This is particularly true of the writings on the subject of guru-disciple.*

**This is probably as much as can be expected considering the prevailing climate.** Whether we term it 'post-modernism' or not, the current intellectual and philosophical climate in the industrialised world has contributed to a particular perspective on the Vedas and the guru-disciple culture which is at its heart. The postmodern paradigm has several elements which may be helpful to the spirituality required to fully understanding the guru-disciple relationship. Conversely, it has some that directly militate against it:

1. **Relational rather than hierarchical** – Postmodern people are suspicious of the mainstream in any area of life and much prefer flat or networked organisations to hierarchies. Postmoderns want to humanise the world and are drawn to marginalised people; they are relationship centred. They give a higher priority to building a relationship than maintaining a building or structure. This view of the world probably helped to create the Hare Krishna movement back in the 1960s and 1970s.

2. However, as the role of the guru in the Hare Krishna movement has become augmented with organisational position and corollary power, there have been more complaints about the 'position of guru' being used to preserve the 'institutional hierarchy.' As the movement has gone from the social fringes to a more 'mainstream'

position, the postmodern observers have re-categorized it from a 'spiritual movement' to a 'religious institution.' Although there is only a difference in size and complexity, that is enough for some to regard the guru-disciple relationship as an instrument of a religious hierarchy – and to react against it.

3. **Spiritual rather than rational** – Postmodern people, it is said, are more inclined to honour feelings along with rationality. They are drawn to signs, symbols and mysticism and love to hear stories of miraculous or mysterious experiences. Social psychologists suggest that this may have something to do with the 'feminisation' of society – and they may be partially right, since some aspects of masculinity are being challenged – but it may also be because spirituality itself has been subjugated to the principle of mere religious conformity for a prolonged period. The mystical element of religion, the tangible experiences of a higher reality, have been so rationalised away that people now crave this very real dimension of life.

4. Though all of this would seem to support people entering into the guru-disciple relationship, it has actually led, in some cases, to blind acceptance of self-declared, somewhat under-enlightened guru figures and belief in their pseudo-spiritual revelations. This alarming state of affairs has, by turn, led to the growth of evangelical rationality, as evidenced by the profusion of the 'anti-God' books written by neo-atheists. Within the Hare Krishna movement, this postmodern trend has often led to initial credulity of the guru's qualifications, without any prior checking, followed by disenchantment some time later. Some post-modern Hare Krishna members have consequently become very influenced by the 'new atheist' writings and have placed rationale as their new guide to reality, completely foregoing their previous convictions in direct mystical experience. In this condition, some have rejected the Vedas entirely.

5. **Explorative rather than possessive** – Postmodern people dislike boundaries. 'To travel is more important than to arrive.' To explore is OK, to say that you have arrived is pride, and to then package what you've discovered is exploitation. They distrust notions of progress and tend to refuse to judge anyone else. They don't like the differences between one person and another or between one religious group and another, and tend to want to de-emphasise them, preferring to think of every person and every

path as equal. Again, this makes the Bhagavad-gita very interesting reading for them since Lord Krishna speaks of the soul present in every physical form and the inherent equality of all life. But the postmodern mind doesn't like there to be any superior path to God-realisation because that makes others 'inferior.' Similarly, they don't like the guru to be a person who knows it all and who can teach them. Rather, they want the guru to be more of an equal - a 'soul friend.' Of course, the guru is the best friend of the soul, but he is more, and must be regarded as more if the real benefit of having a guru is to be ever obtained.

6. **Inclusive rather than exclusive** – Because they don't like to judge or pigeonhole others, postmodern people tend to want to draw out the possibilities in others and seek to include them. Rather than regarding others in terms of their spiritual commitment or membership of a spiritual group, they would prefer to see them in terms of their potential. They are most likely to find some aspects of religious identity – where a spiritual practitioner chooses the company of like-minded others - as cultural aloofness or elitism. Buildings and organisational structures are not as important as the building of communities based on spiritual relationships.

Again, all of this may sound very good but a rejection of good discrimination can cause ineffectiveness in helping others. Different people have different spiritual needs, for instance, and require different approaches of teaching and guidance. And an extreme example of inclusivity in eating, for example, would see a vegetarian postmodern person sit down for a non-vegetarian meal out of respect for the dietary decisions of a friend. But not everyone's dinner is suitable for an aspiring transcendentalist, and judgement is therefore required. Krishna speaks of categories of faith, practise, friends, types of personal discipline and stages of mystical revelation, and reality – according to Him, the One who sees reality as it really is - is made up differences between things, at least as much as similarities.

So although inclusivity is important, not everything or everyone can always be included in everything. Social inclusivity is no doubt the hallmark of Vedic culture since no-one is left out and everyone is on the path back to God. However, the disciplines necessary to develop higher states of awareness rest upon the ability to carefully discriminate between what to do and not; what to study and recite and not; what to eat and drink and what to avoid. After initiation the disciple is meant to honour the instructions of his guru above all others; and to practise the disciplines he has been given as a daily choice. Failure to do this – to try to establish a moral and spiritual equivalence amongst all instructions and all people – simply leads to the ultimate loss of regard for the guru and an inability to honour ones vows.

7. **Culture friendly rather than 'anachronistic'** – Postmodern religion, if a person chooses any religion at all, is religion *a la carte*. People select the ingredients with which they feel most comfortable. That will, inevitably, include elements of contemporary political or philosophical thought, speech, dress and culture being added to traditional time-honoured practises. They tend to view history as progressive and incrementally revelatory, a procession of human enlightenment leading to some ultimate revelation of peace and truth for all humanity. Ideas expressed in the past – simply because they were in the past – are less relevant than those expressed today. What this linear view of history does is to relegate the Vedas to a less enlightened period of human development, a period that produced some good ideas and noble thoughts, but cannot claim to have all the answers.

While intellectually a postmodern thinker may be drawn irresistibly to the logic of *Vedanta* he will almost unconsciously place a limitation on his beliefs since he anticipates another set of 'Vedic' revelations coming along soon. The guru-disciple relationship itself is also subjected to this view of history. The submission required to understand the Vedas may be regarded as an anachronism, as is the guru himself. The spiritual aspirant or disciple regards the guru as a helpful notion – for the people of another country, in another era – but can't see the relevance of such an antiquated relationship in 'today's world.' After initiation, the 'postmodern disciple' may begin to regard the vows he made as historical and therefore less relevant than those he might make today. By constantly reinventing himself in the light of his new experiences and understandings, such a disciple must be extremely careful not to reinvent himself out of his commitment to his guru's instructions.

The added difficulty for anyone approaching the Vedas and the guru today is that none of us are accustomed to serving anyone in order to gain knowledge. If we need to learn something we simply pay a class or course fee, sit in front of the teacher, listen carefully and make notes. We don't have to 'surrender' to the teacher or 'make submissive enquiries,' or make any extra effort to please the teacher by 'rendering him service,' all of which are recommended in the Vedas. There is no relationship we are obliged to enter into, and there is no question of 'obedience.' Logic also commands us to answer the question: "If the Vedas are written down and are now published in the form of a book, why can I not just pick up the book and read it?"

In the modern world, since 1450 at least, we Europeans have learned about the Divine through the medium of the printed word on paper. Great Protestant Christian martyrs were publicly burned to death in England for daring to declare that God could be revealed through English language print. They suffered a painful end for insisting that no priest was required as an intermediary. If any lands are totally unsuitable for the guru-disciple method of teaching it must surely be the Protestant countries. These are the countries which rebelled against the notion that a priest was required to pass down messages from God or to take our prayers to Him. The Vedas would agree – to an extent. They explain that God does indeed reveal himself in the form of the written word – but that we can learn even more if we have a genuine guru.

In the early 21$^{st}$ century the internet search engine promises to provide us all the information we can possibly take in. Never before in human history have we been able to access so much information, store it and share it with whomever we like. The invention of information technology has revolutionised human communication in a way never thought possible some decades ago. Surely this has changed the way we can learn and understand the Vedas?

But there is a difference between information and knowledge, and a difference again between knowledge of something and a true understanding of it. The development of a true apprehension of higher reality comes as a result of incremental mystical revelation. And that, say the Vedas, can only be obtained by serving the guru – the one who is speaking the words of God – and serving him as a representative of God.

# 9

# The need for a guru

*The Sanskrit word guru indicates a teacher. There are many varieties of knowledge in the world and each of them can be learned from some form of teacher – some type of guru. Of all varieties of knowledge, that which can best relieve suffering and provide permanent happiness is the greatest. Therefore the guru who teaches that knowledge is considered to be the most important. The Vedic tradition offers many classical verses to illustrate the logical necessity of finding such a guru, becoming his student and learning from him.*

**As humans, we can explore, interpret, and understand the world by collecting information through our senses and processing it in our brain.** Yet the senses are limited in their range and power, and the sum total of information they can gather cannot encompass the full extent of 'reality.' Even if the range of the senses is increased through the use of scientific instruments, there is still room for observer error and miscalculation.

The tendency to base our comprehension of reality solely upon elementary sensory input and mental processing means that for quite significant periods we are subject to various cognitive illusions. Being in illusion yet willingly accepting it as factual is described as *atma-maya* or 'self-deception,' and basing our decision-making on such self-deception means that we tend to make significant mistakes. As we continue to act in illusion, we create a long sequence of mistakes, where one mistake is based upon the previous, and so on. Involving other people in our mistakes means that we make them complicit in a deception – we effectively cheat them.

The Vedic literature holds these to be cardinal existential problems. While the Upanishads describe the position of the *jiva atmas*, the eternal particles of pure consciousness that become trapped in matter, the Puranas detail the elements of self-deception to which the *atmas* subject themselves. The cumulative illusion begins with *andha-tamisra* or forgetfulness of real identity; becomes deepened by *tamah*, the 'darkness' of eclipsed self-knowledge; then proceeds to the assumption of a new, physical identity or *moha*. Along with this comes the assumption of ownership of enjoyable objects apprehended by the senses. When these are enjoyed the impression of happiness reinforces the new physical identity. This is *maha-moham*. Then, attempts are made to enjoy prolonged ownership of those objects in order to experience repeated happiness. When these result in eventual disappointment, as they must, the 'anger upon frustration,' or *tamisram* manifests. Discharge of anger through thoughts, speech or action causes karmic entanglement in the world and exacerbates existential forgetfulness.

In his brilliant mediaeval treatise, *Tattva Sandarbha*, Srila Jiva Goswami sums up the illusions and their effects in four simple defects of human existence. We are, he says, subject to *bhrama* or false knowledge and mistakes in perception - a confusion or dizziness; we are inattentive to, or negligent of, reality, a condition known as *pramada*; we have imperfect senses and reasoning power known as *karanapatava*; and we are envious of the enjoyment of others and hence we mislead and cheat them: *vipralipsa*.

Accordingly, the philosophical portion of the Vedas begins by explaining that a true seeker of knowledge, a philosopher, should never base his life on an assumed reality that cannot be proven. Something which is false inevitably leads to disappointment, sadness and even suffering. Therefore it is always best to move away from illusion towards reality. But what is reality, and if there are many realities, which reality is most real? How can a philosopher prove that beyond doubt? Since proving anything requires hard evidence, the first task is to analyse upon what evidence, proof or *pramanam*, he bases his understanding of reality. What is trustworthy evidence and how is it gained? What are the many ways he gathers evidence and which, of all of them, can he trust? Classical sources describe ten different means of gathering evidence:

1. *Arsya*: The utterances of a superlative human: a sage or celestial being.
2. *Upamana*, **or comparison:** Knowledge about an unknown object can be gained by comparing it to a familiar object. If we have seen

a cow, for example, but have not seen a forest cow, and if someone tells us that a forest cow resembles a cow, by comparison we can recognize a forest cow.

3. *Arthapatti*, **or presumption:** Here we assume an unknown fact in order to account for a known fact that is otherwise inexplicable. For example, if fat Devadatta does not eat during the daytime, one can safely assume that he eats at night. Otherwise his stoutness without eating during the daytime remains unexplained, as Devadatta cannot get fat by fasting nor can he maintain his weight without eating.

4. *Abhava*, **or non-existence:** Non-perception of a qualified object by a qualified sense is called perception of the *abhava* or the non-existence of that object. For example, a book is a qualified object for the visual perception and the eyes are the qualified senses or means of perception. When one does not see a book on a table he experiences its non-existence. This is classified as a separate category of perception, because there is no actual contact between the object and the sense instrument. Thus what is perceived is the non-existence of the object. Even though the object is not perceived, that in itself is a form of perception.

5. *Sambhava*, **or inclusion:** This *pramana* is based on the experience that the higher quantity includes the lower quantity. A hundred pounds automatically includes ones, fives, tens, and so on. To infer this knowledge, gained by inclusion, is called *sambhava*.

6. *Aitihya*, **or tradition:** This *pramana* applies when something is known by common belief or tradition but the original source of that knowledge is unknown. For instance, there is a popular belief that the Old Fort in New Delhi was built by the Pandavas. We have no written proof or scriptural authority to support this, but the belief has been passed down for generations to the present day by tradition.

7. *Cheshta*, **or gesture:** To acquire knowledge through body language - bodily gestures or symbols - is called *cheshta*.

8. *Pratyaksha*, **or direct perception:** What we directly perceive with our senses may be valid or invalid knowledge; however, only valid knowledge is to be considered as *pramana*. Sense perception is the principal means of acquiring knowledge in this material world. Direct perception is of two types--external and internal. An

external perception is when knowledge is acquired through our senses. An internal perception is when the knowledge is acquired by our mind. In Bhagavad-gita (15.7) Lord Krishna lists the mind as the sixth sense (*manah-sasthani-indriyani*). Through the mind we perceive emotions such as pain, pleasure, love, hate, and so forth.

9. *Anumana*, **or inference:** This is when we acquire knowledge by deduction. Literally, *anumana* means 'knowing after', because the knowledge is arrived at after putting together known bits of information to arrive at an unknown but apparently logical conclusion. Such inferred knowledge is based on the probable relation between what is known and what is deduced. That in turn is based on prior direct perception (*pratyaksha*) or prior verbal testimony (*shabda*). This means the deduced outcome is dependent on the evidence. This concomitant relation between the evidence and the deducted conclusion is called *vyapti*.

Inference is of two kinds, inference for oneself and inference for others. An example of inference for oneself is when a person may make out the concomitant relationship between smoke and fire and arrive at the universal generalization: 'Wherever there is smoke there is fire.' after repeatedly experiencing it in the kitchen and elsewhere. Then if he sees smoke hanging over a mountain in the distance he may recall his prior experience, that wherever there is smoke there is invariably fire, and thus he concludes, 'The mountain is on fire.'

Inference for others consists of a syllogistic formula that has five steps. After arriving at an inferred conclusion a person employs this method, with a view to enable others to arrive at the same inferred conclusion. A syllogism follows this format:

   a. **Proposition:** The Mountain has fire.

   b. **Reason:** Because it has smoke.

   c. **Universal proposition:** Wherever there is smoke there is fire.

   d. **Application:** The Mountain has smoke.

   e. **Conclusion:** Therefore it is on fire.

Any error in perceiving the cause or any deviation in the universal generalization then the conclusion will be faulty. In the above example, if the observer mistakes clouds over the mountain for smoke or perceives the smoke just after rain has extinguished the fire, then his deduced conclusion will be wrong. Hence, *anumana*, like *pratyaksha*, is not a foolproof method of acquiring knowledge.

10. **Shabda, or revealed knowledge**: Shabda literally means sound, but as a pramana it refers to articulate sound which has meaning and which is spoken or written by an apta-purusa, a trustworthy person, an authority. A trusted authority on a particular area of knowledge will have arrived at his knowledge through several of the foregoing methods of pramanam. However, even the greatest human authority will be prone to self-induced illusion. Ultimately, shabda in the strictest sense of the term refers to revealed knowledge about the transcendental reality. This kind of shabda is distinct from the shabda used in mundane transactions, called paurusheya shabda, which is not always trustworthy.

Veda is called *apaurusheya shabda*, revealed knowledge from the divine source, not a human origin, and is received in a succession of self-realized gurus. *Apaurusheya shabda* therefore, because it is free of defects, is the perfect *pramana*. Another term for *apaurusheya shabda* is *shastra*. The distinction between *arsya*, the utterances of sages and celestials, and *apaurusheya shabda*, is that even sages and celestials can be subject to illusion, whereas the origin of the Vedas, the plane of Ultimate Reality, cannot. When the sages and celestials simply repeat the words of the Veda, they themselves act as Veda.

Therefore the philosophical portion of the Vedas, known as the Upanishads, and their analytical commentary known as the *Brahma Sutra* or *Vedanta Sutra*, begin with statements declaring certain fundamental points:

1. Reality cannot be apprehended fully by perception, discourse or logic.

2. *Shastra* – the Vedas and their corollaries – are the infallible sources of knowledge.

3. The meaning of *shastra* can be fully elucidated by a seer, one who knows the different aspects of *shastra* and has direct experience of

*Brahman*, the universal plane of reality beyond sense perception.

4. Such a person should be sought out, enquired from, and served as a teacher, a guru.

For the western reader, unfamiliar with the Vedas, there will be several logical inconsistencies immediately apparent in those four assumptions. Why are only the Vedas an infallible source of knowledge? Surely they are a body of sectarian religious literature written down by fallible humans? Our search for Truth, then, would certainly be more rigorous if we included all of human society's great spiritual works such as the Torah, the Qur'an and the New Testament. And why, if sense perception of the human being is inadequate for penetrating the veil of illusion, should we then seek out another human being who may also prove to be just as fallible as ourselves?

The simple answers might be given as follows: The Vedas are declared to be *apaurusheya*, or 'not written by humans,' and have existed in the form of metric poems and mantras for thousands of years. Their origin is held to be in transcendence itself. The proof of these claims can be discovered only by following the directions contained within them and experiencing that very same transcendence.

Veda simply means 'knowledge' and it exists wherever spiritual truth is uttered. Like the sun shining in the sky, it is not bound by geographical or political borders; it has no nationality or man-made religious affiliation. All great utterances from enlightened humans – all the great historical saints, prophets and sages - can be included as Veda to the degree that their words correspond with the ultimate source of knowledge. Evidence that the Vedas provide adequate direction for enlightenment can be witnessed in the living example of the guru.

Persistence of the Vedic tradition and its philosophical core points to its enduring value for hundreds of successive generations. In each of those generations the guru and disciple relationship has continued, as have the mantras, rituals, stories and philosophical aphorisms, a selection of which follow. It is worth noting that, as one might expect, the Vedas, the declarations of the avatars of Vishnu, and the great sages are all congruent.

It is worth understanding that a guru – a teacher of Vedic mantra, philosophy, theology and ritual - is not simply a pious person who repeats ancient texts without thinking. His training to reach the point of teaching others has been quite rigorous, and physically and mentally demanding. Before even being allowed to read the Vedas, he will have become trained in the rigorous semantic analysis and reasoned debate necessary to comprehend the Vedic aphorisms. Students of all philosophical and theological schools are required to study logic (*nyaya*) and exegesis (*mimamsa*) prior to their entering into Vedic study. The modern term 'hermeneutics' means a methodology for the interpretation of texts. Exegesis is the application of hermeneutics, an extensive and critical interpretation of a sacred text. The definition of the Sanskrit term *mimamsa* means 'investigation and deep thought in order to arrive at rational conclusions.'

The exegetical format is called an *adhikarana* which is comprised of a fivefold process. First comes *vishaya-vakya* – noting the sentence of *shastra* under discussion; then *samsaya* – formulating a doubt as to the correct and relevant meaning; *purva-paksha* – presentation of the opposing interpretation; then *uttara-paksha* – a refutation of the objection and a presentation of the more reasoned interpretation; and finally, *nirnaya* - a sequence of arguments for the conclusion reached. This system helps to establish the truth through reasoned presentation, and means that the guru's students will be able to free themselves from doubt, one of the main obstacles to apprehending the truth.

The other aspect in the guru's life – and the one perhaps much more noticeable – is that he has factually been successful in understanding the Vedas, putting the conclusions into practise, and is reaping the rewards. Although a guru may be scholarly and deeply philosophical, it means very little if he is unhappy. To contact transcendental truth means to become joyful, and this is so obvious in the character of a realised person that even a child could identify a guru by his external symptoms.

For those who understand that ultimately *Brahman* has form and attributes; that the ultimate truth, the highest reality, *Parabrahman*, is a personal God, the guru is one who demonstrates that he has found not only joy, but love. Since love involves not only an expression of devotion, but the realisation that one is loved, the guru must demonstrate in thought, words and actions that he is the recipient of divine love. This gives him a moment-by-moment conviction of the presence of the Supreme.

Part One | The need for a guru

Accordingly, these statements from the Vedas concerning the absolute necessity of accepting a guru, include specific statements regarding the Vaishnava, someone who has realised the personal Supreme.

## Statements from the Vedas

**On the inability of physical perception to apprehend reality:**

*na samdrse tisthati rupam asya, na caksusa pasyati kascanainam*

"His form is beyond physical sense perception. No-one can see Him with material eyes."

*(Svetasvatara Upanishad 4.20)*

*na tatra caksurgacchati na vaggacchati no manah*

"The eye does not go there, nor speech, nor mind."

*(Kena Upanishad 1.3)*

**On the inefficacy of logic and discourse:**

*tarka-pratisthanat*

"Logic and discourse are inconclusive"

*(Vedanta Sutra 2.1.11)*

*acintyah khalu ye bhava , na tams tarkena yojayet*
*prakrtibhyah param yac ca, tad acintyasya laksanam*

"That which is beyond matter and thereby outside the parameter of sense perception is the inconceivable Absolute Truth. Do not attempt to approach it through deductive reasoning"

*(Mahabharata, Bhisma-parva, 5.12)*

*nayam atma pravacanena labhyo,*
*na medhaya na bahuna srutena*

"The Supreme Self cannot be known by any amount of discourse, intelligence or learning."

*(Mundaka Upanishad, 3.2.3 and Katha Upanishad, 1.2.23)*

## On *shastra* being free from the defects of human perception:

*shastra-yonitvat*

"It is only from shastra (scripture) that God is known."

*(Vedanta Sutra 1.1.3)*

## On *shastra* being difficult to understand:

*chandamsi yajnah kratavo vratani,
bhutam bhavyam yac ca veda vadanti
asman mayi srjate visvam etat,
tasmims canyo mayaya sanniruddhah*

'The Vedas describe a bewildering variety of hymns, prayers, sacrifices, rituals, vows, austerities, histories and predictions. Simply by studying the Vedas it is very difficult for conditioned souls clouded by illusion and trapped in this phenomenal world to understand the Absolute, from whom this illusory potency and the material cosmos originate.'

*(Svetasvatara Upanishad, 4.9)*

## On certain qualified persons being able to help us:

'This realization, my dear boy, cannot be acquired by deductive reasoning. It can be properly understood only when an especially qualified person speaks it.'

*(Katha Upanishad. 1.2.9)*

*tarko 'pratistha srutayo vibhinna,
nasav munir yasya matam na bhinnam
dharmasya tattvam nihitam guhayam,
mahajano yena gatah sa panthah*

"Logic and discourse are inconclusive. A person whose opinion does not differ from others is not considered a great sage. Merely by studying the Vedas, which are wide-ranging, one cannot come to the correct spiritual path. Knowledge of this path is hidden in the heart of a self-realized person (mahajana). Consequently, one should accept whatever path these self-realized persons advocate."

*(Mahabharata, Vana Parva, 313.117)*

**On some souls being 'chosen' by God:**

> *nayam atma pravacanena labhyo,*
> *na medhaya na bahuna srutena*
> *yam evaisa vrnute tena labhyas,*
> *tasyaisa atma vivrnute tanum svam*

"The Supreme Self cannot be known by any amount of discourse, intelligence or hearing. Rather, He fully reserves the right to reveal Himself to whom He chooses."

*(Mundaka Upanishad 3.2.3)*

**On the absolute need to accept a guru:**

> *acaryavan puruso veda*

"One who has a spiritual preceptor can know things as they are."

*(Chandogya Upanishad, 6.14.2)*

> *tad vijnanartham sa gurum evabigaccet*

"To understand transcendental knowledge, one must certainly approach a guru."

*(Mundaka Upanishad 1.2.12)*

> *yasya deve para bhaktir, yatha deve tatha gurau*
> *tasyaite kathita hy arthah, prakasanta mahatmanah*

"All the confidential meanings of the scriptures manifest in the heart of one who has as much devotion for his guru as for God."

*(Svetasvatara Upanishad, 6.23)*

*tasmad gurum prapadyeta jijnasuh sreya uttamam*

"Therefore, one who wishes to know about the ultimate goal of life should take shelter of a guru."

*(Srimad Bhagavatam, 11.3.21)*

*tad viddhi pranipatena pariprasnena sevaya*
*upadeksyanti te jnanam jnaninas tattva-darsinah*

"Try to understand this knowledge by accepting a spiritual preceptor, asking relevant questions of him, and rendering service to him. Those who are self-realised can impart knowledge unto you because they have seen the truth."

*(Bhagavad-gita 4.34)*

# Part Two
# The Ancient Culture of Learning

# 10
# 'A' is for Acharya

*Focus on the guru-disciple tradition –and Sanskrit terminology - has grown in today's world. Yet when we use Sanskrit we don't always use the right words. Or we'll use the right word but others don't share the same definition. Confusion and miscommunication is the result. So as a small contribution towards more exact speech I thought I'd explore some terms and how they were traditionally used. It might help us all understand each other a little better. Some of the contents of this chapter are from interviews with the renowned Shankaracharya and Sanskrit scholar Chandrasekharendra Saraswati.*

**Acharya is a word which, like the word guru, is often translated as 'spiritual master.'** The words acharya and guru are often used interchangeably but there is some difference between the two. 'Acharya' is related to words like *'acharana' 'achara'* and *'chara.' 'Chara'* means 'to walk' or 'to go'. *'Charita'* and *'charitra'* mean 'conduct.'

A continuous course of events can be *'desha-charitra'* (the life of a nation) or *'jivya-charitra'* (a biography or life history). An order of movement is a 'walk'. *'Charitra'* means 'walking along a path,' going in a certain order.

The Sanskrit root *'chara'* becomes *'achara'* meaning a 'stream of conduct.' More often, the word *'achara'* is used to indicate a 'stream of conduct within the banks of dharma,' or the life of a righteous person, or 'acharya.'

An acharya shows through the example of his life the practises of the tradition to which he belongs. A definition of acharya is provided in the Manu *Samhita*:

*achinoti hi sastrarthan achare sthapayatyapi*
*svayam acharate yasmad acharya stena kirtitah*

> *"The acharya is thus called because he has studied and understood the meaning of the scriptures, he establishes this meaning in the behaviour of others, and he practises what he preaches."*

The acharya does not simply teach, but shows by example.

In order to teach effectively he must be a *vidvan,* a profoundly learned man. He must be able to clear away the doubts of people with regard to the *shastra* in which he is learned, and he must be able to answer criticism.

The ancient system was for acharyas to teach the *shastra* in which they were expert. For example, Drona Acharya and Kripa Acharya taught what they were expert in - martial arts.

Living with an acharya and studying at his feet is known as '*gurukulavasa*' and not '*acharyakulavasa*'. From this, it might be assumed that, therefore, guru and acharya are the same. So let's have a look at the word 'guru.'

# What is a guru?

Guru means heavy, weighty or big. But it really means one who is 'heavy with knowledge,' or 'one who cannot be moved by lighter argument.' It means who is great inwardly, and whose inner greatness is revealed in his outer conduct.

A guru may not wish for *gurutva* ('guruship') but if he gives *anugraha* (grace) to someone then in that person's eyes he becomes 'guru.'

Getting a mantra, or an art, or knowledge without a guru is forbidden in *shastra*. It is like a wife having a child by her paramour. That son is not authorized – as a legal son would be - to perform the rites according to scripture that a son must perform for his father.

Being initiated into the chanting of mantras and the knowledge behind them is known as *diksha*. A traditionally accepted differentiation between terms is that the acharya is the one who administers *diksha*, and guru is one who teaches a subject over many years.

In southern India, in the Tamil language, the word acharya has become *asiriyar*, and sometimes a newspaper editor is called *patrika-asiriyar* or 'acharya of the newspaper'! In Tamil, the word *'vattiyar'* means an ordinary teacher. The word *'vattiyar'* is derived from the Sanskrit *'upadhyaya'*

# What is the meaning of *Upadhyaya*?

It is Upa + adhyaya

*'Adhyaya'* means any portion of the Vedas demarcated for reading

*'Adhyapaka'* is one who imparts Vedic education

*'Adhyapana'* is the teaching of the Vedas

*'Adhyayana'* is learning of the Vedas

The prefix *'upa'* denotes something that is subsidiary to the main thing being denoted: *anga – upanga, purana – upapurana*, also *guru - upaguru*, or one who is an assistant to a guru.

So *upa-adhyapaka* - or *'upadhyaya'* - means 'one who teaches the Vedas as a co-worker or assistant to the guru'.

There are differences between the acharya and the *upadhyaya*:

The acharya is not one who teaches for his livelihood. He establishes his *gurukula* and teaches for one reason alone: to carry out his brahminical duty of making sure that the *vidya*, or knowledge, in which he is proficient does not cease with him but is kept alive for ever. When a student joins his *gurukula* he does not utter a word about fees or *dakshina*. It is only after a student has completed his education that the acharya mentions it.

The *Manu Smriti* says that one who teaches for a livelihood is an *upadhyaya*. He is not the same as an acharya. One who teaches for a fee is a *bhrtaka adhyapaka*. He teaches one part of the *Veda-vidya* and receives a salary for it in return.

Acharyas for whom teaching was not a means of livelihood dwindled in number in course of time, and the number of *upadhyayas* increased. The name *upadhyaya* itself, instead of denoting a teacher of inferior status, came to denote a teacher of prestige. The original meaning was forgotten and anyone imparting learning came to be called an *upadhyaya*. Even the acharya has come to be called *upadhyaya*.

That is how a number of teachers in northern India who taught the Vedas from generation to generation tagged on the term '*upadhyaya*' to their names – they did not think there was any suggestion of inferiority about it. The Mukherjis, Chatterjis, and Bannerjis in Bengal, for instance.

These names – which have become common surnames over the centuries – are actually contractions of the original terms for different kinds of teachers. The names are actually Mukhopadhaya, Caturopadhyaya, and Vandyopadhaya.

'Mukha' means the Vedas, since they issue from the mouth. 'Catur' means the four Vedas, and 'Vandhya' means a teacher worthy of respect. In Bengali language, Mukha became Mukher, Catur became Chatter, and Vandhya became Bandhya and later 'Banner.'

# Six occupations

According to the *shastras*, to earn his livelihood each man is to be engaged in an occupation in keeping with his *varna*. Brahmanas were known as 'those of six occupations' or *sat-karma-nirata* but in most of the occupations there was no possibility of income:

1. ***Adhyayana*** – learning the Vedas – in this there is no scope for earning money.

2. ***Adhyapana*** – teaching the Vedas – he has to teach an occupation to someone else. He cannot practise that occupation, merely teach it. He must be satisfied with the *dakshina* or fee that is given by the student.

3. ***Yajana*** – performing a sacrifice on one's own – no income

4. *Yaajana* – performing sacrifices for others – perhaps some income.
5. *Daana* – Giving away gifts – no income
6. *Pratigraha* – Receiving charity

There is income in *Yaajana* and *Pratigraha*, but there is a big list of expiatory rites to be performed for accepting various gifts. There is fear that the sins of the donor would be passed on. The brahmana must use the *dakshina* for some meritorious work.

So the only occupation that a brahmana could perform for income safely was teaching – Adhyapana. A noble acharya would only accept a *dakshina* after he, the acharya, and not the student/disciple, was satisfied with their teaching.

The *Manu Samhita* talks about the *dakshina* to be given to the guru after the student completes his studies. According to the student's capacity he can give: cows, land, gold, clothes, grain, vegetables, umbrellas, sandals. Manu also explains that a teacher who fixes his fees beforehand is an inferior kind of teacher and cannot take part in a *shraddha* ceremony, and neither can his student.

# Three qualifications

The acharya must have three qualifications. First, he must be well-versed in a system of thought, in a system of philosophy (*acinoti hi sastrartham*) second, he has to apply in his practical life (*svayam acarate*) what he has learned. Third, he must not only teach his disciples, he must make them live according to its teachings (*acare stapayatyapi*).

One who is proficient in a subject is a *vidvan*

One whose life is based on a subject but who does not teach the sastra is an *anushtata*

If he has realisation of the subject he teaches he is *anubhavi*

He who teaches but does not set an example in his own life is a *pracharaka*

Part Two | 'A' is for Acharya

An acharya is one who is all three – *anusthata, anubhavi and pracharaka*

# The first universities

The heights of education in India must be attributed to the fact that teaching was not considered a business. Education was not institutionalised but left to the care of individuals. It did not deteriorate until a few centuries ago.

It was during the time of the Buddhists that institutions arose for teaching – like the universities of today – at places like Nalanda and Taksasila (Taxila). Before that the practise of a number of teachers teaching at one place had not become widespread. Individual acharyas conducted their *gurukulas* in their ashrams. There might have been one or two *upa-adhyapakas* to assist them.

There was the rare phenomenon of the guru teaching in some *gurukulas* all the 64 traditional arts, with the help of a number of acharyas. In these *gurukulas* senior students probably taught the juniors. The guru in charge was called a *kulapati*.

In the first sarga of *Raghuvamsam*, Vasistha is described as a *kulapati*. Later on, the guru who had 10,000 students in his *gurukula* was called a *kulapati*.

He also fed them all: *yo anna danadi posanat adhyapati* "He who feeds, nurtures and teaches – this is the definition of a kulapati."

But the system could only work with the assistance of royal patronage. The local king, considering the acharya's valuable contribution, undertook to supply what the students needed.

At birth a brahmana has no intrinsic qualifications. At the time of his *upanayana* ceremony, when he receives the *Gayatri* mantra enabling him to 'come closer to God,' he becomes a *dvija* or 'one who has been born twice.' After his education as a *dvija* he becomes a *vipra*. As a *vipra* who applies his knowledge to his life he becomes known as a *srotriya* or 'one who has heard and understood'.

A student is sometimes called a *chatra* (umbrella) because he gets shelter under the umbrella-like teacher

The school was known as the *charana* or 'foot' because it is the thing which upholds all other activities.

The teacher who expounds, '*pravachana*' is known as a *pravakta*

# Length of school terms

Even today, it is customary to have a 12-year course in India's traditional Vedic schools, or Veda-*pathashalas*. It needs eight years to learn the *bhasyas* (commentaries to the scripture) and to understand their meanings. The period of education in the old days was determined by the mental capacity of the student as also according to the subjects he wished to learn. The shortest was nine years. Twelve years became the standard practise. Some courses lasted eighteen years and some thirty-six years. According to Manu, the student could also study for a lifetime. A student was discharged from the obligation of *grihasta* ashram (married life) only after his guru had tested him and satisfied himself that he was of exceptional intelligence. Such a student was called a *naisthika brahmachari*.

For academic purposes the year was divided into two terms. The first was of five months, the second of seven months. The first term was called *upakarma* and the second *utsarjana* or *utsarga*.

The first five months – the *upakarma* period - was for learning Vedic verses. Nothing new was learned in the second period of seven months, but the student would study the six *Vedangas*: *shiksha* (pronunciation), *vyakarana* (grammar), *chandas* (poetic meter), *nirukta* (dictionary), *jyotish* (astrology), *and kalpa* (ritual). On the eve of the *upakarma* term these six studies were discontinued and the study of the Vedas recommenced for five months.

# School holidays

Such *gurukulas* (place of the guru) or *pathashalas* (where the Vedas are recited) exist all over India to this day. Some acharyas are creating even more traditional schools as a revival takes place in Vedic culture. But children must still have holidays, so sixdays a month are days of rest when there are no studies. These are known as *anadhyayana* or 'no recitation' days. There are six days every month: the full moon day, the new moon day, and the eighth and fourteenth lunar day twice in a month. There are also four other days in the year known as *'Caturmasi.'*

Finally, there is a time for most students when formal education comes to an end and they return to their village and take to married life. The rite signifying the conclusion of studies is called *samavartana*. The *brahmachari* is to marry and settle down in the ashram of the householder only after this ceremony. According to the sastras it is a brahmana's duty to teach after he has finished his studies.

# Changing definitions

What has been described so far is the classic ways of the guru-disciple relationship, much of which can still be found even today. Sanskrit is a very precise language although, just as in every living language, some words become transformed in common usage as that which they describe changes, or as the word is taken up by the greater population who may not know the more precise definition. In the next chapter we shall see how the word acharya has been changed in usage, as well as many other Sanskrit words relating to guru and disciple.

# 11

# Shiksha, Diksha, and sliding definitions

*Sanskrit is the language of the Vedas and is also known as deva-nagari, 'the language spoken in the cities of the gods.' With such a divine origin, one might expect the meaning of Sanskrit to remain unchanged over the course of the centuries. And so it has, except for where mere mortals have adopted it for their own uses and adjusted the meanings to fit their own needs. Each religious sub-group genuinely attempts to preserve the pure meaning of each word, but language is dynamic when used in colloquial circumstances, and even slight changes of usage can become incrementally compounded through the centuries. Difficulties arise when the vernacular usage of a Sanskrit word is different from classical usage.*

**The last chapter explored the word acharya.** This is one of the words whose meaning has become adjusted slightly over the centuries. Not a lot, but enough to create confusion in conversation occasionally. Since the word was associated with the classical teacher whose students perpetuated the teachings over many generations, the word came to mean 'the head of an institution' and not merely 'one who teaches by example.' Srila Prabhupada was the acharya of ISKCON from the day of its inception, and that remains his title despite his physical demise. In this sense the ISKCON community uses the term to mean 'the original teacher for whom there can be no replacement.' Members of ISKCON therefore become uncomfortable if any member styles themselves as an 'acharya' – even if that is what the teacher factually is according to the definition given in the *Manu Samhita*.

The term acharya is also applied, quite rightly, to illustrious preceptors such as Madhvacharya and Ramanujacharya. By their codification of philosophy, theology and ritual, and by their strong missionary work and social welfare activities, they are regarded by generations of followers as re-invigorators of their respective *sampradayas*. Some followers even describe them as 'heads' of their *sampradayas*, and then go on to describe their lineages as the 'Madhva Sampradaya' or the 'Ramanuja Sampradaya.'

When wishing to give respect to an acharya of such eminence, it is quite understandable that sincere followers would wish to give them full credit for their contribution. Still, Madhva did not lend his name to a *sampradaya*, and Ramanuja did not start a new one. They are both extremely important members of the Brahma and Shri Sampradayas respectively. Similarly with His Divine Grace A.C. Bhaktivedanta Swami Prabhupada. He accomplished something superlative in single-handedly taking the teachings of the Vedas right around the world. It was something never done before, and, having been done, can never be done for the first time again. Nevertheless, Srila Prabhupada did not come to start a new *sampradaya*. He is an acharya for the world, a founder-acharya for his followers who are grouped collectively as ISKCON, but he is not the '*acharya* of the *sampradaya*.' That position has already been given to Srila Rupa Goswami, who codified the teachings of Shri Chaitanya Mahaprabhu. The distinction is subtle, but important.

Some other common expressions used in ISKCON are *vartma-pradarshaka-guru* meaning 'one who first shows the path.' The word *vartma* means a well-worn track made by a cart, or a path worn smooth by many walkers. In this sense it is used to indicate the path of *bhakti*, well-worn by many previous pilgrims over the centuries. The word *darshaka* means 'shows' and the prefix '*pra*' indicates a moving forward.

Once having been shown the path, the aspirant must walk along it, and another guide must ensure that he does not fall, trip or stray. One who illuminates the path, shining a light on the tricky spots, is the 'path-lighter' or *patha-pradipika-guru*. In their writings, the Six Goswamis also use the term *shravan-guru*, or the one from whom the aspirant regularly hears.

# Shiksha guru

Another well-used term, but one more that has changed usage somewhat, is that of *shiksha-guru*. *Shiksha* has a precise meaning.

The Vedas have a number of corollaries. Six particular texts are known as *angas* or limbs/organs. The *Vedangas* are an essential part of Vedic education and are aimed at fostering complete development of the student. They augment and support the study, preservation and protection of the Vedas. They also help the student put the teachings into practise as a culture. They are as follows:

1. *Shiksha* – guidance on the sound and pronunciation of each syllable of the Vedas
2. *Chanda* – the mastery of rhyme and meter
3. *Nirukta* – meaning of complex words and phrases
4. *Vyakarana* - word and sentence structure
5. *Jyotish* – study of heavenly bodies in order to establish correct time for chanting the Vedas during rituals
6. *Kalpa* – ethical, moral and procedural precepts associated with the ritual practise as a way of life

Each syllable of the Vedas is known as an *Akshara* – an 'atom' – and is considered as such to be the irreducible element of the Vedas. Each syllable must be uttered correctly within the *parimana*, or duration in time, as laid down. This is called *Akshara-Shuddhi* or syllable purity. In addition to the time duration of each syllable, there are rules as to the pitch - high, middle or low. The high, middle or low pitches are called *Udatam*, *Anudattam* and *Swaritam*, respectively. In euphony alone there are various aspects: Enunciation (*Ucharana*), Tone (*Swara*), Duration (*Matra*), Pitch (*Balam*), Eveness (*Samam*), and Compounding (*Santhanam*).

The great grammarian *Maharishi* Panini has written in his own *Shiksha* text how carefully the Vedic mantras are to be uttered. He writes in his *Paniniya Shiksha* as follows:

"The Vedic letters must be spoken very lucidly. The sounds should not be blurred. The sound should not slip down or fade out. On the other hand, they should not be barked out. They should neither be loosely or casually mouthed nor spat out in staccato tones. The comparison is with a mother tiger when she is carrying her cub. The teeth grip the cub firmly but at the same time do not cause any pain. Likewise the words are to be pronounced firmly but delicately."

So *shiksha* lays down the phonetics – the sounds, and the euphony – the pronunciation.

But over the centuries the term *shiksha* also came to mean 'instruction in Vedic knowledge.' Since the techniques of mantra-chanting are also supported by instruction in the theology of the particular mantra, the term *shiksha-guru* was also applied to someone who taught either philosophy or theology in support of a specific branch of recitation. Sometimes a particular body of wisdom, or a particular piece of literature, had deeper meanings that could be understood only by recourse to an expert in the field. It might have some esoteric depth or subtle nuances that could only be revealed by a course of instruction. The *diksha-guru* – the giver of the mantra and primary instructor – might choose to send his disciple to another guru for a limited period. This guru was sometimes known as the *shiksha-guru.*

During the late mediaeval period, particularly in the case of the Mogul-oppressed and somewhat corrupted brahmanas of Bengal, the average ancestral, family *diksha-guru* was often so lacking in the qualifications of an authentic teacher, the disciple would have to find a *shiksha-guru* for even the basic instruction. So the very term *diksha-guru* – which should have indicated a guru with an important function - garnered a meaning of 'official guru, but often not particularly spiritually potent,' while the term *shiksha-guru* morphed in its meaning to become: 'one who gives spiritual instruction and guidance beyond mere preliminary religious indoctrination.'

The relatively recent distinction between *diksha-guru* and *shiksha-guru* was even more exacerbated within the Chaitanya Vaishnava tradition, in which the esoteric truths of the maha-mantra, the names of God, could only be revealed by one who had perfected the chanting. Although *diksha-gurus* were numerous, and initiated many young men in the chanting of the *Gayatri* mantra, very small in number were those great souls who had completely dedicated themselves to constant repetition of the Holy Names, and who were experiencing increasing bliss from the practise. In the northern India of 1600-1900, particularly in Bengal, the number of brahmana priests acting as *diksha-gurus* numbered in tens of thousands, while those enlightened saints who could explain the truths of *Krishna-bhakti* numbered in dozens at most. Many who already had *diksha-gurus* became attracted to the gurus of the Gaudiya Sampradaya and were reassured by them that it wasn't wrong to have a *shiksha-guru* for further instructions, since both gurus were manifestations of the mercy of God and there was no difference between them. There was a slight distinction, however, in that the instructing guru who gave authentic guidance towards God was the very 'personality of Krishna,' whereas the guru who gave the mantra was the 'form of Krishna.'

By the time of Srila Bhaktisiddhanta Saraswati Thakur (1874-1937) the *diksha-guru* was a figure of derision in progressive Bengali Vaishnava circles, someone who was willing to take his disciple's money but offer very little spiritual instruction in return. The Thakur commented on the absence of guidance, while referring to the practice of the guru whispering the mantra in the disciple's ear, that: "*Diksha* does not mean blowing in the ear with some wind." Considering all this, it is no surprise that in tracing the historical lineage of gurus, the Victorian period acharyas – forerunners of the modern ISKCON movement - chose to focus on a connected line of *shiksha-gurus* stretching back through the centuries, a '*shiksha-parampara.*'

# Diksha-guru

One addition to these particular word definitions is that although the names of Krishna are generally referred to as a 'mantra' due to the supremely powerful effect of their recitation, many within the tradition itself do not refer to the names as a mantra but simply 'Nama.' For many Gaudiya Vaishnavas the term '*diksha*' refers exclusively to the giving of the Vedic *Gayatri* mantra and other *Pancharatrika* mantras. Being initiated with the holy name of Shri Krishna is referred to as *nama-grahana* or 'receiving the name.' And, while it was a requirement of *shastra* to be given *mantra-diksha* accompanied by a ceremonial fire sacrifice, there was no similar requirement when a guru gave the name of Krishna.

In his book *Bhakti-sandarbha* sections 283 and 284, Srila Jiva Goswami himself uses the word *diksha* in the specific sense of mantras for deity worship. He writes: "Nonetheless, Vaisnavas following the path of Shri Narada and his successors endeavour to establish a personal relationship with the Lord by receiving the grace of a bona fide spiritual master through initiation, and in this tradition the devotees are obliged at the time of initiation to begin engaging in Deity worship." Since a disciple can only engage in deity worship after receiving the appropriate mantras, the word *diksha* here can only refer to the giving of *Gayatri* and *Pancharatrika* mantras.

## *Ritvik*: The seasonal priest

One Sanskrit word in common usage that has been morphed way beyond its actual meaning is the word *ritvik*. It is used variously, and inventively, to mean 'one who gives *diksha* on behalf of the guru,' 'one who gives *diksha* after the physical demise of the guru,' and then, by extension, any member of a group that extols the validity of such a practise. The word *ritvik*, however, has a very specific meaning.

*Ritvik* is a combination of two words. The first is *ritu* or season; and the second *ijya* or worship. Together they form the word *ritu-ijya* or 'seasonal worship.' Sanskrit hardens the first of two vowels when they appear together so the 'u' becomes a 'v' and *ritu-ijya* becomes *ritvija*. Then a final 'k' is added when referring to the person. Someone who performs seasonal worship is hence a *ritvika* or *ritvik*.

The word is used to mean a highly qualified priest who is contracted by someone else to conduct rituals that occur in certain seasons; on special occasions according to the calendar. Normally the head priest and his assistant are chosen in a short ceremony called *Acharya Ritvik Varanam*. After the rituals are concluded, the priests are remunerated and return home.

Some have tried to draw innovative meanings from the unusual compound term '*ritvik-acharya*'. As can be understood from the definitions above, if a guru or acharya engages a priest to perform occasional ceremonies, including the ritual functions of the initiation ceremony, that priest may be known as a *ritvik*. And if a brahmana is in knowledge of the Veda, teaches it to others, and follows the teachings, he is an acharya. A brahmana can be a *ritvik* or an acharya – and even both in unusual circumstances - but it does not make sense to create meanings for terms not found in a Sanskrit dictionary or in Vedic culture. There are so many other valid words to choose from.

# Sampradaya and Parampara

The words *sampradaya* and *parampara* are often used loosely and interchangeably, as if they both conveyed exactly the same meaning. *Sampradaya* means a school of thought or philosophical conclusion or *siddhanta*, embodied by a community of orthodox practitioners. *Parampara* is, quite literally, 'one after the other' – an historical chain of spiritual preceptors, each of whom was a legacy-holder for the same path and practice.

*Sampradaya* refers to what the sincere aspirant may contact in the here and now, how he may be taught the *siddhanta* in the present day, and locate a current exemplar of the tradition. Whereas *parampara* refers to how the *siddhanta* has been transmitted down through the years. It is a chain of illustrious preceptors, each of whom was connected to the previous one, either through accepting the teachings (*shiksha*) or by becoming initiated with a mantra (*diksha*), and usually both. Some links in the *parampara* may have been established by neither *diksha* nor *shiksha*, but through sannyasa initiation. The *parampara* is a lineage of successive gurus which is established retrospectively, sometimes long after their physical demise. A leading member of the *sampradaya* – usually the acharya himself – looks back over the centuries, traces his finger over the spiritual family tree, and concludes: 'This is how we all got here.'

When we describe a *parampara* we single out certain persons who have contributed the most in establishing the *siddhanta*, reviving it, explaining it to others; popularizing it for the masses, defending it from intellectual attack; and leaving behind a body of literature that served best to perpetuate the *siddhanta* beyond the lifetime of the authors. And in a Vaishnava *parampara* it is also customary to single out those who established temples for public worship; or those who reached high levels of self-realisation and immersion in spiritual practise. Those who were particularly blessed by divine grace are also selected. Yet in choosing some as lineage-holders we simultaneously de-select others. Those who, for some reason, were not selected were not unworthy souls, rather, they were great Vaishnavas, each playing their part in supporting, defending and extending the *sampradaya* in their own time. But others were singled out to have their names as a permanent fixture in the list of the greatest historical contributors. The names of all those in the *parampara* are then passed on to the next generation of disciples for their meditation, study and ritual.

## Part Two | Shiksha, Diksha, and sliding definitions

Hopefully, this brief look at word definitions and the guru-disciple culture will go some way to help us all communicate more precisely.

# 12

# Diksha

*What is the history of the giving of mantras? What is initiation or diksha? What happens at the time of initiation? What does the initiation ceremony consist of? Why are there different opinions about initiation?*

**Initiation is the formal beginning of the relationship between guru and disciple.** Known in Sanskrit as *diksha*, it is the time when the candidate takes refuge in the guru, and receives a mantra together with instruction on its theology, techniques of practise, ritual and moral conduct. The guru will also teach the history of the mantra and its effects on the chanter. Having satisfied himself that the guru is authentic, realised, learned and compassionate, the candidate agrees to serve him, and follow his advice as his lifelong preceptor. In return, the guru promises to teach the new disciple everything he has realised and to always assist him in his progress.

The mantra is given following a preparatory ceremony which may be witnessed by family and friends. The essence of *diksha* is the further transformation of consciousness that begins to take place when the guru and disciple combine in a relationship of mutual service, learning, guidance, blessings and assiduous practise.

A mantra is normally a short Sanskrit sentence taken from the Vedas, often containing the name of the Deity ending in the dative case meaning 'unto', such as Govinda – *Govindaya*, or Vishnu – *Vishnave* and so on. The mantra is not merely a combination of words but the sound representation of the Deity, and therefore the Deity Himself. The name of the Deity is, according to Srila Jiva Goswami, *jivatmaka*, the very life essence of the mantra, and therefore invoking the mantra with one's tongue means to be in the very presence of the Deity. There are consequently rules of conduct to be observed when in the presence of the Deity, and the guru will carefully teach these to the disciple. Unlike the Hare Krishna mantra, which is liberally given to all, most mantras are secret, being given only to those who are sufficiently dedicated to deserve *diksha*.

While the *diksha* ceremony may vary according to the community, the following elements are common:

1. Ritual sanctification of the place where the ceremony is to be conducted
2. Inviting the Deity as a witness
3. Worship with fruits, flowers, incense and lamps
4. Sipping of water with purifying mantras
5. Kindling of a sacred fire and offering grains into the flames
6. Disciple making his symbolic refuge by lying prostrate at the feet of the guru
7. Giving of the mantra by murmuring it into the ear of the disciple
8. Guru blessing the disciple
9. Presentation of gifts to the guru
10. Disciple breaking his fast with a meal of the guru's remnants

The disciple receives a mantra according to the *parampara* of his guru. A Shaivite disciple will receive a mantra dedicated to Shiva, and a Vaishnava disciple will receive a mantra dedicated to Vishnu. Common to all *paramparas* is the 24-syllable mantra known as *Savitur Gayatri* or *Brahma Gayatri*, dedicated to the infinite power behind the Sun. Since this mantra is found in the *Rig Veda* it is also known as the *Vaidik* or Vedic mantra. Since it is the first of all mantras given to students before they receive knowledge it is called 'The Mother of Knowledge,' or *Veda Mata*. It is traditionally given to boys and young men between the ages of 6-24 in a ceremony known as *upanayanam*. When the mantra is given a loop of cotton threads is placed on the upper body, running from the left shoulder diagonally across the chest and around the back up to the left shoulder. This sacred thread is known as the *upavita*, and it is the external symbol that one is a 'twice-born' or a *dwija*. The first birth is from one's mother and father, and the second birth from the eternal Mother and Father, the Vedas and God. After the *upanayanam* ceremony the disciple is qualified to study the Vedas and true education begins.

Almost as ancient as this mantra are the mantras used in ritual worship found in various texts collectively known as the *Pancharatra*. Some of these mantras are also in the same poetic meter as the Vedic *Gayatri* and are therefore also *Gayatri* mantras. Other mantras are in different meters. Mantras from the *Pancharatra* are known as *Pancharatrika* mantras, and they have been given to serious spiritual adepts for thousands of years. If a person is deemed ineligible for the Vedic *Gayatri* he can still be awarded any of the *Pancharatrika Gayatris* and other mantras if the guru chooses. Some mantras contain 6 syllables, some 8, 12, 18 or 32, but all of them have been celebrated throughout the Puranas for their efficacy. The guru may choose to give the disciple a number of *Pancharatrika* and other mantras according to the tradition of the *sampradaya* and his personal wishes.

The Hare Krishna mantra is of equal antiquity, spoken as it was by the speaker of the Vedic *Gayatri*, Lord Brahma. Since it consists of only the pure names of God it is suitable for all to chant. Though not strictly classified as a mantra as defined in the Vedas, it is referred to as such because all mantras are for the elevation of the soul to its eternal position, and the names of God contain the essence of all elevating power. For this reason the 32-syllable Hare Krishna mantra is known as the *maha* or 'great' mantra.

# The Diksha ceremony

The traditional *diksha* ceremony within the Vaishnava community will generally consist of the following elements:

1. *Udaka Shanti* – Sanctification of the spot where *diksha* will take place, and the temporary establishment of the Deity for the duration of the ceremony.

2. *Punyaha Vacana* – Purification of the accessories of the ritual.

3. *Homa* – Fire sacrifice.

4. *Tapa* – marking of the disciple's right and left upper arms or

shoulders with heated silver brands shaped as Vishnu's discus and conch (the *chakra* and *shankha*).

5. *Pundra* – giving the disciple the clay markings of *tilak* on twelve points of the body

6. *Dasya Nama* - giving the disciple a new name consisting of one of the names of God plus the suffix *Dasa* meaning 'servant.'

7. *Mantra Upadesha* – giving the disciple the mantra and explaining how to chant it.

8. *Yaga* – telling the disciple of his new duties as a servant of God. These are five in number:

    a. *Abhigamana* – visiting the temple to have darshan.

    b. *Upadana* – Collecting articles for home worship such as fruit, flowers, Tulasi leaves

    c. *Ijya* – Daily morning worship in the home, including decoration of the Deity, offering foods, and performing *arati*. For some disciples this may also include the daily 'Five Great Sacrifices' or *pancha-maha-yajna*, of service to God, ones ancestors, the great sages, society, and animals and birds.

    d. *Svadhyaya* – Study of scriptures such as the Upanishads, Bhagavad-gita and the Puranas.

    e. *Yoga* – Meditation on the Lord, His divine form and excellent attributes, particularly before the end of the evening.

By the decree of Chaitanya Mahaprabhu himself, the branding of the disciple's upper arms with a hot metal stamp was dispensed with in favour of cooling sandalwood paste designs made by wooden blocks carved into the same shapes. Later on, in the 18th century, the practise was dropped completely as a *diksha* requisite within the Gaudiya-Brahma community. It is retained within the Shri Sampradaya as a one-time event, and within the Madhva-Brahma community as an annual event.

Bhaktivinode Thakur comments, however, that *tapa* (translated as 'austerity' or 'heat') must still be present as part of the process of the disciple becoming purified. Some pains must be undergone by the disciple so that he becomes purified of his attachment to ego and bodily pleasure. Sinful acts must be abandoned and the disciple must rise early in the morning, undergoing any discomforts needed to serve the guru's order. Through the heat of this personal austerity, *tapa* can be preserved as an element of *diksha*.

It is almost standard within the ISKCON community for a person to have been given *pundra* or *tilak*, long before initiation, as well as Tulasi neck beads. This is in keeping with the theology of the Hare Krishna mantra being the liberal dispensation for the age. Instead of the maha-mantra being kept secret, it is generously distributed to all. So a disciple may eventually 'receive' the maha-mantra from the guru years after having heard it for the first time. The understanding here is not that the disciple is receiving a mantra for the second time, but that he or she is being given access, through the guru's blessing, to a higher understanding of the same mantra. This higher understanding is only made available to those who agree to follow the process of chanting the mantra and to carefully avoid the commission of mental, verbal and physical offences to the predominating Deity of the mantra, Shri Krishna, and to his servants, the Vaishnavas.

The Vaishnava community has offered initiation into the chanting of Vishnu's names to recognise the eligibility of all souls to dedicate themselves to the supreme person. Most gurus will offer some form of initiation after the candidate has undergone a suitable period of preparation. Different attitudes, however, prevail over the respective position of the Vedic *Gayatri* and those who can receive it through the *upanayanam* ceremony.

Vedic scripture describes that the *prarabdha karma* or the sum total of accumulated karmic reactions present at birth will give very strong tendencies to the individual. Those tendencies will influence the individual's thought, speech, action and work throughout life. Principles of social organisation described in the Vedas talk in terms of four classes of individual, each of whom is influenced by a certain set of karmic reactions and subsequent tendencies. The four classes of individual each have certain religious duties ascribed to them. The *upanayanam* ceremony is offered to the three higher classes, the brahmanas, *kshatriyas* and *vaishyas*. Those who have become 'twice-born' by virtue of *diksha* and a purified existence are recognised as having been elevated even within their class status, since *diksha* is regarded as a reformatory process that creates a better human being. Since the entire business of human life is to make spiritual progress while living peacefully, the business of organising human society can be made more factually progressive when it is guided by those who are 'twice-born.' Vedic culture holds that human society should never be led by the popularly-elected merchant class as it is today. In ancient India the social strata were thus carefully defined so that society would have qualified leaders and move always upwards towards God.

But sometimes saints were found in the 'lower classes,' and scoundrels were to be found in the 'upper classes,' and so Vaishnavas throughout history found themselves in the position of speaking out and establishing that the real mark of an 'upper class' human being was not whether they had been initiated with a *Gayatri* mantra, but whether they had taken advantage of the mantra and become better people. What were the personal qualities they exhibited in their dealings with others? Were they compassionate, kind, generous and devoted to good deeds? Or were they arrogant, haughty and uncaring of the suffering of others? If it was the latter then to be a so-called 'twice-born' was to be a hypocrite; and if it was the former then the person was factually 'upper class,' regardless of their external social status.

# Reforms

In their bid to help reform society, the Vaishnava community has consequently sometimes honoured the Vedic ideal of class, and sometimes not at all. Sometimes, those who were already given Vedic *Gayatri diksha* and become 'twice-born' were given *pancharatrika* mantras, yet those who were not 'twice-born' were also given them. In other circumstances those who received *pancharatrika* mantras might never be given the Vedic *Gayatri*, yet some were. Different attitudes prevailed at different periods of history.

By the time of the 19th century, what was once a noble ideal for organising human society had degenerated into a rigid caste system with some astonishing examples of human ugliness. The Vaishnavas responded accordingly. The reformer Bhaktivinode Thakur, even though he was fully qualified to wear the *upavita* or sacred thread, did not wear one, and neither did his disciples. By this gesture he signified a commonality between himself and his disciples, no matter from what social caste they originated. Through his actions and teaching he emphasised the position of a Vaishnava as being equal to a brahmana. It also reinforced the notion that Vaishnavas, as a class, could not strictly be considered as part of ordinary *varnashram* society, having already relinquished their material aspirations.

His son, Bhaktisiddhanta Thakur, by contrast, chose to wear a sacred thread and devised another strategy for dealing with the issue. He reasoned that the chanting of the maha-mantra served to develop all good qualities within the chanter, including those elevated human qualities possessed by the 'twice-born.' Yet since a candidate had to become first qualified for the Vedic *Gayatri*, he asked his followers to dedicate themselves to chanting the names of Krishna for some time until the suitable qualities developed within them. After such a transformation had become evident, the male followers – from whatever social background - were given both Vedic *Gayatri* and *Pancharatrika* mantras at the same time. Females were given the *Pancharatrika* mantras. As an external symbol that they had received the Vedic *Gayatri*, he also gave his male disciples the *upavita* to wear. By this external symbolism he signified the same message as his father – that the position of the Vaishnava – from any social level - was at least as good as the so-called 'upper classes.'

His decision to give the Vedic *Gayatri* to people of classes of person other than those born in upper class families was met with outrage by the priests of the day. Their status was threatened, as was their financial income and that of their descendants. Some of them employed gangs to hurt his disciples with stones and other physical attacks; and there was even a contract taken out to kill him. But he and his disciples survived, and the entire enterprise, known as the Gaudiya Mission, went on to enjoy considerable success.

Thus for Bhaktisiddhanta Thakur and his followers, being given the holy names of Krishna in the form of the maha-mantra became 'first initiation' and being given the Vedic *Gayatri* and *Pancharatrika* mantras became 'second initiation.' The *Gayatri* mantras, both Vedic and *Pancharatrika*, are regarded as being supportive of the main mantra, the maha-mantra. The maha-mantra was to be both softly spoken in private meditation and loudly broadcast to the public. The *Gayatri* mantras, both Vedic and *Pancharatrika*, were to be recited inaudibly, as per tradition.

Bhaktisiddhanta Thakur even went one step further in his reformist activity, so committed was he to remove the deep-set notions of class distinction. When someone came to him who had already received *Gayatri diksha* in childhood, he initiated them again, thus separating them from any obligations to their former guru, often a family priest who would have given little or no training. So when a young man, Abhay Charan De, came before him that is what Bhaktisiddhanta Thakur did. Abhay Charan De had previously been initiated by such a family guru, Mahendranatha Das Goswami, but Bhaktisiddhanta Thakur gave him the Vedic *Gayatri* again. Similarly B.R.Sridhara Swami was also given the *Gayatri* again, although he had been initiated in his youth by his *gurukula* guru.

The Thakur gave first initiation quite easily and stipulated a differing number of rounds on the wooden *japa* beads for his disciples. His father had described four rounds as a *grantha*, and the first level of commitment. So the Thakur also asked for this as a minimum number of rounds for busy family people. But he also urged them that the actual standard was to 'chant the holy name of Krishna constantly.' For the sannyasis, the renounced and the elderly he insisted on 64 rounds, some eight hours daily chanting, although a dispensation for those who were actively doing missionary work was that they could chant a minimum of sixteen rounds of beads.

## 'Sixteen rounds'

Abhaya Charan De – who would later become known as Srila Prabhupada and start his own worldwide mission – thus preserved his guru's emphasis on sixteen rounds in creating a body of preachers, and also followed him by giving first '*Harinama*' initiation followed by '*Gayatri*' initiation some six months later. Interestingly, by doing this he also followed the scriptural edict that both guru and disciple should mutually examine one another for at least one year before *Gayatri diksha* is given.

Similarly, ISKCON also follows the traditional system of *diksha* - but in two halves. The first half, consisting of *Tapa, Pundra and Dasya Nama* makes up the 'first initiation' and then *Mantra Upadesha and Yaga* comprise the 'second initiation.' The preliminary ceremonials are common to both, although ISKCON is unique in the Gaudiya community as also having a fire sacrifice or *homa* as part of the ceremony for giving the maha-mantra.

The instruction manual for *diksha* is a book known as *Hari Bhakti Vilasa*, written and edited in 1534 by Sanatana Goswami and Gopala Bhatta Goswami under the direct order of Chaitanya Mahaprabhu. As a handbook for Vaishnava practise it is broad in scope and includes quotations from more than two hundred scriptures. In once sense it is not merely a Gaudiya manual – since the Gaudiya community was only just being formed at the time – but a handbook that unites all Vaishnava *sampradayas* in its inclusivity.

It devotes the entire second chapter to *diksha* and covers the need for *diksha*, the appropriate time for it, and the details of the wide variety of ceremonies held to mark such an important occasion within different spiritual communities. Although there are many colourful details and *tantric* rituals that can be employed, the Goswamis conclude that the best time is when the guru gives his consent, and the best place is a holy place.

In ISKCON the candidate is required to have demonstrated an initial taste for spiritual life by chanting, choosing to associate with other devotees, engaging in devotional service and giving up bad habits. At the ceremony of first, or *Harinama* initiation, the candidate must be freshly bathed and dressed in new cloth. After sipping water, three strands of Tulasi neckbeads will be given to him. The guru gives a lecture, often on the ten offenses to the names of Krishna, a list taken from the *Padma* Purana. The candidate is then called forward and offers *pranama* by bowing down to the guru. He or she is then asked to recite the 'four regulative principles,' four restrictions that are to be followed thereafter. Then the guru will give the disciple's new name, a name that often begins with the first letter of the old name. After this the guru hands the disciple a string of wooden *japa* beads upon which he has chanted. A fire sacrifice follows, after which is kirtan. The new disciple offers the guru a small *dakshina* of money as a gift.

Second initiation follows at an unspecified interval, although Srila Prabhupada said that it was not universally necessary for all his disciples, and that discretion should be applied as to who should be given it: 'Only those who are serious.' Whereas the maha-mantra is public, the *diksha* mantras are secret, given by the guru in a private place. Beginning with

Srila Prabhupada and ISKCON, female disciples have also been given the Vedic *Gayatri* mantras, although not the sacred thread.

# 13

# Qualities of the guru and the disciple

*The mediaeval poet, philosopher, and Vaishnava guru, Vedanta Deshika (1268-1370) is a highly regarded acharya of the Shri Sampradaya. He appeared more than two hundred years after Srila Ramanujacharya. His writings on the guru found in his work Nyasa Vimsati were incorporated into the Hari Bhakti Vilasa by Gopala Bhatta Goswami (1503-1578). Here he supplies qualities of the guru and qualities of the good disciple.*

## Fourteen Qualities of the Guru

1. ***Sat-sampradaya siddham*** – He is firmly established in the *sampradaya*.

2. ***Sthira dhiyam*** – His mind remains firmly fixed, even in debates based on deceitful reasoning.

3. ***Anagam*** – He is free from sin, and never swerves from *shastra*.

4. ***Srotriyam*** – He is fully conversant with the Vedas and *Vedanta*.

5. ***Brahma nistham*** – He has resolute devotion to God, free from blemishes.

6. ***Sattvastham*** – He is dominated by *sattva guna*.

7. ***Satya vacam*** – Free from deceitful speech, he always tells the truth.

8. ***Samaya niyataya sadu vritya sametam*** – He is adept at *anushtanams* (religious practices).

9. ***Dambha asuyadhi muktam*** – He exhibits no inauspicious

characteristics such as egoism or jealousy.

10. *Jita visayi ganam* – He does not engage in conduct prohibited by the Bhagavat *shastra*s. Has controlled senses.

11. *Dirgha bandhum* – He is a friend and guide for all those who have sought his refuge, always seeking their welfare, and lifting them up to the ultimate destination.

12. *Dayalum* – He has spontaneous compassion and kindness for his disciples.

13. *Skhalite sasitaram* – He corrects his disciples and recommends improving actions for them.

14. *Svapara hitaparam* – He determines what is mutually good for him and his disciple and acts accordingly.

# Fifteen qualities of the good disciple

1. *Sadh buddhi* – Good intelligence.

2. *Sadhu sevi* – He has the disposition to mingle with, and serve, the *sadhu*s.

3. *Samucita charita* – He is marked for his righteous conduct, both personal and social.

4. *Tattva bodha abhilasi* – Has an eagerness to learn spiritual teaching.

5. *Susrusu* – He excels in helping the guru in his *seva*.

6. *Tyakta mana* – He has become humble or at least free from the gross manifestations of pride.

7. *Pranipatena para* – He has implicit obedience to the guru and bows down in his presence.

8. *Prasna kala pratiksa* – He waits for the right time to clear his doubts about what he has learned from the acharya.

9. *Santa* – He is peaceful and self-controlled.

10. *Danta* – Controls both his mind and speech.

11. *Anasuya* – Free from jealousy.

12. *Saranam upagata* – Always eager to hear 'instructions of divine grace' from his guru.

13. *Sastra visvas sali* – Has total faith in shastra.

14. *Paristam prapta* – Ready to undergo any tests set by the guru for assessing his state of preparedness to be accepted as a deserving disciple.

15. *Krita-vid sisya* – He will be a grateful disciple for the knowledge to be received from the acharya.

Vedanta Deshika concludes: *"Tattvata – abhimatam sikshaniya."* (Truly, such a person with these qualities is fit for instruction by the acharya).

# 14

# What does a guru teach?

*Guru means 'teacher,' but what is he supposed to teach you, and how often? How do you know if he is teaching you correctly? How do you know if you are a good student? What is the relationship of learning to spiritual progress? This chapter explores the ancient and modern teachings of the Vaishnava guru.*

*In the last chapter we examined the writings of the great acharya Vedanta Deshika and this chapter begins with his delineation of the essential instructions the Vaishnava guru must teach a disciple.*

## Four key instructions of a Vaishnava guru

1. The creation, sustenance and dissolution of everything that is animate and inanimate are under the total control of the Lord and His consort. We have to comprehend the Lord as:

    a. *Jagat Karanan* – The Creator of all

    b. *Jagat Rakshakan* – The Protector of all

    c. *Sarva Samharakan* – The Destroyer of all Creations

    d. *Karma Pravrtti Niyamakan* – The Commander of all acts initiated by the soul

    e. *Sarva Karma Phala Dhayakan* – The Granter of the fruits of all karmas

2. Understanding this unique role of the Lord, please do not consider anyone else as your goal.

3. Do not seek anyone other than Him as a means to reach Him.

4. Knowing that both fear and fearlessness about *samsara* arise from

Him, please do not break His commands in *shastra*.

## The teachings of Madhvacharya

A guru in the line of Madhvacharya would be expected to teach his disciples what Madhva taught his. Baladeva Vidyabhusana, trained in the line of Madhva, explains his core teachings as follows:

1. Krishna, who is known as Hari, is the Supreme Lord, the Absolute.
2. That Supreme Lord may be known through the Vedas.
3. The material world is real.
4. The *jivas*, or souls, are different from the Supreme Lord.
5. The *jivas* are by nature servants of the Supreme Lord.
6. There are two categories of *jivas*: liberated and illusioned.
7. Liberation means attaining the lotus feet of Krishna, that is, entering into an eternal relationship of service to the Supreme Lord.
8. Pure devotional service is the cause of this relationship.
9. The truth may be known through direct perception, inference, and Vedic authority.

## Five key conversations

Lord Shri Chaitanya Mahaprabhu also positioned himself in the preceptorial line of Madhvacharya and taught all of the above. In addition he taught the fundamental place of the recitation of the names of God; the congregational chanting of God's names as the religion of the Age of *Kali*; the supreme nature of the Srimad Bhagavatam; the supremacy of Krishna; and the ultimate place of Krishna's consort, Radha. There are several important 'teaching conversations' he had with different followers, five of which contain essential lessons in both the theology and practise.

Lord Chaitanya spoke with Sarvabhauma Bhattacharya, the royal philosopher of King Prataparudra and a brilliant logician, and with

Prakashananda Saraswati, the celebrated follower of Shankaracharya. He convinced both that the personal Godhead was higher than the impersonal aspect of *Brahman*. While travelling in the south of India, his talks with the Krishna devotee Ramananda Raya began at a fundamental level and then, prompted by the Lord's insistence, culminated in the highest conceptions of *bhakti*.

With the two brothers, Sanatana Goswami and Rupa Goswami, formerly very highly placed governors in the administration of the Muslim Nawab Hussein Shah, Lord Chaitanya spoke in such a way as to give a thoroughly systematic course of instruction in the philosophy, theology, and orthodox practise of Vaishnavism, particular focused on devotional love of Radha and Krishna.

His teaching of the first brother, Rupa Goswami, took place in the holy city of Prayag, over a ten-day period. Lord Chaitanya began by describing the embodied soul; different levels of consciousness of the embodied souls, and how the cycle of birth and death ceases when the soul is given the 'seed of *bhakti*.' Developing this imagery, the Lord described how the devotee, the gardener, should water the seed and guard against any weeds while waiting for the fruit to appear. He then went on to describe the different relationships, or *rasas*, which the soul can have with Krishna.

On a separate occasion the Lord taught Rupa's brother, Sanatana, in the same city. Sanatana, like his brother, had been regularly hearing Srimad Bhagavatam from spiritually advanced brahmanas, and even before he taught him, Lord Chaitanya Mahaprabhu immediately requested him to compile a book of Vaishnava practise: "...*Vaishnava achara bhakti smriti shastra*..." The Lord's teaching began by his describing the constitutional position of the soul and quickly went on to explaining Lord Shri Krishna's internal and external energies; His expansions and incarnations; the Spiritual Sky and the supreme beauty of Krishna. He then taught that devotional service is the highest form of yoga, and how the spiritual aspirant must reject any self-motivated practises of karma, *jnana*, or mystic yoga. Lord Chaitanya taught Sanatana how dormant consciousness of Krishna is awakened by the mercy of a pure devotee of Krishna, then explained to him the characteristics of a pure devotee and the six symptoms of souls surrendered to Krishna.

He then said: "I wish to speak briefly of the various practises of devotional service," and proceeded to list the sixty-four items of *bhakti*, the most important five being: "One should associate with devotees, chant the Holy Name of the Lord, hear Srimad Bhagavatam, reside at Mathura and worship the Deity with faith and veneration...even a slight performance of these five awakens love for Krishna." Lord Chaitanya Mahaprabhu continued by describing the gradual increase in love of God that takes place within the practitioner of the items of *bhakti*, and finished by describing some of the many qualities of Krishna and Radha.

When Sanatana Goswami asked him how to write such a difficult book, Lord Chaitanya reassured him and began to describe the book he wanted. "In the beginning, describe how one must take shelter of a bona fide spiritual master. Your book should describe the characteristics of the spiritual master and the disciple. Then, before accepting a spiritual master, one can be assured of the spiritual master's position. Similarly the spiritual master can also be assured of the disciple's position..." The Lord continued explaining the contents of the book, covering every aspect of a devotee's practise: brushing teeth, bathing, putting on *tilak*, performing temple service and collecting all the items for Deity worship. There should be sections, the Lord said, for daily, fortnightly, monthly and annual activities and events such as festivals of Krishna's appearance. Finally, the Lord explained, everything in the book should be supported with evidence from the Puranas.

Sanatan Goswami responded by writing both the *Hari Bhakti Vilasa*, a book on Vaishnava behaviour, and the *Brihad Bhagavatamrita*, a book about the journey of the soul to the highest realm. His brother, Rupa Goswami, wrote the *Bhakti Rasamrita Sindhu* and the *Upadeshamrita*, and also several dramas that reveal the divine *lilas* of Radha and Krishna. The resulting literature of both brothers contains references from more than two hundred standard Vaishnava and Vedic texts. Within the disciplic line coming from Shri Chaitanya Mahaprabhu, the books of Rupa and Sanatan are thus considered to be the standard authorities for the practise of *bhakti-yoga,* or devotional service to Radha and Krishna. Due to the teachings contained in these books, and the knowledge and spiritual inspiration they provided to generations of devotees, the pastimes of Lord Shri Krishna became widely known once again, and the small village of Vrindavan became the city of five thousand temples it is today.

Part Two | What does a guru teach?

# The teachings of Srila Prabhupada

In his life and teaching, Srila A.C. Bhaktivedanta Swami Prabhupada faithfully taught the lessons of all his spiritual preceptors. He either translated into English, or taught through discourses, the works of Rupa and Sanatana Goswami, and the conclusions of their nephew, the great mediaeval philosopher, Jiva Goswami. Rupa Goswami's treatise on devotion to Krishna, *Bhakti Rasamrita Sindhu*, became *The Nectar of Devotion*, and his short volume of essential instructions, *Upadeshamrita*, became *The Nectar of Instruction*. But he went further – he taught the antecedent literature as well. He carefully translated and gave his disciples a lengthy commentary on the Srimad Bhagavatam and the Bhagavad-gita. He took great care to provide them with the most important Upanishad, the *Isha Upanishad* (rendered as *Isopanishad*) and even wrote a separate commentary on the Tenth Canto of the Srimad Bhagavatam, seamlessly blending translation and commentary into a prose rendition, entitled *Krsna, the Supreme Personality of Godhead*. He summarised the most important conversations of Lord Chaitanya in *Teachings of Lord Chaitanya*, and then went on to translate the entire teachings and life of the Lord in the multi-volume *Chaitanya Charitamrita*.

He introduced traditional worship of the Deity throughout the world, and indicated to his disciples that they should follow the *archana* prescriptions found in the ancient *Pancharatra Agama* and rendered by the Goswamis in their book, the *Hari Bhakti Vilasa* and later, shorter works such as the *Archana Paddhati*.

As such, a modern guru in the line of Chaitanya Mahaprabhu, the Goswamis and their representative Srila Prabhupada, would surely be found teaching the contents of the ISKCON founder-*acharya's* works. He would be able to cross-reference them and be able to quote sufficient references from memory, including the original Sanskrit or Bengali. He would teach correct pronunciation and teach his students how to defeat arguments posed against the Vaishnava conclusion. Although he might not know other works extensively, the modern guru should also know and have an appreciation for the *Mahabharata* and *Ramayana*.

The guru should surely teach how to engage in the recitation of the names of Krishna and be able to provide the disciple with adequate instruction on practical techniques of chanting the maha-mantra, avoiding mistakes, apathy, inattention and so on. The guru might also teach songs of the Vaishnava acharyas and their meanings.

If the guru gives the *Gayatri* mantra then he must teach the disciple how to chant it, how to follow the rules on timing and so on. And if the disciple is to engage in worship of the Deity, the guru must also teach the various modes of worship; how to gather paraphernalia for worship, and the various rituals, ceremonies and festivals associated with the particular Deity.

# Modern practice

In contemporary practice, all these different aspects of teaching may not be taught by one person. In fact, it is quite common for the guru to entrust education of his disciple to the care of others. But it is certainly the guru's responsibility to ensure that his disciple is being fully educated in the philosophy, theology, practise and ritual of devotional service to Krishna. If he is not teaching the disciple personally, he must know who is and exactly what they are teaching. Correspondingly, it is the disciple's duty to ensure that he or she is learning everything they need, and in a systematic manner, and to present to the guru a report of what they've learned.

Srila Prabhupada was concerned that his disciples learn his books thoroughly and be able to quote them as a lawyer knows and quotes his law books. He instituted a system of exams for his disciples and was troubled when his sannyasis did not seem to know enough to be able to present the teachings in a proficient manner. He thus urged his followers to spend time each day reading the books that he had given them.

In the beginning of spiritual life, faith is strongly established through a good foundation of Vedic knowledge, since such knowledge serves to remove doubt, fix the mind on transcendental objectives, and counter internal and external arguments. It enables the practitioner to be convinced and to convince others of the reality of Krishna. And in the advanced stages of spiritual life, descriptions of Krishna's qualities and activities provide the greatest pleasure.

# 15

# How does a guru teach?

*The guru teaches the disciples the Vedas – but the manner of his teaching is unique.*

**Everyone who has ever been to school knows the normal manner in which students are taught.** The teacher presents the information and the pupils listen carefully. They look at illustrations, charts and graphs, then repeat extracts of the text by rote, learn formulae, write essays, do hands-on experiments and answer exam questions. At some point in all of this something sticks in their minds and they have 'learned.'

The guru does all of this, and more – he is a teacher, after all. He uses many techniques in order that his students learn the Vedas and the corollary rituals, behaviours and disciplines. Yet the real way of learning the Vedas, or truly understanding them, can be through nothing short of enlightenment, the awakening, or illumination that descends upon the soul as the grace of a higher intelligence.

The path of gaining higher, spiritual knowledge, in contrast to gaining ordinary or academic knowledge, is said to be 'descending' rather than 'ascending.' The Sanskrit word *arohana* means 'ascending,' as in the expression *sam-arohana* or 'mountain climbing.' The word also means 'ladder.' *Avarohana*, by contrast, means 'descending', and the expression *avaroha-pantha* means the 'traveller of descending knowledge.'

The spiritual path is one of descending grace, and of allowing the guru to give knowledge, casting aside ego. His Divine Grace A.C. Bhaktivedanta Swami Prabhupada had much to say about the difference between a teacher of ordinary knowledge and a teacher of spiritual knowledge:

> "*For advancement of material knowledge there is a need for personal ability and researching aptitude, but in the case of*

*spiritual knowledge, all progress depends more or less on the mercy of the spiritual master. The spiritual master must be satisfied with the disciple; only then is knowledge automatically manifest before the student of spiritual science."*

*"The process should not, however, be misunderstood to be something like magical feats whereby the guru acts like a magician and injects spiritual knowledge into his disciple, as if surcharging him with an electrical current. The bona fide spiritual master reasonably explains everything to the disciple on the authorities of Vedic wisdom. The disciple can receive such knowledge not exactly intellectually, but by submissive enquiries and a service attitude. The idea is that both guru and disciple must be bona fide." – (Srimad Bhagavatam 2.1.10)*

The Vaishnava guru does not teach the Vedas merely as an academic subject in which he has become proficient; he teaches it as a pathway of divine revelation that he himself has walked and from which he has personally prospered. As one of the results of divine revelation is an acute awareness of the severity of earthly bondage, he teaches so that the student can be free from a worldly predicament. The guru is after the transformation of the disciple, not merely transmission of information. Because the guru is realised in his personal capacity, he also teaches with genuine compassion for the student. Srila Prabhupada writes:

*"The bona fide spiritual master's concern is how the devotees who have surrendered to him as a representative of the Lord may make progress in devotional service." – (Chaitanya Charitamrita Adi 1.61)*

The guru, however, is not an unworldly figure, aloof in his study of ancient texts and far removed from practical affairs and the minds of ordinary people. He knows the psychology of each disciple and speaks to that student appropriately to help him. He also guides the student towards activities that will serve to help him personally:

*"A bona fide spiritual master knows the nature of a particular man and what sort of duties he can perform in Krishna consciousness, and he instructs him in that way." – (Srimad Bhagavatam 3.22.7)*

*"It is the duty of the spiritual master or teacher to observe the psychological movement of a particular boy and thus train him in*

*a particular occupational duty."* - (Srimad Bhagavatam 4.8.36)

*"It is the duty of the acharya...to find the ways and means for his disciple to fix his mind on Krishna. That is the beginning of sadhana bhakti."* – (Nectar of Devotion)

The spiritual master is also meant to be sufficiently detached from the pleasures of the world that he finds no interest in anything material. The Vaishnava guru automatically displays this in his daily life, and tries to inculcate the same spirit in his disciples, knowing that attachment for any material pleasures of the world will merely force the disciple to return again, after this life is over.

*"Children play on the beach and make houses out of sand, but after a while the father comes and says, 'Now, my dear children, time is up. Stop this business and come home.' This is the business of the guru – to teach his disciples detachment. The world is not our place; our place is Vaikuntha loka."* – (Teachings of Lord Kapila.)

Once an individual has asked to be admitted into the guru-disciple contract, it also means that he is asking the guru to guide, correct, and even, on occasion, rebuke him as his disciple. Although this may not be a regular occurrence, it is nonetheless necessary as a part of the gentle art of personal transformation: "The father, the spiritual master, and the supreme executive officer of the state are always well-wishers of their sons, their students and their citizens respectively. As such, the well-wishers have a right to chastise their dependents." – Indra speaking to Krishna in *Krsna the Supreme Personality of Godhead*.

But the guru should only offer a rebuke if he, in his turn, has been so dealt with by his own guru and has reaped the reward of compassionate correction. He cannot be a stern taskmaster if he does not exemplify the personal characteristics that he demands from his students. The disciple learns many lessons simply by studying the character of his guru and his behaviour, especially in challenging or difficult circumstances. The guru must not simply be a teacher by voice, but a teacher by example. A famous conversation takes place between Sanatana Goswami and Haridas Thakur:

*"Some behave very well but do not preach, whereas others preach but do not behave properly. You simultaneously perform both*

> *duties in relation to the holy name, by your personal behaviour and your preaching. Therefore you are the spiritual master of the entire world." – (Chaitanya Charitamrita, Antya 4.102-3)*

Srila Prabhupada echoes Sanatana Goswami's analysis by saying: 'The qualifications expressed in this connection are that one must act according to the scriptural injunctions and at the same time preach. One who does so is a bonafide spiritual master.'

The guru is meant to engage his disciples in worship of the consecrated image of the Lord, a process explained in the *Pancharatra* literature known as *archana*. This involves much practical activity such as collecting fruits, vegetables and flowers; making garlands, sewing clothes to dress the image, grinding sandalwood; cooking and cleaning. Then there is the physically demanding process of the worship itself with ceremonial bathing, dressing and decoration of the image, the offering of home-made ghee lamps and serving the public who visit the temple:

> *"Simple theoretical book knowledge is not sufficient for a neophyte devotee. Book knowledge is theoretical, whereas the archana process is practical. Spiritual knowledge must be developed by a combination of theoretical and practical knowledge, and that is the guaranteed way for attainment of spiritual perfection." - (Srimad Bhagavatam 2.3.22)*

Above all, the guru or acharya, the spiritual master, is most concerned that anyone who has come to him for learning the science and art of devotion should gradually be elevated, by a wide variety of means, to the platform of factual Krishna consciousness, the goal of life. The great writer on *bhakti*, Srila Rupa Goswami, states as follows:

> *tasmat kenapy upayena manah krsne nivesayet*
> *sarve vidhi-nisedhah syur etayor eva kinkarah*

> "An acharya should devise a means by which people may somehow or other come to Krishna consciousness. First they should become Krishna conscious, and all the prescribed rules and regulations may later gradually be introduced." – *(Chaitanya Charitamrita, Adi 7.37)*

Part Two | Teaching techniques of the gurus

# 16

# Teaching techniques of the gurus

*Teachers of every subject use a variety of educational styles. By employing a range of techniques they help their students rise gradually through levels of knowledge and a nuanced understanding of the subject. If the subject has a practical application the student learns new practical skills and acquires competency in their execution. Along the way, new perspectives open up, and the student's values adjust accordingly.*

So, what are the techniques by which a guru teaches the Vedas? And how does he teach the devotion of *bhakti-yoga*? There are many classical techniques that gurus have passed on to their disciples through the ages, simply through the act of teaching them. The disciple learns through those techniques and, in turn, uses them to teach his own disciples. Srila A.C. Bhaktivedanta Swami Prabhupada employed a vast array of classical teaching styles, and was therefore a unique exemplar of a traditional guru. The large number of disciples who grasped what was a deeply philosophical and nuanced worldview bear witness to his effectiveness as a teacher. Some, but certainly not all, are listed here. Contemporary gurus will certainly employ all, or at least some, of these in their teaching.

**Argument** – the form of argument employed by the guru does not involve a loss of temper or displays of aggression. This form of active dialogue takes the form of a protagonist raising an objection and the guru dismissing the objection using several forms of logic or counter-quotation. When staged between two parties, each of whom has thoroughly researched their philosophical position, the ensuing debate is very mentally strengthening for both participants and observers.

**Conversation** – Naturally, the guru speaks about the goal of the spiritual life and does so with enthusiasm. The guru who teaches through silence is a thoroughly modern invention. By talking to his disciple, the guru shares his knowledge, experience and wisdom. By questioning his disciple and listening to him, the guru learns more about his student and his level of understanding.

**Correction** – the disciple must allow himself to be corrected by the guru. His master may correct his errant thinking, his words or his actions. Being corrected by the guru is considered by the student to be a reward, even if such correction might be harsh. The corrections issued by the guru range from a gentle chiding all the way through levels of rebuke to a severe verbal chastisement.

**Correspondence** – the guru personally writes to his disciples leaving them with permanent sources of inspiration and encouragement.

**Demonstration** – The path of *bhakti-yoga* involves physical activity directed toward the satisfaction of Krishna. These activities are known as devotional service and the disciple can learn not only the techniques of ritual and ceremony but also the mood of care and love with which the guru performs these actions.

**Encouragement** – The spiritual path can be divided into clear stages, each of which the disciple must pass through. Every stage involves some fear, since the disciple will have to sever certain attachments in order to progress. The guru helps by giving the disciple courage to face the next step. The giving of courage is known as encouragement.

**Example** – the guru is nothing more than a disciple who teaches, and so his life must be a living example of his guru's instructions to him. By watching his actions – even when he does not speak – his disciple can learn much.

**Lectures** – when the guru speaks to a gathering of disciples or to the public, there is often a commensurate heightening of presentation and subsequent comprehension. The guru manifests enthusiasm and knowledge in the face of the assembly, and takes time to present persuasive arguments to many people at once.

Part Two | Teaching techniques of the gurus

**Natural analogies** – this verbal technique employs drawing as many points of comparison between a sometimes abstract philosophical point and a naturally occurring phenomenon. If done correctly, that which is known creates an understanding of that which is currently hidden from the disciple.

**Recitation** – It is said that 'Recitation is the Mother of Learning' and this is nowhere more true than in the guru's ashram. Disciples recite their allotted portion of the Vedas as a daily discipline, committing vast amounts of text to memory at a young age. Once imbibed, it will always be ready for recall.

**Redirection** – the guru may, occasionally, assign the disciple a completely different task from his normal routine. By changing the disciple's activity the guru stretches him and forces him to call upon new abilities.

**Removal of Doubt** - When appropriate, the guru helps to remove the doubts of the disciple, both in the goal of spiritual life and the means to achieve it. He also helps to remove the disciple's doubts about his own qualifications to follow his guru's instructions.

**Service** – the disciple comes to the guru with 'a mountain of pride' from previous births in the world, and somehow or other it is the guru's task to try to reduce this burden of selfishness in his students. Service to others – whether willing or not – helps to develop humility, and when pride diminishes illumination of true knowledge increases. So the guru engages his disciples in menial tasks. He may also set them challenging or seemingly impossible tasks.

**Singing** – devotional love is expressed often through the voice, in prayer, chant, or musical singing. Disciples learn much through their master's voice, not only the content of the song but from the emotional content.

**Walking dialogue** – the guru and the disciple walk together, and the movement helps in both the presentation and the assimilation of the subject matter. When surrounded by nature, the guru may point out an example in nature that illustrates the points under discussion.

**Writing** – The guru meditates on what he wishes to present to his followers then, taking help from the writings of the predecessor acharyas, he carefully writes down his detailed explanations and observations, coupled with his deep realisations. The book links the disciple with the Veda texts, the lineage of acharyas and his guru, all at the same time.

# 17

# The reprehensible delusions of guruship

*The mediaeval teacher who gave these cautionary instructions for gurus wrote many important works on the practise of bhakti. His name is Pillai Lokacharya, a southern Indian Vaishnava in the Shri Sampradaya, and he lived from 1217 until 1323. He wrote eighteen major works and Srila Bhaktivinode Thakur liked his summary of Vaishnava philosophy known as Artha Panchakam. The Thakur was the first to have it translated from the original Tamil into Bengali language. Years later, in the presence of Srila Bhaktisiddhanta Saraswati Thakur, two Shri Vaishnavas resided in one of the Gaudiya Math temples and discussed it with the devotees there for several days. One of Pillai Lokacharya's main works was the Shri Vachana Bhushanam, which summarizes the teachings of Shri Ramanujacharya (1017-1137). In that book is found the following short section. It has been translated by Shri Rama Ramanuja Achari and I reproduce it here with a few additional comments.*

Pillai Lokacharya has described in Shri Vachana Bhushanam three reprehensible delusions which must be avoided by the guru at all costs. These are:-

**Verse 308: The delusions of 'preceptorship' or thinking of oneself as the preceptor:**

*A guru should think of himself as simply a conduit of the Lord's grace and not as a teacher of sacred lore. This awareness prevents the guru from developing the egotistical notion of being a great and learned person and having custodianship of spiritual knowledge.*

At first, this seems a strange proposition from a Vaishnava acharya. The very word guru means 'teacher' and the definition of a Vaishnava guru is that he is a teacher of sacred lore. If he doesn't teach that then he's not a guru. He must also be a preceptor, or a living example of scriptural precepts. If he doesn't live what he teaches – if he's not a preceptor – he cannot be a guru. If he is a good disciple of his own acharya he must also be a custodian of a great spiritual legacy; it was carefully given to him by his own guru in *parampara* with the confident expectation that he, the faithful disciple, would offer it to others. This verse doesn't mean that the guru should disregard his responsibility to teach others and abandon his disciples. But he should always remember that 'learned preceptor' is only how the disciple sees him. When he thoughtfully considers his own role, he should not regard himself as great and learned, merely a humble disciple and messenger of his own guru. And because his own guru is receiving the Lord's grace, his guru may mercifully bestow some of this grace upon him, allowing him to act as a conduit – a pipe or channel – through which the Lord's mercy can flow.

### Verse 309: The delusions about the role of the disciple:

*The guru should not think of the disciple as his own personal adherent – the disciple should rather be thought of as a co-disciple of the same acharya. Thus the guru avoids the potential for exploitation inherent in the relationship.*

The entire material world is operating under a fatal misconception. Bound up tight into a bodily identity, each soul thinks: "This body and mind is everything that I am, it is me, and these material things are mine, and these other persons are mine, too. I could be much happier if many more things were arranged for me to enjoy, and even happier if others would make me the centre of their lives. Surely, if they would love me and serve me more I would find lasting happiness."

But the reality is the very reverse of this perspective. The individual soul is not the centre of the universe, even though he may feel that his own particular universe revolves around him. Lasting happiness can be achieved not by being served by others, but by serving others and, in particular, the most significant Other. The path to freedom from predominating self-absorption, and the way to lasting happiness begins when the soul realises: "This temporary body and mind is not 'me,' and therefore nothing is 'mine.' The Supreme is the centre of the universe, and my happiness will come from divine service to that centre."

Therefore, there is potential danger for the guru if he thinks: 'This disciple is mine,' since he sets up a proprietary relationship within his mind. How can he 'own' another person and describe that person as 'mine?' And if on the basis of a sense of ownership he then allows himself to be the object of service for the disciple, there is a further danger that he may exploit the situation and thereby forget his own position as a servant of God. So here Pillai Lokacharya proposes a solution: that the guru simply regards the student as a 'co-disciple' of his own guru. By looking upon the disciple as a spiritual brother in service to his own acharya, he can be free from any tendency to regard the disciple as his personal servant.

However, throughout the Vedas the disciple is instructed to render services to the guru, viewing the guru as a human representative of the divine. Cleaning, cooking, washing, carrying, collecting and chopping wood, begging donations of money, grains, fruits and vegetables – all these traditional services are described. The guru's duty is to accept this service. Particularly if he is elderly, the guru may actually need these services to physically maintain his teaching institution. So when the disciple collects wood for the guru's daily fire ceremony, the guru is meant to burn it; and when the disciple cooks for him, the guru is meant to actually eat it. So the guru accepts service from the disciple, yet he must not consider him a servant; and he must teach him as a student – which involves looking for gaps in his learning or defects in his character – all the while regarding him as a spiritual peer. It all sounds like an impossible, torturous paradox.

The reconciliation is not a material, mental adjustment. As is often the case in these circumstances, the only solution is a spiritual one. By deep consideration of his fortunate identity as a disciple of his acharya, the guru will come to the only conclusion possible: that the students surrounding him – who choose to regard themselves as his disciples - are only there because of the spiritual wisdom of his acharya. Were it not for his acharya's deep knowledge and compassionate teaching, his rigorous character formation of him as a young disciple and his personal guidance and spiritual blessings, none of the students would even be there. He considers that it is therefore not to him that they offer their menial service, but to his acharya. But they do so *through* him. He acts as a channel for their service which he passes upwards to his guru, and for receiving the grace of his guru which he passes back down to them. Accordingly, their gratitude, honour, respect, dedication and love are also passed upwards, since these profound feelings are, by rights, also intended for his spiritual master. In this way they are factually co-disciples, although it is never correct for them to consider themselves as such. But from the guru's point of view they are; and he may even consider that: 'My acharya has sent me these students to teach – how kind he is.' The guru's acceptance of their service is simply another duty he performs for his acharya.

But this is not a level of self-abnegation that can arise and be sustained in the guru through mere willpower. It must have a spiritual source and come effortlessly. It can only be achieved when the guru has an ongoing spiritual connection with his acharya, when he experiences his grace in daily life, and when he constantly reflects on his good fortune.

**Verse 310: The delusions arising from the process of instruction of a *shishya* - these are of four categories:**

1. Seeking to gain financially from the disciple, either by gifts or tuition fees, *dakshina*.

2. The delusion that one is actually facilitating the liberation of the disciple.

3. The delusion that one is assisting the Lord in his saving of souls.

4. Seeking or expecting social companionship or service from disciples.

Firstly, the high quality guru will neither ask for, nor expect, *guru-dakshina*, until the studies of the disciple are complete. The guru must see that his instructions have been absorbed by the disciple, that his character has developed and that he has spiritualised his life. This may take some years. There are daily donations the disciple accrues for his guru by begging, and these help with maintenance only. They are not the same as the *guru-dakshina*, which is a concluding gift in gratitude for years of tuition. If the guru regards his disciple as a source of additional income, above and beyond what he needs for simple maintenance, then he may gradually develop the mentality of a businessman. As soon as this occurs the guru stops correcting his disciple and begins to flatter him. Both guru and disciple then become weakened by that insincere transaction.

Second, the guru may be praised by his disciples as being the one who is taking them to Vaikuntha, the eternal abode of God. Although it is their sacred right to address him in this way, if he begins to believe them, that he is the giver of liberation, then he has assumed one of the qualities of God to be his own. Only God gives spiritual liberation to the living being, and the guru, though he may be praised by the disciple as a saviour of sorts, must always remember that he is nothing but a representative. Just as a policeman must always remember that both he and his uniform merely represent the ultimate power of the state, so the guru must remember that his power is merely borrowed. Failure to remember this – whether by guru or policeman – results in corruption and a consequent fall from position.

In addition, the guru should not imagine, says Pillai Lokacharya, that he is somehow assisting God in the task of liberating souls, or that without him God would not be able to perform the task. God, known as Mukunda, is quite capable of liberating all souls whenever He wishes and ultimately has no need of the guru at all. The guru plays his part by voicing the sacred scripture to the disciple and correcting him externally, but the eternal guru within, the *Paramatma*, is enlightening the disciple and leads him through successive stages of surrender.

However, in his book *Madhurya Kadambini*, the great eighteenth century Vaishnava author Srila Vishvanath Chakravarti Thakur gives more credit to the guru. He explains that "Krishna is neutral, but His mercy follows the devotees' mercy, and a devotee preacher functions on the *madhyama* platform where he discriminates who is receptive to mercy." So in his opinion, Krishna brings us to a guru, who connects us to Krishna. By the recommendation of the guru, and generally only in that way, does Krishna deliver us. So in that sense the guru also delivers the disciple, but he is not meant to consider himself in that role.

Finally, Pillai Lokacharya says that the guru must not attempt to turn his disciples into comfort-providers or seek to derive emotional companionship from them. The disciples may indeed provide comfort and companionship, but if the guru actively looks for it, or expects it from them, he is at fault. It may develop within him an artificial dependency that will prevent him from correcting his disciples when needed, and may deter him from his absolute and complete dependence on God. Although the guru has been advised to regard his students as 'co-disciples of the same acharya,' that doesn't obviate him from the responsibility – on behalf of his acharya – to confront them with their faults, to challenge or rebuke them when necessary, and to use every means at his disposal to correct them so they stay firm adherents to the spiritual path. Correcting a disciple may be very risky in a relationship based upon friendship, but it must be done. Failure to correct or challenge disciples may indicate that the guru has an unacknowledged emotional need for the company of friends, and this can act as an obstacle in his teaching.

Pillai Lokacharya's observations are relevant in any historical era, and his suggestions are pertinent for us today. Certainly, in the life example of His Divine Grace Srila Prabhupada we saw all the above recommendations demonstrated in action. Although he was very much honoured by his thousands of disciples, and though he accepted all manner of services from them, he always regarded them as having been sent by his spiritual master. At one point he told them that they had been with him in their previous life and were now 'all together again.' Yet despite this generous and collegiate view, Srila Prabhupada never refrained from correcting or rebuking his disciples, sometimes to the point of angrily shouting at them. Yet once the correction had been issued, sometimes mere moments later, he returned to a peaceful demeanour. Thus he showed that 'chastising' a disciple was a function of his service to them, and not an ordinary emotional outburst.

And though he allowed them to care for his physical needs and to relate to him as friends, he never once became dependent on them. No-one was ever too important a disciple that they could not be dismissed. The prime consideration for Srila Prabhupada was always the long-term spiritual health of the disciple, and the collective health of his Krishna consciousness movement. The result was that, in general, his disciples were cautious in his presence, fully knowing that they needed him much more than he needed them. In his presence they felt that although physically they were with him, his consciousness was always detached from the ordinary workings of emotions and senses, fixed and unwavering on another level entirely. Through this he practically demonstrated the Krishna consciousness of which he spoke, and successfully provoked within them a desire to reach it themselves. Srila Prabhupada was thus a living, contemporary demonstration of the perennial behaviour of a Vaishnava acharya.

# 18

# Where can I find a guru?

*By asking friends and colleagues, consulting a trade directory, phone book or the internet, we can easily locate any kind of expert. We can discover their reputation, their level of qualification, whether they are approved by their regulating body and whether or not they have satisfied customers. We can also discover the costs involved. But how do we find a guru? The answer is that it is a relatively easy matter, but only achieved after a radical transformation of consciousness.*

**The first step is to be convinced that you actually do have a problem that needs fixing.** You need to feel that something is not quite right, and that a conversation with a specialist might throw some light on it. But you have to diagnose your problem accurately.

For instance, a big wet patch in your ceiling is not a 'ceiling problem' but a water leakage problem. The real problem is elsewhere. Spiritual problems can also be misidentified as 'emotional' problems. Existential anxiety manifests through the emotions and mental states – but it is a spiritual problem, and only someone well-versed in the study and experience of meditative states of consciousness can help you. A plumber, a dentist, a teacher of science, a psychotherapist or a clairvoyant cannot help.

Does a guru always have to be another person? Can you not learn without a teacher? Well, your logical analysis of your predicament is in itself a kind of guru, since with the help of your mind and rational thinking you can make a series of choices that will help you move in the right direction. Indeed, without logical analysis and rational thinking brought to bear in decision making, it is impossible to preserve the discretion needed to safely move forward.

And when, using our own reasoning power as a guru, we conclude that the way forward is some form of spiritual effort, that's when things start to happen. The curious phenomenon that begins to take place at this point is that, rather surprisingly, the universe does begin to respond to the intensity of our determination by presenting us with opportunities for different kinds of information – books, conversations, talks, discussions and interesting people – sources of incremental discovery that either we avoided before, or that just didn't seem available at the time.

This increase in awareness is followed, at some point, by moments of extreme clarity. The intensity of spiritual aspiration deep inside us is extrapolated into our environment, and it seems as if nature itself becomes a guru. A beautiful sunrise, a bird's song or a tree in the landscape, all seem to lift our level of perception. We see things in them we hadn't noticed before. They seem to enlighten us. We climb a hill and the surrounding countryside reveals a new dimension of reality, or we take a walk along a beach and the horizon seems to open up our mind to new thoughts and feelings. We are illuminated, at one with the universe, and we experience a momentary glimpse of transcendence.

But attempts to replicate this phenomenon seem to fail. We climb the same mountain and nothing in particular happens. Our fleeting moments of *nirvana* in a beautiful cathedral one morning are followed by a subsequent visit when we notice only the dank, musty smell and the leaflets pinned to the notice board. Our super-sensory awareness does not take place again, either at our own bidding or as a response to the natural phenomena. Frustratingly, the same spiritual experiences, which were previously so real, cannot now be reproduced. Why this should be so, we're left struggling to understand.

But we persist with our enquiries, and gradually, things become a little clearer. Our conversations become deeper. We read books and we listen carefully as others speak about their own experiences. As time passes, particular lines of enquiry seem to be more relevant to us than others. We receive the intellectual conviction our analytical mind requires. We experiment with meditation methods and discover that something helps us to replicate spiritual feelings. But we don't want to be cheated on our spiritual path, so we proceed with caution while investigating these new ideas. On the other hand, we conclude that what we're experimenting with seems to make logical sense, and so we draw towards us some new friends who seem to be living examples of the ideas we now value. Then, almost as if we hadn't realised it, one particular friend seems to be our guide; not exactly a guru figure, but someone who'll help us to find the one we're looking for.

Its around this time that the idea of having a spiritual teacher makes even more good sense to us. Whereas previously even the concept of having a permanent spiritual guide may have seemed culturally strange to us, or perhaps an admission of weakness or inability, now the idea is welcome. There is a famous classical reference to this tipping-point on the path, and it comes in the account of the sage Prabuddha's discussions with a king named Nimi, found in the latter section of Srimad Bhagavatam. He advises the king that through a logical analysis of the fragility and temporary nature of ordinary happiness and the brevity of human life, one naturally arrives at the conclusion that one must seek out a spiritual master.

And then, in a case of real life emulating classical text, the guru 'arrives' in our life. Sometimes it happens quite suddenly, but when it does happen, we know about it. Something has definitely changed. We may be surprised that we hadn't made the connection before. Externally, the person we now regard as our guru may not have been the person to whom we previously paid much attention; or we may have passed up several opportunities to meet with him before. But now it is somehow different. Now we can see who he truly is: someone who is learned in the tradition; who lives it, who has helped others and who has the time and generosity of spirit to help us personally move forward. There again, perhaps if we are persistently self-referential, we will conclude that it is **him** that has changed. He was neither wise nor compassionate before, but now that he has made spiritual advancement he is just fit for our purposes. Whichever the case may be - we have found our guru.

# The sequence of gurus

In his final conversation with his friend Uddhava, Lord Krishna explains this sequence of gurus. He describes how, at first, one's own mind can be the guru and then, when there is illumination within, the universal guru seems to speak from the trees, mountains and rivers. Finally, the great secret is revealed, that God dwells within, the supreme soul of the entire universe located alongside the tiny individual soul, *Param atma* alongside *Jiva atma*. Spiritual knowledge, memory and forgetfulness all come from him in response to the soul's innermost desires. And then, when the soul desires nothing else, the *Paramatma* expands in the form of the guru. Either the soul encounters an entirely new person in his life, or it dawns upon him that the one individual he has known for a long time was his spiritual teacher all along.

This revelation of the guru, however, is not cheap. The classic accounts describe that a certain spiritual intensity of effort is required. The consciousness of the self as a consumer of the external world must be abandoned in favour of the attitude of a supplicant. A sense of urgency, helplessness, and intense longing are all described in classical literature as helpful, too.In the eleventh canto of the Srimad Bhagavatam, where this important conversation with Uddhava is found – the 'Uddhava-gita' – Lord Krishna explains this progression as follows:

> *"Generally those human beings who can expertly analyze the actual situation of the material world are able to raise themselves beyond the inauspicious life of gross material gratification. An intelligent person, expert in perceiving the world around him and in applying sound logic, can achieve real benefit through his own intelligence. Thus sometimes one acts as one's own guru."* - (Srimad Bhagavatam 11.7.19 - 20)

He then continues his explanation by telling the story of a certain King Yadu and what happened when he met a highly spiritually advanced young brahmana. The brahmana does not appear to be following any particular discipline, yet all spiritual qualities have become manifest in him as he wanders, childlike, through the world. The king wishes to know how this was achieved, so he asks him: "How did you acquire this extraordinary intelligence? What is the cause of the great ecstasy you are feeling within yourself?" The brahmana replies that he has taken refuge of many gurus and, having gained transcendental understanding from them, he now wanders the earth in a liberated condition. He then lists his gurus:

> *"The earth, air, sky, water, fire, moon, sun, pigeon, python, the sea, a moth, a honey-bee, an elephant and a honey-thief; a deer, a fish, a prostitute, a bird, a child and a young girl, an arrow-maker, a serpent, a spider and, finally, a wasp. By studying all of them I have learned the science of the self. Please listen...as I explain to you what I have learned from each of these gurus."* - (Srimad Bhagavatam 11.7.33 - 36)

The narration is long but enlightening. The essential lesson is that when the soul searches for repeated sensory enjoyment, everything he encounters remains merely a dull source of either pleasure or pain. When that same soul chooses to search for spiritual liberation, every object around him becomes a guru.

However, Lord Krishna concludes with the very same instruction as he gave to Arjuna on the battlefield some thirty-six years previously: that the sincere seeker of spiritual emancipation should approach a living example of spiritual enlightenment, a saint who is the embodiment of spiritual qualities; someone who has developed compassion and the spirit of kindness towards others, and who can act as a true preceptor. To clarify things to Uddhava, and to make sure he finds the right person, he lists the major qualities of a saint, someone in the possession of which is just suitable to be accepted as a guru for life.

# 'Find a guru'

Like the young brahmana in the story, saints are awakened to their own relationship with the divine and they consequently see all things in the world as being connected with the ultimate source. The direct experience of their own, intimate connection with that source gives the saints great inner peace and joy, and that radiates from them. This is directly tangible to those who keep their company, and when they observe their joy, they become happy too. And while it is true that we can connect with the divine by reading holy writings, the divine is also found in the lives of those saints who repeat holy words – and live them. And a living example of precept - a compassionate and friendly preceptor - can be a greater teacher for us than all the lessons we try to learn from the holy writings.

A guru is much more than a spiritual friend, a *pandit* or a priest, all of whom may act, through knowledge or ritual, as human intermediaries between man and God. The guru is special because he is an instrument in the hands of God, someone who knows that he does not possess anything material, and is not possessed by anything or anyone within this world. He knows that he is wholly possessed by God only and acts only for him.

The curious fact is that even though Krishna himself – the supreme Godhead manifest within the world – is standing before Arjuna directly, right inside his war-vehicle; even though he has already explained his transcendental identity as the source of all knowledge; still he counsels Arjuna to 'find a guru.' His advice does not change with Uddhava. Krishna wants Uddhava to 'find a guru.' Thus Krishna serves to preserve the ancient guru-disciple tradition, even though circumstances would seem not to require it. Yet the Lord stipulates one very special characteristic of the person he recommends as worthy to be a guru: he must be a *prapanna*, a soul surrendered to God.

After a recounting of the lessons learned from each of the brahmana's twenty-four gurus, Lord Krishna says in conclusion:

> ... *mat-parah kvacit mad-abhijnam gurum*
> *santam upasita mad-atmakam*

> "...One should approach a spiritual master who is full in knowledge of Me as I am, who is peaceful, and who by spiritual elevation is not different from Me." - *(Srimad Bhagavatam 11.10.5)*

The specific words the Lord uses here is *mat-parah* – or 'one who is devoted to me,' and *mad-abhijnam* – 'one who knows me as I am.' He goes on to describe the qualification of a suitable disciple: that the disciple who goes to find a guru should be 'free from false prestige' and 'should be endowed with feelings of loving friendship toward the spiritual master, and should always desire spiritual advancement.'

It is then that Uddhava asks Krishna what the qualities of a *prapanna* are – one who has no other shelter in this world but God, who is completely surrendered to Him, and who loves Him. Krishna replies by describing the twenty-eight qualities of a *sadhu*:

> "O Uddhava, a saintly person is merciful and never injures others. Even if others are aggressive he is tolerant and forgiving toward all living entities. His strength and meaning in life come from the truth itself, he is free from all envy and jealousy, and his mind is equal in material happiness and distress. Thus, he dedicates his time to work for the welfare of all others. His intelligence is never bewildered by material desires, and he has controlled his senses. His behaviour is always pleasing, never harsh and always exemplary, and he is free from possessiveness. He never endeavours in ordinary, worldy activities, and he strictly controls his eating. He therefore always remains peaceful and steady. A

saintly person is thoughtful and accepts me as his only shelter. Such a person is very cautious in the execution of his duties and is never subject to superficial transformations, because he is steady and noble, even in a distressing situation."

"He has conquered over the six material qualities – namely hunger, thirst, lamentation, illusion, old age and death. He is free from all desire for prestige and offers honour to others. He is expert in reviving the Krishna consciousness of others and therefore never cheats anyone. Rather, he is a well-wishing friend to all, being most merciful. Such a saintly person must be considered the most learned of men. He perfectly understands that the ordinary religious duties prescribed by me in various Vedic scriptures possess favourable qualities that purify the performer, and he knows that neglect of such duties constitute a discrepancy in one's life. Having taken complete shelter at my feet, however, a saintly person ultimately renounces such ordinary religious duties and worships me alone. He is thus considered to be the best among all living entities."

# 19

# Within you, without you

*In his teaching of the nature of the guru, Srila Prabhupada naturally echoed the conversations between both Uddhava and Krishna, and Arjuna and Krishna. He spent time elaborating how, at the right time, God who dwells within us manifests physically outside us. The guru manifests in response to our desire. This principle is commonly overlooked or misunderstood. Some imagine they have no need of a guru, while others imagine that they can accept initiation from a guru 'within the heart.' Still others imagine that the physically manifest guru simultaneously dwells within the heart. So for everyone's benefit, Srila Prabhupada consistently explained the standard Vaishnava teaching of God and guru. Here are a selection of quotes from his talks, letters and writings.*

**The following is taken from the first book he wrote in 1960, *Easy Journey to Other Planets*:**

> "Krishna reveals Himself from within to one who is serious about God realization. Both Krishna and the spiritual master help the sincere soul. The spiritual master is the external manifestation of God, who is situated in everyone's heart as Supersoul."

**From the Srimad Bhagavatam:**

> "It is here recommended to Dhruva Maharaja that he meditate on the supreme guru, or supreme spiritual master. The supreme spiritual master is Krishna, who is therefore known as chaitya-guru. This refers to the Supersoul, who is sitting in everyone's heart. He helps from within as stated in Bhagavad-gita, and He sends the spiritual master, who helps from without. The spiritual master is the external manifestation of the chaitya-guru, or the spiritual master sitting in everyone's heart. - (*Srimad Bhagavatam 4.8.44*)

When we rightly take the direction of the Supersoul, our life becomes successful. He is directing from within and from without. From within He is directing as chaitya-guru, or the spiritual master sitting within the heart. Indirectly He is also helping the living entity by manifesting Himself as the spiritual master outside. In both ways the Lord is giving directions to the living entity so that he may finish up his material activities and come back home, back to Godhead. - (*Srimad Bhagavatam 4.22.37*)

One who is sincere and pure gets an opportunity to consult with the Supreme Personality of Godhead in His Paramatma feature sitting within everyone's heart. The Paramatma is always the chaitya-guru, the spiritual master within, and He comes before one externally as the instructor and initiator spiritual master. The Lord can reside within the heart, and He can also come out before a person and give him instructions. Thus the spiritual master is not different from the Supersoul sitting within the heart. - (*Srimad Bhagavatam 4.28.52*)

## From the *Chaitanya Charitamrita*:

It is not possible for a conditioned soul to directly meet Krishna, the Supreme Personality of Godhead, but if one becomes a sincere devotee and seriously engages in devotional service, Lord Krishna sends an instructing spiritual master to show him favour and invoke his dormant propensity for serving the Supreme. The preceptor appears before the external senses of the fortunate conditioned soul, and at the same time the devotee is guided from within by the chaitya-guru, Krishna, who is seated as the spiritual master within the heart of the living entity.- (*Chaitanya Charitamrita, Adi 1.58*)

One should not take any responsibility on his own but should be a soul surrendered to the Supreme Personality of Godhead, who will then give him dictation as the chaitya-guru, or the spiritual master within. The Supreme Personality of Godhead is pleased to guide a devotee from within and without. From within He guides him as the Supersoul, and from without He guides him as the spiritual master. - (*Chaitanya Charitamrita, Adi 8.79*)

## From classes and a conversation:

...Krishna, He is within our heart. Hridyantah-stah. Therefore, as soon as we become a little inclined towards Krishna, then from within our heart He gives us favourable instruction so that we can gradually make progress, gradually. Krishna is the first spiritual master, and when we become more interested, then we have to go to a physical spiritual master. That is enjoined in the following verse:

*tad viddhi pranipatena pariprasnena sevaya
upadeksyanti te jnanam jnaninas tattva darsanah*

*(Lecture on Bhagavad-gita 4.34 — New York, August 14, 1966)*

So Krishna is advising that "I am in everyone's heart." You can take advice from Krishna. Krishna is ready. Krishna's another name is chaitya-guru. Chaitya-guru means the guru who is situated within your heart. Krishna comes out as instructor guru or initiator guru outside, and he is sitting within the heart as chaitya-guru. Krishna is ready to help you, help us, every one of us, in two ways: by the external guru and internal guru. Internal guru, He is Krishna Himself, and external guru, His manifestation, the spiritual master. So we should take advantage of two gurus and make our life successful. *(Lecture on Bhagavad-gita 13.3, September 26, 1973)*

We see, Krishna was present before Arjuna, but nobody was present before Brahma. Therefore it is said, *tene brahma hrida adi-kavaye, hrida*: "through the heart." Because Krishna is situated in everyone's heart. Actually, He is the spiritual master, chaitya-guru. So in order to help us, He comes out as physical spiritual master. *(Lecture on Srimad Bhagavatam 1.2.4)*

So guru is also incarnation of God, mercy incarnation of God. Guru means that... God is within you, chaitya-guru, the guru, or the spiritual master, within your heart: *isvarah sarva-bhutanam hrid-dese 'rjuna tisthati (Bhagavad-gita 18.61)*. So this Paramatma is also incarnation of God. And the same Paramatma, when He comes before you, being very much merciful upon you, to teach you from outside, that is guru. *(Lecture on Srimad Bhagavatam 1.3.26 October 1, 1976)*

> Prabhupada: Therefore God is called chaitya-guru, the spiritual master within the heart. And the physical spiritual master is God's mercy. If God sees that you are sincere, He will give you a spiritual master who can give you protection. He will help you from within and without. Without in the physical form of spiritual master, and within as the spiritual master within the heart. *(Room conversation with Irish poet, Desmond O'Grady, May 23, 1974, Rome)*

In these enlightening passages Srila Prabhupada explains how we receive guidance on the spiritual path. The *Paramatma*, or Supersoul, is the manifestation of God who accompanies us on our journey through the material world. As God he is the ultimate spiritual guide and sits within the heart, always helping us in accordance with our desire to be helped.

At the time when we most desire it, his compassion manifests in the form of an external teacher who will give us the same message as the guru within. The guru within – the *chaitya-guru* – is entirely spiritual, whereas the guru without is a physical manifestation. His complete connection with God allows him to be described as a spiritualized physical manifestation, but physical nonetheless. To him we can ask all our questions and receive unequivocal answers from an authoritative source. We can serve him and also receive correction when required. He is an eternal soul within a temporary physical body, but one who can, if we choose to accept him in that role, act as an intermediary with the guru within. He appears 'before the external senses', yet through our enquiry and his kindness, the effect of his company is felt deep within.

Although Srila Prabhupada describes that the *Paramatma* 'comes out' in the form of the guru, and that therefore he is a 'manifestation', even an 'incarnation' of the mercy of God, it should not be concluded that the guru is God. The theology is quite clear: God may direct the individual soul through the guru, but the guru remains a dependent, *jiva atma* - a servant of God. One should not, even with the best of intentions, begin to ascribe the qualities of God to the guru. This may spring from genuine devotional sentiments, but it is theologically incorrect and can lead to forms of impersonal thought.

It is God who is seated within the heart, not the physically manifest guru, and it is only God who is omniscient and omnipresent. Srila Prabhupada took care to explain this difference. 'How do you know what your disciples are doing?' he was once asked. As if to offset any future misunderstandings, he replied: "The postman tells me."

The search for a guru is a rewarding one although, at times, it may be fraught with difficulty as we are tested and challenged in many ways. There may even be frustration as we encounter those who seem at first to be gurus but who prove disappointing to us. Yet we cannot ultimately be thwarted because our most important journey is an internal one, a journey towards complete harmony with God. As always, God helps us in all ways and so, provided sincerity of purpose is maintained and we do not become crippled by doubts or distractions along the way, nothing can hinder our efforts.

# 20

# Little ants on a leaping lion

*Who is the more important in the life of the disciple, the historical acharya or the physically present guru? The discussion has been going on for at least a thousand years.*

**The year was 1315 and the great Shri Vaishnava poet, Vedanta Deshika (1268-1370) was writing a book about the transmission of spiritual knowledge.** He was trying to think of an analogy for the importance of devotion to the acharya, the foremost spiritual preceptor, when he remembered something that Mudaliandan, the nephew of Ramanujacharya, had said:

> *"When a lion leaps from one hill to another, the little ants on its body are transported with him. Similarly, when Ramanujacharya leaped over this world of repeated birth and death, we were saved because of our connection with him."*

The saving grace of the guru and the reciprocal devotion of the disciple has always been an essential feature of Vaishnavism, particularly when the guru is a powerful and revolutionary teacher such as Ramanujacharya (1017-1137), who left such a tremendous impact upon the entire tradition. Ramanuja's contribution to his *sampradaya* and the cause of Vaishnavism was immense, and his legacy has lived on for a thousand years. His writing and teaching of the Vaishnava theology consolidated an ancient tradition, making it even more accessible; and his codifying of ritual and worship, and putting in place sustainable management systems for hundreds of temples, ensured that his impact would be felt for generations. It is no exaggeration to say that well over half a billion people living today are, in some way, the beneficiaries of his life. There is an incident that illustrates the place he occupies in the minds and hearts of his followers, even today.

Once, he was relating the well-known story of Vibhishana's meeting with Rama on the eve of battle. Vibhishana was the brother of Ravana, who had kidnapped Sita, the young wife of Rama, and now Vibhishana wanted to join Rama's forces and help him conquer Ravana. But members of Rama's army doubted his intentions and labelled him a spy. They explained to him that joining the entourage of Rama was not such an easy proposition, and they then began listing Vibhishana's many disqualifications.

While Ramanuja was narrating this story, he saw that one member of his audience was standing up and leaving. Noticing the man's troubled expression, he enquired as to what was the concern that he should leave his discussion. "By hearing Lord Rama's associates describe Vibhishana's disqualifications," he said, "I think that I shall never attain Lord Rama's company for I also have the very same disqualifications. The sincerity required before one can gain the company of Rama, means that I will not attain His eternal company at the end of my life."

Ramanuja replied with great concern, "My dear friend, please come back, sit down and be peaceful. I shall personally speak on your behalf to Rama. I shall take you with me at the end of your life and thus be your guarantee of salvation." The followers of Ramanuja back then took this promise seriously, and today, many centuries later, they still do. Ramanuja, as one of the prominent acharyas of the Shri Sampradaya, still offers the assurance of salvation for every initiated disciple. During the initiation ceremony in some branches, the guru asks the disciple: "Who is your guru?" The disciple replies: "You are my guru." The guru then corrects him, saying: "Sripad Ramanujacharya is your guru…and I am also your guru." The disciple will then be given his new name, ending in Ramanujadasan 'the servant of Ramanuja.'

Yet although he was such an inspirational and unifying force for generations of Shri Vaishnavas, discussions on the precise position of Ramanujacharya also became the cause of some divergence within the community. It was Ramanujacharya who claimed that he was the link with God for all who followed him, and yet to continue the *parampara* he had also empowered seventy-four of his senior disciples as *simhasana-dhipatis*, or 'throne-holders' who would conduct initiations after his demise.

After some centuries had passed, various theological differences arose between the followers of the acharya, very gradually creating rifts in the community. Some Shri Vaishnavas stressed that the causeless grace of God was the all-important factor in spiritual emancipation, and that there was no independent means by which this grace could be achieved. Only God has the power and the free will to award it. Others argued that personal surrender to God (*prapatti*) was the most important consideration, since our efforts can attract God's grace.

Another issue was the saving grace of the guru. Was it the grace of the acharya, Ramanuja, coming down to the disciple that was the most important factor for spiritual emancipation, or was it the physically manifest guru who was instructing and guiding the disciple within the world? Who was the greatest conduit of divine grace? On the one hand, Ramanujacharya had promised that he would personally intercede with God for his followers, and seems not to have put time limits on this promise; on the other, he installed seventy-four gurus for all practical educational, training and sacramental purposes.

When considering these questions in the 14th century it might have been reasoned that the redeeming power of the acharya - himself so close to God - was the foremost guru in the life of the disciple. Certainly those who regarded causeless grace would have been attracted to this viewpoint. On the other hand, those who regarded personal efforts as an essential prerequisite to the descent of divine grace might have reasonably deemed tuition and guidance from a physically manifest guru as most important, since these help to precipitate personal effort. These divergent ideas, it should be noted, were not distinctly different philosophies creeping into the *sampradaya*, merely differences in emphasis of parts of the same philosophy. Yet gradually these differences of opinion did go on to result in two distinct schools, one in the north known as the *Vadagalai*, who tended towards regarding the predecessor acharya as more important than the guru, and the southern community known as the *Tenkalai*, who stressed the guru as the focal point of one's surrender and therefore as more directly relevant than the acharya.

I should remind readers at this point, since the parallels with modern-day ISKCON will not have escaped them, that it does not appear that the southern Vaishnavas disregarded their acharya simply because they accepted their contemporary guru as their point of surrender. Neither did those of the northern school become dismissive of initiation because they had accepted the grace previously offered by their acharya. Rather, everyone worshipped Ramanujacharya and, at the same time, everyone became initiated by one of the contemporary lineage holders. That was, and still is, the Shri Vaishnava culture.

Everyone understood the necessity of having a guru so that they could learn proper pronunciation of the Vedas, the correct understanding of Vaishnava doctrine free from the beginner's tendency to speculate, and the daily practises and rituals of *sadhana-bhakti*. By having a guru they could watch and learn from a living exemplar of the tradition. They knew how essential the preceptor was in the correction of bad habits and egoistic tendencies, and how his living example offered them a role model. They also understood the obvious principle that the student needed to have a relationship of friendship and service with that guru so that the guru would bless the student.

Scripture recommends that we take shelter of, and surrender to, such a physically manifest guru who God sends to us; and scripture also reveals that grace can come to us from any previous acharya - particularly one from whose words we gain so much enlightenment. God can use anyone He likes as an instrument of our salvation, after all. The *purva-acharyas* and the guru complement each other. We should resist the temptations of *raja-guna*, the predominating influence that polarises viewpoints and pulls people apart, setting them up against one another. The progressive path is that of *sattva-guna*, influenced by which one always tries to see how apparent differences can be harmonised.

Yet eight hundred years later, similar discussions persist within the community of followers of His Divine Grace A.C. Bhaktivedanta Swami Prabhupada. To them his position is as unique as Ramanujacharya: within just twelve years he created a worldwide movement of Vaishnavism which, in only fifty years, has grown to a community of one million followers. He left behind him eighty books which have been translated into more than ninety languages. Surely if any acharya in the last one thousand years is deserving of the appellation of 'conduit of divine grace' it is him. But like Ramanujacharya, Srila Prabhupada also left behind him the instructions and mechanisms for the creation of gurus who would succeed him. They too are accepted as conduits of divine grace by their disciples.

Many prefer to regard Srila Prabhupada as their main connection to grace, placing him in a position akin to Ramanuja, while others regard their *diksha-guru* as the principal manifestation of divine grace, with Srila Prabhupada as their guru's connection. There should actually be no competition between these two views as they are based solely upon realisation and preference. And certainly they should not be regarded as a basis of any animosity between those who hold differing views. God Himself gives faith and however it manifests it should be celebrated.

One who accepts Srila Prabhupada as the acharya is factually accepting him as his guru. How could it be otherwise? It is he who has supplied a million people with accessible knowledge and an example of pure devotion to Krishna. It is he who fashioned a worldwide mission for the spreading of Krishna consciousness, and who left a legacy of temples and centres dotting the world. When any of his followers is successful in bringing a soul to spiritual life, it is through the power of Srila Prabhupada's words which he or she has repeated. And certainly we are all depending on Srila Prabhupada to intercede with Krishna so that we can attain His shelter. He is surely our guarantee of salvation if we follow his instructions and personal example in our daily life.

And yet saying all this does not, as some claim, obviate the need for another guru in the life of the disciple. Srila Prabhupada explained that the guru is the 'external manifestation of the *chaitya* guru, the *Paramatma* within the heart,' and someone who thus 'appears before the physical senses of the disciple.' Why should this be if the active necessity is for the disciple to gain knowledge and divine grace? Well, the guru's task, as well as giving divine knowledge, is to offer practical guidance to the disciple, to show how to render service to the Lord, and then occasionally to correct the disciple, or even to rebuke him. While this can be obtained from books and, in modern times, recordings, the simplest way to have a spiritually productive relationship with a guru is to have one where the conditioned, physical senses will be confronted, at least periodically, with his physical presence.

Despite the protests of some who wish to be connected only with such an acharya as Srila Prabhupada, it is not that the physical presence of a guru in one's life can be so readily rejected. Even if the stature of the guru cannot compare with that of the historical acharya, which, quite frankly, is to be expected, still there is a pressing need for a relationship with a guru who is ' before the physical senses.' Even at the risk of being considered a fool who needs the periodic company of a personal spiritual teacher in order to prosper, it is better than being overly intelligent and dispensing with thousands of years of Vaishnava tradition and plain necessity.

Srila Prabhupada had no spiritual limitations, yet he had physical limitations. He could not distribute the books he'd written in all the countries of the world, and so engaged his willing disciples as his arms and legs to do it. One who has accepted the role of guru in the present day is thus also a mere instrument in the acharya's hands. Although others may view him as 'guru', he knows that he remains an instrument, and consequently regards himself always as a humble disciple.

Sometimes, under the influence of *raja-guna*, the element of material nature that pushes us into divisions, a false dilemma is posed: "Do you want to be a follower of Srila Prabhupada or do you prefer to follow a modern day guru? Take your choice!" This is a false dilemma born out of the mind's inability to hold two apparently contradictory allegiances at once. It is not a case, actually, that we should have to choose one and be bereft of the other. They are both necessary, and both complement each other.

In my own personal case, some time ago I had cancer which was successfully treated. The medical team included some highly specialised surgeons who tended to me once or twice, operated, and then saw me once afterwards. But the bulk of the healing work was performed, every single day for many weeks, by competent and experienced nurses. Both types of medical workers were essential for saving my life and for my ultimate well-being, and I am extremely grateful to both. The surgeons could not see me every day to change my dressings, but the nurses could. The nurses could not perform the operation but the surgeons could. It would be a false dilemma to ask me to choose one or the other. I needed them both for the specialised tasks they could perform.

Srila Prabhupada is the acharya for everyone who takes to contemporary Vaishnava life in his preceptorial line. And the term acharya certainly includes the term guru. So Srila Prabhupada is everyone's guru. And yet if a disciple is scripturally instructed, personally and practically guided, and sometimes corrected, they also have a guru in the person who is doing all that for them. The person who gives the mantra is also the guru.

If that is the case, then the disciple is recommended by scripture to serve and enquire submissively from that preceptor. Besides, in the desperate condition of *bhava-roga*, the 'disease of material existence,' and with such a short life span, do we not need as much help as we can get?

When faced with exactly the same conundrum centuries ago, Vedanta Deshika liked the metaphor of the little ants on a leaping lion. The ants have their helpful relationship with each other - and that is valid - yet they all have a relationship with, and an immense debt of gratitude to, the lion, upon whose back they sit. I suggest that, eight hundred years later, we can still understand our relative positions by reference to this wonderful imagery. So let us all take the help of everyone we can in our community of brother and sister ants - and then cross over the yawning chasm of *samsara* by clinging to the back of the great leaping lion.

# 21

# The parampara family tree

*When we think of spiritual life, we tend to think first of our own practises within our contemporary community. But the anxiety for the greatest devotees of Krishna is how to ensure the teachings and living examples are passed on to the next generation, and after that, for many generations more. It is no easy task, and even Lord Krishna says that He must come to the Earth, age after age, to re-establish the teachings that have been lost. One important feature of preserving teachings through history is therefore the chain of teachers, the parampara.*

**The Sanskrit word *parampara* literally means 'one following the other' or 'uninterrupted series,' and refers to a chain of teachers in which the student, when qualified, becomes the teacher for a new group of students.** If the chain is unbroken, and if each teacher has taken care to pass on exactly what they've learned, the *parampara* can eventually consist of a large number of human connections over hundreds of years, successfully sharing accumulated wisdom to successive generations. The chain can consist of parent-child links, schoolteacher-pupil or spiritual preceptor-disciple links; whatever combination has preserved, transmitted and protected the knowledge, skills and values for a branch of human society. The word *parampara* can equally be applied to a line of teachers of pottery, music, dance, architecture, martial arts, or a line of spiritual teaching.

As we investigate a *parampara*, we look back through time to learn the names of great teachers who safeguarded the knowledge in the past so that others could receive it in the present. Being a retrospective analysis of the flow of knowledge through history, it is quite common that certain prominent figures within the *parampara* attract attention for their wisdom, commitment, ingenuity or resilience in the face of obstacles. The names of such notable teachers are often taught to pupils in order to impress upon them what an illustrious lineage they belong to. By learning of their great forebears, the pupils are given inspirational role models and become grateful of their ancestors' efforts to preserve and transmit their specialised knowledge. The pupils are also made aware of the need for themselves to assume the role of knowledge-preservers and transmitters for the next generation.

Although the word *parampara* is normally used to indicate the teacher-student tradition in the culture of India, the principle it describes is universal. Many traditions throughout the world preserve the names of their most celebrated exponents for all the same reasons. Not for nothing does the Prime Minister of Great Britain have heroic oil portraits of all the previous premiers hanging in chronological order up the main staircase of Number 10 Downing Street. Over in Rome, the Pope goes one better: he has portraits to inspire him, but also life-size white marble statues of all the former pontiffs in the apostolic *parampara* of Saint Peter. Not arrayed up the staircase, perhaps, but certainly somewhere within the 114 acres of the Vatican.

Yet a *parampara* is not a chain of post-holders of an institution, even though a line of noble men and women going back through history may be identified. A transmission of knowledge, skills and values must be conveyed through the chain in order for it to be a *parampara*. In the case of the Prime Ministers of the United Kingdom, the chain is all those who have been elected to office by exercise of the democratic vote of the British public. No political philosophy or statesmanship is passed down from one Prime Minister to another. Indeed, given the nature of politics, each successive PM may have radically different views than the one before him. Cumulative knowledge and precept is developed independently of the post-holders, within the systems and structures of the British governmental institutions, the laws that support them, and within the collective memories and culture of the citizens themselves.

In the case of the Roman Catholic Church, the line of popes is an apostolic succession, a line of those who represent the original apostle, Saint Peter. Yet even within this religious organisation it is not that a sacred transmission of knowledge takes place between popes. Rather, a College of Cardinals exercises their considered vote and selects one other cardinal who will fill the post – the post of 'Head of the Catholic Church.' Naturally, they take into consideration a host of important factors including the candidate's personal sanctity, his adherence to creed, and his abilities in leadership and pastoral care. Creed and ritual is cumulatively developed within the body of the Church, separate from the pope, and this may also change over time.

To be a *parampara*, there must be some identifiable skill that remains unchanged, some technique or specialised knowledge. For instance, it is a well-known fact that the *sthapatis* of the village of Swamimilai, near Kumbakonam in Tamil Nadu, India, create their remarkably beautiful bronze statues using techniques basically unchanged since the Bronze Age. Techniques have passed from father to son since prehistoric times, as has the language they use to describe the divinities they create.

Sometimes, the teachings of a tradition can be traced through men and women who had no institutional support or patronage at all. They lived, taught and died in relative poverty. And sometimes, because of this, they remain nameless; only the teaching survives as proof of their dedication. Where particular teachers did create an organisation to survive them and better preserve the teaching, they may have successfully perpetuated transmission; the knowledge being preserved intact not simply by the pupils of the master, but by a range of systems and structures. Written teachings, educational courses, and institutional devices can often help to preserve and protect a body of wisdom. Sometimes, however, the very reverse is true: the human power structure that accompanies the institution can obscure the purity or content of the original wisdom. History is filled with examples of such successes and failures. The real institution that a teacher leaves behind is therefore not the powerful posts and material resources; it is the vitality of the teaching and the scale of its dissemination to enthusiastic new students.

In the case of a *parampara* set up to preserve the teachings of a particular school of the Vedas, we would look for the authentic connection with the relevant *shastra*. Traditionally, that meant the acharya of the school knowing the relevant Veda sections and being able to recite them by heart. Exact pronunciation is a key element in a Veda *parampara* since the true Veda disappears where there is mispronunciation. Elaborate systems for correct pronunciation have thus co-existed for thousands of years and the acharya must teach them to his students until he is satisfied that they also know them perfectly. Philosophically, the acharya must also preserve and disseminate the details of his school's understanding of the *Vedanta Sutra*. He must also demonstrate techniques, rituals and customs that elevate his students to the plane of transcendence and he himself must be a living example of what he teaches. Finally, all these items must be passed down from guru to disciple, century after century, without deviation from the original teacher.

A Vaishnava *parampara* does all of this and also preserves the rituals of temple installation, worship of the sacred images within the temple, the theology of the Supreme Personality, and the modes of devotional service between Man and God. Vaishnava behaviour and morality, both personal and social, is preserved along with the supportive traditions, festival observances, and such items as songs, music, and food.

There are many other fascinating features of a *parampara* which either help or hinder its survival. By looking at important elements within the ancient Indian guru-disciple tradition we can understand how important the guru-disciple connection actually is. The following is by no means an exhaustive list.

# The originator

Somebody, somewhere, was the first person to give the teachings to human society. In a Vaishnava tradition that position is held first by a divine person, and then secondly by a liberated soul intimately connected with the divine. Vaishnavism is the way of life dedicated to Vishnu, or God Himself, the supreme source of all knowledge, especially the knowledge of the nature of God and how to reach Him. Vishnu is always accompanied by Lakshmi, His eternal consort, and He is the father of Brahma, the first created being. Brahma, in turn, is the father of four prominent sons – the Kumaras – and he is also the generator of Shiva. These four: Lakshmi, Brahma, Four Kumaras and Shiva, are the originators of four separate branches of teaching which have, as their common element, the soul's devotional service to Vishnu.

# Popularisers, innovators, and other important teachers

When we look at the Vaishnava family tree, we'll see that the names of particular teachers are highlighted. Those who were the greatest exponents and the ones who taught it most successfully to others, for instance, are of particular interest. Then there are those who made the teachings accessible to others, perhaps for the first time. This may be due to writing in a vernacular language, introducing the teachings to a new audience, or writing popular songs and plays which, when performed, attracted the public's attention to Vishnu. They are also those who created novel methods for broadcasting the message of the Lord beyond their location, either by sending messengers, creating temples or by holding popular public festivals.

## The 'Telescope effect'

When a few dozen names are selected out of hundreds of authentic masters of Vaishnavism, we indirectly create a list of many who were 'almost famous.' They were great in their day, but in comparison to the greatest heroes of the history of Vaishnavism, the most popular saints and the true innovators, they don't endure as household names in the contemporary world. This might be termed the 'Telescope Effect.'

An old-fashioned telescope is made of several sections of decreasing width that slide into one another. When you've finished looking through it, you collapse it to form a compact metal tube. We tend to do that with history, too. Decades of history are collapsed into a few short sentences summarising major battles, scientific inventions, political successes and failures and cultural swings. With the telescope effect, even the few dozen selected names of the most famous Vaishnavas in the entire history of the religion can be further contracted down into a brief mention of just three or four. In this way, even the brilliant and the exceptional are passed over. This produces apparent 'historical gaps' of sometimes hundreds of years in a list of teachers spanning thousands of years. Sometimes only the masters who made a uniquely notable contribution are listed.

## Different branches, same trunk, same root

There are many branches of the Vaishnava family tree. As each guru teaches many disciples, so those disciples also have their own disciples, and different branches are created. There may be very slight differences in teaching or practice due to differences of emphasis placed by the teachers on various aspects. Sometimes this occurs due to pressing needs or when some aspect has been forgotten and needs to be revived.

Disciplic branches of the Vaishnava family tree can be seen coming from the disciples of Madhvacharya; the associates of Chaitanya Mahaprabhu; and in more recent times, the disciples of Srila Bhaktivinode Thakur and Srila Bhaktisiddhanta Saraswati. Although the branches may be many, the trunk and root of the tree – those parts which nourish the branches - are the same.

# The Family tree 'zig-zag'

If you were to highlight all the important exponents of one family tree, you might find that many of them were situated in different branches of the tree. It gets complex. If you traced your finger down through the family tree, joining up all the gurus who truly preserved the essence of Vaishnavism, the greatest contributors, you'd find that your finger moved not in a straight line, but in a zig-zag motion, moving from branch to branch. The 'zig-zag' is slightly surprising, given that preservation of teachings might be expected to be more in a direct line, and is most often portrayed as such.

# The diksha parampara and the shiksha parampara

When a guru gives a mantra to a disciple, the action is known as *diksha*; and when he provides instructions on the meaning and techniques of chanting the mantra his action is known as *shiksha*. In a majority of cases there would be one guru to provide both, but in some cases two different gurus.

Sometimes a *diksha-guru* would deliberately send his disciple to another guru for specific instructions. The *diksha* guru might be regularly teaching his disciple *shiksha*, but, knowing that another guru was an expert in a particular text, he would send his disciple to him for a course of tuition. Thus the fortunate disciple would have two gurus.

In some instances, the *diksha-guru* might provide the mantra and, perhaps due to infirmity or ill health, be unable to provide instructions for an adequate period. This would be particularly so in the case of the premature death of the guru. In other cases, the *diksha-guru* might have been a family priest who was relatively unaccomplished at teaching the nuances of the *Vedanta Sutra*, for instance. The disciple would then, often in his maturity, seek out a highly educated brahmana to teach him. Finally, in yet other cases, the disciple might have the great fortune to meet an empowered and enlightened devotee of Vishnu; someone whose transcendental symptoms indicated his high level of spiritual devotion. Taking advantage of his company, the disciple would then gain great blessings from the confidential *shiksha* of his guru.

In all these cases, it may be easily understood why the *shiksha-guru* played a more important role in the disciple's formation and education than his *diksha-guru*. In the Gaudiya *parampara* it is held that because *diksha* is a one-time event, and the *shiksha* a lifetime course, that of the two gurus, the *shiksha* is more important than the *diksha*. Of course, both are essential.

A *parampara* in which all the guru-disciple links are those of *diksha-guru* to disciple (mantra-giver to mantra-receiver) is known as a *diksha-parampara*. A *parampara* in which the links are by instruction is known as a *shiksha-parampara*. In reality, however, the two *paramparas* tend to run concurrently, since most gurus give both *diksha* and *shiksha*. However, in the Gaudiya *parampara* it can be seen that many guru-disciple links were *shiksha* only and so it is sometimes referred to as a 'predominantly *shiksha parampara*.'

# The '*Parivara*' and the '*Vamsha*'

The movement of Shri Chaitanya Mahaprabhu entered into mediaeval Indian society, a culture wherein many would be initiated in childhood and by a variety of *diksha-gurus* in a wide array of *paramparas*. When a person became inspired to follow Chaitanya Mahaprabhu he or she would request instruction and guidance from one of his senior followers, thus accepting them as *shiksha-guru*. New followers would consider themselves disciples of the *shiksha-guru* and serve them in just the same way as they had served their *diksha-guru*. Membership of the Gaudiya Vaishnava community did not therefore depend on initiation. However, in the second and subsequent generations from Chaitanya Mahaprabhu there were greater numbers of followers who also became initiated by the disciples of those early followers.

A disciple is known in Sanskrit as a *shishya*, and thus the *parampara* composed of *diksha-gurus* and their disciples is also known as a *shishya-*

*parampara*. In Bengal this was collectively known as a *parivara* or 'retinue.'

Because the brahminical tradition allowed for a father to initiate his own son, and for the son to then initiate his own sons, there was, in the years after Chaitanya Mahaprabhu, a *parampara* composed of father-*diksha-gurus* and son-disciples. This family line of descent was known as a *vamsa*. Sometimes it was also known as a *bindu-parampara*. But the father who initiated his own sons would also initiate disciples, too, thus creating a *shishya-parampara* or *parivara*. In this way, every *vamsha* or family succession would also have a *parivara* or discipular succession closely associated with it.

Unfortunately, in the way that religious history often runs, some Vaishnavas considered that the biological descendants of the associates of Chaitanya Mahaprabhu were 'superior' gurus. God had chosen them to be born in the family of a great, transcendental ancestor and had thus blessed them more than others. As the centuries went by, the argument for their superiority became even more clamorous. They were the only legitimate gurus, it was said, and only they had the right to initiate. But it was patently not the case – as was evidenced by their often unremarkable behaviour and poor knowledge. Although being a biological descendant of a great Vaishnava certainly confers a noble ancestry, it does not bestow any particular spiritual quality upon the descendant. The young man whose great-great-grandfather was a high court judge will still have to go to law school, just like anyone else. Similarly, the young man whose great-great-grandfather was an eminent acharya with thousands of disciples cannot expect to be honoured as an acharya just because of the family tree. He must become trained, practise spiritual discipline, and begin to exhibit the qualities of an acharya before he can be recognised as one. Failure to do so will lead to a 'truncated *parampara*.'

# The truncated *parampara*

Sadly, sometimes a smaller branch of a *parampara* comes to an end. The guru has disciples, but none of them have their own disciples. The branch dies and bears no fruit. In other cases, the entire *parampara* itself dies. This can be brought about by a variety of circumstances. Sometimes if there is corruption in the teachers themselves, or in the chain of teachers, the followers may complain that the chain is no longer required; it no longer helps them. The mediaeval Protestant movement was inspired, in part, by the need to reduce the stature of the Pope and the priestly class. They were both regarded as superfluous in the matter of understanding the Bible.

In the history of the Sikh chain of gurus, there was such intense competition for the position of guru and supreme spiritual leader that the line came to an end after the death of Guru Govind Singh in 1708 – even though there were a total of twenty-two successors vying for the position. The last guru decided that to prevent any possible problems in the future the voice of the guru would be superseded by the voice of scripture – the collection of teachings written and compiled by the first guru, Guru Nanak. The line of living gurus may have come to an end but the creation of the 'everlasting guru' in the form of the written word, the *Guru Granth Sahib*, is regarded by Sikhs as the definitive moment in their history.

Islam had an even more tempestuous time arriving at a plan for succession. In the first few years after the death of Muhammad in 632 AD there were four caliphs, or supreme leaders, whose rule of the lands under Islamic conquest lasted until 661. But three of those caliphs were assassinated and, after a civil war lasting five years, Islam had broken into three main sects. There was intense disagreement as to who would be the true successor of the Prophet. The puritanical Khariji sect deemed that any Muslim who committed a major sin was an apostate and therefore an enemy and unfit to be the caliph.

After the assassination of Uthman, the third caliph, Muhammad's nephew and son-in-law Ali ibn Abi-Talib was installed as the fourth caliph. But not everyone was happy. Uthman's cousin, Mu'awiya ibn Abu Sufyan, the governor of Syria, rebelled against Ali, demanding vengeance for Uthman's murder. The dispute continued until Ali himself was assassinated by one of the Kharijis, and the position of supreme leader was taken up by his sons, Hassan and Hussein. By 680 both sons were either poisoned or killed in battle. Those in 'the party' (Shi'a) of Ali broke away to become a minority sect known as the Shi'a or Shi'ites. Later on, in 765, other Shi'as devoted to the seventh caliph, Ishmael, created their own sect known as the Ishmaelis. Those in the majority, who remained, as they saw it, on the 'well-trodden path' or *sunna*, became known as the Sunnis.

After the passing of the founder-*acharya* of ISKCON in 1977, there were also many years during which the healthy continuation of the *parampara* was threatened by groups of dissenters. One proposal was that, as in Sikhism, the books of Srila Prabhupada were, in effect, the everlasting guru; any gurus of the future were not actual gurus but more like priestly representatives. Some years later, as in Islam, two or three factions argued that other gurus should now be recognised as the supreme leader. This led to acrimony and community divisions.

The practicality of continuing the disciplic succession can render a simple principle unnecessarily complex. Theological speculation, personal ambition and community politics can often act as obstacles to a simple, natural flow. Yet despite the tendency of followers to disagree over doctrinal and political differences, there are nonetheless distinct advantages in having a living chain of preceptors, and the continuation of the *parampara* is regarded by the followers of the Vedas to be an intrinsic component in the welfare of human society.

## *Parampara*: A human necessity

Srila Bhaktivinoda Thakura, the great Victorian guru in the line of Chaitanya Mahaprabhu, also wrote on this subject in his book *Jaiva Dharma*. There, in response to the question, 'Why is there a disciplic succession?' he writes:

> "In this world, many people are contaminated by the impersonalist doctrine and thus fall into a life of sin. If there were no disciplic succession, or institution of devotees free of this contamination, then it would be very difficult for ordinary people to find saintly association. This is why the *Padma Purana* tells us, 'Any mantra that does not come in disciplic succession is considered to be fruitless. Therefore, four divine individuals will appear in the age of Kali to establish disciplic schools.' Of these four schools, the oldest is the Brahma Sampradaya. This disciplic succession has existed since the time of Lord Brahma and is still strong. Whatever scriptures — whether Veda, Vedanta or other — are taught in a particular school maintain their original form; no interpolations are possible in these texts. Thus there can be no doubt about the mantras that are found in the books of these ancient schools. Thus a disciplic succession of saintly persons is an absolute necessity for human society and that is why the institution has existed since the earliest times."

# Sampradaya

A *sampradaya* is a school of philosophy embodied and exemplified by its teachers. The *sampradaya* is the orthodox message and practise that is transmitted through the centuries by the human mechanism of the *parampara*.

From the early Middle Ages, a *sampradaya* was recognised as such when it was able to provide a commentary on the *Vedanta Sutra*. The *Vedanta Sutra* is itself a commentary on the Upanishads and other Vedic literature. The writer of the commentary, or *bhasya*, had to carefully define the relationship between souls, God and the world, and the nature of the illusion which prevents the souls from directly experiencing reality as it is. A distinct *bhasya* that had been checked by experts for logic, clarity and adherence to grammatical rules firmly established the community of the writer as a distinct *sampradaya*; whereas failure to do so meant that the community had to subsume itself within another *sampradaya*.

Thus when Adi Shankaracharya (788-820 AD) wrote his *Sariraka Bhasya* commentary on *Vedanta Sutra*, he established his community firmly as a *sampradaya*, as did Ramanujacharya (1017-1137) when he wrote his *Shri Bhasya*. Madhvacharya (1238-1317) was in the Brahma Sampradaya and wrote his four commentaries on the *Vedanta Sutra*, beginning with the *Brahmasutra Bhasya*. Some 250 years later, within the community of followers of Chaitanya Mahaprabhu, the *Bhagavata-purana*, or Srimad Bhagavatam, was acknowledged as the natural commentary on *Vedanta Sutra*. It had been written after the *Vedanta Sutra*, and by the same author, Srila Vyasadeva, and was therefore itself the natural and conclusive commentary and the perfection of *bhasya*. The Srimad Bhagavatam even began with the same first aphorism of the *Vedanta Sutra: janmadyasya yatah*. Early followers reasoned that no other commentary was required, so a separate *bhasya* was never written.

Yet because there were philosophical differences between the teachings of Chaitanya Mahaprabhu and Madhvacharya, when the *sampradaya* credentials of the Gaudiya Vaishnavas were challenged in the late 1700s, they could not establish the validity of their claim. If they were Madhvas, the other Vaishnavas insisted, why did they not accept his teachings? And if they were, in fact, the 'Chaitanya Sampradaya' and a distinct community, why did they not have a commentary on *Vedanta Sutra*?

Part Two | The parampara family tree

Under the direction of his guru, the now aged Visvanatha Chakravarti Thakur, the younger Baladeva Vidyabhusana wrote a commentary on *Vedanta*, giving it the name *Govinda Bhasya*. He wrote it in an astonishingly short time, under inspiration of the beloved deities of Rupa Goswami, Radha Govinda. Yet even though he could have had his community recognised as the 'Chaitanya Sampradaya' he maintained that they were of the Brahma Sampradaya and wrote that the *parampara* was that which came through Madhvacharya and his disciples.

Chaitanya Mahaprabhu himself saw the *sankirtan* movement as the prime benediction for humanity in the age of *Kali*, and the chanting of the names of Krishna as the essential religious practise for the age. As such, it was to be the movement that brought all the Vaishnava *sampradayas* together and unified them on a common platform. It was not that the other Vaishnava communities would have been in any disagreement about the chanting of the Holy Names. Such descriptions of the efficacy of *Harinama japa* and *kirtan* were already written in the Puranas that they all honoured. But the different theologies laid stress on different elements of the soul's relationship to God, and the practises necessary to attain the highest realisation of that relationship.

Lord Chaitanya Mahaprabhu therefore took different elements from each *sampradaya*; elements that he considered the strongest theological points and practises for attainment of Krishna *prema* – pure love of Krishna. He accepted the basic doctrine of Madhvacharya, while at the same time recognizing certain aspects contained in the teachings of the other three. Lord Chaitanya brought these teachings together in the perfection of dharma. His own words, as quoted by Shri Jiva Goswami, are as follows:

> "From Madhva I will take two essential teachings: his complete rejection and defeat of the Mayavadi philosophy and his service to the deity of Krishna, accepting Him as an eternal spiritual personality. From Ramanuja, I will accept two teachings: the concept of devotional service, unpolluted by karma and jnana, and service to the devotees. From Vishnuswami's teachings I will accept two elements: the sentiment of exclusive dependence on Krishna and the path of raga-marga, or spontaneous devotion. From Nimbarka, I will take two very important principles: the necessity of taking shelter of Srimati Radharani and the high esteem of the gopi's love for Krishna."

Therefore, although Baladeva Vidyabhusana established the credentials of what could have been the 'Chaitanya Sampradaya,' he simply reiterated the statement of Kavi Karnapura two generations before him and declared it to be a part of the Madhva Sampradaya. Madhva's disciplic succession included the two luminaries, Laksmipati Tirtha and Madhavendra Puri, who had given initiation to Isvara Puri, the guru of Chaitanya Mahaprabhu.

There were other groups of Chaitanya Vaishnavas over in Bengal who were simply not interested in declaring themselves part of the Madhva Sampradaya. It did not concern them. Madhvacharya lived four hundred years ago and way down in the south of India, thousands of miles away, they reasoned. What was the connection? The spiritual family tree descended from Chaitanya Mahaprabhu, the very incarnation of Radha and Krishna, and that was enough for them. But as the decades went by, some of the practises of this 'Chaitanya Sampradaya' significantly strayed from moral and religious orthodoxy, and by the mid-1800s, Bhaktivinode Thakur again affirmed that the line of Chaitanya Mahaprabhu had descended from Madhvacharya.

Part Two | A very different diksha

# 22

# A very different diksha

*Ideas about exactly what was conferred on the disciple through diksha sometimes changed through history. Popular notions, superstitions and flights of the imagination often coloured the understanding of the initiates. The line of Srila Prabhupada descends from great Vaishnavas who worked tirelessly to dispel such misconceptions.*

**In the very early years of the Gaudiya Sampradaya, the majority of followers were initiated by their own family or community gurus and simply became followers of Chaitanya Mahaprabhu at a later stage in their life.** They kept their respective mantras and distinct forms of *tilak*, but took the teachings of Chaitanya and the Goswamis as their inspiration. Many did not feel they had to become initiated again in order to be sincere followers. Three distinct communities had evolved: in the Orissan seaside holy place of Jagannatha Puri were renunciates and sannyasis living together in their ashrams; in Vrindavan the white-clad hermits; and in Bengal the householder village followers of Nityananda Prabhu.

Between the writing of the *Hari Bhakti Vilasa* in 1534 and the writing of the *Chaitanya Charitamrita* in 1616, there was further consolidation and standardisation of theology, practice and missionary efforts. Some of this took place during and after the Keturi festival in the 1560s. The Vrindavan followers and the devotees from Bengal and Orissa came together in the presence of Jahnava Mata, the wife of Shri Nityananda Prabhu.

Gopal Guru Goswami was a disciple of Vrakresvara *Pandit*, an associate of Lord Shri Chaitanya Mahaprabhu. The story goes that when he was a young boy Chaitanya Mahaprabhu was kind to him, giving him first the affectionate name 'Gopal' and then, when the boy quoted from the scriptures, the name 'Guru.' Later in his life Gopal Guru had a dream of Chaitanya who told him to initiate the first person he saw when he woke up the following morning. The next day he looked out of his door and there stood a young brahmana who had come to see him. That was Dhyanachandra.

Gopal Guru Goswami wrote a *paddhati*, a handbook, to help his followers to contemplate the divine activities of Radha and Krishna. This *lila-smarana*, or divine remembrance, was to be done in addition to chanting at least sixty-four rounds of *japa* each day. His disciple Dhyanachandra Goswami expanded on his guru's writings and wrote a handbook for contemplative practise in 1620. Within this book he describes eleven qualities of the liberated souls who serve the assistants of the gopi maidens in the eternal realm of Vrindavan. He advised each disciple to meditate on his inner self as one of those assistants, known as *manjaris*.

As the years passed by, it became the custom for gurus to give the 'eleven qualities' or *ekadasa-bhava*, to their disciples at the time of initiation; and it became the custom for the disciples, quite naturally, to imagine that their guru was indeed one of those *manjaris*. Such a guru who is firmly situated in his eternal, spiritual identity is known as a *siddha*, or a 'perfected one.' It therefore became a presumption on the disciple's behalf that the guru was not merely giving him an aid to contemplation, but actually 'revealing' his inner identity to him. Despite different disciples receiving the same set of qualities, and therefore the same identity, this conception became a standard in that particular line. And as each guru could, and did, have hundreds of disciples, who would then go on to have their own disciples, within two hundred years the succession had grown into a large family tree. From one handbook had grown a dynasty, and it became known as a *siddha-pranali*, or 'channel of the perfected ones.'

At the same time, human beings being what they are, there were some feelings of exclusivity within those who had taken *diksha* within this *siddha-pranali*, especially those who could trace their line of perfect gurus back to an associate of Shri Chaitanya Mahaprabhu himself. Some particularly high level of self-absorption seems to have been displayed by those who came in the familial line of Nityananda Prabhu, through his son Virabhadra Goswami. As biological descendants they even claimed sole authority to initiate since they were 'family members' of Nityananda, or *Nityananda-vamsha*.

Into this mixture came another problem – and it was a big one. In order to deeply meditate on Radha and Krishna's *lila* one is supposed to have already advanced spiritually. But after several generations, many gurus would give the highest meditations to entirely undeserving candidates. Some disciples did not chant even four rounds of daily *japa*, what to speak of sixty-four. And many fell into immoral conduct.

Thus a noble attempt to follow the Goswamis seems to have been successful for only a few, and it endured for perhaps two hundred years, but by the latter decades of the nineteenth century things were in a woeful state. The vows of celibacy that the renounced were meant to follow were as tattered as the white cotton garments they wore. The illegitimate children spawned by the union between the 'goswamis' and the female renunciates had, over several generations, grown so numerous as to form an entire sub-caste dynasty – all claiming to be 'upper-class,' by dint of their heredity, no matter the absence of their spiritual practise.

# "Blind sampradaya"

Bhaktivinode Thakur described any *sampradaya* that removed spiritual vision and gave only ignorance of Radha and Krishna as a 'blind' *sampradaya*, or *apasampradaya*. In his writings he categorized thirteen of them, and described the many ways in which their theology and practise deviated from the teachings of Chaitanya Mahaprabhu. Some of them mixed Vaishnava concepts with Buddhist beliefs, some with Sufi conceptions, and other groups mixed devotion to Radharani with darker, Tantric practises. One of the *apasampradayas*, known as the Bauls, was a group of wandering minstrels and sang their songs of devotion mixed with all kinds of materialistic lyrics. They had originally developed when Sufi travellers, exiled from Persia, sang songs from village to village in order to earn money. They were not devotees of Krishna, but discovered that singing songs about Krishna brought them an income. Later, more materialistic Hindus took note of this style and wrote many popular ditties with attractive melodies. Bhaktivinode Thakur's songs, in contrast, described the feelings and practises of pure devotional service, and to counteract the pernicious influence of these groups, he had his own songs printed up and widely distributed. His followers sometimes set their guru's devotional songs to the popular melodies of the Bauls.

The Thakur wanted to popularise the teachings of Chaitanya Mahaprabhu, who taught that love for Krishna should not be mixed with selfish desires for sensual gratification, yogic powers or impersonal liberation. He taught that those disciples who thought that simply by the act of initiation they had been made a party to the intimate realms of Goloka Vrindavan were being duped by the guru; indeed they were complicit in the deception because they were being carried away by their imaginations. It was never possible to simply imagine oneself in the pastimes of Radha and Krishna and to arrive there by dint of the powers of the mind. It had to be revealed by the Lord as an act of grace, and that would take time and effort. Impatience and the desire for pure devotional service did not make a good combination. Those who similarly imagined that their devotional feelings or occasional tears were symptoms of great spiritual attainment were taking it all too cheaply, he said, and he labelled them *prakrita-sahajiyas*, or materialistic 'ease-lovers.' Feelings for Krishna were always good, he explained, but one must know his level and not imagine that he has progressed beyond that. There is a difference between a green, unripe mango and a fully ripened fruit, and one must know the symptoms of each.

Gaura Kishora dasa Babaji was aware of this state of affairs by dint of his occasional residence at Radha Kunda, the holy lake of Srimati Radharani in Vrindavan. Once when he was asked if he could also give *siddha-diksha* and reveal the *ekadasa-bhava* to a particular candidate he replied firmly:

> *"The Hare Krishna mantra is a siddha mantra. Within this mantra are the siddha-rupa of Shri Krishna and the siddha-rupas of all living entities. If you chant the maha-mantra purely the syllables of the mantra will gradually reveal the spiritual form, qualities, and pastimes of Shri Krishna. This chanting will also reveal your eternal spiritual form, service, and the eleven particulars of your spiritual identity."*

Bhaktisiddhanta Saraswati decided that enough was enough. The movement of Chaitanya Mahaprabhu could not be championed by spiritually weak representatives. Fuelled by his father's strong condemnation of such 'blind *sampradayas*,' and Gaura Kishora *dasa* Babaji's endorsement, he understood that the pseudo-contemplatives had lost their authority and brought wholesale disrespect upon the Vaishnava community. People everywhere regarded Vaishnavas as immoral beggars.

Part Two | A very different diksha

So he wanted to re-establish a strong religious community led not by reclusive contemplatives or charlatan brahmanas but by a religious order that initiated newcomers into the unadulterated teaching and practise of *bhakti*, and one that was very firmly part of ordinary society.

And 'ordinary society' in India includes monks. There are four classical life-stages: the student, the householder, the retired, and lastly the monk or sannyasi. After a lifetime of learning, the sannyasi travels and follows a renounced life, but he is not a reclusive. Clad in saffron coloured cloth and carrying a bamboo staff, he serves society by travelling, teaching and inspiring others. Bhaktisiddhanta Thakur wanted his missionary organisation – the Gaudiya Math – to be a dynamic movement of faithful, properly trained members led by travelling preachers, mainly sannyasis and student-monks, or *brahmacharis*.

At that time in India there was another successful organisation with somewhat similar aims: the Ramakrishna Mission. They had started decades previously and were already well-known. They wore orange robes and had a strongly organised movement with many branches, and they were popular with the public for their spiritual teaching and charitable activities. One of the members of the Ramakrishna Mission had left that organisation and joined Bhaktisiddhanta Thakur, and he was already contributing by giving the newly-formed Gaudiya Math organisational shape and leadership.

Srila Bhaktisiddhanta conceived of creating not merely orange-clad *brahmachari* students, but fully-fledged sannyasis. There was, however, no tradition of sannyasa within the contemporary Gaudiya community. Centuries previously, those sannyasis that had joined Chaitanya Mahaprabhu had already been initiated into the sannyasa order either by sannyasis in the Shankara tradition or by those who came in the *parampara* of Madhvacharya. Chaitanya Mahaprabhu himself had been awarded the sannyasa order by a monk in the Shankara tradition. The celebrated Six Goswamis had not urged their followers to become sannyasis, and one of them had even commented that the 'wearing of reddish cloth may contribute to pride.' Neither his father, Bhaktivinode Thakur, nor his guru, Gaura Kishor Babaji were sannyasis, and the other great spiritual confidante of his father, Jagannatha Das Babaji, had also been a reclusive saint.

Not only was he considering a distinct break with the 400 year-old tradition of the Gaudiya Sampradaya, he was proposing the creation of an entirely new order – a new community of sannyasis – with no inherent historical tradition. Aside from the saffron cloth, a feature that was prescribed by scripture for wandering mendicants, what would his sannyasis look like? What would be their principles of renunciation? What would be their ritual? What additional mantras? And which sannyasi would train and prepare them, then initiate them? It could not be a sannyasi of the Shankara school, since the Vaishnava teaching stood in opposition to their interpretations of the *Vedanta Sutra*; and it could not be a swami of the Madhva school, since there were significant points of theology that stood in contrast to the teachings of Chaitanya Mahaprabhu. He wanted to continue the *siddhanta* and practises taught by Mahaprabhu and his immediate followers, the Six Goswamis; but he wanted that *siddhanta* and ritual to be taught by a new order of monks, strictly following the principles of renunciation. Only in this way would the teachings of the Gaudiya Sampradaya become forever separated from the pride, syncretism and debauchery into which they had sunk over the centuries.

So he turned to an unlikely source of information. He and a few followers travelled to the south of India where he consulted members of the Shri Sampradaya, followers of Ramanujacharya (1017-1137) whose sannyasa order had remained strong and highly moral for the past nine hundred years. The Shri Vaishnavas numbered in hundreds of thousands, were geographically widespread, and were a well organised and socially integrated community which upheld the supremacy of devotional service to Vishnu.

Although Srila Bhaktisiddhanta Thakur did not accept the ultimate philosophical conclusions of the Shri Sampradaya, he nevertheless valued their preservation of the fourth order of spiritual life and the details inherent in its practise. After this consultation he returned to Bengal and took sannyasa himself. This decision served to quickly reclaim the social and moral authority of Chaitanya Mahaprabhu's teachings within the contemporary society of his day and to give the Vaishnava community a fresh social position and respectability. In turn that reclamation helped to re-establish the philosophical basis of the true meaning of authentic *diksha* in the Gaudiya line, freeing it from centuries of misconception and layers of sentiment and superstition. Throughout his life Srila Bhaktisiddhanta Thakur remained a fierce critic of the pseudo-Vaishnava gurus of Bengal as well as the new ideas that were entering Bengal society from the British-influenced intelligentsia. He regularly gave initiation to those who already had *diksha* from a family priest or another *sampradaya,* and began the missionary efforts to send teachers of Krishna consciousness beyond India.

# Part Three

# Creating and sustaining community

# 23

# The guru spreads his arms

*A guru lives to teach his students. He takes great care to guide them towards becoming teachers themselves, and is overjoyed when they take his message to new places. Sometimes, through his faithful students, the guru fashions a network of teaching-places, spiritual schools that create a legacy for coming generations. Widening the scope of his teaching while he lives, and making it available for many others after he dies, is all part of the guru's compassionate work. This chapter looks at how that has been done over the past thousand years.*

**A guru lives to give systematic knowledge, relevant guidance and inspirational encouragement to all who wish to receive it from him and who are qualified to become students.** He gives whatever he has with compassion, love and discipline, and he sets before his grateful receivers a living example of what it means to be in consciousness of God and His laws. To better share his gifts with others, the guru invites them to come and live with him. Because they are being given shelter, or in Sanskrit, *ashraya*, the place where he teaches his students is known as an *ashram*.

The guru is also kind to others, even if they don't live with him, and therefore he makes additional arrangements for people living some distance away from him. His senior disciples travel and may also set up ashrams under his order. This collection of ashrams, each of which can provide the company of the guru through his representatives, is sometimes known as the *parishad* or 'group', or *sangha*, the 'association'. The guru may have many graduate students who live at some distance yet keep their connection to him through occasional visits and correspondence. Collectively, these may be referred to as the guru's *parivara*, his 'retinue' or 'entourage.' If the members of the *parivara* come together more regularly for meetings the names *samaja*, 'assembly,' or *sabha*, 'society' may be used. If the *sabha* members form themselves into sub-groups, assuming different tasks to be performed in between meetings, they may become known as the *samstha*, or 'organisation.'

The English word for a messenger being sent out by his master is *missionary*, and the collective name for several messengers working together is a 'mission'. If they're successful in attracting people to their cause, so much that many seem to be coming all at once, we sometimes call that a 'movement'. And when such a spiritual enterprise has been established, or instituted, for some years, the English language refers to that as an 'institution'. When a movement of people becomes focused on veneration of a saint or guru, the English word 'cult' is used. And when they worship that saint congregationally with common songs, prayers, and rituals – and have been doing so for some years - we more often use the term 'religion.' Srila Prabhupada used all the above terms – Sanskrit and English - to describe his followers as they worked together to spread the *sankirtan* message of Shri Chaitanya Mahaprabhu. He didn't flinch when using the word 'cult' despite its negative connotations during his time; and similarly the word 'institution' was freely used, without any allusions to more mundane enterprises.

Whatever words are used to describe gatherings and collectives of inspired people, the phenomenon repeats itself through history. Someone has a positive message and wishes to pass it on to others. He has to first show that his message is relevant and useful, logically persuasive and life-enhancing. Having done that, he needs to spread his arms, so to speak, to reach out and touch others. He does this by travelling - by speaking to a family here and a crowd there - by explaining his ideas to influential people, to fellow philosophers and powerful leaders. Then he does it by writing and by engaging followers in carrying his message – both verbal and written - to places he cannot physically go. And for sustainability he must create something that ensures his message - and his messengers - will continue long after his death. Creating this human vehicle is crucial. With it, the message survives the successive generations sufficiently to create a permanent cultural phenomenon. Without this human movement of messengers, the message itself can vanish.

The story of gurus and the movements they created through history is a very interesting one, and would fill many large volumes. For our purposes, it is sufficient to say that there are four main historical periods, and in each one the guru and his disciples lived and worked together in slightly different ways. It helps when asking important questions on the nature of the institution a guru creates around him, the legacy he leaves, and where you might find your own place, to know something about these different ways.

The first period can be termed **Ancient**, the second **Early**, the third **Mediaeval**, and the fourth **Modern**. Let's say that Ancient is in the times described by the Puranas; Early is India from the time of Gautama Buddha (600 BC) up to the time of Adi Shankaracharya (788-820AD); Mediaeval from Shankaracharya through to Shri Chaitanya Mahaprabhu (1486-1534) and the end of the 1500s; then Modern up until current times. I'm sure that serious historians might frown at these simplistic definitions, but they can always correct me after they read this chapter.

# Ancient period

In ancient times, the guru often had his school in the forest. The tranquillity was helpful for uninterrupted study, since for reciting the Vedas it was best to locate quiet places with as few disturbances as possible. While inhospitable places like mountain caves traditionally provided yogis with tranquillity and shelter, the gurus liked the forest because it gave access to water, fruits and other fresh foods, and the all important firewood for the daily fire sacrifices. Indeed, the ancient verse in the *Mundaka Upanishad* urges the student to find a guru and to go there with 'firewood in hand' (*samit-panih*). Disciples lived with their guru and served him daily by cleaning, cooking, fetching water and collecting and chopping firewood. They learned their subjects by listening carefully to him, memorizing through repetition, and by asking intelligent questions.

When the students grew up they would marry and take on different occupations. Sometimes even a young prince was a student at a forest school for some months, or a year or two. The guru might continue counselling his grown-up pupil and, on occasion, stay at his palatial residence for a few days. Later on, as king, the former student would build a school for his guru in a spot slightly closer to the city, but where he could be supplied with all the items necessary. These schools could grow to quite a size, and some of them had hundreds of students.

The famous Durvasa Muni travelled with all his disciples, a large flock that numbered in the thousands. In his case it was always a mixed joy for the king to receive his master, since all the disciples would have to be fed and accommodated as well, and Durvasa rarely gave notice of his arrival. We also read of Sandipani Muni who was the *kulapati* (head teacher) of a very large establishment where many gurus lived and taught a total of 74,000 students. However, the average guru and his ashram were much smaller.

It is important to distinguish between the roles of the householders and the sannyasis. The gurus were mainly householders, since teaching young students for years required a stable environment where food could be found without too much effort, a living situation which, though simple, wasn't too uncomfortable, and sufficient regularity in the daily and yearly routine. Sannyasis, on the other hand, were duty-bound not to have any place they called home, to beg daily for food from different houses, and to travel widely, giving inspiration and counsel for a day or two only. The longest period they could remain in one place was one week. They might have one assistant with them, but the rules made long term tuition of disciples impossible. Initiation meant being initiated into a course of study, with the relevant mantras and rituals pursuant to the course. So sannyasis would not generally initiate, although examples can still be found.

Before the death of the guru, he would select someone to inherit his title, his teaching position and his physical assets, humble though they might be. That meant that, usually, the leading disciple, the most learned disciple, the most trustworthy disciple, would be chosen. From then on the initiations and main teachings would be given by that leading disciple - the new acharya. In the event of other leading disciples being qualified, they might leave the ashram and set up a new ashram, attracting their own disciples. In this way the teachings would proliferate.

# Early period

In what I have called the 'Early' period, from Buddha to Adi Shankara (600 BC to 800 AD) we find Buddhism spread throughout India. Royal patronage and strategic planning created many university towns where Buddhist monks not only learned the philosophy and practises of Buddhism, but professions and trades of all kinds. When they left the university to become householders they took with them the means of livelihood as well as a thorough grounding in Buddhism. This helped to spread Buddhist teachings throughout the country and beyond.

Buddhist monks - those who chose to remain as monks and not marry - also took to living together in large population areas where they could support their monastic life by the daily alms round. They called these *guhas* or 'caves'. A cave was one of the traditional places where travelling sannyasis would gather together and live for four months during the rainy season. This *chaturmasya* period was the only time that wandering sannyasis would all live together. Most of the Buddhist monks that lived in India were Indian by birth and knew about this rainy season tradition, so they called their living areas *guhas*, too. This is an important development because previously those who wanted to lead a spiritual life either married, lived in the forest or in a small village setting with their wife and taught their disciples there, or else they became sannyasi monks and travelled without educating disciples. For perhaps the first time, in a regulated way, those who wore saffron robes lived together in an urbanised area and taught people about the spiritual life.

# Mediaeval period

The mediaeval period, lasting from the time of Adi Shankara Acharya (788 – 820) through until the time of Shri Chaitanya Mahaprabhu (1486 – 1534) and the end of the 1500s, is characterised by the gradual eclipse of Buddhism in India, the spreading of Adi Shankara's 'Crypto-Buddhist' teachings and a resurgence of the Puranic and Pancharatrik teaching in the form of the four schools of Vaishnavism.

Since this chapter only concerns the physical institutions of the gurus, I will merely summarise Shankara's teaching by saying that whereas Buddhism did not draw upon the Vedic texts, and did not concern itself with them, Adi Shankara's *Advaita* (non-dual) conception, or *mayavada* did. So Adi Shankara taught strongly and enthusiastically from the Vedas and Upanishads, and helped to transform the intellectual climate for hundreds of years into the future, to the point where Buddhism hardly existed in the country of its origin.

Adi Shankara Acharya borrowed from the Buddhists in the way his followers lived and taught. Since Buddhist monks had chosen to live in important population and pilgrimage centres, so would he and his disciples. There was Dwaraka, in the far west of India, the place where Lord Krishna lived for a hundred years; Shringeri in the south; Jagannatha Puri on the east coast, the place of Jagannatha; and Badari in the Himalayas. Adi Shankara re-invigorated and elevated the Vedic sannyasa order to the point where most of the population felt that to properly take sannyasa, one had to become initiated by a follower of Adi Shankara. These highly learned sannyasis then set up their ashrams in the pilgrimage places, each one becoming the 'Shankaracharya' of the region.

The big change that came along with Adi Shankara was that now education in Vedic philosophy and science was taught by saffron-clad sannyasis with their bamboo staves. To be trained by one of them was to be able to hold your head up high and declare with pride the name of your swami guru. Although the Vedic schools with their married gurus still existed, the more prestigious option was the sannyasi followers of Shankara, who naturally gave initiations to all comers.

Co-existent with Shankaracharya and for some years after him was a succession of Vaishnava mystics known as the Alwars. Twelve of them were prominent and they lived from around 500 to 950AD. Some of them knew each other but most did not. Although they did not collaborate, they sung of the same supreme person. They left behind them 4,000 hymns which were compiled into a body of work by Natha Muni, whose grandson was known as Yamuna Acharya (918-1038). Yamuna was the preceptorial inspiration of the great Vaishnava reformer Ramanuja Acharya (1017 – 1137). Ramanuja's great contribution to the development of the Vaishnava *sangha* was that he chose to reform, regularise, or in some cases re-establish, ritual worship in many of 106 major temples, situated from the very southern tip of India right up to the north. By doing so he gave life to the tradition and strengthened the teaching of *bhakti*. He wrote nine brilliant books in which he set out an alternative and completely valid interpretation of the Upanishads, demonstrating that the ultimate reality is Narayana, the original person. Through royal patronage he furthered the teaching of the Vedas according to the *siddhanta* of Vaishnavism, and helped to develop the city of Shri Rangam – where he lived for sixty years – into a temple town of some twenty thousand inhabitants. He was also a sannyasi and during his life gave sannyasa initiation to many hundreds of disciples.

Ramanuja's other major reform that was really 'spreading the guru's arms' was his argument that the 4,000 hymns of the Alwars were 'a second Veda' and therefore an equally important revelation. Since these

The Guru and Disciple Book

were written in the Tamil language it was then possible for all kinds of people to study them and teach them, not only the priestly class. Indeed, the Alwars themselves were from different social classes. Some were brahmanas; one was a king, one a musician and one a reformed thief. Ramanuja taught that *bhakti*, or offering all one's actions to the Divine, and serving God through hearing about His incarnations and singing about Him, was the one path that all could follow, regardless of birth or social circumstances. The sum total of this teaching was to ensure that the *bhakti* revolution became a very large and popular movement, with simple and effective enough ideas for all to practise and teach.

Ramanujacharya left behind him seventy-four *simhasanadhipatis* or 'throne-holders' who would continue to give initiations after him. Some of these were sannyasis but most were married men. They lived in and around the holy places he had popularised. This mass movement, coupled with a broad appeal to all classes of people, with stories and songs and divine poetry, ensured that the foundations were set for centuries to come. Whereas Adi Shankara had been intellectually appealing, Ramanuja was not only intellectually superior, but also expanded the appeal of his teachings to include the common man and woman.

Only a century later came Madhva Acharya (1238 – 1317) who was born, and lived, in and around Udupi in Karnataka, south-western India. One of his immediate neighbours was the Shankaracharya of Shringeri, only thirty miles to the north. With one of the four headquarters of *Advaita* philosophy on his doorstep, Madhva, who came in the lineage of Lord Brahma, opposed the philosophical monism of his neighbour by teaching a strongly dualistic version of Vaishnava philosophy, and he taught it extremely vigorously. A miraculous appearance of the Deity of Lord Krishna made the town of Udupi a famous pilgrimage place. And there was a second miracle. The same Krishna turned round to give audience to a poor man, a *shudra*, who could not enter the temple. This event made Madhva's compassionate teachings resonate with the poor and the masses.

Eight of Madhva's sannyasi disciples and their ashrams framed the main temple in the town square. Each ashram had a small temple inside it, which was also open to the public. As the years went by, each head of the eight temples cared for the main shrine for a period of several years. This was eventually set as a two year period in a fourteen year rota. This has given Madhva's ashram system stability and durability for the past eight hundred years. There are many sannyasis who have come from

## Part Three | The guru spreads his arms

the Madhva school, making it a very large movement. Although less geographically widespread than Ramanuja's, Madhva's large number of followers have continued to be a strong force in India.

One sannyasi who was undoubtedly knowledgeable of both these Vaishnava communities was Madhavendra Puri (1420-1490). Although nominally a swami in the Shankarite line, he exhibited a superlative devotion for Krishna. Indeed, there seems to have been a great number of swamis who turned to *bhakti* in that period. One of Madhavendra Puri's disciples was Isvara Puri, who became the guru of Shri Chaitanya Mahaprabhu (1486-1534).

Lord Shri Chaitanya Mahaprabhu, curiously enough, exemplified in his life different kinds of Vedic ashram teaching. Up until the age of twenty four, as a young married man, he both learned and taught in one of the many Vedic schools around the area of Navadwipa. So great were the number of students in this area, who came from all over India, it became what we would refer to today as a 'university town.' Upon taking sannyasa he travelled for six years throughout India like a traditional sannyasi and taught and inspired everyone he met. For the last eighteen years he lived in partial seclusion in the large pilgrimage place of Jagannatha Puri. There he gathered around him the devotees who would continue his movement after him, training them carefully in all the nuances of the teaching and practise. He also sent his dear companion Nityananda Prabhu back to Bengal (which in those days included modern Bangladesh) to teach others in the many villages there.

He taught that the all-attractive Lord Krishna is the supreme person, and that He can be reached in mystical union by discussing the stories associated with Him, worshipping His sacred image, in the home or the public temple, and by reciting and singing His divine names, particularly in the form of the great mantra – the Hare Krishna mantra. In this, Lord Chaitanya made Vaishnava teaching and practise even more accessible for all classes of people, and gave the one process that ordinary people would find instantly effective and spiritually rewarding.

After his disappearance from the world in 1534, there were three different modes of the *sankirtan* movement; three ways in which the followers lived together to support each other's spiritual practise. In the seaside pilgrimage place of Puri was the '*guha*' ashram mode, with sannyasis living together in a big, important town. In rural Bengal were the householders with sixty-four gurus giving initiation in different villages under the direction of Nityananda Prabhu. These villages were spread over a wide area. Over in Vrindavan, more than a thousand miles from Bengal – a huge walking distance in those days – were the Goswamis such as Rupa and Sanatana who lived the lives of hermits, neither householders nor sannyasis, but living in poverty, sleeping under different trees each night. Each branch gathered followers – some quicker than others – but it would be some decades before all three groups came together and discussed what common teachings they would jointly present.

# Modern period

The teachings of Chaitanya Mahaprabhu became widely proliferated in the 1600s and 1700s, even travelling as far as today's eastern Indian states of Assam and Manipur. But there was a tendency for the most advanced members of the lineage to practise as hermits in seclusion, perhaps with a modest ashram of followers around them. This suited individual contemplation but not widespread expansion. The drift away from widespread dissemination towards the eremitic lifestyle was somewhat understandable: the Hare Krishna mantra was to be chanted for many hours each day, and those who could take up this daily practise needed to be relatively free of family duties and were thus often older in years. Travelling conditions were harsh, and the social and political climate generally unfavourable.

Muslim conquerors had first made incursions into India in 664 AD. The Arab warlord Al Muhallab ibn Suffrah had attacked southern Punjab and returned home with ample rewards for his efforts. From that time on there were successive waves of Afghans, Turks and Persians attacking India, looting and destroying religious buildings and culture. The coastal region – around what is now Kolkata (Calcutta) – was important for trade, from China to the north and Asia to the east, and ships could also sail around the southern tip of India to the Middle East. Bengal was finally conquered in 1204 and became a region under Islamic law with numerous incidents of forced conversions of Hindus – particularly those who had the audacity to spread their teachings. Vaishnava gurus and others had to pay financial tributes known as *jizya* to their Muslim overlords, and the teaching of the Vedas and temple worship became overlaid with a financial imperative.

Part Three | The guru spreads his arms

Gurus customarily initiated their sons who would then become titular heads of a particular holy site. The sons also inherited the Islamic tax payable for that site, but sometimes had no strong inclination to follow in their father's religious footsteps. As reluctant inheritors of their father's title they nevertheless continued initiating followers, accepting donations from them and rendering a portion of the income as tax to their Muslim overlords. They managed to survive physically, but as the decades progressed many lineages gradually became spiritually weak.

Wherever there is Muslim dominance and oppression, the local people become inclined to ideas and styles of worship that will help them to cope. In the far west of India, the Hindus developed a more martial spirit and diffused the hard and fast Vedic ideas so that the resulting theology would form a barrier to Islam. They became known as the Sikhs. In the far east, the popularity of the aggressive-looking *Kali* enjoyed a resurgence, and various sects formed that practised darker rituals, known collectively as 'left-handed *tantra*,' or *vama-marga*.

Along with Muslim culture came the Sufis. Spurned by other Islamic leaders, they took to earning their livelihood throughout Bengal and beyond. Some Sufi mendicants sang their songs and begged to make a living. But begging from Hindus was much more successful when the Sufis sang Hindu songs. And so began another period of widespread dissemination of quasi-Vaishnava teaching through the medium of Sufi bards and poets. This inevitably diluted the teachings and the situation persisted the longer the Vaishnava saints were in seclusion.

Then, after hundreds of years of domination, along came the East India Company and finally the British Raj. The British had been in Calcutta since 1690 and there had been a growing British presence throughout the 18th century. In 1757 at the Battle of Plassey, the East India Company and Clive of India defeated Siraj ud-Daulah, ruler of Bengal, and the British influence increased. Gradually the intellectuals of Bengal became acclimatised to their new fair-skinned lords and along with them the teachings of the Christian faith. They began to adapt Hinduism to accommodate certain points of Christian doctrine, particularly in the urbanised regions surrounding India's capital city, Calcutta. Denial of temple deity worship, the 'worship of graven images,' and new forms of Vaishnava-Christian syncretism became the fashion amongst the English-speaking Bengalis, collectively known as the *bhadralok*.

Into the confusing mixture that was Victorian India entered Srila Bhaktivinode Thakur (1838 – 1916) who brought about changes in several ways. As an English speaker he wrote books in the language of those in power, explaining the logic of the Vedic and Vaishnava path in a way that appealed to their logic and reason and those Bengalis who followed them. He also wrote books in the vernacular, both for the common reader and the seasoned practitioner. He travelled for his job as a deputy magistrate and conducted group *sankirtan* meetings for village gatherings wherever he went, some five hundred in total. Some of the groups he founded are still running today. He wrote many songs in the simple Bengali language, with melodies derived from the Sufi-influenced pseudo-Vaishnava groups that were so popular. And he wrote pamphlets, poems, essays, and engaged in public speaking – and initiated followers, too.

His son, Bhaktisiddhanta Thakur, developed some of his father's groups into fully-fledged *maths*, ashrams for students with public temples attached to them, and he developed many more. In a space of eighteen years he had inaugurated sixty-four centres throughout India and Burma, and had sent missionary sannyasis to Berlin and London. He was the first guru to teach using gramophone recordings, BBC radio, agricultural shows, a daily newspaper, waxwork exhibitions, printing presses installed in temples, a steam ship, a car, modern western dress, and the very first to desire and initiate a mission to London in 1933. His contribution to the Gaudiya lineage was to restore the order of *tridanda* sannyasa (Vaishnava sannyasa) an important move he made after extended consultation with members of the Shri Sampradaya down in Madras.

The followers of the Ramakrishna Mission were growing in number in the Bengal of the 1920s and their holy men all dressed in saffron robes. Srila Bhaktisiddhanta also decided to dress the *brahmachari* students in the saffron colour of sannyasis, thus creating a highly visible, and respectable, army of followers. He chose to award brahminical initiation to even those from non-brahmana homes and to speak vigorously against those who practised the corrupt forms of Vaishnavism, even at the risk of a loss of immediate popularity. Later, he sent his sannyasis over the sea to preach as part of a co-ordinated missionary movement – something that had never been attempted before.

The India-wide success of the Gaudiya Mission, as it was called, was a phenomenon that previously had taken other religious movements one or two generations to accomplish. Bhaktisiddhanta Thakur had done it in less than twenty years. It was a religious phenomenon. Just before his death in 1936 he asked his leading members to co-operate and to preserve a unified mission, but unfortunately, not long after, his movement began to pull apart under the strain of competing ideas for organisation and spiritual leadership. By the late 1940s it was a shadow of the great enterprise it had once been.

Twenty years later, his disciple, Srila A.C. Bhaktivedanta Swami Prabhupada, continued this line of vigorous innovation – while preserving both spiritual purity and organisational cohesion – by translating the great Srimad Bhagavatam into English for the first time and creating an international organisation. He wrote and lectured prodigiously, and carefully guided his young western disciples. He physically circled the world fourteen times in twelve years, inspiring followers to open over one hundred centres and rural communities, and he organised a hierarchical system of governance in each of those centres. The entire organisation was topped by a board of governors which he named after his guru's own expression for such a body: the Governing Body Commission. His guru had borrowed this term from the well organised, British-run India Railway Company.

Srila Prabhupada's unflagging desire was to create a mission reaching all the countries of the world, an institution that would survive his death and continue to preserve and transmit the teachings of Chaitanya Mahaprabhu to newer generations. He was always acutely aware of how in-fighting and lethargy had overtaken his guru's institution, so he repeatedly cautioned his young disciples on the importance of working in a spirit of co-operation, and to be conscious that his Society was built on the foundation of 'love and trust.'

ISKCON's success is a surprise for academics in the West and religious traditionalists in India. For academics who prefer to classify it as a 'new religious movement' it should – statistically at least – have fallen apart after the death of its charismatic founder. That the organisation has continued to grow, albeit shakily at times, is a source of fascination for them. For the Hindu traditionalists in India, even the attempt by Bhaktivedanta Swami to create a non-traditional religious corporation with branches in every country – including the countries of the cow-eaters - was a very brave move indeed. That he chose to do it, at first, with western converts, and actually succeeded, is even more astonishing, and that those converts then came to India and consolidated Vaishnavism in the very land of its origin is nothing short of a miracle.

Now in over six hundred locations, with books published in a hundred languages, the pure Vaishnava *siddhanta*, the ancient Sanskrit language, the beautiful temple worship, festivals, art, music and food, and the age-old life of the Vedic forest ashram have all truly come out of India. The guru's arms have fully extended and wrapped themselves around the entire planet.

# 24

# Not everybody likes organisations

*In order to accomplish challenging tasks, people organise themselves, forming teams and systems. But not everybody likes organisations, and nobody seems to like 'organised religion.' What exactly is it that makes people feel uncomfortable? And if the guru has successfully spread his message around the world using an organisation is that wrong? Is there a better way?*

**Their discomfort is quite predictable. In fact, there are many studies by sociologists and social anthropologists to suggest that we humans show an aversion to any social grouping larger than a small cluster.** It seems that we're all programmed to be members of family-size groups and small villages, and trying to fit into anything bigger doesn't sit well with us.

After several decades of analysing data collected from tens of thousands of respondents in many countries, social scientists have settled on a discrete hierarchy of social groupings. First, they say, is the 'core group' or 'support clique'. This is the group of intimates from whom the individual would seek personal advice or help in times of severe emotional and financial need. The number in this group is only 3-5 persons.

The next social grouping is the so-called 'sympathy group', made up of all the good friends with whom one has special ties. This varies from 12-20 but figures suggest 15 as the most common size. One step up from this is the 'band' at 30-50 persons. This is the group of friends that serves to secure the basic necessities of life for the members. Larger than this is the 'clan' or 'village', a group composed of the average number of 'acquaintances' with whom coherent personal relationships can be maintained. These relationships involve a sense of mutual obligation, trust and reciprocity. In this group the individual knows who everyone is, knows their own relationship to that person, and knows the relationship of each member of the group to others. In this group, survival of the group's values and purposes can be ensured by the relationship ties between the members. The size of this group – on average – is 150.

This figure, although originally a theoretical projection based on other factors, seems to be borne out in practice. Independent of any knowledge of academic research, the Christian religious groups known as the Hutterites and the Amish limit their communities to 150, too. After three centuries of experience, they have found that it enables social cohesion. Anything larger than this, they say, and the energy and discipline of the community begin to dissipate. Tribes in the Amazon jungle and in Africa have also found it a workable size for their communities. It was also the average size of English villages described in the *Domesday Book* of 1087, and, rather curiously, it is also the size that businesses start to need formal management systems if they are not to fall apart as they continue to grow.

Observant people who like mathematics have also pointed out that these 'circles of acquaintanceship' increase by a factor of approximately 3 each time (5-15-50-150). Each successive circle includes the members of the smaller circle. Psychologists have also noted that with each circle the average emotional intensity of the relationship declines, as does the frequency of personal meetings. 150 people seems to be the limit of one person's 'psychological capital' – as well as their available time!

Small groups create an emotional connection and provide the mutual support necessary for many projects to prosper, including spiritual life. Interestingly enough, a look at the reported sizes of ISKCON centres in its early years reveals an average size of 8-15 per community. When many pioneer members are asked about the movement during that period they comment that: 'ISKCON had more of a family feel back then.' The suggestion is that size seems to be an indicator of emotional appeal and connectivity between the members. Yet larger groupings were also indicated by the founder. His Divine Grace A. C. Bhaktivedanta Swami Prabhupada talked a great deal about the members of his organisation forming 'Vedic villages' where a peaceful agrarian lifestyle could be pursued. When he was questioned as to how many people would form such villages he replied: 'Fifteen families.' Given that grandparents traditionally live with the family, as well as the son's wife and children, the figure in a 'Vedic village' could quite easily be 150.

Proponents of the 150 model of social cohesion assert that groups larger than 150 members generally require more restrictive rules, laws, and enforced norms to maintain a stable, cohesive group. This might explain why even successful religious 'institutions' remain unloved by many of their members. The size of the institution ensures a loss of emotional intensity between the members, and very infrequent meetings with most of them. Added to this is the physical and emotional distance between the average member and those in positions of power and influence, coupled with the fact that those very distant persons are seen as the origin of seemingly overly-prescriptive rules and bye-laws. The rules may be required in order to produce stability and compliance, but they do little to create a sense of emotional connection within the average member.

Indeed, no spiritual aspirant is truly excited by the prospect of being a member of a 'religious institution.' Institutions have no intrinsic charisma. The aspirant is quite happy as a member of the guru's retinue, and the smaller that retinue the better. Small means that the student can be close to the guru, and hence close to the source of spiritual inspiration that he seeks. Institutions, in and of themselves, are not spiritually attractive. It is the relationship with the spiritual teacher that is the prime motivating factor for the follower and provides the sense of spiritual connection. Support and guidance is given by other disciples in the 'sympathy group'. With these essential elements in place, the disciple may even question whether such a large religious institution is required at all, let alone his membership of it.

Yet the guru's mission is also to broadcast and propagate the teachings - to as many newcomers as possible. That enormous task requires the training of future teachers and celebrants, preparation of various types of publications, and the building of temples and other venues so that people can congregate and become educated and inspired, no matter what their level of spirituality or commitment. If the mission is to survive, it also involves organising 'support groups,' 'sympathy groups' and 'villages' so that future would-be disciples can be part of a social network and helped toward discipleship, and existing disciples and their families can live peacefully and be supported through the inevitable challenges of life. The disciple's role in all this is to help the guru and to alleviate his burden. When the larger mission of the guru is understood by the disciple, and he can see a role for himself in it, he may choose to expand his identity to accommodate membership of a larger grouping that will help him serve the guru's mission.

# The organisation

A group of people who share the same interest and purpose may, for the smooth running of their activities, form themselves into sub-groups, each of which performs different tasks. Like the organs of the human body, the sub-groups work in specialised ways in order to accomplish the success of the entire organism – the body. When such a larger group is divided into a number of smaller sub-groups with defined roles, we call that an organisation. Therefore an organisation is not a structure to be lightly dispensed with in the name of greater spirituality. It can be most helpful. In fact, there are many good reasons why it is essential. There are some ancient prototypes for Vaishnava organisations, as we saw in the last chapter.

Eleven years after the departure of Shri Chaitanya Mahaprabhu, the young Jiva Goswami, nephew of Srila Rupa and Srila Sanatana Goswamis, inaugurated an organisation he called the *Vishva Vaishnava Raja Sabha*, 'The Universal Society for the King of Vaishnavas'. In 1544 the organisation had some extremely distinguished members. Not only the Six Goswamis of Vrindavan, but Shri Nityananda Prabhu and his twelve close friends, the remaining members of Shri Chaitanya Mahaprabhu's sixty-four associates; as well as Lokanatha Das Goswami; Bhugarbha Goswami and Kasisvara Goswami. There is some surviving evidence that the organisation had several divisions for promoting philosophical education, worship standards, defence of Vaishnava theology against opposition, public preaching and so on. The leaders of these divisions also gave awards for achievement in the respective areas.

More than three hundred years later, Srila Bhaktivinode Thakur re-established the *Sabha*. After his father's time in this world had come to a close, and feeling the need to make the organisation even stronger for the coming years, his son re-launched it. On the 5th of February, 1919, Srila Bhaktisiddhanta Saraswati Thakur inaugurated the *Vishva Vaishnava Raja Sabha* once more. Speaking at the property known as 'Bhaktivinode Asana' at 1, Ultadanga Junction Road in Calcutta, before a large assembly of Vaishnavas, he said:

"Even though this Sabha is eternally established, it has descended into the world three times. Eleven years after the disappearance of Shri Mahaprabhu, when the world was beginning to darken, six wonderfully bright stars arose in Shri Vraja-mandala and were engaged in the service of Gaurachandra…

"Shri Chaitanyadeva is Krishnachandra Himself—the King of all the Vaisnavas in the world (Visva-Vaishnava-raja). The gathering of His devotees is the Shri Visva-Vaishnava-raja-sabha; the foremost ministers amongst the members of the society are Shri Rupa Goswami and his honoured Shri Sanatana Goswami. Those who consider themselves to be the followers of Shri Rupa are the members of this Shri Visva-Vaishnava-raja-sabha. The leaders amongst them are Shri Shri Prabhupada Srimad Raghunath Dasa Goswami and Shri Shri Prabhupada Srimad Jiva Goswami."

"The people who were accepted as disciples by Shri Rupa-Sanatana—the leaders of the sabha, later became the directors of the sabha. By taking shelter at the pure feet of Shri Rupa and Shri Raghunatha, Sripada Krsnadasa Kaviraja Goswami Prabhu… became one of the directors of the Shri Visva-Vaishnava-raja-sabha. Again, Shri Narottama Thakura Mathodaya—the crest jewel of transcendental devotees, decorated the crown of this Vaishnava-raja-sabha in the post of its director. Later, such kings of devotees as Shri Sripada Visvanatha Cakravarti Thakura spread their moon-like rays upon the sabha."

"In 1885 a brilliant star of the universal Vaishnava firmament re-illuminated the Shri Vishva-Vaishnava-raja-sabha. During that period many people in the great city of Calcutta received light from this sabha…Just as autumnal clouds suddenly spread in the sky and cover the moon's rays, so materialistic, non-Vaishnavas in the dress of Vaishnavas cause hindrances to that transcendental light in society. Today, it is four years since the servant of the King of universal Vaishnavas and the leader of the followers of Shri Rupa departed from this world, and sometimes his light is becoming covered by mist; seeing this, the group of people sheltered at the feet of the followers of Shri Rupa have become firmly resolved to protect the light of discourses on Hari from the strong gale."

"The transcendental flower of Krishna-prema that was budded forth by the Acharyas...was shown to the world by Srimad Bhaktivinode Thakur and after his disappearance it has begun to fully bloom. The followers of Shri Rupa have protected that beautiful and fragrant flower from the attack of depraved people and have thus given aid to the olfactory function of the bees swarming at Shri Gaura's feet."

In his speech, recorded in a Calcutta newspaper, Srila Bhaktisiddhanta Thakur spoke strongly that the job of the organisation was to protect the delicate flower of Krishna *prema* from the attack of 'depraved people,' the 'materialistic, non-Vaishnavas in the dress of Vaishnavas (who) cause hindrances.'

Srila Bhaktisiddhanta Thakur provided his understanding of the membership criteria of the organisation: *"Those who consider themselves to be the followers of Shri Rupa are the members of this Shri Vishva Vaishnava Raja Sabha."* He also mentioned that those who were accepted as disciples of Shri Rupa *'later on became the directors of the Sabha'*. It is interesting to note that, for him, the organisation was not a grouping created by humans, so much as humans in service to a divine fellowship that had descended into the world. Protecting as it does the pure teachings of Shri Chaitanya, the appearance of ISKCON in the world 47 years later must have been, logically, the fourth appearance of the *Vishva* Vaishnava *Raja Sabha*.

Even in the 21st century, so many years after the life of Shri Chaitanya, it would serve the true understanding and purpose of the *Vishva* Vaishnava *Raja Sabha* if the thousands of members of ISKCON bore in mind the privilege of being a part of such a glorious movement for the spiritualisation of human society. Rather than viewing ISKCON externally as a human institution, it would enhance our transcendental vision to contemplate on it as a vehicle of divine grace that some are privileged to serve.

# The perils of 'organised religion'

Although Srila Bhaktisiddhanta Saraswati Thakur gave a contemporary human framework to the 'divine descent' of the *Vishva* Vaishnava *Raja Sabha* in 1919, and although his mission was certainly organised, he wanted to clearly distinguish it from religious organisations in which there was no genuine spiritual vitality, or in which the original, noble ideals had been eclipsed by mundane, temporal concerns. He personally struggled with many such organisations in the India of his day. When religious conventions become the norm and are followed by the masses, he argued, yet the religious leaders themselves are covered by material illusion, or *maya*, that religious institution becomes the greatest fraud, the greatest obstacle to spiritual progress. So in January, 1932 he published 'Organised Religion' in 'The Harmonist', his magazine. In that article he warned:

> "The mere pursuit of fixed doctrines and fixed liturgies cannot hold a person to the true spirit of doctrine or liturgy. The idea of an organised church in an intelligible form, indeed, marks the close of the living spiritual movement. The great ecclesiastical establishments are the dikes and the dams to retain the current that cannot be held by any such contrivances. They, indeed, indicate a desire on the part of the masses to exploit a spiritual movement for their own purpose. They also unmistakably indicate the end of the absolute and unconventional guidance of the bona-fide spiritual teacher."

Srila Bhaktisiddhanta Thakur knew that even the highest revelation of the Vedas could, in the hands of unqualified religious leaders, be the cause of the masses drifting far away from the Vedas. So he warned that even ecclesiastical bodies and conventions could, over time, prohibit the free flow of 'unconventional grace.' According to him, the essential components in ensuring that the religious organisation remains the servant of the *sampradaya* were the pure hearts and behaviour of the leaders; their fidelity to Vaishnava theology and practise as taught by Shri Chaitanya; their bravery to speak strongly against opposing elements and their compassionate and widespread missionary activity.

When the inattentive spiritualist, through over-familiarity with God, begins to behave as if he were the master of God rather than the servant; when he begins to use the Vedas, the Deity and the sacred mantra as if he were their proprietor; when instead of employing his disciples in his guru's mission, he uses them for his personal pampering, this is the beginning of the end for his own enterprise.

Srila Bhaktisiddhanta Thakur used to employ a number of clay 'waxwork' exhibits to preach his message around the villages of Bengal. Housed in glass-sided exhibition cabinets, and taken by wagons, the show proved very attractive for local people. One cabinet, however, made many of the local brahmanas angry. It showed a brahmana with three lines of forehead markings – a devotee of Shiva –behaving in a despicable manner. The diorama was based on the following story:

> Once there was a rich man who had a very nice temple inside his home. On the altar were several large black shaligram stones from the Himalayas. These round stones are described in the Puranas to be directly Vishnu Himself and as such, are held in the highest estimation by worshippers. Because he was always very busy, he engaged a brahmana to come to his home each morning and perform the worship. So every day the brahmana was coming, and several hours later there was the fragrance of camphor, sandalwood, and incense. The altar was decorated with flowers and the rich man was very happy. He paid the brahmana for his services and the brahmana was also happy.
>
> One day the rich man thought that he would look through a crack in the door as the brahmana was performing the worship. To his horror, he saw that the brahmana was doing the worst thing possible. The brahmana had taken the largest shaligram stone from the altar and was using it to break open the nuts for the daily offering!

Some of the local brahmanas, mainly Shaivites, after seeing this particular waxwork, became so enraged at the slur on their community that they filed a court case for libel. When the case came to the magistrate, Srila Bhaktisiddhanta was informed that if the image was not removed he would be liable for a heavy fine. His response was simply to have the waxwork brahmana's forehead repainted so that instead of three-line *tilak*, it depicted him with two upward lines. In this way he showed a brahmana devotee of Vishnu engaging in offensive behaviour. He remarked that since even Vaishnavas were not beyond this kind of behaviour it was quite fitting that the forehead marking was changed. The local brahmanas were pacified and the travelling show continued.

This short chapter, in summary, was to explore a common resistance to identifying oneself as a member of a large religious organisation – even when it was created by the guru. The phenomenon is quite natural, and needs to be understood. For our own spiritual welfare there is a great need to be part of a smaller, human-scale group of supportive friends. That should be our primary concern. However, there is also a need to serve the guru in his attempt to bring the message of Bhagavad-gita to a greater audience. This collective endeavour is the guru's compassionate vehicle, the extension of his legacy to the world. It is also helpful for personal progress to be a functioning part of such a larger body. In serving the world we also have our own needs met.

How can small groups, working together as part of a large organisation, resist the temptation to drift apart from each other? How can their members avoid the urge to exploit the resources of the organisation for their own ends; and how can spiritual vitality be preserved so that the organisation meets its noble goals? Some suggestions are given in the next chapter.

# 25
# Sustainability through governance

*Every large group that aims for sustainability requires a set of values to which each member voluntarily subscribes. Those values help to determine how the members interact. When each member of the group honours those values, the entire group can reach the goals for which it was formed. Governance is the system through which the group's values can be upheld and the integrity of the group preserved.*

**One of the essential functions of the human body is that it be regulated, balanced, controlled and governed.** The purpose of governance within the body is to keep all the organs working together at the right temperature, to balance the intake of oxygen and excrete any toxic accumulation. When governance is good the entire body can maintain its physical existence, carry out its collective functions and perpetuate itself through to the next generation. Governance within a human body requires a functioning brain, and governance within a human organisation is very similar.

Governance is the way in which an organisation is directed, controlled and led. It defines relationships and the distribution of rights and responsibilities among the members and supporters. The governance 'organ' of the organisation also determines the rules and the processes through which the organisation's objectives are met. It not only provides the means of attaining those objectives, but also monitors performance. It also defines where accountability lies throughout the organisation.

In addition, the governance 'organ' may do any of the following:

1. Safeguard the intangible and physical assets of the guru.

2. Remind members of the ethical code that outlines acceptable behaviour.
3. Help to communicate any finer points of theology throughout the organisation.
4. Create plans for the organisation and set goals.
5. Register and resolve grievances.
6. Facilitate the means of selecting or electing leaders.
7. Discipline the members.

ISKCON's governing 'organ,' the Governing Body Commission or GBC, performs all of the above and more; it would seem that the organisation should be well governed. But ISKCON suffers from its own success. The movement has expanded considerably since its creation, and its governance mechanisms struggle to keep pace with its growth. The GBC was created in the early 1970s to govern an organisation much smaller than the ISKCON of today. Back then the GBC was comprised of a dozen or so leading members. Now the governing body has multiplied by a factor of three, but ISKCON's membership internationally has multiplied by a factor of fifty. Although its leaders do not wish to unnecessarily expand the members of the governing body, some attention is required to ensure the safe growth and good health of ISKCON on into the future. As of the time of writing, that attention is being paid. The abilities of a 1970s organ are being scaled upwards for future growth.

But even with the best governing body at the head of the organisation; and even though all the governance functions are undeniably essential, still the members of a governing body may never be loved, appreciated, or even understood. Indeed, their motives may always be suspect. In addition to the emotional distance involved in such a large organisation, and in addition to infrequent communication between the governing body and the members, there are also some features of ISKCON that are peculiar to many religious bodies.

Religious organisations tend to be a bit on the conservative side, looking as they do to preserve the great legacy of the past and keep it going for future generations. Srila Prabhupada said that the disease of his western followers was that, like their countrymen, they had a strong tendency to make changes where they were not required. So ISKCON's governing body must control the members' tendency towards unnecessary change. While the leaders of a religious organisation should always be prepared to make certain adjustments to accommodate developments in culture, politics, social attitudes and language, they should be equally careful not to change the fundamental principles. Getting this balance right ensures accessibility and relevancy for new audiences, while getting it wrong ensures the loss of the very heart of their religious tradition. History has shown that great legacies can be dissipated in just one or two generations.

The very success of a religious institution can spell problems in preserving a legacy. With the success created by early pioneers comes growth and positions of power. While the pioneers may fully understand how much human effort it took to grow the organisation, the next generation of leadership often doesn't. They step into their positions in a powerful, global organisation with sometimes very little comprehension of the sacrifice that was needed to create it. The result can be a negligence of certain essential human qualities and organisational safeguards. Power and personal privilege are great temptations for the negligent, as is political party spirit and subsequent in-fighting. The theology can be manipulated to suit various enterprising leaders and used to shore-up personal advantage.

Within ISKCON, these manifestations are dealt with, to a certain extent, through the GBC exercising control and discipline. On occasion, a GBC member needs to be corrected by his colleagues. However, for the average member of ISKCON, it does not take too many impositions of discipline or new bye-laws for the GBC itself to seem a repressive, backward-looking group of theological nit-pickers. Of course that is not true, and individually at least, the members of ISKCON's governing body are well-balanced, happy, spiritually enlivened and personable people. When they act together, however, with due diligence to the weighty responsibility of leadership, their physical and emotional distance to the average member becomes compounded by their resolutions. Although the GBC's decisions are made for the benefit of all of ISKCON's members, the positive emotional reciprocation from those very members may not be hearty.

So an ISKCON member may have a deep respect and abiding affection for his guru as an individual; but a curious and disproportionate lack of the same when his guru – and others like him – sit together to make responsible decisions for the good of the organisation. The Pope has the same problem. Everybody seems to love the Pope, but not his 1400-strong Roman Curia, the governing body and administrative apparatus of the Catholic Church. Of course, it may be that the Pope has his own personal issues with the Curia, too, but without them leadership of a 1.2 billion member organisation would be much more of a strain for him.

It is not only the size of ISKCON that has changed over the years. As well as the rapid membership growth, there has been a complete inversion of the living situation of its members. In my youth in the 1970s, practically every single member lived in community, all over the world. Our ashrams were full to bursting, but we knew nothing else. There were so few who didn't live this way that we referred to any others rather disparagingly as devotees who 'lived outside the temple.' The expression was often accompanied by an eyebrow raised in disapproval, as if the demarcation line between devotees and non-devotees ran around the perimeter of the temple garden.

Now, the latest calculation is that a mere 4% of members live in temple ashrams – a complete reversal within a generation. This is not surprising considering ISKCON's phenomenal rate of outreach and subsequent growth, and the slow pace of community development compared to the growth in membership. It may also have something to do with the fact that our ashrams, even today, can be quite austere and regimented places, a perfect haven for the deeply committed and the enthusiastic young newcomer, but not places where the majority of members can spend more than a week or two.

What this means is that in order to be relevant to the majority of ISKCON's members, the GBC must concern itself with the challenges faced by them, in the situations where they live. Although the ISKCON centres and temples, and a few farms and schools, are the tangible and legal assets of the organisation, the growing number of members are the real capital of the organisation. Failure to address issues common to the majority will make the GBC appear even more inaccessible and irrelevant to the members' lives.

And the members themselves must ensure that friendly, supportive and spiritually enlivened individuals have an honoured place within their respective 'circles of acquaintance' - their 'support', 'sympathy' and 'village' groups. Failure to do that will make the beliefs and practises of Krishna consciousness appear increasingly remote and irrelevant. When that happens, the very concept of ISKCON membership becomes meaningless.

Because of the lack of connection between the increasing number of members and the body (whether real or imagined), ISKCON is sometimes criticised by members, frustrated by the pace of change, as lacking in emotional connectivity but high in institutional policies and procedures . Indeed, because of this, some go so far as to describe that they are members of the 'Hare Krishna Movement' but not the 'ISKCON institution' as if there were, in fact, two mutually exclusive groups, the one familial and the other bureaucratic. In fact there are not two groups - except in the mind of the observer. The individual projects his needs outwards and conceives that he belongs to an organisation of his own, personal creation.

Yet we all join groups where we feel our needs will be met; and when those needs are no longer met, we leave the group. That ISKCON should at least satisfy our spiritual needs is reasonable; and what each of us wants, quite reasonably, is what was advertised when we first encountered the devotees: the awakening of our dormant perception of Krishna, the ultimate origin of all, the eternal person, and the reservoir of all pleasure. We want to have our lingering and tricky questions answered and the internal assurance that we're on the right path. We want the love, support and fellowship of others who can help us on that path, and the affectionate and compassionate guardianship of an enlightened spiritual preceptor. What we don't want – at least some of us - is to be a member of an international organisation.

# Half-chicken logic

This is a bit like saying that we want to breathe, but we'd rather not have lungs. Yet without lungs we can't breathe, and without air the lungs have no meaning. Lungs and air are in a reciprocal relationship and are inseparable. Oxygen is what we crave, and those two pink, blobby, bloody sponges inflating and deflating within our chest enable us to extract that vital substance from the air. Lungs may not look attractive, but without them we're dead. In India, the mango tree is given as a similar example of internal symbiosis. The mango tree produces the sweetest, most delicious 'king' of all fruit, but everything else on the tree tastes bitter. Reject the mango tree for its foul taste and you'll have no sweet fruits; reject the lungs for their ugliness and you'll have no breath. This phenomenon of something we don't want producing something we do is quite common in nature; rejecting the former because we want the latter is the path of the less intelligent, as recounted in the following story.

There was once a farmer who had one chicken who was larger than all the others. The chicken laid enormous eggs which gained him handsome profits at the local market. However, the chicken ate more than all the other hens and thus cost the farmer dearly. The farmer considered the situation logically and decided to preserve the rear of the chicken which made him money, but to remove the front of the chicken, which cost him money. He cut the hen in half with an axe. His false logic was rewarded with nothing at all – the chicken was dead. He no longer had to spend money feeding the hen, but he no longer made a handsome profit. His lack of understanding of how one thing is produced from another had produced a foolish action. In ancient India this was called '*ardha-murgi-nyaya*' or 'the logic of half-a-chicken.'

The thing we want is known as *upeya*, or the goal; the thing that gives us what we want is known as *upaya*, the means of achieving the goal. Quite often the *upaya* is desperately unattractive, but because it produces the *upeya* we should never reject it.

Membership of a spiritual organisation – or to use that pejorative expression - a 'religious institution,' seems to be counter-intuitive when what we're really looking for is the complete personal freedom offered by spiritual life. Being a member of such a human organisation involves adhering to rules and bye-laws, making friends with people we may not like, and placing ourselves within a group that may, at times, make mistakes, all of which do nothing for our sense of divine freedom. But just as in chickens, mangoes and lungs, an organisation does help us to reach our goal in many ways.

Many years ago I met a musician connected to the rock group Led Zeppelin. He explained that while what the members of the group wanted was the freedom to do as they wished, because the means of achieving that freedom was their music, they practised a very rigorous daily discipline involving hours of rehearsals. "They live like monks in a monastery," he explained, "They do everything together." I remember the story up until today because it was told to me at a time when I was struggling with my own distinct lack of organisational identity. While I understood the need for personal disciplines as a part of my daily *sadhana*, I was less convinced about the continued need to be a part of a large institution – especially an institution which had, by that time, disappointed me. But somehow that inside story of the gods of rock helped me. They had to put aside their short-term, personal goals for the sake of achieving something greater together. The success of the group was more important than their individual desire. In the end, the success of the group enabled each of them to fulfil all their personal desires.

Remaining a member of a group such as ISKCON also requires going beyond a limited, individualised comfort zone. It requires seeing oneself neither as the enjoyer nor the rejecter of institutional identity, but simply a servant of a higher purpose to be attained by co-operatively working with others. Even in a small shop front in New York, Srila Prabhupada was brave enough to style himself and a small handful of followers an 'international society,' a preposterous claim were it not for the unlikely fact that it became truly international very quickly.

# The devil and the saint

Of course, history books are not usually so kind to 'religious organisations.' And in today's world there is widespread and ingrained suspicion of institutions generally, and religious ones in particular. We don't trust the combination of religion and power, however great the original prophet, saint, or guru was, and however noble the cause.

There's an old Irish story:

> A saint was walking down the road, a peaceful smile on his face. A farmer sees him: "Where are you going dear saint?" he says. "I'm going to start a religious movement," replies the saint, and carries on his way. Then the farmer sees the Devil walking some distance behind the saint, obviously following him. "But you," says the farmer, "where are you going, and why are you following

him?" "Me?" replies the Devil with a cunning grin, "Why, isn't it obvious? He's going to start a religious movement – and I'm going to help him organise it!"

But while there are numerous historical accounts of the institutionalisation that has so crippled the legacies of even the best of saints, it is also a fact that, at some point in its successful expansion, a movement of spiritual people must give itself a shape and systems in order to maintain its natural growth. Mother Nature herself has ordained that living structures of greater complexity require enhanced and regulated systems if they are to grow. So it is with organic movements of people.

Religious movements are companies, and they bear certain similarities to any other company. Their product is an inspired community of faith rather than the manufacture and distribution of electronic widgets, yet just like ordinary companies, they pass through different stages of growth, enter periods of crisis, and must change and adapt in order to grow. Religious movements are born through inspired leadership, pioneering and personal sacrifice. While those remain necessary for its future, the organisation will come to a stage where charisma and creativity are no longer enough - sheer numbers make a more formalised management system necessary. That means that the pioneer members must delegate authority to others, creating a new tier of leadership. Failure to do that results in a hindrance to growth.

But delegation involves a risk that those new authority figures may channel the organisation's resources away from the original aims. When the governing body fears they are losing control and try to solve the crisis with more red tape, it can also precipitate another crisis where leaders feel stifled. The solution is often a simplification of formal systems, an increase in education, and greater levels and frequency of communication. More collaboration is also required at this time. After a certain period, it may be time for some more inspired, charismatic leadership and greater focus on pioneering.

Yet the vitality that runs through such an organisation, in all periods of its transformation - the elements that actually give it life - must be the qualities of the soul as outlined by Gautama *Rishi*:

1. *Daya* – Compassion for all beings
2. *Kshanti* – Forbearance, a patient endurance
3. *Anasuya* – Lack of Envy
4. *Saucham* – Purity of body, thoughts and actions
5. *Anayasa* – Freedom from the exertion engendered by personal ambition and greed
6. *Mangala* – Auspicious and pleasant nature
7. *Akarpanya* – Generous
8. *Aspriha* – Not clamouring after undesirable things.

Nothing else will keep a spiritual organisation factually spiritual. The proof that this is happening will be that people are coming forward to become devoted to Krishna – and remaining so.

The steady growth of ISKCON can be attributed to Srila Prabhupada's deliberate founding of his Society as an organised mission of pure followers dedicated to systematic propagation; an international body of spiritual practitioners who reach out to others to deliver his teachings. By the dedication of the early followers, his movement became established in hundreds of cities. The great challenge to ISKCON now, wherever it has spread in the world, is to ensure that both the practise and the outreach are continued through the next generation and beyond.

ISKCON is, by a strict dictionary definition, both a spiritual movement and a religious institution. The founder-*acharya* of ISKCON understood the inevitable strains that tend to occur when thousands of diverse individuals from a wide variety of social backgrounds, ethnicities and political persuasions all work together. He told them that being part of a spiritual movement – where the members were all trying to improve themselves despite their temptations - was actually the most difficult proposition in the material world. He remained concerned about his united, international society becoming fractured by philosophical dissension and political in-fighting. He said that they could definitely be successful if ISKCON was run not only with spiritual purity, 'love and trust,' and the service mood of Vaikuntha, but with 'organisation and intelligence'.

Part Three | Sustainability through governance

But sometimes members of organisations do become polarised around certain issues, and then the organisation fractures. The next chapter examines that tragic feature of organisational drift and how it may be avoided.

# 26

# Are you church or chapel?

*It was the great question of a childhood upbringing in Cornwall, and a choice that had to be made. But why did I have to choose? Sadly, religious traditions do divide and splinter for the flimsiest of reasons, but it is much better if we can all get along with each other. By resisting the temptation to fight and separate, thus interrupting the flow of divine wisdom, we can keep our spiritual traditions dynamic and create a better world.*

**"Are you church or chapel?" was the question posed to my mother when we moved into a house in a small Cornish village.** Whether we were church or chapel was an important question, for it defined the social circle we would be joining, our emotional support team, and ultimately our chances of salvation. The Church of England and the Methodist Chapel were the two places of worship in the village, one the establishment religion and the other dissident. The chapel stood at one end of the single street in the village, and the church was firmly at the other end. The blacksmith's shop, with its fiery orange furnace, the heavy clink of hammer on anvil and the burning smell of sizzling horses' hooves, stood right in the centre.

Half a century later, I still live in a small village, this time just four miles from the edge of the north London suburbs. You can't get horseshoes made in this village, but there are no less than seven places where they will make you a cappuccino. How times have changed. Despite the passing of years and the lack of good blacksmiths, there are still variant theologies poised at either end of the high street, not only Christian but Jewish as well. At opposite ends of the parade of shops are the United Synagogue and the Reform Synagogue. Which reminds me of an old Jewish joke. When rescuers finally discover the lone Jewish survivor of a shipwreck on a desert island, they find that he's used bamboos and coconut leaves to build himself two synagogues, one at either end of the

Part Three | Are you church or chapel?

island. "Why two?" they ask, "There's only you here." "Oh, this one is where I pray," he replies, "and that other one is the synagogue I wouldn't be seen dead in!" I think you have to be Jewish (or married to one) to fully grasp the sad irony of that joke, but the meaning is clear: human beings tend to pull any religion in two, and for as much as they love one they tend to spite the other. The reality is not far from the joke. Some years ago, the Jewish population of the island of Bermuda was a mere 110 – and there were, indeed, two synagogues.

Just last week I was in Liverpool where there are two grand cathedrals, both built over many years and at enormous expense. They are connected by one short street that runs between them – Hope Street. Although named after a local merchant, the theological implications of the name have not been lost on the local clergy. Both the Roman Catholic Church and the Church of England live in hope of a full reconciliation between their respective denominations. Sadly, they have been trying for some time without success. Religion, you see, would be so easy if it weren't for human beings. We are influenced predominantly by *raja* and *tama guna*, the two forces of nature that ceaselessly pull us apart and then set us against each other. In this condition we are almost bound to project our own selfish concerns onto the pure messages of God. In doing so we appropriate the Divine and fashion Him in our own image then, because we are all individuals who, mostly, can't agree with anyone else completely, we enter into conflict. Whatever the reason may be, we become heated in our opinions, find friends to support us, and then pull apart into distinct groupings.

What divides religious people? Often, it can be the very small things: bells, smells, decorations and robes, priests and songs, or whether being baptised with water is for babies or adults. Or the bigger things of which these are parts: Theology, liturgy, governance, gender issues, and whether God has a living representative on Earth and so on. But it doesn't end there. History has shown that, in every religion, each division becomes rent by fresh divisions and the two become three, four and more. New theologies are developed to support human preferences, and the clear water of pure revelation becomes muddied by tribal thinking. In this way, the one great man who spoke the Sermon on the Mount is now represented by 41,000 different Christian denominations.

The one Catholic Church, presumably in a bid to stave off the debilitating effects of multiple splintering, has given permission for no less than 23 different 'Rites,' 38 separate 'Orders,' and 272 distinct 'Congregations,' all with different costumes, customs, prayers and organisational structures.

The tendency to divide is, of course, seen everywhere. We have become so accustomed to it that we may hardly even notice it at all. If we do, it may not even alarm us. Take sport, for instance. It wasn't long after I joined my school rugby team that I learned that there were, in fact, two games of rugby: Rugby Union and Rugby League. The game originated in 1823 but 72 years later, in 1895, the 'Great Schism' took place, never to be repealed. The 'working class' northerners had felt it necessary to separate from the 'upper-class' southerners, and the League and the Union were created accordingly. The game of rugby was itself an 'upper class' separation from the original game of football, played by all boys. In that game, the pulling apart continued to be a long-standing tradition of the game. Footballers were often pulled into two rival teams. A fan had to make his mind up who to support. There was, for instance, Liverpool and Everton in the same city; Rangers and Celtic in the same city of Glasgow, the two teams split along religious and social lines; and Manchester United and Manchester City, all rival teams for one town.

But it is when the divisions occur in religions that the potential for rivalry can escalate into something far more serious. Religion is no game, and the issues involved are all of the ultimate importance. The issues are so serious to the adherents of denominations that strongly opinionated members of opposing religious tribes can often go to war with each other, each convinced that they have the blessings of the Divine. In my own lifetime I have personally experienced street battles between Catholic and Protestant in the towns of Northern Ireland; have been there when an IRA bomb exploded in the centre of Belfast; and have witnessed tensions between denominations of Jews. I have read of open conflict between factions of Tibetan Buddhists, and I am all too aware of the immense chasm that exists between Sunni and Shi'a strands of Islam, with periodic warfare between them in different parts of the world. Vaishnavism has not always been immune from these schisms. The followers of the teachings of the great Ramanujacharya (1017-1137) were united for seven centuries, but then succumbed to (verbal) conflict over cardinal philosophical points, eventually becoming the *Tengalai* (Southern School) and the *Vadagalai* (Northern School) sometime in the 17th or 18th century.

In the Hare Krishna movement, the splintering tendency was regularly subjugated by the single, commanding voice of its founder-*acharya* who confessed, "I am always afraid of this crack." His urgent and repeated pleas for peace and unity amongst his followers didn't stop some from splintering away during his life, and certainly hasn't prevented them from doing it since. And, just as in Christianity, Islam and Judaism, where all fractures are done in the name of God, his son, prophet or blessed and inspired rabbi, in the Hare Krishna movement it was, and continues to be done, in the name of 'what Srila Prabhupada really wanted.' And so it was that the 'true' followers of Srila Prabhupada began a campaign against all his other followers when they failed to support their views on how initiations would be conducted after his physical demise. It was also how the similarly 'true followers' of Srila Prabhupada justified their transformation of a hitherto unknown Indian sannyasi into an international figurehead of messianic proportions. For them, who needed him to be so, the sannyasi became 'the real inheritor of Srila Prabhupada's legacy.' Now deceased, the rifts that he and his followers managed to create, pulling apart communities, marriages and families, are all but impossible to heal. ISKCON has thus lost hundreds of members to this and several other breakaway movements – movements of varying degrees of integrity and endurance – all of which claimed to have adopted their stance because of a more refined understanding of the founder-*acharya*'s instructions. Such is theology, and such is life.

ISKCON members could help themselves by learning a bit more of religious history. They should know that all of this has happened before. They need to learn sufficient Vaishnava theology to identify and understand the veracity of ideas that arise from time to time within their own community. They should be aware when someone seeks the imposition of Judaeo-Christian notions upon Vaishnavism, such as the '*ritvik*' idea of a truncated *parampara*, or the deification of an ordinary sannyasi as a messiah. Splintering of a religious grouping is also exacerbated by poor spiritual leadership, sexual and financial scandals, poor governance and managerial ineptitude. ISKCON would be helped greatly by putting measures in place to prevent all of these. In addition, and because members of any group will periodically enter into conflict, the ISKCON machinery must allow room for overheated members to find their place, always using the oil of reason to reduce friction, and the water of understanding to cool things down.

Like the Vatican and its shepherding of a disparate flock of many-hued sheep, we may end up with several dozen 'orders' within the Hare

Krishna movement, but at least they will be working under the same name and style. Theologies have a tendency of variation according to the very genuine physical needs and faith-levels of their proponents. As such, they won't always mesh together, and practices may not always conform to strict *orthopraxis*, but splintering might be prevented, and we may all be spared the debilitation of any further reduction in size and influence. Splintering diminishes the strength of collegiate effort and repeated division is a scourge that ultimately ends in a loss of power and increased apathy. If people can be united to do good in the world it is helpful for everyone concerned.

So, was it church or chapel? It was chapel. Actually, to be more accurate, it was both. I went to the Methodist chapel on Sunday where I enthusiastically sang Wesleyan hymns and learned the elements of faith free from unnecessary rituals, bell-ringing or stained glass, and then I went bell-ringing every Monday evening in the Church of the Holy Name, where I pulled thick, well-worn ropes beneath the bell tower to my heart's content, sending loud, thunderous peals throughout the village.

# Part Four
# Shades of saffron

# 27

# Sannyasa dharma

*Practically everyone has now heard the title 'Swami' and knows that it is mostly used in reference to a spiritual person, a holy man, who travels and dresses in orange robes. It is worth investigating the ancient order of sannyasa to see how they lived, before we continue to examine some modern versions of the sannyasa life and how they are related to the guru-disciple relationship.*

**According to Sanskrit etymology, the word *samnyasa* or 'sannyasa' means 'renunciation' or 'abandonment'.** It is a tripartite compound of *san* (collective), *ni* (down) and *asa* (from the root *as*, meaning 'to throw' or 'to put'). So a literal translation of the word would be 'laying it all down'.

Sannyasa is part of the *varna* and *ashram* system, an occupational and life stage social organisation found within the Vedas and practised for thousands of years. The purpose of any kind of progressive human society, the Vedas say, is so that by collective endeavour the maximum number of people can be simultaneously healthy, peaceful, prosperous, and spiritually enhanced. The *varna-ashram* system flows naturally according to psycho-physical propensity and life-stages, and provides the maximum level of opportunity for yoga and spiritual attainment, the ultimate purpose of human life.

There are four life stages for brahmanas in the *varna-ashram* system. The student life of the *brahmachari* is meant for studying and developing good character; the married life of the householder or *grihasta*, for raising a family, developing wealth, performing religious deeds and giving in charity; the life of the retired person, the *vanaprastha*, is meant for performing austerity and developing gradual detachment; and the life of the sannyasi for withdrawal from the world and a life of renunciation.

# The sannyasi guidebook

There is a teacher – and a manual – for everything in life, and similarly there is a great deal of advice on how to be a sannyasi. One of the more famous manuals originated from someone who created hundreds of sannyasis himself: the great mediaeval Vaishnava, Srila Ramanujacharya (1017-1137). The great acharya had several people in his life that he regarded as gurus. One of them, Yadava Prakash, was a philosophy teacher when Ramanuja was a boy. At that time, the teacher regarded him as an annoying child who did not fully understand the Upanishads. Later on in his life, however, he had a complete change of heart and submitted himself as a humble student of the grown-up Ramanuja. When Ramanujacharya required a guidebook for his renounced monks, he asked his former teacher to use his knowledge of the scriptures to compile one. The result was *Yati-Dharma Samuccaya*. The Sanskrit word *Yati* is another word for sannyasi, or renounced person. The book includes many details derived from the writings of ancient sages. It explains how a man should live when in the fourth stage of life, what he should wear, how he should beg for his food, how he should eat and travel, and how he should keep his consciousness elevated and his behaviour chaste to the life of an ascetic. Here are some brief extracts:

# Appearance

One who is an ascetic should carry the triple-staff, or *tridanda*.

One should either be shaven-headed or one may wear one's hair in a topknot. If shaven-headed he must shave his head on the lunar day that falls between the 14th day of the growing moon and the first day of the dark (new) moon. He should not shave during the four-month long monsoon period.

One should dye one's cloth using the reddish-orange rock *gairika* (an oxide of iron).

These three things may be white: one's *upavita* (the sacred thread draped on the left shoulder of all brahmana males), the strainer (small cloth to strain out insects from drinking water), and one's teeth.

# Behaviour

The sannyasi should be homeless, and be free from pride and anger. He may stay only one night in a village, but five in a town. He must not enter a home where the husband is not present, but may enter the threshold if it is raining.

# The Ten vows

A sannyasi must take ten vows as follows:

1. Not to injure anyone – human or animal - in word or deed. This includes the following nine elements:

    a. Causing anyone anxiety

    b. Causing pain

    c. Causing someone to weep

    d. Calumny – making malicious statements so as to injure someone's reputation

    e. Destroying someone's happiness

    f. Conquering someone

    g. Drawing blood

    h. Making someone grovel

    i. Obstructing someone's welfare

    j. Killing or acting as an accessory to killing: (i) To kill (ii) To give consent that another may kill (iii) To butcher that which has been killed (iv) To buy meat (v) To sell meat (vi) To cook meat (vii) To assist in cooking (viii) To eat meat.

2. To tell the truth

3. To be honest in one's dealings

4. To live in poverty

5. To live in obedient service of one's guru

6. To observe inner and outer cleanliness
7. To suppress anger
8. To refrain from wrongful conduct in mental, verbal and physical acts
9. To always avoid carelessness.
10. To live in chastity. There are eight elements of 'broken chastity', as follows:

    a. To remember previous sexual actions
    b. To recount them to others
    c. To engage in amorous play with a woman
    d. To look at a woman
    e. To speak in secret with a woman
    f. To formulate one's intentions for sexual action
    g. To make a firm resolve
    h. To perform the act

The opposite of 'broken chastity' is chastity.

# Possessions

Water-pot (known as a *kamandalu*); water-strainer; fine thread and needle; clothes dyed reddish-orange; a sling bag; a begging bowl (*kundika*); a loincloth; a sitting stool; sandals; a ragged shawl; a cloth yoga band to fix the posture during meditation; an umbrella; and a string of rosary beads.

Of these, five possessions are obligatory: one's sacred thread or *upavita*, the *danda*, the strainer, loincloth and waistband.

# Danda

The *danda* is composed of three bamboo sticks each three-quarters of an inch thick. They should reach up to the hair and should contain 6, 8 or 10 joints that do not protrude. 2 or 5 strings, known as *mudras* tie the three sticks together top and bottom. String made from cow's hair must be tied below the second section from the top.

"One who accepts in his mind the rod of chastisement for his speech, body and
mind is known as a tridandi -- one who has accepted the threefold rod of chastisement." (*Manu-samhita* 12.10)

# Begging

The sannyasi must live by begging. All his meals must be begged, but only once in the day at certain times. There are five types of begging:

1. *Madhukara* – Begging 'in the manner of a bee', from either 3, 5, or 7 houses only. Such houses must not be deliberately selected.

2. *Prakpranita* – 'Offered in advance.' Sometimes the sannyasi may wake and find that the food has already been left for him, right where he slept.

3. *Ayacita* – 'Unsolicited.' The sannyasi has performed his morning rituals and is about to set off for begging, but food is given before he goes on his alms-round.

4. *Tarkalika* – 'Contemporaneous' – The sannyasi is proclaimed by a brahmana householder even as he approaches him.

5. *Upapanna* – 'Offered' – He is given food after begging. This may also include being fed at an ashram or monastery, where the food is brought by local devotees.

Each type of begging is good, but the timing must be observed: "Beg when the smoke from cooking fires has stopped rising, when pestles have stopped pounding, the meal for the family has come to an end and the remnants have been put away." (So says the sage Manu)

The controlled sannyasi will beg and eat only after midday. These are the divisions of the day: *Pratah* is the morning, *Sangara* the mid-morning and *Madhyama* the middle of the day. *Aparahna* is the afternoon and *Sayana* the evening.

The manual describes these periods so that the sannyasi will know when he is allowed to beg for food. Roughly translated the excerpt reads as follows: "One *muhurta* is 48 minutes. Each of these divisions lasts for 3 *muhurtas* or 3 x 48 minutes. Each division is then approximately 2 hours and 24 minutes. Accordingly, the time for begging, or *Madhyama*, 'Midday,' extends from 4 hours 48 minutes after sunrise until 7 hours 12 minutes after sunrise.

The sannyasi must make no provision for the next day. He must beg from brahmana homes only if possible. He must not carry food to his next destination or for the next day. He must carry no separate salt and must not eat at night. He must avoid any house where fish or meat is cooked, and he should eat no meat or honey, even if they are offered to him. If he is given food and also begs for more and hence eats twice, he must do a penance of reciting 10,000 *Gayatri* mantras.

"Yogis beg in the morning, but men of true knowledge beg in the afternoon."

## Begging bowl

In *Kali Yuga* an ascetic must not eat out of his begging bowl directly, but beg with it held in the left hand. The contents may then be transferred to a leaf when the ascetic is in a quiet place.

## The fallen sannyasi

A man who has fallen from his sannyasa vows is to be known as a dog, or *vantasi*, a 'vomit-eater.' The king will brand him on the forehead with the mark of a dog's paw.

"The man who falls from his vows will live as a worm in excrement for 60,000 years and then, in his next births, become a mouse, a dog for twelve lifetimes, a vulture for twenty years, a pig for nine, a thorn tree, an Ashoka tree for 1000 years, whereupon he will be born as a demonic, non-vegetarian brahmana." – Sage Satatapa

# Disqualifications for taking sannyasa

Renunciation can only be practised by those who can renounce the objects of their attachment. A eunuch, or anyone who is not attracted by women, cannot renounce and therefore cannot take sannyasa: "The rule of celibacy disqualifies a eunuch because he does not have the capacity to engage in sex. Abstention is only a vow for those with the capacity."

A eunuch is as follows: "When a man remains as unmoved when he sees a young woman as when he sees a baby girl or an old woman he is called a eunuch."

# When to become a sannyasi

*"One can become a sannyasi immediately after student life,"* says the sage Vasistha.

*"One should be married first, and then become a sannyasi,"* says the sage Yajnavalkya.

# After the death of a sannyasi

*"Burial,"* says the sage Bodhayana.

*"Cremation,"* says the sage Atri Muni.

# 28

# Sannyasa: the real and the false

*The life of a sannyasi is an arduous path to take, as we've seen in the last chapter. But the inner consciousness of the sannyasi is the main element of it all, rather than the external orange robes, the bamboo sticks and the begging bowl. This was the argument of Srila Bhaktisiddhanta Saraswati Thakur, the spiritual master of ISKCON's founder-acharya. So why did he introduce the orange robes and the triple staff into the Gaudiya Sampradaya after a gap of four hundred years?*

**Adoption of the sannyasa path does represent a spiritual step forward.** It provides a dramatically altered lifestyle in which a desired radical change is most likely to be brought about. Sannyasa signifies a man's complete withdrawal from the affairs of the world, along with his sense of control and personal power over his environment. It is achieved by placing all his life – even the food he eats - solely in the charity of strangers and the support of the natural world. Placing his future in the hands of the Divine, it is a facility for a man's consciousness to change before the end of his life.

However, true renunciation of the world is a level of consciousness that arises within oneself, and it takes place whenever one has realised the flickering nature of worldly happiness. Such a level of consciousness is not limited by any external factor, and so the spirit of sannyasa can arise whatever the material circumstances in one's life. Once having understood the true nature of the world a person can continue to work in a spirit of detachment. This is the consciousness of the true sannyasi, as explained by Shri Krishna in the Bhagavad-gita:

*kamyanam karmanam nyasam
sannyasam kavayo viduh*

> *sarva-karma-phala-tyagam*
> *prahus tyagam vicaksanah*

"The giving up of activities that are based on material desire is what great learned men call the renounced order of life (sannyasa). And giving up the results of all activities is what the wise call renunciation (tyaga)." *(Bhagavad-gita 18.2)*

The entire dialogue of the Bhagavad-gita takes place because Arjuna wants to abandon his life as a warrior, arguing that it will be a spiritually superior choice to fighting. Shri Krishna stresses that even something as mundane as fighting done in a spirit of genuine detachment is a superior path. The consciousness behind the action, and not the action itself, is the measure of the morality. Therefore, although Krishna is the original creator of the sannyasa order of life, He argues that it is the type of consciousness that makes the detached sannyasi and not the robes, the homeless wandering and the begging bowl.

This does not mean that all the scriptural prescriptions for the sannyasi are made irrelevant by the teachings of the Bhagavad-gita, but it does mean that the spirit of sannyasa life can also be had if one, in any condition of life, 'gives up activities based on material desire' and acts completely without selfish interest. Since selfish interest is bypassed whenever one acts to serve the Supreme, acts of divine service, or *bhakti-yoga*, result in elevated states of God-consciousness. This level of spiritual consciousness - the very opposite of the ordinary self-consciousness induced by bodily identification - is the perfection of renunciation of the world and hence the factual supreme goal of the sannyasi.

The Vaishnava accepts that everything within the universe is owned and controlled by Vishnu, or God, and that he cannot renounce anything because it never belonged to him. Renunciation for the Vaishnava is not, therefore, the giving up of something, but the full comprehension of its owner, the renunciation of the tendency to enjoy that object, and the return of the object to the owner by offering it in divine service. The conclusion of this line of thought is that the pure Vaishnava is the true sannyasi, whatever stage of life he might be in.

The Goswamis of Vrindavan made these theological points very clear. Rupa Goswami wrote as follows: "Not being attached to anything yet properly using everything in relation to Krishna is *yukta-vairagya*, renunciation suitable for *bhakti*. Renunciation, by persons desiring liberation, of items related to God, considering them material, is called *phalgu-vairagya* (insignificant and worthless renunciation)"

Four hundred years later, Srila Bhaktisiddhanta Saraswati Thakur created his mission for widely broadcasting the teachings of Chaitanya Mahaprabhu and the Goswamis. Accordingly, when he published his newspaper, *The Gaudiya*, he featured two Bengali verses of his own composition alongside Rupa Goswami's *yukta/phalgu* maxim on the header of each newspaper. Translated, his verses read as follows:

> "All sense objects which are used without personal attachment and in relation to Krishna are non-different from Krishna. It is a mistake to reject anything suitable for serving Krishna, considering it an object of sense gratification."

So although he'd created a missionary movement led by celibate monks, he nevertheless employed everything possible in the service of preaching his gospel. Although *sadhus* traditionally walked from village to village, slept under trees, and didn't mix with worldly men, Srila Bhaktisiddhanta had his missionaries living in cities, sometimes in apartments or spacious temples; and had them using cars for transport as they went to visit important men in the city. In Calcutta he even had a river launch, a steamship, and dressed his followers in tailored shirts and overcoats, presenting themselves with visiting cards to big businessmen. His followers went so far as to present kirtan on the BBC radio using traditional Indian instruments and a European piano. He was prepared to do whatever was required to facilitate the spiritual awakening of others – even when it seemed to contradict standard behaviour for holy men.

When he sent disciples to London in 1933 he cautioned them about not appearing unkempt, because people in London were: "...hasty to judge a person by his external appearance." Even at home in British-ruled Calcutta he wore a London-made, Savile Row overcoat and explained: "I have to go various places for propagating *Hari-katha*, so I must present myself as a learned and decent gentleman; otherwise non-devotees will not give me their time."

When questioned about all these innovations to the traditional life of Indian holy men and whether it wasn't all a step too far, he remarked: "It depends on the capacity of the individual." He reasoned that if everything belongs to Krishna, then everything can be used to serve Krishna. And since spreading the message of Krishna is the best service to Him, there should be no question of not utilizing everything possible in the preaching mission.

But he recognised the risk in allowing his followers who were not free from selfish desires contact with money, buildings, vehicles, and worldly men – and their wives; and he cautioned them: "not to become entrapped in the deceitfulness of subtle enjoyment, and thus while ostensibly performing *Hari-seva* actually become inimical to it."

# Gaudiya Math

So why did Srila Bhaktisiddhanta Saraswati feel it necessary to introduce the order of sannyasa into the line of the Chaitanya Vaishnavas? Four hundred years had already gone by without it, and it was neither a theological nor a social requirement for Vaishnavas. In northern India, the orange clothing was commonly identified with the followers of Adi Shankara, the teacher of atheistic monism, a teaching completely opposed to Vaishnavism. And in the *Chaitanya Charitamrita*, the leader of the Vaishnava community, Sanatana Goswami, is recorded as saying to his friend, Jagadananda *Pandit*: *rakta-vastra vaisnavera parite na yuyaya* – "This saffron cloth is not fit for a Vaishnava to wear..."

So although Shri Chaitanya Mahaprabhu had joined the sannyasa order, the Six Goswamis, his principal followers and codifiers of his theology and ritual, did not. From that time onwards it was the custom for renounced Vaishnavas in the Gaudiya *parampara* to simply adopt the Goswamis' hermit life and, like them, to wear knee-length off-white loin cloths. It is just conceivable that Bhaktisiddhanta Saraswati could have conducted all his preaching activities without any sannyasis at all.

But the social, religious and intellectual circumstances of Bengal demanded something more. The so-called followers of Chaitanya Mahaprabhu were withdrawn, inaccessible, and often morally incapable of representing the tradition. Some of them flouted even standard moral principles and led lives far beyond the pale of respectable society. So reprehensible were they – and so numerous - that even the very word 'Vaishnava' was despised in some quarters. Millions of people had their religious needs met either by brahmanas expert in rituals or family gurus who were inheritors of their father's title. Religious instruction was in the hands of men who were often no better off, spiritually, than those they sought to teach. There were some good ones, but their 'disciples' were simply registered students who neither studied nor followed the moral precepts. The very survival of the line of Shri Chaitanya Mahaprabhu was at stake.

Srila Bhaktisiddhanta Thakur wanted to create an accessible, authentic, spiritually strong and socially respectable movement. He wanted to distance himself and his followers from the degraded pseudo-followers of Chaitanya, and he wanted thereby to preserve the purity and reputation of his own spiritual forebears such as Gaura Kishor Das Babaji and Jagannatha Das Babaji.

So he did something quite radical. He re-created tridandi-sannyasa within his Gaudiya line, beginning with himself. After consulting with sannyasis in the Shri Sampradaya in the south of India, he first took sannyasa himself, then gradually initiated his qualified disciples until there were eighteen sannyasis in total. At that time in Bengal the Ramakrishna Mission was popular. They weren't technically sannyasis, but all the celibate members dressed in the traditional orange of a sannyasi. When one of their leading organizers joined him as a disciple, the decision was made and all of his *brahmachari* disciples also wore the saffron cloth, too.

# Complaints

But there were complaints and arguments all over Bengal against what many viewed as inappropriate dress and behaviour. Srila Bhaktisiddhanta Thakur was making ordinary men into brahmanas and was now initiating his disciples into the sannyasa order. What was going on? Most Bengalis had never been to the far south of India and not seen Vaishnava sannyasis of the Shri and Brahma Sampradayas. They simply had no knowledge of any such thing as an orange-clad Vaishnava. They had many arguments against it:

Sannyasa was part of the *varna-ashram* social system – and weren't Vaishnavas above and beyond this? The orange cloth was only for *mayavadis*, those preaching an impersonal philosophy – what business was it of those who believed in a supreme person to wear this colour?

And finally, none of the Six Goswamis had taken sannyasa; Sanatana Goswami had deemed it unacceptable; and hadn't Chaitanya Mahaprabhu himself quoted from scripture saying that five things are forbidden in the Age of *Kali* - and one of them was taking sannyasa?

Srila Bhaktisiddhanta Saraswati Thakur dealt with all these arguments, and more. He replied that a person's qualification as a brahmana should be ascertained by his character and behaviour – springing from his purity – and not from his caste by birth. He quoted a famous sage in defence of his awarding brahminical initiation to those from different rungs of Indian society:

> *jata-karmadibhir-yastu samkaraih samskrtah sucih*
> *vedadhyayana-sampannah sad sat karmasvasthitah*
> *saucacarasthitah samyag vighasasi guru-priyah*
> *nityabrali satyaparah sa vai brahmana ucyate*

"One whose birth and subsequent works have all been purified by the appropriate samskaras, who has the qualities of purity and cleanliness, who is devoted to Vedic study, who performs worship of the Supreme Lord Vishnu, and who instructs others in that worship, who is a paragon of the six activities of a brahmana, whose behaviour is never impure, who eats the remnants of his guru's prasada, who is dear to the guru, who always carefully follows his vows, and who is fixed in the truth is known as a brahmana." *(Bharadvaja Muni)*

He said that the true, 'topmost' Vaishnava is beyond the *varna* and ashram society since he has already reached the platform of *bhakti*, but that a Vaishnava who wishes to keep himself humble will consider that his guru is on such a level but he himself is within the boundaries of social norms, simply aspiring for elevation. This will keep him free from pride. Although the mayavadi sannyasis believe that as soon as one takes sannyasa he is 'as good as Narayana,' the Vaishnava could never think like this. Therefore the Vaishnava does not take sannyasa out of pride, but out of humility. Whereas the mayavadis, upon taking sannyasa, remove their *sikha*, the short lock of hair on the back of the head, and their *upavita*, the sacred thread, the Vaishnavas kept both.

When Chaitanya Mahaprabhu referred to sannyasa being forbidden in the Age of *Kali* he was referring only to *phalgu-vairagya*, or false renunciation; the *markata-vairagya*, or 'monkey-renunciation.' The monkey is also saffron in colour, he also lives in the forest and sleeps under trees – or up them – but he keeps six girlfriends. This type of pseudo-renunciation will become widespread in the *Kali Yuga*, and it is not required.

The sannyasis of Saraswati Thakur were a body of renunciates who established the real spirit of *vairagya* as opposed to those who simply spoke of it. They were travelling preachers and extended the mercy of Chaitanya Mahaprabhu throughout Bengal and beyond – even to Europe. They became respected, influential and popular; they gained the appreciation of the intellectuals and the masses – and as a result the Gaudiya Mission spread like a saffron fire. By the time of his passing in 1937, the mission was represented in sixty-four cities and towns and was comprised of thousands of adherents.

# 29

# Undercurrents

*The ancient codes of sannyasa are for the purpose of fostering genuine detachment from the world, a level of consciousness that can also be developed by serving Krishna. When the Vaishnavas become sannyasis they are, presumably, doubly-blessed: once by the ashram itself, and twice by the results of their devotion. So when many sannyasis join together to work collectively to foster this consciousness in others, it would seem that nothing could go wrong...*

**Srila Bhaktisiddhanta Saraswati became a sannyasi in March of 1918, aged 44.** On the same day he inaugurated the Shri Chaitanya Math in Mayapur. His recently departed father, Srila Bhaktivinode Thakur, had given him the instruction to present pure devotional service, publish Vaishnava books, serve the holy dhama of Shri Mayapur, and to re-establish a purified form of *varna-ashram* culture which he termed *daiva-varnashram*. By the end of his short life in 1937, aged 63 – after a missionary career of less than twenty years - he had spread the teachings of Lord Chaitanya Mahaprabhu throughout India, and to Burma, Germany and England; established sixty-seven centres, published many books and countless periodicals; initiated some 3,000 disciples, hundreds of them *brahmacharis*, and awarded sannyasa to eighteen of his most dedicated followers.

But it had been a constant struggle, not only with the various corrupted religious groups of the time, but with supporters and members of his Gaudiya Math organisation. Practically from the beginning he attracted those who, after a year or two of lukewarm spiritual practice, fell into apathy, lethargy, philosophical disagreement, and self-interest. They competed for position within the fledgling organization, used the power so gained to influence others, fought over limited resources, and entered into direct conflict with each other. Some raised funds on behalf of the mission and set aside a portion for themselves, while others fell into old habits of various kinds. Even some of the eighteen sannyasis, the very spiritual leaders he depended on to develop the mission and perpetuate it after him, succumbed to weaknesses of various kinds over the twenty year period.

Of course, what he'd done had been a very precarious exercise. Adjusting the traditional rules of sannyasa in order to preach the message of Chaitanya, consequently demanding an even higher level of consciousness from his sannyasis – it was a great endeavour fraught with risk. Instead of physically withdrawing from the external world, sannyasis were now dealing with it every day, in the largest cities of India. Instead of walking from village to village and begging for food, they were travelling in trains – even riding in cars, unheard of for a *sadhu* – and being served meals in the homes of rich men. They were addressed as *maharaja*, or 'great king,' sometimes lived in palatial buildings, and attracted crowds who came to hear them speak. And those members of the public who were impressed with what they heard donated funds liberally. Some of them, faced with all of this, succumbed to temptation.

Yet had it not been this way, had the Gaudiya Math of Srila Bhaktisiddhanta Saraswati not been arranged just as it was, with exactly the public presence, profusion of publications, temple building and level of geographical outreach – it is unlikely that the message of Chaitanya Mahaprabhu would have survived in India, let alone spread internationally. He was aware of the needs of the time, yet he also knew that perhaps not all who followed him shared exactly the same lofty ideals – or staying power. So he taught, spoke, lectured and wrote with vigour; and he guided, corrected and rebuked his leaders when they strayed, which they did often. His writings and transcribed conversations bear witness to a troubling undercurrent of spiritual weakness – even amid so much spiritual and organizational success.

Just twelve years after the inception of his organization in 1930 he dictated an anonymous article for the *Gaudiya*, the movement's magazine. The aim was to remind errant followers of the purpose for which they had joined him. He wanted to highlight the mistake of performing energetic physical service for the guru and his mission without actually heeding his instructions to become more involved in hearing and chanting about Krishna, the very purpose of the entire endeavour. When, after the article was published, the complaints began about what Math members felt was an audacious article, he replied:

"Whoever cannot tolerate this article has never taken birth in the Gaudiya Math. It was right to publish this, so that there may be reform. If there is no energy in the powerhouse, then even thousands of light bulbs cannot give illumination. Similarly, without purity and sincerity, there is no use in having many followers and a big institution."

By 1932, certain leading disciples were already grumbling that their guru was mis-spending all the funds they had raised on preaching programmes and printing. They felt it would be better if he kept the money in the bank. His reply came in a lecture: "My aim is not to make provisions and lay bricks for rascals who may come in the future. Possibly the structures already made will one day become dens of *ganja* and vice."

In the same year he had occasion to speak once more about a worrying tendency. A sannyasi returned from a preaching event and told the members of the ashram: "I delivered a superb speech that was much appreciated, so I shouldn't take ordinary rice *prasadam*. Cook *puris* for me." When Srila Bhaktisiddhanta Saraswati heard of this he became disappointed and said *karilam sannyasi haya gelo vilasi*: "I made them renunciants, but they became voluptuaries."

On another occasion he stood in a doorway witnessing two of his sannyasis loudly arguing with each other. Neither saw him standing there. When they did, they both fell to the floor in embarrassment, bowing down before him. At their apology he said, "No, no it is not your fault, it is mine. Shri Chaitanya Mahaprabhu took *maharajas* and made them into beggars; but I have taken beggars and turned them into *maharajas*."

In a letter of 25th April, 1933 he wrote:

> *"The Math is not a place...to display foppery. Those who want foppery...can go back home and care for their family. Sannyasis who do not indulge in foppery should be recognized as Gaudiya Math sannyasis. The rest should be sent back home. Instead of wearing red, they can be clad in white cloth...and sent back home. Even if consequently our manpower depletes, still it is better. If those who have taken shelter of the Math but are motivated by their bellies and genitals are driven away, the expenses of the Math will be reduced and also worldly disturbances."*

Part Four | Undercurrents

"Those who come to render devotional service are brahmacharis, grihastas, vanaprasthas, and sannyasis. The Math will not give shelter to persons who do not perform devotional service, for they are enemies of the Math. 'I have rendered so much service to the Math, so I will ride in the car, boss others around, and demand respect. I must have a big share in the leadership and management of the Math' – that mentality should never be encouraged. Such is the talk of mundane householders. Those serving the Math should do so with no expectation of return."

By 1934 the large, showpiece marble temple in Calcutta's Bagh Bazaar was beginning to be a source of contention for the members who occupied the rooms there. They argued as to who would have which room. Disappointed, Srila Bhaktisiddhanta Thakur often quoted the Bengali proverb *dustau garu ceye sunya goyala bhalo*: "Better to have an empty cowshed than a troublesome cow." Expanding on this proverb he explained:

"There is no need for 'bad cows' that harm others. A single 'good cow' is sufficient. We want a living source, not so-called sannyasis. If our mission does not flourish with a real living source, then we will distribute the stones and bricks to the poor for one *paisa* each, or rent the temple to them. If there is no good soul in the mission, I do not want it. I don't need 'bad cows.'

It was around this time, towards the end of his life, that two parties developed around two leaders of the Gaudiya Math. Both men had been previously praised by Srila Bhaktisiddhanta Saraswati, one for his work in the practical organisation of the manpower of the *Math*, and his considerably successful fundraising; the other for his philosophical astuteness, his writing capabilities and his successful teaching and personal charisma. Both men were noted for their surrender to their guru and their devotion to him. Members rallied around one or the other according to whom they felt was the true inheritor of the legacy of their acharya. Eventually, in the late 1930s and the early 1940s, the Gaudiya Math was rent in two by the divisions of opinion. Shortly thereafter, the Gaudiya Math fractured into several uncooperative movements, each a mere shadow of the original.

Religious movements, no matter how pure the intentions of their founder or the veracity of their theological claims, are limited in their scope and endurance by the purity of intention and conduct of their members – particularly the leaders. Even good people are prone to weaknesses, and history has shown that those weaknesses don't change very much; no matter what century it happens to be. Five hundred years ago, Shri Chaitanya Mahaprabhu mentioned three causes of male distraction from the spiritual path; *dhanam, janam* and *sundarim*, or wealth, followers, and beautiful women.

When Srila Prabhupada travelled to the USA in 1965, he went with personal experience of the mixed fortunes of the Gaudiya Math. He'd been a participant and an observer ever since he'd first become a member in 1922. Over the span of forty years he'd seen the once brilliant movement become tarnished and dysfunctional. He was bitterly disappointed, but determined to make his own contribution to his guru's mission in the new world.

Part Four | White skin, orange cloth

# 30

# White skin, orange cloth

*We've seen in the last chapter how Srila Bhaktisiddhanta Saraswati resurrected the sannyasa ashram in early twentieth century Bengal, and used the ancient disciplines of the renunciate life to create a strong core for his missionary movement. Following his lead, Srila Prabhupada also created a section of sannyasis within his ISKCON movement. In this chapter, some of his struggles to develop and maintain it are presented in his own words.*

**Srila Bhaktisiddhanta Saraswati was spreading the teachings of Chaitanya Mahaprabhu in an India where many already regarded the saffron-robed mendicant to be a figure of derision or a beggar who made no contribution to society.** The state of sannyasa had gradually drifted from its original purpose because of the preponderance of unscrupulous men who had adopted the dress simply to maintain themselves. Srila Bhaktisiddhanta wanted to make a difference, and to restore sannyasa to its former, noble position. But he exercised caution. Although he had 3,000 disciples, he gave sannyasa to only eighteen, and even then he regularly took issue with the way they behaved. His personal correction of his wayward sannyasis was to last only until 1937 when he passed from the world.

As time passed, there were repeated issues of power struggles, party politics and independent accumulation of finances. By the time A.C. Bhaktivedanta took sannyasa himself in the late 1950s, the state of the once united Gaudiya Math was a disappointment for many of its members. He openly criticised his sannyasi godbrothers for what his guru had termed their 'foppery,' and challenged them that although they hadn't continued the energetic preaching mission of their spiritual master, they were still raising funds in the name of missionary activity and keeping 'tens of millions of rupees in the bank,' while initiating disciples 'in the manner of businessmen.'

The Guru and Disciple Book

When he wrote his 'Light of the *Bhagavata*' in 1962 he described the state of the *varna-ashram* system, and with it the plight of the sannyasi:

> "In Kali Yuga, however, the entire system has gone topsy-turvy. The student lives in luxury at the expense of the father or the father-in-law. When the educated, indulgent student becomes a householder by the strength of university degrees, he requires money by all means for all kinds of bodily comfort, and therefore he cannot spare even a penny for the so-called vanaprasthas and sannyasis. The vanaprasthas and sannyasis nowadays are those who were unsuccessful in family life. Thus the so-called sannyasis try to construct another home in the name of the sannyasa ashram and glide down into all sorts of luxury at the expense of others. So all these varnas and ashrams have now become so many transcendental frauds. But that does not mean that there is no reality in them. One should not conclude that there is no good money simply because one has met with counterfeit coins. The sannyasa ashram is meant for complete freedom from all anxieties, and it is meant for uplifting the fallen souls, who are merged in materialism. But unless the sannyasi is freed from all cares and anxieties, like a white cloud, it is difficult for him to do anything good for society."

While it may be imagined that Srila Prabhupada was offering a comment merely on the plight of sannyasa in Indian society, his comments can also be taken as a general statement of a universal rule: that men who have renounced the world will, without the exercise of due diligence, drift inexorably in their interactions with others towards self-serving forms of religious business transaction, accumulation of fame and followers, and will inevitably move toward establishing a subtle or gross connection with women.

In creating his ISKCON, thirty years after the passing of Srila Bhaktisiddhanta Thakur, Srila Prabhupada wanted to fulfil the mission of his spiritual master on an international scale. He also wanted to strenuously avoid the 'foppery' and other human weaknesses that had hindered the Gaudiya Math and helped bring about its fragmentation. ISKCON was to be a fresh creation, made up of highly committed members. So from very early on, to further the preaching activities and develop the four ashrams, he initiated selected disciples as sannyasis. Yet even as he did so, he cautioned them – and all his followers – that the life of a sannyasi was one of strict discipline. He started talking about it in his first public lectures:

> "Then this is a hint by Lord Chaitanya that a sannyasi who has renounced everything, if he lives very gorgeously, with good dress, and good house, and apartment... No. This is not approved by Chaitanya Mahaprabhu. Then what is that? Whatever is absolutely necessity, he should accept, not more. Yes. That is renounced order of life, not that in the name of renounced order of life he should live at the expense of the householders, very gorgeously. No. This is not sannyasa. It is not accepted by Chaitanya Mahaprabhu's sampradaya." *(Lecture, 21st November, 1966)*

But even as he created his first sannyasi in August 1967, he was to discover that it would be no easy task to discipline them. Kirtanananda was one of his first disciples, and Srila Prabhupada felt he would be suitable for travelling and starting new centres. So when, while in India, Kirtanananda asked if he could become a sannyasi, Srila Prabhupada agreed. But by October he was receiving complaints that the new sannyasi had disobeyed him by returning to the USA rather than opening a centre in London, as he'd been instructed. In New York, he seemed to be teaching a brand of impersonal philosophy, and had encouraged devotees to shave off their *sikhas*, remove their *tilak* and stop wearing robes. Srila Prabhupada's response was swift: "This is very much disturbing to me and has caused me much pain...for the time being he has cut all link with me, therefore any instruction given by him is unauthorized and should at once be rejected. He has no right to dictate as he has without my sanction...He is too much puffed-up...I am very sorry that he is exploiting his present position as a sannyasi."

It was still the very early days of ISKCON, and the founder-acharya wanted to ensure that his movement got off to a good start. The fact that his first sannyasi had already taught a deviant philosophy, assumed a special status simply because of his new ashram, then sought to misrepresent his guru – these things did not bode well for the future. That one disciple should, using the position of the spiritual master, place himself in a superior position was something that Srila Prabhupada had seen in the Gaudiya Math years ago. So he wanted to nip such ideas in the bud, and he wanted to create more equality amongst his own disciples, stressing that consciousness of Krishna was the main factor, not the ashram. After reinstating Kirtanananda Swami in ISKCON he again had occasion to write a letter of correction, just two years later, on the 30th August, 1969, from Hamburg, Germany:

"In our society I do not know what you mean by cooperation with Kirtanananda Maharaja. In our society everyone, either a *brahmachari* or sannyasi or *grhastha*, who has dedicated his life and soul for this movement, they are all on the same level of sannyasi. For the present moment, nobody can claim an extra honour from his Godbrothers. Everyone should treat his Godbrothers as Prabhu. But nobody should try to claim any extra honour on account of an official position. I do not know why Kirtanananda Maharaja says that his authority overrides yours. At the present moment everyone is working under my authority. Similarly, Kirtanananda also should work under my authority. So the condition imposed by Kirtanananda as stated by you does not look well..."

Claiming extra honour due to an 'official position' was not, however, the only problem with the early sannyasis. Most of the devotees were young, and for a young sannyasi, celibacy did not prove as easy as it first seemed. In 1968, one sannyasi had already left his celibate life and become married. The story is told by Satsvarupa Das Goswami in the Srila *Prabhupada Lilamrita*

"One of Prabhupada's sannyasi disciples, Hanuman, had fallen down from the sannyasa standard and had married. Such a thing had never before happened in ISKCON. But now, on Prabhupada's first day in Mexico, Hanuman, dressed as a householder, came to see his spiritual master. After the crowd of guests had left Prabhupada's room, only Hanuman and a few senior men remained. "Srila Prabhupada," Hanuman began, "Lord Chaitanya Mahaprabhu had one disciple in the renounced order, Chota Haridasa, whom He rejected from His association because he became too much lusty after a woman. I was also one of your sannyasa disciples, and I too became lusty after a woman. I was wondering if you have also rejected me from your association."

A heavy silence followed as everyone looked at Prabhupada, who sat with his head down. After a long pause, Prabhupada looked up at Hanuman and said quietly, "Lord Chaitanya is God. He can spread this movement all over the world in one second without the help of anyone if He likes. I am not God. I am simply a servant of God. I require so much assistance to help me spread Krishna consciousness all over the world. If someone renders even some small service to help me, I am eternally indebted to him. You have rendered so much assistance to me, how could I reject you?"

The sannyasis were intended to travel and preach, spreading the movement by attracting new devotees of Krishna and opening new centres. But as sannyasis they were also meant to live very simply, without fixed accommodation, and funded only by donations from those to whom they gave some knowledge. Srila Prabhupada's idea was that this knowledge exchange could take place by book distribution, but for some sannyasis this was not easy. Some then travelled from temple to temple, inspiring the devotees, who then paid for them to travel to their next destination. Sometimes a sannyasi would stay longer in one place, helping out with the management of the fledgling centre. But the ISKCON centre was not meant to become his new 'home', the members of the centre his new 'family,' and the assets of the centre were never intended to be at his personal disposal, for that was in contravention of the requirements of sannyasa life.

> "Actually, sannyasa, or renunciation of material household life, necessitates complete absorption in Krishna consciousness and immersion in the self. One does not take sannyasa, freedom from family responsibility in the renounced order of life, to make another family or to create an embarrassing transcendental fraud in the name of sannyasa. The sannyasi's business is not to become proprietor of so many things and amass money from the innocent public." *(Srimad Bhagavatam 3.24.34)*

> "Therefore for a sannyasi it is recommended that he should not live more than three days in a place, because as soon as he lives more than three days, he'll get some attachment. Attachment. So he is forbidden." *(Lecture, 24th August, 1968)*

To a temple president, who had been funding the travelling of the sannyasis, Srila Prabhupada wrote:

> "Regarding the sannyasis, they should be independent. Why they should take help from you? They are strong men, so they should manage on their own strength. That is the test of their effective preaching work." *(13th November, 1970)*

Another service for the sannyasis was to ensure that the teachings were being taught as written by Srila Prabhupada in his books. Their job was to be learned, expert in preparing and delivering classes, and vigilant that spiritual standards were being kept in each centre they visited. But in 1970 there were some incidents whereby Srila Prabhupada's position as the ultimate authority of ISKCON was minimized, and certain of his leaders were implicated. Disappointed, Srila Prabhupada decided to not remain In the USA as planned. Then, at a festival on the New Vrindavan farm community, Kirtanananda Swami along with Sudama Swami, Brahmananda Swami and Vishnujan Swami had announced that by Srila Prabhupada's recent departure from America, he had rejected his disciples for failing to recognise that he was not merely Krishna's representative, he was actually Krishna himself. When Srila Prabhupada heard this he immediately recognised it as an impersonal doctrine veiled in devotion. He promptly excommunicated them. He wrote to some followers:

> *"You are all my children and I love my American boys and girls who are sent to me by my spiritual master and I have accepted them as my disciples....At the present moment in our ISKCON campus, politics and diplomacy has entered. Some of my beloved students on whom I counted very, very much have been involved in this matter, influenced by Maya."*

They were allowed to return some time later, but he'd acted swiftly in order to protect other members of his Society from impersonal doctrine and to signal his displeasure in their pronouncements. Through this action he had also signalled that his sannyasis had no intrinsic, special position, only that they were, like all his other disciples, members of ISKCON – and members that could be disciplined.

The constant jockeying for position and control; the teaching of philosophy that was a shade or two removed from the original; and the occasional amassing of personal wealth at the expense of the organization, all of these were to become a standard feature of sannyasi life in ISKCON throughout the 1970s. And then there were the repeated cases of shattered vows as the renunciates left their vows of celibacy. Many of Srila Prabhupada's 5,000 letters reflect his attempts to simultaneously inspire, encourage yet also regulate his sannyasi disciples, his leaders – and to explain to all his disciples the function of the sannyasa order. But his instructions to them were also written into his books, too. Some of his commentaries to the verses of Srimad Bhagavatam were written in the same week that he'd received the news that another of his sannyasi disciples had left his vows. Srila Prabhupada would then incorporate a cautionary instruction into the body of his commentary as a lasting teaching.

# 31

# The GBC

*It was also in 1970 that Srila Prabhupada created a governing body for his ISKCON. By doing this he fulfilled both his guru's intention of having an international society run by a 12-man body and also created the mechanism whereby his movement could be governed by collegiate and parliamentary processes in his absence. According to his document of 28 July 1970, he appointed twelve members, none of whom were sannyasis. The 'Governing Body Commission' or 'GBC' was to improve the standard of temple management and financial and legal accountability; to safeguard the existing temple properties; supervise the promotion of Krishna consciousness, particularly through the publishing and distribution of books, and the opening of new centres and education of the devotees.*

**Although there was not a single sannyasi selected to be a member of the first Governing Body Commission, it transpired that over the next few years that several *sannyasis* proved themselves to be particularly helpful in governance work.** They joined the GBC. Some of the original, married members of the GBC also became sannyasis and remained on the GBC. Over time the constituency of the GBC became predominantly sannyasi. The distinctive lifestyle differences between the pioneering, preaching, travelling sannyasi and the managerially competent, governing body member – who was also a sannyasi – became somewhat fused. Sannyasis were now both travelling preachers and involved in institutional governance. But Srila Prabhupada still wanted to preserve the essence of the sannyasa life, no matter what service the sannyasis performed in his movement:

> "I've sent the sannyasis letters requesting them to preach from different centres. I'm glad that Subala das Swami has gone to Amsterdam. Similarly the other three may go to other places. Why are they together? Sannyasa means they should travel extensively,

create new centres and new devotees – that is sannyasa business. Also they can create life members." *(28th October, 1970)*

"Sannyasi must be independent and not rely upon temples to pay his expensive travelling costs, simply he must take Krishna's mercy whenever and wherever it is offered." *(29th July 1972)*

In 1973, despite some sannyasis being on his GBC, Srila Prabhupada confirmed that the sannyasa lifestyle must remain the same as he'd originally explained it:

"It is nice that Subaldas Maharaja is travelling. As sannyasi, he should travel. The more a sannyasi travels and preaches, the more he becomes experienced and unattached." *(Letter 18th October, 1973)*

And in November he wrote the same thing in a letter to Revatinandan Swami:

"I am glad that you are travelling and preaching. This is your main business. For a sannyasi the more he wanders and preaches, the more he becomes experienced. The people benefit, he benefits, and from a material point of view he'll profit. So constantly travel and distribute books as much as possible."

With his young disciples jostling for power, and certainly using either their institutional office or their ashram status as leverage, Srila Prabhupada also had to sort out disputes between the temple heads and the travelling or managing sannyasis:

"In regards to your question about how the relationship between a sannyasi and the temple president should be, my hope is that you will all be able to cooperate together. The temple president is in charge and the sannyasi should not contradict the instructions. Although if he does see something wrong, or if he sees a fault or defect, he should bring it out directly to the temple president. And then work it out in a Krishna conscious way. Not that he will try to override the temple president's authority. I want that you all work together cooperatively." *(Letter, 28th February, 1974)*

By the time that Srila Prabhupada wrote the following words, there was considerable income being generated by thousands of devotees distributing his books. Yet he was insistent that even though some of his sannyasis were now dealing with money they should stay true to their roots:

> 'A sannyasi is supposed to beg from door to door. He does not beg simply because he is hungry. His real purpose is to enlighten the occupant of every house by preaching Krishna consciousness. A sannyasi does not abandon his superior position and become a beggar just for the sake of begging... They are not actually beggars; their real business is to deliver fallen souls. Therefore they may go from door to door just to introduce a book about Krishna consciousness so that people can become enlightened by reading. Formerly brahmacharis and sannyasis used to beg from door to door. At the present moment, especially in the Western countries, a person may be handed over to the police if he begs from door to door. In Western countries, begging is considered criminal. Members of the Krishna consciousness movement have no business begging. Instead, they work very hard to introduce some literatures about Krishna consciousness so that people can read them and be benefited. But if one gives some contribution to a Krishna conscious man, he never refuses it.' (*Chaitanya-caritamrta Madhya lila 8.39*)

Srila Prabhupada explained the proper relationship between a sannyasi and money, and the motives he should have as he begs for that money. He had previously written that a sannyasi was supposed to 'contribute some literary work for the benefit of society' but if he writes his own book – the funds raised actually belong to his guru, or to his guru's mission:

> "I know you are a very good cook and I can understand that you have found the books useful for distribution. I have no objection to your printing it with the name Revatinandana Swami's Cookbook, but the royalty should go to the Bhaktivedanta Book Trust. Just as I am publishing the Bhagavad-gita As It Is with the Macmillan Company, but the royalty is going to the BBT. I think this method is appropriate. If you yourself take the royalty it will be personal interest in money and trade, and this will deviate your principle of sannyasa. Sannyasi means he is in the renounced order and lives by begging alms for the bare necessities of life. It is not good to make trade to get money for personal expenditure. If the royalty is given to the BBT, we will keep a separate account

from this royalty and necessary expenditures for your preaching may be supplied from the BBT." *(9th January, 1974)*

There were times, however, when even Srila Prabhupada seemed at a loss as to how to restrain his sannyasis, such as in this 16th October 1975 letter to Jayatirtha Das:

"The local management has to be done by temple president, GBC should see whether management is going on nicely, and if there are any discrepancies that will be discussed at the GBC meeting in Mayapur. That is the process. Sannyasis are meant for preaching only. That is the principle. But, contrary to the principle if things are being embezzled then how can I save them. How one man can manage the whole world affairs? This is my concern."

In general, Srila Prabhupada would insist that his sannyasi preachers maintained the traditional robes, a rule that he relaxed for *brahmacharis* (although, as always, he wanted them to wear *tilak* on their foreheads, and a shaved head with *sikha*) but when one particular new sannyasi was having great success at selling books in normal clothing he relented in his case. He wrote in his comments to the incident of Hiranyakashipu accusing that his son, Prahlada, had been secretly taught by Vaishnavas in disguise:

"For paramahamsas, or sannyasis in the Vaishnava order, preaching is the first duty. To preach, such sanyasis may accept the symbols of sannyasa, such as the danda and kamandalu, or sometimes they may not. Generally the Vaishnava sannyasis, being paramahamsas, are automatically called babajis, and they do not carry a kamandalu or danda. Such a sannyasi is free to accept or reject the marks of sannyasa. His only thought is 'Where is there an opportunity to spread Krishna consciousness?' Sometimes the Krishna consciousness movement sends its representative sannyasis to foreign countries where the danda and kamandalu are not very much appreciated. We send our preachers in ordinary dress to introduce our books and philosophy. Our only concern is to attract people to Krishna consciousness. We may do this in the dress of sannyasis or in the regular dress of gentlemen. Our only concern is to spread interest in Krishna consciousness." *(Srimad Bhagavatam 7.13.9)*

Although the founder-acharya of ISKCON may have been somewhat flexible with his sannyasis regarding their becoming involved in management, handling money, and even, on occasion, their dress code, he was inflexible on a sannyasis connection with women:

> "So far your suggestion that they sew clothes for the sannyasis' deities it is not possible. Sannyasis may have no connection with women." *(Letter to Jayatirtha, 13th January, 1976)*

By 1977, many sannyasis had come and gone. Under his pragmatic instruction, some had at least become religiously married and remained within his Society. But he was troubled that the sannyasa ashram had not been successful:

> "And this kind of hypocrisy--they have taken sannyasa and mixing with woman. This is not to be allowed. If you want woman you get yourself married, live respectfully. We have no objection. But this hypocrisy should be stopped. There have been so many fallen down. First of all, there will be no sannyasi anymore. I have got very bad experience. And at least, we are not going to create new sannyasis. And those who have fallen down let them marry, live like respectable gentlemen. I have no objection. [...] Get one wife and live like a gentleman. Similarly woman. Live with one husband fastidiously, with children. What is the wrong there? We have so many grhastha devotees. [...] But what is this nonsense that you take sannyasa and make relation with...? This should be completely stopped." *(Conversation, 7th January, 1977)*

> "Sannyasi should go on preaching, preaching, preaching, preaching. Practically, I was sitting here in Vrndavana, in Radha-Damodara temple. So at the age of seventy years, nobody goes out, at least from Vrndavana nobody goes at the age of seventy years. But Krishna asked me. I thought that I must go, Guru Maharaja wanted it, Chaitanya Mahaprabhu ... Let me try. So if I had not gone, then this institution would not have developed. So this is practical. Mahatah nirvicharanam. Mahatma, they must move. So when there is absolute necessity they may stay. Otherwise, they must move -- move on, move on, move on, move on, move on. No staying, that is principle. No staying. I am this old age, I cannot move; still I am travelling all over the world. I am simply

interested that whatever I have done, it may not be vanquished in my absence. Let me go and encourage them. Otherwise, I have no capacity to move now. But still I am moving. Only for this purpose. So a sannyasi must move. A sannyasi must not stay anywhere more than three days. That is the principle." *(From the Transcendental Diary by Hari Sauri Das)*

# 32

# Saffron cardinals

*Critics of ISKCON say that the Society has a 'guru problem' in that many of those who give initiation seem to have encountered spiritual difficulty. But because the overwhelming majority of gurus are sannyasis, it might also be said that ISKCON has a sannyasi problem. Indeed, perhaps that is the real problem. Sannyasa is an ancient tradition that endured through mediaeval times, was adopted for the Gaudiya lineage in modern times, and was introduced as a vital component along with the inception of ISKCON. What is the current state of the sannyasa ashram within the Society, and how are sannyasis functioning as gurus? Could the situation be improved?*

**It's clear from the ancient rules that renunciation was the hallmark of a sannyasi and defined his existence.** That spirit of renunciation played out practically in his mode of living as he begged for his food, slept under trees, and walked from village to town, enlightening those householders he met along the way with the spiritual wisdom he'd accumulated during his life. He sought to extricate himself from any lingering attachment to the comforts of home, money, popularity, and the pleasures of family life.

Later, Vaishnava acharyas philosophically defined true renunciation as the practise of offering everything to the Supreme Person, regarding everything as His property, and acting always for His pleasure. Whether that offering of one's life was in the forest or in the middle of a crowded city, the criterion was always whether or not it was pleasing to Him. Since helping others towards a greater consciousness of Krishna is certainly pleasing to Krishna, a sannyasi can do anything that furthers that cause. And if several renunciates can work collectively and achieve more, that is a distinct advantage.

Yet when they do form a cooperative venture, and do it successfully, the thousands of grateful souls respond by asking if they also can join them and take part in their missionary work. And that is where sannyasis may find themselves as leaders or managers of a religious institution.

There's nothing intrinsically wrong with that – if it works well. When it doesn't work it can be a great disappointment for all concerned. Organisations based on the teachings of Krishna are somewhat rare in the world, and they are intended to provide hope in the face of contemporary personal and social trouble. When sannyasi leaders within such an institution fail, their failure creates widespread confusion and despair.

Unfortunately, in its now almost 50-year history, ISKCON has been no stranger to leadership failure. A steady trickle of sannyasis departing from the life of celibacy has left in its wake many despondent members, particularly when those sannyasis were also functioning as gurus. In fact, the phenomenon has given birth to intense theological debate, political wrangling, and institutional splintering with consequent membership loss. ISKCON is by no means the only religious body to grapple with the problem of 'shattered vows.' Celibacy as a way of life is a great sacrifice, and difficulties are experienced within every spiritual tradition.

But the followers of Srila Prabhupada expected more. There was great hope that through devotion to Krishna a different kind of spiritual practitioner would be produced; a stronger, more committed person who would be resilient in the face of earthly temptation. There was great hope that by many such spiritually strong persons working together a different kind of religion would be created. ISKCON is a great spiritual success story, and as a whole it is prospering and enjoys steady growth. But almost annually one section of members is thrown into turmoil because of spiritual scandal. So what is the deeper problem, and is there a solution?

# Management and control

The founder-*acharya* of ISKCON faithfully replicated the Gaudiya Math sannyasi within his new movement, a continuation of his spiritual master's mission. If there was anything different it was that his sannyasis were to be international pioneers, principally preaching in the English language, and of course, they were American and European converts to Vaishnavism. He wanted them to become learned in his books, teach and inspire others, and to preach in new places with vigour and determination, recommending to the other leaders where a new branch of the organisation could be opened.

In time, because they often were his best and most committed disciples, Srila Prabhupada asked them to relieve him of the burden of management. Their role was adapted slightly to include management as well as preaching and inspiration. A sannyasi in ancient times would be reluctant to manage anything but his begging bowl, but the mediaeval tradition of a sannyasi in an organisational leadership position was sufficient reason for Bhaktisiddhanta Saraswati Thakur to choose sannyasis to head up his organisation's branches. He then went on to select twelve of them to form a governing body for his organisation, with a married man as the overall manager. Although the original members of ISKCON's governing body were not sannyasis (it was, after all, only four years since its founding) in a relatively short time the GBC was comprised mainly of renunciates. This was still very much Srila Prabhupada's plan.

After the physical departure of the founder-*acharya* of ISKCON, and for at least a decade, the movement's membership continued to increase rapidly. As the movement spread geographically the number of branches swelled, and the governing body of a dozen or so members was supervising an international movement many times the size of the one it was created to govern.

## 'Shudras and sannyasis'

Lord Chaitanya Mahaprabhu had said that even a *shudra* could become a guru if they knew the science of Krishna; and a sannyasi could also become a guru. Anyone, regardless of their social position, if they knew the science of Krishna, could function as a guru. These two categories of person – *shudras* and sannyasis - do not traditionally give initiation to disciples. The *shudra* because he may not be learned, having not been given Vedic *diksha* and thereby access to systematic education in the Vedas; and the sannyasi because he is always travelling and cannot provide his disciples with a course of study in the Vedas. But if they knew the science of Krishna, even they could become gurus.

So in addition to everything they were already doing, the sannyasis of ISKCON became gurus. Not all of them at once, but enough that a standard pattern developed. Srila Prabhupada had already said the 'sannyasi is the spiritual master of all the other *ashrams*,' and it was a natural assumption on the part of ISKCON's growing membership that the sannyasis being the recognised spiritual leaders, managers and ultimate governors of the Society that they also take on this important role. Srila Prabhupada had been a travelling sannyasi, and had set the role model of spiritual leader, ultimate manager and guru. It was quite reasonable to assume that becoming a guru within ISKCON was the exclusive entitlement of the sannyasis. There was even strong pressure on householders already in positions of spiritual leadership to become more 'qualified' by taking sannyasa, whether they were completely ready for it or not.

And so sannyasis began to be surrounded by disciples, many of them young women. It was probably the first time in the history of the world that young sannyasis had come in such close proximity to such large numbers of young women, all of whom naturally adored their guru. But Krishna consciousness is very powerful – more powerful than any material allurement – and it worked. Newcomers joined in their hundreds, and intrepid preachers took books, deities, *prasadam* and festivals to different parts of the world.

But with success came money. Thousands of enthusiastic new disciples selling books every day meant that large quantities of funds were pouring into ISKCON. While most of it was directed, as Srila Prabhupada ordered, towards investment in opening new branches and developing book publication and sales, some of it began to be directed to the sannyasis who were initiating. Sannyasis were traditionally meant to beg from householders and to acquire only what they needed with nothing left over for the next day. But sannyasis who were managers and who also had householder disciples were something different entirely it seemed. They didn't have to travel in order to enlighten others, or if they did they simply moved between one group of disciples and the next. They didn't have to beg at all because funds would come to them in the form of contributions from their disciples. And they didn't have to eschew the company of women, quite the opposite; they were being requested to counsel and guide their female followers.

Money, followers, females and living in one place for more than three days. The very ingredients which might spell the downfall of a sannyasi in ancient times were now present in an intoxicating mixture right before his modern counterpart – and it was all, seemingly, authorised by guru and God.

# 'Clergy burn-out'

ISKCON was already what is described by academics as a 'high-commitment' religious institution. Followers chant a mantra for two hours a day and follow vows that even a Jesuit would not entertain.

In the case of the sannyasis, to the already 'high-commitment' we must also add 'high-risk.' Young men, some of them at the peak of their sexual powers, from American backgrounds that provided them with no cultural context for their adopted life; placed into positions of organisational power; surrounded by the trappings of wealth and adored by followers, many of them young women. Over time, it became a burden that was all too much for some of them.

In the world of civil engineering, when a bridge is built, there is a maximum weight it can handle before it starts to become, as the engineers express it, 'subject to stress.' If that continues for some time, 'stress fractures' will appear, and if not dealt with, the bridge will collapse. In their social and spiritual role, sannyasis are meant to be like bridges, connecting us from this world to another. When they take on too much they become stressed and eventually, no matter how good they are, the cracks will begin to appear.

Nobody sets out to create a spiritual scandal. That's often the very last thing to happen, the end of result of a long period of stress. Before that comes temptation, inattentive spiritual practice, materialistic contemplation, mental or verbal offenses to the Vaishnavas which, when they accumulate, cause even greater attraction to sensual enjoyment and so on. For a middle-aged sannyasi, undergoing his midlife crisis or a full blown 'dark night of the soul,' there might be intense feelings of loneliness, despair and some regret for the life he chose all those years ago. He may be unable to see his way forward. If he has no-one in whom he can confide then his position is greatly stressful. If he has close friends but cannot reveal his mind for fear of losing his institutional position he may simply repress all his desires and fears. Later on they will burst out of him in an unpredictable way and everyone will be shocked at what lay lurking within him.

Part Four | Saffron cardinals

# Unexamined patterns

ISKCON is not always good at spotting patterns in the lives of its members. This is because its members are all meant to fit into a noble, scripted behaviour written about by Srila Prabhupada and spoken of in ancient scripture. When its members fail to measure up to ideal expectations it is all too easy to excuse it as an isolated, individual failing. But several decades of such 'isolated incidents' have shown that there is indeed a pattern and it requires immediate attention. Remedial measures are urgently required. Failure to act has repercussions for every member of the Society and its reputation; and with loss of organisational reputation comes a drastic loss of public good will.

Let us begin our examination of current ills in need of a remedy by examining the travelling plans of the average sannyasi in ISKCON. Whereas in former times the saffron-clad monk would be a village-to-village traveller, the modern sannyasi is very much an international preacher. There's a reason it has evolved into its present state. From its pioneering years, ISKCON sought to bring Krishna consciousness to all continents. The GBC divided the world into numerous 'zones' and assigned supervision of each to a GBC member. Due to GBC members being occasionally added and subtracted, 'zones' being re-configured or exchanged annually, and a general lack of any long-term, integrated strategy, certain sannyasis ended up with two zones in diametrically opposite parts of the world. When those same sannyasis became gurus they were naturally the first choice for the aspiring disciples of that zone, and after giving initiation they were compelled to regularly visit those parts of the world. It became quite common for a sannyasi to fly thousands of miles every year, at considerable expense.

But before we talk of expenses, let's contrast the life of a sannyasi with another man of God. If our man of God were, say, a Catholic priest he would be celibate, live simply in a house shared with two other priests and preach to the congregation on behalf of the organisation. He would teach the scriptures, perform sacerdotal functions such as weddings and funerals, and engage in pastoral work. He'd be paid a modest amount from the centralised funds of the organisation, and be supplied his clothing and allowance for a holiday. The local congregation would provide him a car plus fuel, and take care of the electricity and heating bills of his shared house. The priest would not charge fees for his teaching, performance of ritual, or solicit donations for his pastoral or confessional services. Funds raised as he went about church business would be submitted to the church.

The ISKCON sannyasi is also celibate and well-educated in scripture, but in contrast is paid nothing by the organisation. He is meant to live, as per tradition, by begging from those he teaches. But whereas in ancient times that meant the ten or twenty villagers he met along his path, in today's ISKCON it translates into the sannyasi's complete freedom to solicit funds from the entirety of the organisation's membership. That fund-raising capability is particularly enhanced if the sannyasi is also a guru. Because he is given nothing, but placed in a position of management, it can pressure him to make calculated, pecuniary 'arrangements' so that his basic needs are covered. In his relationship with his disciples he is more or less pushed into a position of requesting them for regular financial help. Disciples, naturally, are somewhat duty-bound to ensure that their guru does not go hungry. The sannyasi, like the priest, does not charge for his teaching, performance of ritual, or solicit donations for his pastoral or confessional services. And a sannyasi does not normally perform sacerdotal functions such as weddings and funerals. But any other funds he receives as he goes about ISKCON business are often not submitted to ISKCON, but retained by him personally.

# The 'Circuit'

If the sannyasi guru has only a few disciples or supporters located in different places, then in order to secure even his basic needs he will have to travel between locations – and the disciples may have to pay the international air tickets. This leads to him arranging a 'preaching circuit' which, naturally, precludes him from pioneering in new places. Indeed, it has meant that pioneer preaching as an outreach activity of the Hare Krishna movement has decreased in direct proportion to the number of sannyasis who have established their 'circuits.'

In practise, the combination of a sannyasi living in 'poverty' and a large number of willing and helpful disciples with well-paid careers has led to accumulation of personal wealth on a considerable scale. The situation of sannyasis with several thousand disciples, all of whom give regular donations for their spiritual master, has resulted in substantial personal bank accounts for a few renunciates. Somehow, this is probably not the intention of the ancient rule that a sannyasi 'live by begging.'

It has also led to independent temples and 'projects' paid for by the guru's personal assets and registered in his name. Funds are diverted from ISKCON's members towards something that is not ISKCON. The desire for a sense of personal proprietorship, free from the anonymity and regimentation of institutional membership is evident in just how many independent 'guru projects' there actually are. In some countries it can even be said that ISKCON has become the poor sister of the guru's personal enterprise. This can only be described as corruption. By resorting to this behaviour, the sannyasi guru creates separatism during his life and prolonged court cases after his death.

# The absent guru

To teach a systematic course of education and to guide a disciple in their life requires at very least some regular classes and pastoral interviews. In practise, however, this function is performed in ISKCON by local teachers and guides. As the years have progressed the local teachers, many of whom are married, have all become very well educated in Vedic scripture and have devised many of the movement's successful educational courses. Responsible for systematic education in doctrine and practise, life stage guidance, crisis counselling, and spiritual encouragement, and factually the teachers and guides of most ISKCON members, these local gurus – gurus in the real sense of the word - are yet to be recognised as such.

Meanwhile, the disciple, who lives on average three thousand miles from the guru, has to be content with an all-too-brief class or evening gathering with the sannyasi spiritual master, perhaps only once a year. The contemporary guru's role is thus much more inspiration than education. Yet this is also part of a long-standing tradition; most of Srila Prabhupada's 4,800 disciples were trained to read and discuss his books, listen to his recorded lectures on cassette tapes, give each other lectures based on their reading, and to regard this as their primary source of education. They only saw him personally once a year. Consequently this has somewhat persisted in ISKCON as a traditional model of the guru-disciple relationship. But with around seventy initiating gurus now, the contemporary disciple cannot be blamed for expecting slightly more. And many are disappointed that the accessible guru with whom they thought they were forming a relationship is pressed to attend to other work, or to visit rich patrons in the vicinity in order to raise funds for his 'project.'

# Niggling doubts

Consequently disciples often feel under-cared for, particularly if they don't live close to a local Vaishnava community. They may have studies that involved them relocating or a job that prevents them from keeping regular company with devotees. This results in a feeling of alienation for the disciple, and a loss of a sense of belonging. When a faith crisis arises, as it inevitably does, the disciple's daily spiritual practises suffer. The unspoken truth is that those who are factually helping the average disciple go unrecognised and financially unsupported, while the guru is honoured and supported for doing what may, to the disciple, seem very little.

The niggling doubts of one disciple, when multiplied many thousands of times throughout the movement, become a wave of disenchantment which severely hinders the missionary efforts of ISKCON. The reason is obvious: why would anyone remain enthusiastic about enlisting new members when their faith in the movement's ability to help them is so low?

This has led to a poor regard for the governing body generally. That the GBC is comprised of predominantly saffron-clad males, some of whom did not process through family life, has convinced many committed members that their predicament as fathers and mothers of children is neither sympathised with, nor understood. Children's education throughout ISKCON has collapsed, partly due to the widespread child-abuse of a generation ago and the subsequent scandal that broke when the adult victims prosecuted. Many regarded the GBC intransigence in originally dealing with the incidence of abuse as due in part to their lack of connection with the concerns of parents and children. Women's issues, too, are felt not to be a priority for a predominantly celibate male governing body. In this, perhaps ISKCON has something in common with its Catholic counterpart.

Whether or not these accusations are correct, they are the feelings voiced by a significant portion of ISKCON's membership, and as such they cannot be ignored. There is a point at which even a large number of enthusiastic new converts cannot outweigh the discontent of the older, more experienced ones. ISKCON must prepare itself for the future, and for its future healthy growth. Women must be encouraged to take a full role in leadership and management, and family life must be honoured and supported in practical ways. The teachers and guides of ISKCON, the educators, pastoral counsellors and spiritual mentors, must all be valued for the essential contribution they make to members' lives.

## Future church, future problems?

At any one time there are some men on a 'waiting list' to take sannyasa. Due to instability in previous years, no member of ISKCON is allowed to be considered for sannyasa vows until the age of 40 and even then they must be supervised further for between one and five years. Due partly to this policy and better training and supervision, the number of sannyasis abandoning their vows has been minimised.

But there is much more to be done. In order to prevent ISKCON of the future becoming bloated with partially-renounced, under productive and overpaid men in orange cloth there must be a radical re-think of their service engagement within the organisation. Many aspire to become sannyasis because it remains a position of some prestige within ISKCON. The organisation is now affluent enough that by choosing the right locations as part of his 'circuit' the sannyasi can look forward to a later life free from at least the basic struggles of existence.

A surfeit of men arranging their lives in such a way is of no benefit to ISKCON at all. Rather, it takes the entire movement away from its primary focus. While Srila Prabhupada travelled almost single-handedly to every continent and established Krishna consciousness there with just a few disciples, there remain many parts of the world now where the ISKCON movement has no presence at all, even after nearly fifty years. This pioneering effort must be preserved lest we turn into a corpulent and rather self-satisfied church. While it is admittedly difficult or almost impossible to spread the teachings of Krishna in some hostile territories, it is the primary duty of a sannyasi to do this. They must travel and preach.

Yet 'travel' for a sannyasi should not always mean 'international air travel at considerable expense.' Neither does it mean that the sannyasi always has to leave the country of his birth in order to preach. There is more than enough service engagement to do in his motherland, and it is better to employ one's language skills and local knowledge there.

# In summary

In considering all the elements in the life of a sannyasi, the conclusion is that there are well defined codes of conduct and they must be adhered to in order for the renunciate to be worthy of the ashram. Whether he follows the ancient rules of Yajnavalkya Rishi and the other great sages; the Gaudiya Math rules set by Srila Bhaktisiddhanta Saraswati Thakur; or Srila Prabhupada's own, highly charitable and flexible rules for ISKCON sannyasis, he must follow one set of rules – or will otherwise be a sannyasi in name only. Intrinsic to the sustainability of the sannyasa ashram is his ongoing commitment to breaking free from the hold of previous attachments symbolised by comfort, security, and the need for emotional support or sexual contact. Yet all these can be severely compromised in the name of expedience, practicality and the needs of the mission. Status and position, control of money, security of living situation, and emotional interaction with women; these are all problematic for the sannyasi and hence for the faith of those he leads.

When a sannyasi has a surfeit of money at his fingertips, a house that he deems to be his own, and a proliferation of female disciples, it upsets a delicate social contract necessary for *varnashram* to flourish. And spiritually it leads to weaknesses. Either he becomes emotionally or physically compromised, or the disciple does. Many are the young women who have succumbed to the charms of a relatively young renunciate, and of course, vice versa. In ancient times, physical punishment was in order for the sannyasi that broke his vows, and it wasn't a pleasant experience. Thankfully, ISKCON has no plans to introduce any such form of punitive measure, believing as it does – and as its founder-*acharya* patently did – in the value of forgiveness, repentance, remorse and reformation. But prevention is certainly better than a cure: if sannyasis can simply be free to preach, unburdened by the stresses of inappropriate levels of managerial responsibility and the need to secure personal funding, they can act with maximum productivity for the ISKCON mission.

Part Four | Reflections and reforms

# 33

# Reflections and reforms

*If a Jumbo jet filled with passengers fell out of the sky, the event would alarm the world. The air accident investigators would not stop searching until the cause had been found. If it happened again the following year it would result in widespread fear of international air travel. The analogy is appropriate to our subject. Every year for a number of years now, and too often to deny a pattern, one sannyasi guru has 'fallen' resulting in numerous spiritual casualties and a widespread loss of trust. It is therefore a matter of urgency to establish the cause and find a solution. In the course of my research I have had numerous personal interviews with sannyasis and other spiritual leaders of ISKCON. Their conclusions have led to the writing of this chapter.*

**In the spring of 2013, while in southern India, I was introduced to an elderly sannyasi who was presiding over a five-day temple installation ceremony.** He radiated warmth and friendliness, and fairly glowed from a lifetime of personal austerity. I discovered that he was 84 years old, and had taken sannyasa at the tender age of 14. As the head of a large, traditional faith community since his twenties, he'd led an impeccable life of virtuous behaviour, theological study and spiritual teaching and worship.

A few days later I went to see his traditional boys' school, a *gurukula*, where perhaps two hundred boys and youth were learning the Vedas and practising the daily life of Vaishnava *sadhana*. The sannyasi's personal shrine, his travelling altar, was set up inside the main shrine room. I was allowed to come up and have a closer look. There on the altar was the sacred image of Krishna worshipped by the great saint Madhvacharya in the 14th century. The sannyasi was continuing the worship that had been performed by men like him every day for centuries. After eight hundred years the sannyasis of his line were still strong in their practises. Only a handful of men had departed from the strict path of a sannyasi in all that time. Was there anything that ISKCON could learn from this achievement?

It turns out that ISKCON has indeed been learning from a variety of sources - and improving - over the almost fifty years of its existence. The learning experiences have been somewhat painful and would have been perhaps more quickly arrived at had there been more of a tradition from which to learn. After a fitful start to western sannyasa during its early formative years, and repeated sexual scandals during the ensuing years, ISKCON's leaders formed a body for examining candidates for the sannyasa ashram. Known as the Sannyasa Ministry, it was created in 1992 by senior sannyasis, and immediately put in place procedures to assess eligibility of the prospective new monks.

# Checks and balances

How does one really know that a boy of fourteen is eligible to become a sannyasi, and that he will still be one seventy years later? To make a mistake would be ruinous for the boy's life, and disastrous for the faith community. The same question may be asked of those who selected the present Dalai Lama at the age of two.

Believers in reincarnation will understand that some men have a head start in the matter of detachment from material pleasures. Sometimes a man who was a monk in his previous life comes back again. He gets another chance to do good works on the Earth, again as a monk. He brings all the results of his good karma with him, and it is revealed in his strong spirituality, even from early childhood. How can he be identified? This is where astrology, and other arts such as palmistry, can help. Done properly, astrology can reveal both the past life and the future course of the present life. Accumulated tendencies that have already begun to manifest in his current life as *prarabhda* karma will become extrapolated in the current life as strong inclinations leading to almost inevitable actions. The astrologer studies the boy's chart for signs that he has exceptional inclination for the renunciation of sensuality and the spiritual path. In most cases they are right.

ISKCON also employs astrology now, but only as an additional measure to a number of more earthly considerations, the first of all being his age. Not two or fourteen in this case, but 40. The candidate must already exhibit impeccable spiritual practises and be aged 40 or more. If formerly married, he must have made adequate arrangements for the maintenance for his wife and family. He must be prepared to travel and teach, both existing members and the public, and while doing this he must act under the instructions of another, more experienced sannyasi, who acts as his mentor.

The prospective sannyasi must include at least two months every year when he travels to places where the Vaishnava community is not developed. The remainder of the year he travels to existing temples. The governing body of ISKCON, the GBC, receives reports from almost everyone that the candidate sannyasi visits during his waiting period, which may last up to five years. Although anyone with information and feedback may communicate with the GBC, certain members' reports are given priority. The candidate's mentor; the temple presidents of the temples he regularly visits; and a specially-selected 'ten man committee' all provide their impressions of him.

Just as one is given initiation into the spiritual life by a guru, so the candidate will be given initiation into the sannyasa order by an older sannyasi, known as the *'sannyasa-guru.'* The *sannyasa-guru* will also carefully inspect the candidate throughout the assessment period. Finally, he will provide a written report to the GBC. Based on the cumulative response to the candidate's behaviour, teaching and preaching, the GBC will approve him as a sannyasi.

# The 'Dangerous age'

The year 1992 marked a watershed in the history of the sannyasa order in ISKCON. Since that year, marking the beginning of thorough examination of prospective sannyasis, the attrition rate has remarkably diminished. Almost all members of the sannyasa order who took their final vows after that date have been successful. Sannyasis that leave their vows now tend to be those who became initiated into the order before that date. This success rate tends to suggest that that the measures of scrutiny formulated by the Sannyasa Ministry have indeed been the much needed solution to the problem of sannyasis departing from their vows.

However, because the age of sannyasis departing from their vows is now in the mature range, perhaps 55-65, the statistics may also indicate that they are leaving their life of renunciation even after many years. Certainly this is the case in the Roman Catholic Church, where (as one Catholic priest recently informed me) the 'dangerous age is between fifty to sixty-five, because a priest may reflect on his life and decide that he's missed out on a certain aspect of human intimacy and warmth – and he's still not too old to do something about it.'

This 'dangerous age,' as the priest put it, is not confined to the Catholic community. In his autobiography entitled 'The Ochre Robe', Agehananda Bharati, a western convert to Shankara *Vedanta*, writes of his own six-hour interview before he took sannyasa from a swami of the Shankara line. He explained that the swami asked him how he was finding the vows of celibacy. When he replied that he was, at the age of 28, finding the vows 'no trouble at all' the swami replied that the most difficult period would be between the ages of 45 and 60 'when the senses of the body rebel and the mind panics.' At that time, even a controlled person fears that he is about to leave the world without any further opportunity for the gratifications of sensuality or love.

So ISKCON sannyasis are certainly improving in their fidelity to their vows. Yet it is not yet time for breathing a sigh of relief; it will be another twenty years before we know for sure that their success has continued beyond the difficult later years of life.

# When sannyasis become gurus

Both from extensive scholarly research and anecdotal evidence, the increased difficulty for sannyasis seems to come when they have included the role of guru to their many roles. This role, more than any other, increases their contact with women in the form of female disciples and, if they have extensive management responsibility, in the form of female secretaries. Being surrounded by followers normally means financial support along with the sense of proprietorship and entitlement that often induces. The constant positioning of the sannyasi as guru may lead to the 'delusions of guruship' mentioned in a previous chapter.

Naturally, no single element of the sannyasi's modern life: the preaching, travelling, management, leadership, guruship and so on - even the counselling of women and men who depend on him for guidance and advice, or even the regular funding – no one element can be singled out as the conclusive factor that inevitably leads to downfall. But the aggregate of all the factors seems to have contributed to the demise of many – by their own admission in candid interviews.

In sociological research conducted by an ISKCON academic, six former sannyasis who were also gurus explained during frank interviews that the challenges inherent in being a sannyasi were definitely exacerbated by their becoming a guru. They felt that their internal commitment to renunciation was compromised when they received honour as a guru and spiritual leader. When each was asked what were the 'main reasons' for their departure from their vows they each gave a number of clear, definite answers. Their answers have been compiled, in order of priority, as follows:

# Reasons for leaving

1. Immature motivation. Taking sannyasa for the wrong reasons.
2. Ordination while young.
3. Difficulties in personal relationships with peers.
4. Loneliness at a time of difficulty; no spiritual support when they needed it.
5. Lack of role models; a clear social system within which to act, and clear rules of behaviour.
6. The Classical Temptations: Sex, Wealth and Fame.
7. Pride which led to mental and verbal offenses to other Vaishnavas. 'Taking more respect than I was due.'
8. 'Mid-life Crisis.'
9. Excessive self-confidence and lack of preventative measures.
10. Lack of experience of a higher, spiritual taste.

# Solutions and reforms

When asked for solutions, a wide range of former sannyasis, contemporary sannyasis, and a variety of leaders and senior members of ISKCON all seemed to identify roughly the same areas needing improvement:

1. Systematic education of sannyasa candidates and general members as to the behaviour of sannyasis and their respective roles. ISKCON does not have a curriculum for their sannyasis, although most of them are well-educated through their personal studies. The only formal qualification for an ISKCON sannyasi is the *Bhakti Shastri* degree, the same qualification as a candidate for second initiation.

2. Ordination at a mature age, and a mature stage of life.

3. There is need for a *Dharma Shastra*, a guidebook, for modern times. Although there is such a manual for ancient and mediaeval sannyasis, there is need for a handbook that takes into consideration the context of the contemporary world and its new challenges. In particular, the extra pressures under which a sannyasi acts when part of a missionary organization. The book should include rules for eating, travel, housing, company, counselling women, contact with families and children, funding oneself, and saving and spending money, and a reasonable limit on the number of followers.

4. There is need for a healthy organizational culture where undue stress is not placed on a minority of high-status members. There must be support that helps to prevent unhealthy patterns of behaviour. It must be recognised that unhealthy behaviour affects the entire spiritual community and hence its growth, so it is everyone's obligation to contribute to the organisational culture.

5. It is a myth that sannyasis are infallible beings, and a myth that they become infallible after being designated as a 'guru.' There must be a personal counsellor system for sannyasis, and complete confidentiality for them to reveal their minds to their counsellor. In the event of a personal crisis, there must be adequate support and counselling – no public revelations in the spirit of 'transparency' as this was rarely Srila Prabhupada's way.

6. Sannyasis and all members must keep their *sadhana* – their personal spiritual practises – and their *sanga* – their network of spiritual friends, their spiritual company and fellowship – as a priority in their lives.

Part Four | Reflections and reforms

7. There must be ongoing research on existing models of sannyasi behaviour until we are satisfied that we have correctly identified any remaining problems and their solutions.

# The 'Guru problem'

As explained before, sannyasis that also become gurus within ISKCON (as around half of them have done) are subjected to an extra level of responsibility which doesn't always serve the spirit of renunciation. There are many elders of ISKCON who identify not merely a 'sannyasi problem' within the movement but an ongoing 'guru problem.'

It is not that the individual sannyasis who become a guru for their disciples are in themselves 'problems.' They are strong and compassionate Vaishnavas, dedicated to serving Srila Prabhupada and his mission. But the culture of guruship within ISKCON is overdue an adjustment, a fine-tuning that would make it more suited to the noble purpose that is needed. There are certain inherent problems in how ISKCON seeks to train, educate, appoint and supervise those who formally care for the spiritual guidance and welfare of its members. Though problems have been identified and discussed, the remedies have either not been agreed or universally embraced.

Those enthusiastic for reform in ISKCON, including many of the sannyasis themselves, have put forward many suggestions which include, but are not limited to, the following:

1. In ISKCON there is a disproportionate and inordinate level of attention and authority given to the initiating (*diksha*) guru and his charisma, and a corresponding and inappropriate lack of recognition to those who instruct the disciples (*shiksha-gurus*) on a regular basis. This may be simply because of the perspective of the movement's newest members, but it should be formally adjusted. The primary role of sannyasis should be to give instruction (*shiksha*) and the local *grihasta* devotees can give initiation (*diksha*).

2. Sannyasis should be theologians, teachers and preachers, and be less involved in management.

3. Sannyasis who do have their own disciples should limit themselves

to an appropriate number that they can actually care for. When a sannyasi takes too many disciples it can affect his consciousness or result in physical illness. In extreme cases it can be a contributing factor to his gradual spiritual weakness. Sannyasis must be more cautious in initiating and counselling women. They must also be somewhat careful in venturing extensive marital or child-rearing advice, particularly if they have not previously been married.

4. Gurus in general – but particularly sannyasis who are also gurus – should be teaching their disciples how to relate to different categories of local Vaishnavas. They should teach their disciples how to recognise the symptoms of those who are more spiritually advanced, those who are equals, and those who are their juniors. They should teach them to help their juniors, make friends with their equals, and take shelter of those Vaishnavas who are more advanced. Failure to do this has the result of disempowering the relationships that would be of most help to the disciple.

5. The guru himself must give full credit to those who are actually helping his disciples. If he does not then ingratitude may arise within him, and he may develop a critical attitude leading to *Vaishnava-aparadha*, a consequent lack of attraction for spiritual practise and eventually a growing attraction to sense gratification.

6. Despite recent organisational and linguistic adjustments, the guru is still being regarded as one who has been 'certified' as being on a particular stage of spiritual competency. This is not the case. Even though the GBC body makes an arms-length 'no objection' vote that the individual can begin to initiate disciples, this should not be understood as a form of certification. It would be more helpful to its reputation if the GBC had as little to do directly with the 'approval process,' since it is often blamed if a guru subsequently falters. Rather, accreditation of the guru's theologicalcomprehension can be conducted by a GBC-appointed educational board (with the Bhaktivedanta degree as a prerequisite, as requested by Srila Prabhupada); his example of *sadhana* and behaviour approved by committee local to his residence or travelling circuit, and his characteristics as a suitable preceptor ascertained by the prospective disciple, as per the recommendation of *shastra*.

7. Gurus who are sannyasis need to be more careful with their accumulation of 'personal wealth' and should direct funds given

Part Four | Reflections and reforms

to them to an independent entity. At the very least they must be completely transparent with their personal assets and should subject them to public scrutiny.

There are many reforms that are needed within the contemporary Vaishnava community. By identifying what is required, and through helpful and respectful advice, patience, and compassionate dealings, we can all gradually improve, personally and collectively. Perhaps in 800 years the world will not judge ISKCON too harshly for what happened in its first 50.

# Part Five
# Gurus, scandals and issues

## 34

# Why would anyone become a guru?

*When otherwise good people are placed in positions of power over others they often become proud. Pride can lead to temptation and moral corruption, even exploitation. Therefore pride, coming before a fall, is a perennial obstacle on the spiritual path.*

**No wonder, then, that throughout history, people who knew a thing or two about the perilous human condition – and were a little more interested in the spiritual side of life - tried various methods for becoming free from pride.** The trick was to be extremely careful with the trappings and temptations of power. In order to equalize the power differential, religious people sometimes took to vows of poverty, positioned themselves alongside the poor, or became devoted servants of the sick and the needy. Some chose to live in places where there were just no other human beings to dominate: the mountain hermitages and the forests. Meanwhile, the city-dwelling Roman popes, poised before the adoring masses gathered in Saint Peters Square, engaged an assistant to whisper to them that all the adulation was no more than dust. Other reformers, dismayed at the corruption in the organised churches, periodically flattened their institutional hierarchies, and deliberately formed theologies and brotherhoods that stressed equality.

For the aspirant transcendentalist, the pride that may arise from position is regarded as such an intoxicant that even the thought of the respect of others fills him with a strong desire to turn and run the other way. Being honoured by others can immediately fill the heart with pride, and once there, and as long as the honour persists, it is very difficult to remove. Conversely, it is said that freedom from pride is the key to the gates of paradise. Therefore a *sadhu* traditionally avoids anything – and anyone - that may pollute his heart.

Part Five | Why would anyone become a guru?

# A representative of God?

So why would such a genuinely spiritual person allow himself to be respected as a spiritual master? Surely being a 'master' of any kind is one temptation too many? The view of the person who regards himself as a disciple is that the guru is the earthly representative of God, an even greater position than a mere political or intellectual leader. Consequently, the disciple places himself in the lowest position of subordination and the guru in the highest of all positions. The one being honoured as guru then becomes complicit in such a viewpoint. A situation just waiting to become a problem, for isn't absolute power in the eyes of others absolutely dangerous?

On the other hand, for those who are tempted by the prospect of being honoured and served by others, the role of guru acts as a magnet. For them it is a very good proposition. What other institution would guarantee the permanent adoration of other human beings? First in line for the position of guru must surely be the pathological narcissist, for whom being the centre of attention is a deep craving. History is filled with examples of priests, prophets and god-men who, having had a little charisma, bewildered others into following their whims, sometimes with disastrous results. Even worse have been those who had the endorsement of an established religious institution behind their position. But given that not everyone who assumes the role of guru is driven by a desperate need to be surrounded by admirers, or to solve their financial problems, and given that the guru-disciple relationship is so risky - what could be a motive for allowing oneself to be honoured as a guru?

In traditional communities, a senior disciple will only allow new students to regard him as their guru if the predecessor guru has appointed him as such or, in the absence of a clear order, if he is chosen from amongst his peer group as suitable for the task. The most common procedure in the case where there is a singular guru or *acharya* at the head of an ashram or institution is that the guru selects one of his senior students himself. The student must be learned in that school's particular branch of the Veda. He should fully understand the details of the school's philosophical *siddhanta* and be someone who can, through citation of relevant portions of *shastra*, defeat logically any opposing arguments. The disciple must also be a good practising exemplar of the disciplines and rituals of the tradition and someone who has the *anugraha*, the inherent 'grace,' to be able to deal affectionately with people.

The selection of a successor might take place long before the guru's physical passing, or it could be a deathbed decision. The guru then passes on certain hereditary rights to the chosen disciple, along with the right to occupy the seat of *acharya*. On the guru's physical demise, the chosen disciple automatically assumes the role as an act of heartfelt and grateful service to his guru. In other cases, the guru may choose more than one senior disciple, particularly if the school has multiple locations. In the case of Sripad Ramanujacharya, he was chosen by his peers to be the *acharya*, then before his death chose seventy-four disciples to succeed him. They were to teach new students logic, mantras, theology and ritual. They were also to look after the ritual worship in selected ancient temples spread throughout India. They became known as *simhasana-dhipatis* or *acharya-purusas*. Descendants of the original seventy-four still serve in that capacity today, nearly 900 years later. In keeping with the tradition, the family descendants of the original seventy-four gurus give initiation to the family descendants of the original disciples. Both gurus and disciples can trace their lineage back to the 12th century.
In a similar manner, Swami Ramananda (1300-1411), inspired by the teachings of Ramanujacharya, yet not a part of his lineage, chose twelve disciples to succeed him, each of whom was already distinguished by their widespread teaching of the guru's message.

But even in the absence of the guru's clear order, a good disciple wishes to extend the fame of his guru by preserving his legacy and expanding the *sampradaya* by teaching and helping others in their spiritual life. And part of that teaching is the initiation of the student into the mantras and practises of the particular school.

The much-maligned word preacher, or *pracharaka* in Sanskrit, means one who, by his words, exhorts others to raise themselves to a higher level of spiritual practise. Such preaching by a spiritually empowered person produces changes in the hearts of the listener. They become converted to the practise of spiritual disciplines and identify themselves with a particular Vedic lineage. When such an expert preacher produces a number of converts, he solidifies their intellectual conversion by requesting them to take up the daily recitation of a particular mantra. This will empower them to fully comprehend the spiritual nature of the texts and disciplines they've already taken up, and raise their consciousness to the level whereby their newly formed conviction remains strong. Since giving a mantra to a student is termed *diksha* or initiation, it is evident that initiation is an important component of preaching. Since traditional

Part Five | Why would anyone become a guru?

Vedic culture requests that respect be offered to the giver of the mantra, becoming a guru is a natural corollary of preaching.

So the only reason that a saintly person would allow others to view him as someone grandly styled as 'the earthly representative of God' is if he regarded that role as a necessary service to his own spiritual master. Only by being a good disciple can he possess the mentality necessary to be a good guru. And if assuming the role of a spiritual teacher helps him to serve his guru – and if he can do it without becoming compromised – then he will do it. What motivates the humble *sadhu* to act in this way is threefold: his desire to perpetuate the teachings of his own guru, through words and life example; the desire to share with others the experience of having a guru - a treasured experience that he gained from his own preceptor - and to safeguard the legacy of his guru on into the future.

Certainly this aspect of establishing his guru's mission was something important to Srila Prabhupada, since his own preaching was also accompanied by initiating. His assumption of the role of guru and the simultaneous initiating of young converts was a characteristic of his international movement which he began in 1966. However, even before this, when he wrote his *League of Devotees Prospectus* in 1952, he included 'spiritual initiation' as one of the purposes of his new organisation. In a long, alphabetical list of clauses, he outlined what the activities and criteria of membership would be. When he reached (o) he wrote:

> (o) *To revoke the quality of goodness (satwaguna) in every member of the League individually by the process of spiritual initiation (Diksha) by establishing him in the status of a qualified Brahmin (good and intellectual man) on the basis of truthfulness, forgiveness, equality, tolerance, education, purity, knowledge (specific and general) and faith in the transcendental service of Godhead.*

Even though Srila Prabhupada had received no direct order to 'become a guru', he had received the order to spread the teachings of Shri Chaitanya in the English language. To him, initiation was merely a subsidiary aspect of that service, not something separate.

When he wrote his spiritual master a long poem of separation in December, 1958, twenty-two years after his passing, he also commented

## The Guru and Disciple Book

on how his mission was struggling in his physical absence. The problem was, he wrote, that not enough qualified members were preaching and making disciples:

> *"To chant the holy name of the Lord is the explicit command of my worshipful spiritual master. I could never honestly neglect that order. Your greatest acclaim is that you propagated the topmost religious culture. Anyone who accepts the holy name from you becomes spiritually qualified. If all those who attained this qualification were to go out and make disciples then the miserable conditioned souls would all be delivered from this world of birth and death."*

The qualification for 'going out and making disciples,' at least according to Srila Prabhupada in 1958, was merely that the person had received the maha-mantra from Srila Bhaktisiddhanta Saraswati Thakur: *maha-mantre mane yei tara adhikara*. Though his words were designed to unsettle his listeners, Srila Prabhupada sent his eight stanzas to his godbrother, Keshava Maharaja, who duly published it in the Gaudiya Patrika (Volume X, number II) of February, 1959, in time for the disciple's gathering at Vyasa Puja that year.

While most writing on the guru-disciple relationship is written as advice to the aspiring disciple, it is worth considering for a moment the feelings of those who are viewed as gurus. They see themselves as disciples, not gurus, after all, and may be uncomfortable with the accumulated trappings that tend to come along with the guru role. They may have had doubts about their suitability for the task, and it might be with reluctance that they first assumed the role of preceptor. And they may shake their heads in puzzlement at how others regard them. Nevertheless, as the old Indian proverb goes: "When a dancer ascends the stage, she cannot then cover her head out of shyness." A person who has agreed to become a spiritual teacher must then teach, and do it with the necessary discipline required of a master; and if he becomes the head of an institution then he must give instructions, discipline and orders to the members of that institution. But there is still need for natural caution.

Srila Prabhupada's godbrother Bhakti Rakshaka Shridhara Maharaja, who had been initiated in 1926, was somewhat reluctant to take up the role of guru for the new candidates after the passing of his spiritual master. Srila Bhaktisiddhanta Saraswati Thakur had departed the world in 1936 and as a disciple of just over ten years at the time, B.R. Shridhara Maharaja felt it too weighty a responsibility. But there was an incident that moved him in that direction. B.R. Sridhara Maharaja tells the story himself:

> "At that time, when going through the books of Jiva Goswami, I found he had written that those who have money but do not spend it for the Lord, they commit *vitta-sathya*. Similarly those who have some knowledge and experience about bhakti, about Krishna and the devotees, but do not like to help others, they commit *jnana-sathya*. At the same time I had in my memory from my early days a story from the Puranas where it is mentioned that a particular brahmana was a big scholar but he gave no education or help to anyone. As a result, in his next life he received the body of a mango tree which bore many beautiful fruits, but not even a single bird would touch them. Then one day Anantadeva noticed the tree while on his way to see God. When he enquired about it, the Lord replied, "He was a great pandit but he did not instruct or give his share of learning to anybody. He was so miserly in his scholarship that in his next birth he was put in such a position as this tree.""

Another thought came to Sridhara Maharaja:

> "Another thing also came to my mind, that a doctor is not omniscient, but should he not try his best to cure a patient? As much as he has capacity he must try to help, otherwise the world will be at a stand-still. It is not that everyone will say, 'Only if I have complete and full knowledge will I approach to help another,' for that is not possible in this world. Everyone has some relative position. With this also coming to my mind I began in a mild way to help."

What seems to have confirmed his train of thought, and his decision to initiate students, was his pilgrimage to a holy place. One time he travelled to Ekachakra, the birthplace of Shri Nityananda Prabhu. He wanted to pray for permission to take up residence in Navadwipa Dham, the birthplace of Chaitanya Mahaprabhu. While lying prostrate and praying, the thought came to him: "You are praying for my mercy yet you are reluctant to give what you yourself have gained?" Upon his return he had made up his mind. It was 1947, eleven years after the passing away of his guru. He began initiating disciples from that point on.

How Srila Prabhupada thought is quite clear from an incident that took place very early on in his life as a sannyasi. It was a full seven years after his first, unsuccessful attempt to create an international organisation for Krishna consciousness and he was, at that time, 63 years of age. He had been initiated into the sannyasa order by Srila Bhakti Prajnana Keshava Maharaja on September 17, 1959, and shortly thereafter went on a short preaching tour to Agra, Kanpur, Jhansi, and Delhi. Some of the *brahmacharis* from the ashram, many years his junior, accompanied him. At the conclusion of the evening in Agra, the northern Indian town famous for the Taj Mahal, some members of the audience came forward and asked if he, the new Bhaktivedanta Swami, would initiate them. When he agreed to their proposal the *brahmacharis* objected, explaining that only their guru, Keshava Maharaja, initiated new candidates. At the end of the tour he went to see the Maharaja to ask his opinion. When he responded that, yes, he was the one who gave initiation for the ashram and its branches, Srila Prabhupada humorously asked: "Oh, you have got me married, but now I can't have any children?"

Srila Prabhupada returned to his quarters at Vamsi Gopalji temple in Vrindavan. He began translating what would be his life's work, the monumental Srimad Bhagavatam, and regularly took the early morning train up to Delhi for preaching. In 1960 he took a room above a Radha-Krishna temple in the city's Chippiwada neighbourhood. It was there that he often typed for 11 or 12 hours a day.

His next written homage to his spiritual master, entitled *Vaisistyastaka* and delivered at the Vyasa Puja ceremony in 1961, was again a sharp challenge to those in the Gaudiya Mission whom he felt were either deviating from his guru's order, or who were initiating disciples out of their need for personal maintenance and not out of a desire to increase the preaching. After reminding his godbrothers that Srila Bhaktisiddhanta Saraswati had, in order to increase the missionary work, taken the unusual step of breaking with tradition and 'installed his sannyasis in the middle of cities in marble mansions, visited British governors, and even sent them overseas,' he castigates his fellow sannyasis for now sitting comfortably, hoarding money, and increasing the number of disciples 'in the manner of businessmen.'

> "*All these new things that we have fabricated are not our spiritual master's preaching methods. This charade of posing as gurus is the business of the deviant caste goswamis. Everyone has become a*

*sense enjoyer and given up preaching."*

According to these poems by Srila Prabhupada, initiating disciples was expressly for the purpose of increasing the missionary effort, and not for personal gain. It was a selfless act of dedication to the mission of the guru, not a strategy for attracting personal servants or an increased bank balance. In keeping with this view, Srila Prabhupada would initiate disciples and immediately engage them in missionary efforts. So it was that seven years later, in 1966, after several years writing and preparation, he initiated his first western disciples and simultaneously inaugurated his international society.

From his teachings and personal example, Srila Prabhupada certainly seems to have considered the matter of initiating to be entirely congruous to preaching and managing a missionary society. For him the duties of teaching, writing, preaching, travelling, managing and initiating were all equal aspects of furthering the mission of his guru, and he treated them equally as components of his service as a disciple. When he spoke, he spoke as a disciple of Srila Bhaktisiddhanta Thakur; and when he wrote his books he did so as a faithful messenger of his guru's conclusions. When he managed his young ISKCON society, it was on behalf of his spiritual master who always wanted a mission in the western world; and when he gave initiation he did so as a service to his spiritual master, not for any self-interest. Although Srila Prabhupada accepted service from his disciples he remained detached and never became the enjoyer of facilities or status offered by them. In an instant he could rebuke or even excommunicate certain disciples if he felt they had become a threat to his guru's mission. And he regarded his followers as souls sent by his guru to help him in his guru's mission. On one occasion he declared that his disciples were with him in his previous life, and that now: "We are all together again."

So the answer to the question: 'Why would anyone become a guru?' lies, as always, in the capacity of the individual for selfless love and service to his guru, and extending himself with compassion to the next spiritual generation. Becoming a guru for any other reason sets one on the road to ruination. But for service to the guru and his mission one may successfully become the spiritual master of thousands.

# 35

# Gurus of the future

*There is a well-known story of Srila Prabhupada's conversation with an elderly Jewish gentleman while sitting on a park bench in New York. Noticing his unusual clothing the man, a Mr. Ruben, asked him who he was and what he was doing in New York City. Many years later, the same man recounted the conversation: "He seemed to know that he would have temples filled up with devotees. He would look out and say, "I am not a poor man, I am rich. There are temples and books, they are existing, they are there, but the time is separating us from them."*

**The founder-*acharya* of ISKCON had a clear vision of the future of his mission, and envisioned it continuing for centuries beyond his lifetime.** It is no surprise, then, that he would describe his own disciples becoming gurus themselves and continuing the disciplic succession. Far from leaving the order to become guru until just before he passed away, Srila Prabhupada mentioned it many times. Here is just a small selection of relevant extracts from his lectures, room conversations, and letters.

## 1967

> *"I wish that in my absence all my disciples become the bona fide spiritual master to spread Krishna consciousness throughout the whole world."*
>
> **Letter to Madhusudana Das, 2nd November, 1967**

## 1968

> *"I am training you all to become future spiritual masters, but do not be in a hurry...If you immediately become guru, then the service activities will be stopped; and as there are many cheap gurus and cheap disciples, without any substantial knowledge...all*

*spiritual progress choked up."*

**Letter to Achyutananda Das and Jaya Govinda Das, 21st August, 1968**

"Our method is very simple. If one is fortunate enough to meet a bona fide spiritual master and if he acts strictly under his discipline, he also becomes within a very short time another spiritual master."

**Interview in Seattle, 24th September, 1968**

"...Another examination will be held sometime in 1971 on the four books, Bhagavad-gita, Srimad Bhagavatam, Teachings of Lord Chaitanya and Nectar of Devotion. One who will pass this examination will be awarded with the title of Bhaktivedanta. I want that all of my spiritual sons and daughters will inherit this title of Bhaktivedanta, so that the family transcendental diploma will continue through the generations. Those possessing the title of Bhaktivedanta will be allowed to initiate disciples. Maybe by 1975 all of my disciples will be allowed to initiate and increase the numbers of the generations. That is my program."

**Letter to Hansaduta Das, 3rd December, 1968**

# 1969

"...and the next year we shall hold an examination on Teachings of Lord Chaitanya, Nectar of Devotion and Vedanta Sutra, and those who successfully pass will be awarded with the title of Bhaktivedanta. By 1975, all of those who have passed all of the above examinations will be specifically empowered to initiate and increase the number of the Krishna consciousness population."

**Letter to Kirtanananda, 12th January, 1969**

"Regarding your question about the disciplic succession coming down from Arjuna, it is just like I have got my disciples, so in the future these many disciples may have many branches of disciplic succession."

**Letter from Los Angeles, 25th January, 1969**

"So in this disciplic succession, Lord Chaitanya, from Lord

*Chaitanya the six Goswamis, and similarly, coming down, down, Bhaktivinoda Thakura, then Gaurakisora Dasa Babaji, then my spiritual master, then we are next generation, my disciples. So there is a disciplic succession."*

**Lecture in London, 23rd September, 1969**

*"Every one of us should become spiritual master because the world is in blazing fire... So all my students here who are feeling so much obliged...I am also obliged to them because they are helping me in this missionary work. At the same time, I shall request them all to become spiritual master. Every one of you should be spiritual master next."*

**Vyasa Puja address, Hamburg, 5th September, 1969**

# 1971

*Prabhupada: "Yes. All of them will take over. These students, who are initiated from me, all of them will act as I am doing. Just like I have got many godbrothers, they are all acting. Similarly, all these disciples which I am making, initiating, they are being trained to become future spiritual masters."*

**Room Conversation in Detroit, 18th July, 1971**

*"So far naming your child is concerned, you as her parents should give her a suitable name...then when she grows up and takes initiation from a bona fide spiritual master, she may be given a new name at that time."*

**London, Letter to David R. Schomaker, 9th August, 1971**

# 1972

*"Some time ago you asked my permission for accepting some disciples. Now the time is approaching very soon when you will have many disciples by your strong preaching work."*

**Letter to Acyutananda Swami, 16th May, 1972**

*"So we have got this message from Krishna, from Chaitanya Mahaprabhu, from the six Goswamis, later on, Bhaktivinoda*

Part Five | Gurus of the future

*Thakura, Bhaktisiddhanta Thakura. And we are trying our bit also to distribute this knowledge. Now, tenth, eleventh, twelfth... my guru maharaja is tenth from Chaitanya Mahaprabhu, I am eleventh, you are twelfth."*

**Los Angeles arrival lecture, 18th May, 1972**

*"As I am an old man, I am travelling all over the world. Now to give me relief, the GBC members...I shall expand into twelve more so that they can exactly work like me. Gradually they will be initiators, at least first initiation."*

**Conversation with the GBC in Los Angeles, 25th May 1972**

*"So far designation is concerned, the spiritual master authorizes every one of his disciple. But it is up to the disciple to carry out the order, able to carry out or not. It is not that spiritual master is partial; he designates one and rejects other. He may do that. If the other is not qualified, he can do that. But actually his intention is not like that. He wants that each and every one of his disciple become as powerful as he is or more than that. That is his desire. Just like father wants every son to be as qualified or more qualified than the father. But it is up to the student or to the son to raise himself to that standard."*

**San Diego, June 29, 1972**

# 1973

*"To become spiritual master is not very difficult thing. You'll have to become spiritual master. You, all my disciples, everyone should become spiritual master. It is not difficult. ....... Keep trained up very rigidly and then you are bona fide guru, and you can accept disciples on the same principle. But as a matter of etiquette it is the custom that during the lifetime of your spiritual master you bring the prospective disciples to him, and in his absence or disappearance you can accept disciples without any limitation. This is the law of disciplic succession. I want to see my disciples become bona fide spiritual master and spread Krishna consciousness very widely, that will make me and Krishna very happy.....*

*So I hope that all of you, men, women, boys and girls, become spiritual master, and follow this principle. Spiritual master, simply, sincerely, follow the principles and speak to the general public."*

**Vyasa Puja Lecture, London, 22nd August, 1973**

*"Krishna has been so kind upon me to have sent so many sincere disciples to help me push on this movement on behalf of my guru maharaja...I am dependent upon you, my older disciples, to carry it on."*

**Letter to Jayananda, 1st December, 1973**

# 1974

*"I feel happy that after my departure things will go on. I am happy that I have got so many sincere devotees who will carry on. That is my happiness."*

**Letter to Madhudvisa Das, 18th September, 1974**

*"From Madhavananda I have heard that there is some worship of yourself by the other devotees. Of course it is proper to offer obeisances to a Vaishnava, but not in the presence of the spiritual master. It will come to that stage, but now wait. Otherwise it will create factions."*

**Letter to Hansaduta Das, 1st November, 1974**

# 1975

*"All of our students will have to become guru, but they are not qualified. This is the difficulty."*

**Letter to Alanath, 10th November, 1975**

*"You are an old experienced devotee and I have personally trained you in so many things, so now it is your responsibility to train others, otherwise what is the meaning of my training you?*

**Letter to Gurudas Swami, 12th November, 1975**

*"Every student is expected to become acharya. Acharya means one who knows the scriptural injunctions and follows them practically in life, and teaches them to his disciples... I want to see my*

*disciples become bona fide Spiritual Master and spread Krishna consciousness very widely, that will make me and Krishna very happy... Keep trained up very rigidly and then you are bona fide Guru, and you can accept disciples on the same principle. But as a matter of etiquette it is the custom that during the lifetime of your Spiritual master you bring the prospective disciples to him, and in his absence or disappearance you can accept disciples without any limitation. This is the law of disciplic succession."*

**Letter to Tusta Krishna, 2nd December, 1975**

# 1976

*"You each be guru. As I have five thousand disciples or ten thousand, so you have ten thousand each. In this way create branches and branches of the Chaitanya tree."*

**Speech in Mayapura to the GBC members, 1976 (Reported by Hari Sauri, Satsvarupa Das Goswami)**

*"So we got this information from His Divine Grace Bhaktisiddhanta Sarasvati Thakura, and that knowledge is still going on. You are receiving through his servant. And in future the same knowledge will go to your students. This is called parampara system. Evam parampara prap... It is not that you have become a student and you'll remain student. No. One day you shall become also guru and make more students, more students, more. That is Chaitanya Mahaprabhu's mission, not that perpetually... Yes, one should remain perpetually a student, but he has to act as guru. That is the mission of Chaitanya Mahaprabhu."*

**Lecture, 10th December 10, 1976, Hyderabad**

In his recorded lectures, conversations and correspondence, Srila Prabhupada can be heard describing a future when his disciples would accept disciples themselves and continue the succession. And there were other occasions, unrecorded, when he said as much to his senior followers. Jayapataka Swami, Bhakticaru Swami, and Gour Govinda Swami were all given the verbal direction to initiate disciples, always with the proviso that it could only be 'in the absence or disappearance of the spiritual master.'

Yet Radha Govinda Das, later Swami, was personally instructed, not once but twice, to begin initiating disciples. During a personal conversation with Srila Prabhupada in Vrindavan, October, 1977, after asking his guru to accept seven young men from Bihar as initiates, he was told in Hindi: "I am sick now, you are preaching in Bihar, you initiate them." Thinking that he had misunderstood Srila Prabhupada's intention, Radha Govinda returned later with a senior man, Akshayananda Swami. When his guru again heard the request, he became angry with the messenger: "I told him to give. I am not going to give!" After due consideration and further consultation, Radha Govinda Das gave initiation that December, although his action did not come to light until sometime later.

Bhakticaru Swami was initiated in 1977 and went to serve his guru personally. He explains a similar instruction: "I took sannyasa a few months after *diksha*. I went into the kitchen to cook, and at one point Srila Prabhupada said to me: 'So now you are sannyasi, and sannyasi is guru. You can initiate but not while the spiritual master is present. That is the formality.'"

What Srila Prabhupada clearly said to his disciples in 1977 is now unfortunately contested, largely because of attempts by revisionist historians to reconcile his last instructions with the severe disappointments in spiritual leadership that were to begin some years later. It should be noted, though, that there was a consistency in what Srila Prabhupada said, right through the years. Beginning in 1967 through to 1977 he makes it clear: to serve the spiritual master's mission one becomes a faithful preacher and increases the number of devotees. Those devotees are given mantras, making the mantra-giver the *diksha-guru* of the receiver. That is the ancient and God-given method and it is required of all of us to preserve it now so that it may help future generations.

Part Five | The July 9th letter

# 36

# The July 9th letter

*One particular letter written by Tamala Krishna Goswami and signed by Srila Prabhupada garnered a largely undue amount of attention through the late 1980s and the 1990s. For some, it became the 'Final Order' of how His Divine Grace wanted initiations to be conducted in the future. The protagonists of the ritvik theory, somewhat conspiratorially, declared that the contents of the letter had been suppressed or hidden away from the members of ISKCON for many years. This was not exactly correct, however, since in the pre-digital years, much information was simply not widely available or internationally distributed. I personally read that letter shortly after it arrived on the doormat of our temple, and present my thoughts about it here.*

**I was 20 years old in 1977.** An enthusiastic young *brahmachari* monk, I travelled throughout Britain and Ireland in a Ford Transit van filled with Srila Prabhupada's books. There were normally four of us to a vehicle. We loaded up the van on a Sunday afternoon and tried to empty the van of books by the time we returned the following Saturday night.

It was a simple life and involved a certain amount of hardship; sleeping on makeshift platform beds made up of cardboard book boxes, waking up before four o'clock on cold mornings, and bathing in icy rivers. We lived on a simple diet of pressure-cooked rice and vegetables. I don't remember much culinary expertise. Dried dates with butter or cottage cheese, or sometimes marzipan eaten straight from the block, were our occasional delights.

Our spiritual impetus came from the knowledge that Srila Prabhupada would be hearing of our book distribution results within a week or two of our reporting them. He wrote the books and we sold them for him; then he thanked us for helping him give Krishna consciousness to the world. It was a spiritual reciprocation that had us always trying to do more for him. Just knowing that he was somewhere in the world, not only writing books for us and the spiritual benefit of the world, but praying for our welfare and blessing our endeavours spurred us on. We had youthful energy and idealism on our side, and there was fresh evidence every week that his writings were making a difference in people's lives.

We also had a capable and intelligent leader in Jayatirtha Das. Arriving in England from the USA in 1975 with his beautiful and gentle wife Manjuali, he was tall, slender, with long, delicate fingers. Jayatirtha had a Mediterranean complexion from his American-Lebanese parents. He spoke intelligently, had an extensive vocabulary, and was a well-mannered gentleman with a sharp business sense. He had distinguished himself in the rituals of traditional worship while serving the temple deities of Shri Shri Rukmini Dwarkadish in ISKCON's western headquarters in Los Angeles. He had shown himself to be a progressive thinker who got loyalty and practical results from those he led.

He'd also, rather remarkably, been featured on the cover of the *Wall Street Journal*, for his great success at growing the Spiritual Sky Incense Company from a bundle of sticks to more than a million dollar business. It had been Srila Prabhupada's idea that incense could be made and sold by the devotees in order to fund the temples, and Jayatirtha had delivered that from the movement's world headquarters. The journalist noted with some appreciation that although the company's turnover was substantial, the CEO's entire wardrobe consisted only of 'three sets of robes'.

Coming to England, he'd quickly summed up what was required and began a campaign of energetic fundraising, simultaneously restoring and redecorating the temples while inspiring members to explore new, creative methods of distributing the teachings of Krishna consciousness.

And then one sunny, late afternoon in July - it could have been a Sunday - four of us were asked to come upstairs to Jayatirtha's room at the Bhaktivedanta Manor. He wanted to speak with us. His room was at the end of the corridor outside Srila Prabhupada's rooms. The warm sun streamed in through the windows and we sat down cross-legged on the carpet facing him. Jayatirtha was sitting on a cushion behind a low desk. In the sober conversation that took place I remember two things distinctly: the first was that he wanted us to all read personally a letter that had arrived a few days earlier; the second was that he seemed concerned to point out that the contents of the letter would not change our relationship with him.

He passed it to me and I noticed the headed notepaper from the Krishna Balarama Temple in Vrindavan, India. I don't remember him ever sharing any of his correspondence with us either before or after this time, so I presumed the letter was of some extra importance. I scanned its contents briefly before passing it over to my friends. The text of the letter, written by Srila Prabhupada's secretary Tamala Krishna Goswami, was an explanation of how initiations were to be conducted, followed by a list of names of leading devotees, including Jayatirtha. He seemed very serious, slightly uncomfortable, and was at pains to reassure us that: "Things will continue as normal, nothing will change."

At the time I didn't understand why we needed an explanation. He was already a well-known leader in the movement and had been given great responsibility by our guru. Everything he touched seemed to become successful and he was obviously giving great satisfaction to Srila Prabhupada. The letter, as far as I could understand, was simply describing an administrative detail; yet another service that eleven senior and trusted devotees would be doing. I felt proud that our spiritual master had selected Jayatirtha, our local man, to be one of the eleven leaders in the movement designated for extra responsibility.

As it was, Jayatirtha was already acting in the capacity of forwarding names to Srila Prabhupada. On occasions he was even choosing spiritual names for the candidates, a practise that had been in place already for some years. My own name was chosen by another senior devotee and then forwarded to Srila Prabhupada for approval. Sometimes Srila Prabhupada changed the names that others had selected – even on the day of the initiation after he'd read the name out – and at other times he accepted the suggested name. And of course, Jayatirtha, expert as he was at ritual, had already presided at many initiations. So the letter seemed to be describing that the names would not have to be forwarded to Srila Prabhupada for approval. It was a detail, and I was puzzled as to why it required a private meeting.

We filed out of the room shortly afterwards, not quite understanding the full implications of the letter, and never in my wildest imagination could I have conceived that in the remote future the letter would assume for some the status of a final and binding written order.

So we didn't really discuss the 'July 9th letter' at all after that Saturday afternoon. Life was simple. We were all brothers and sisters serving Srila Prabhupada together. Some of us were selling his books in the high streets of Britain, some serving in the temples, and some in leadership positions were receiving letters from our guru.

What happened next was of far greater importance to us. Just a few weeks after the letter had been sent from Vrindavan, Srila Prabhupada came to stay with us at Bhaktivedanta Manor. He arrived on the 28th of August and stayed until the 13th of September. It would be his final visit outside India. His body had visibly changed from when I had seen him last back in March at the annual Gaura Purnima festival in Mayapura, India. His eyes were sensitive to light and his feet swollen. He was physically carried, either in an adapted chair or a wheelchair. He spoke with some difficulty at times.

When Jayatirtha entered his rooms, Srila Prabhupada treated him with more than normal affection. He said: "You are my *tirtha*, and I have come to take shelter of you." The tears fell from Srila Prabhupada's eyes as he embraced his disciple and wet the shoulder of Jayatirtha's cotton shirt.

This display of emotion for those who served him was, at very least, an indication to an observer that Srila Prabhupada loved his disciples and had gratitude for their service and trust in their devotion to him. The fact that some of them occasionally disappointed him, and some severely tested his tolerance, does not alter the fact that he was extremely grateful for all their faithful service rendered over years.

It is a sad fact that after 1977 many of those he trusted would become weakened in different ways and some would either leave his movement or mislead others within it. But even knowing what we know now does not change the fact: that he had a firm friendship with most of his leaders and was grateful to them for helping hundreds of others come to know Krishna. Whatever history does, it should not rob Srila Prabhupada's early leaders of his blessings, or our appreciation of their efforts.

Part Five | The July 9th letter

And the July 9th letter was simply one more way in which the founder-*acharya* was expressing not only his instructions to his leading disciples, but his trust in them. Whatever leadership, sacerdotal or organisational role these named individuals were to play in the future, they would simply do it – as they had always done – as an adjunct to Srila Prabhupada's singular leadership.

That was what it meant to be a servant of the spiritual master. Whatever he asked for, that is what you did – or tried to do, to the very best of your ability. Sometimes his plans would change, and then the entire body of followers would change their plans, too. When he wanted *prasadam* available for all guests at every temple, at any time of day, the entire movement changed to accommodate his desires. It was his movement, not ours. Srila Prabupada was our spiritual master and we were, in every conceivable way, his surrendered disciples. All of us, including the named eleven, were giving our young lives to his service. We ate food only after ritually offering it to a picture of him; we woke up in the cold early morning only for him, and accepted the hardship of approaching thousands of pedestrians with his books so that we could serve him. We listened to his recorded classes and kirtans every day; his photograph graced the vehicle we lived in, the temples we worshipped in, and every book we sold. We were, in effect, acting wholly under his order, acting as his youthful arms and legs.

We felt privileged to be in his movement, the movement that he had started from the very beginning, then guided and shaped. He wrote the books, transmitted the teachings and gave the orders, continually presiding over his often errant followers. Everything in the movement belonged to him: every building, farm, school, restaurant – and every organisational post of authority. He could make or break any of his 'leaders' in a matter of minutes. Wherever power was exercised throughout his growing movement it was because Srila Prabhupada had empowered individuals to do so; they had no power of spiritual or moral authority in their own right. Every action was justified or conducted in the light of a: "Srila Prabhupada said…"

Had I known what would begin to take place just a few years after his passing away on November 14th, 1977, the letter of July 9th would indeed seem portentous, even ominous. But none of us knew what would happen, certainly not the named eleven. The letter was accepted as one more in the series of thousands of letters Srila Prabhupada had written or requested to be written over the previous twelve years. Significant only in that it expressed some administrative details and the chosen men who would be performing a well understood function.

Srila Prabhupada was describing something in the letter that would attract disproportionate attention due to his disappearance just four months later. But nobody thought of the letter as a final instruction of any kind. His illness was serious but he had been seriously ill and recovered before; and it didn't enter our minds that he would depart. Even the thought was inconceivable. In my mind he would recover just as he had done in 1974 when I had first met the devotees. On my first morning with them a telephone call came to give the good news that Srila Prabhupada had recovered from an illness. All the devotees exploded into a spontaneous kirtan. It was one of the things that had first impressed me about them. I thought that, once again, the spiritual master of the Hare Krishnas – now my spiritual master - would again recover so that he could complete his life's work, the Srimad Bhagavatam. Shri Krishna Himself, the Supreme Personality of Godhead, was in charge of sickness and health – surely He would allow His dear most servant to complete his translation?

It is easy now, with the confidence that hindsight often gives us, to imagine that there was a an attempt to pervert the true spirit of what Srila Prabhupada relayed to the leaders of his movement through his secretary Tamala Krishna Goswami. I don't believe it. There was no conspiracy. The letter was accepted as his order, as were all the letters he'd written, but not as the 'final order' concerning initiations. He had already expressed his intentions for the continuation of initiations long before; in classes, commentaries, administrative meetings and personal conversations.

Neither can it be said that the subsequent weakness of leaders should be traced to their defiance of this one letter. As sad and confusing as the next few years would be, the falls of the leaders were due to much more basic, and much more human, reasons.

Part Five | So what went wrong?

# 37

# So what went wrong?

*Srila Prabhupada wanted his qualified disciples to become gurus for a new generation of followers. He told them all as much from 1967 onwards – only two years after he inaugurated ISKCON. By the time of his disappearance in November, 1977, he'd explained the subject many times in lectures, conversations and letters. However, after a few years, even while the movement was prospering, it was clear that something was wrong. Some of those who had taken up the role of guru were abandoning their responsibilities. Dissatisfaction and philosophical confusion were steadily growing – and everyone seemed to have an opinion as to why. What went wrong?*

**One of the less charitable, and rather dramatic, accounts of this period of ISKCON's history runs as follows:** "Immediately after the disappearance of Srila Prabhupada, the movement was divided into eleven fiefdoms, each ruled over by an autocratic acharya who ruled the members in his zone like a dictator. All the '*zonal-acharyas*' had velvet thrones and gold-plated cutlery, while the poor devotees had hardly anything to eat. Because of this oppressive treatment, thousands left ISKCON, and the movement has never been the same since."

Like all revisionist histories, this one requires further investigation to separate the facts from the fiction. There were serious problems for a number of years, that is true, but they were neither immediate nor universal. Some members did leave the movement, for a variety of reasons, yet many more joined. While it serves the purpose of certain campaigners to accentuate the scandals of the era, all the facts should be known before a conclusion can be drawn.

So what did happen? Let's begin by backtracking a little. To answer the question: "What went wrong?" you first have to know what it would have looked like if it all went right. The following facts are generally accepted:

1. According to *shastra* – the scriptures explaining how gurus and disciples live, teach and perpetuate their spiritual culture through history – a guru's disciples will accept their own disciples after their master has passed from the world.

2. Srila Prabhupada wanted his disciples to continue the movement he started.

3. He desired that the movement continue to grow by attracting more new members.

4. He wanted the books, philosophical presentation and strong preaching style to be preserved.

5. He wanted the temple worship to be at least maintained, but improved if possible.

6. He thought that the movement he started could continue not only with purity of disciples' behaviour, but equally importantly, with "Organization and intelligence."

7. At some stage – we don't know exactly when – his disciples would take up the role of spiritual masters for the new members.

8. These new initiates would be 'disciples of the disciples' of Srila Prabhupada, and the next generation of gurus would initiate them on his behalf.

9. Some of his disciples were insufficiently spiritually advanced to take up this role, but he said it was still possible for them to act as gurus if they were 'strictly following.'

10. In April, 1977, Srila Prabhupada says that he will choose some disciples to become gurus; that he was waiting for that, but: "the training must be complete."

11. In May, 1977, he says that future devotees will be 'disciple of my disciple' or his 'grand-disciples.'

12. In July, 1977, he lists eleven names of disciples who will help with the backlog of new candidates for initiation. From then on, names of the new candidates do not have to be sent to Srila Prabhupada for approval, but they can be approved locally by these eleven men. The letter does not appoint the eleven as gurus, it merely appoints them as continental representatives who will perform

that one task in addition to the other tasks involved in the training and initiation of new disciples, many of which they were already performing: preparing the candidates, choosing their spiritual names, chanting on the *japa* beads, conducting the initiation fire sacrifice, asking the candidate to make their vows and handing them their beads.

13. On October 18th, 1977, less than a month before passing away, he refers to the eleven men on this list as his 'deputies' and says that he has stopped initiating 'for the time being,' and that: "I have deputed some of you to initiate," adding that: "If, by Krishna's grace, I recover from this condition I shall begin again."

14. On November 14th, Srila Prabhupada passes away in Vrindavan.

Writing as someone who was there at the time, I must first explain that we were all in great shock and grief when Srila Prabhupada passed from our vision. He'd been everything to us, and now he was gone. Most of us had found it incomprehensible that Srila Prabhupada would ever leave us, or that, if he ever did, it would be at some more opportune time, probably when he had finished translating the Srimad Bhagavatam, and some other books besides. And what about the farms and the *varna-ashram* colleges, the big temple in Mayapur and Krishna consciousness being taken to all the countries of the world? It was devastating to learn that our master and guide would be seen and heard no more. How could we even think of a future without him?

Over the years I have read many inappropriate accusations from relative newcomers that we, as his disciples, were merely experiencing mundane grief, that we were in 'bodily consciousness,' and that we were too neophyte to understand that our guru was 'living still in sound.' Such pseudo-philosophical smugness is not helpful, and is incorrect. As Srila Prabhupada wrote many times, the guru is a physical manifestation who appears before the external senses of the disciple in response to his ardent spiritual desire. He is the external appearance of the *Paramatma*, the Guru within, and that being the case, he is the arrangement by God for the disciple at that time. It is not that the physical manifestation, or *vapu*, is of no consequence simply because the guru's instructions, or *vani*, are more permanent. When the guru disappears the disciple is grief-stricken because he knows he will never be seen in that form again. That particular expression of Krishna's affection upon him is now unavailable. However, his relationship with his guru becomes internalized and the guru's instructions – and his memories of times spent with the guru – become his treasures.

So as November and December turned into January there was an enormous, gaping vacuum – a huge hole in the movement where the acharya had been. Everyone felt it. The Hare Krishna movement that we all knew was a movement with Srila Prabhupada in the centre, at the top, and all around. He was Krishna's representative on Earth and our connection with the spiritual world. He wrote the books, introduced us to an ancient spiritual culture, explained definitions of Sanskrit words, gave enthralling classes, chastised errant members and brought them back in line, opened temples, performed initiations – he did everything and he was everything. Now there was no Srila Prabhupada. How would we go on?

Nature hates a vacuum, and that was probably why we attempted to fill it in the only way we knew. The hierarchical system that Srila Prabhupada set up trained all members of ISKCON to regard their spiritual authority as a representative of the founder-*acharya*. Not only did devotees now expect the highest level of such authority - the GBC body - to keep the movement going as managers and spiritual leaders, they also needed them to answer some serious questions. There were many devotees waiting to take initiation, and at least eleven names had been approved, back in July, to help with the initiation procedure. Were they gurus now? They were something – but no-one was quite sure what. They had been singled out from everyone else - wasn't that an indication of their stature? Prabhupada himself had named them his 'deputies' – but did this indicate that he approved them for the most responsible service – initiation?

# Logical assumptions

This was the first confusion. In May, 1977 Srila Prabhupada said that he would select some of his disciples to act as guru, but by November the only selection that vaguely resembled anything like that was the choosing of eleven to act as continental representatives in the matter of initiation. He had already said for years that disciples could initiate – but not in his presence. And now he was no longer present. It seemed logical, at the time, to connect those two facts: (1) Srila Prabhupada wanted his disciples to have disciples and said that he would choose some to act as gurus. (2) Srila Prabhupada chose eleven of his senior disciples to take responsibility for the entire initiation procedure. It was a simple assumption to make that Srila Prabhupada's passing automatically promoted those eleven into the role of guru.

So they met together and discussed the situation. Various shades of philosophical and organisational understanding were put forward; some of the eleven were reluctant to take up the role of guru, and they spoke up in protest at their unsuitability. Others were rather more interested in taking up the role, and one or two were positively impatient for it. One thing that everyone was agreed on was that a united conclusion was required for the sake of the movement. After all, it was one united movement that Srila Prabhupada wanted, and only one philosophical conclusion was therefore possible. So differences of opinion gave way to uniformity. By early 1978 there were eleven gurus.

## Two powers merge

The second confusion was the merging of the separate and distinct roles of spiritual leadership and organisational governance. Both are positions of power, but they are two different types of power. The first is temporal power – power borrowed from the size and structure of the organisation and the person's position within it. The power is given by the organisation and can be taken away by the organisation. If someone leaves the position, he leaves the power behind him.

The second type of power is spiritual power – a power that comes from deep within the individual and which is evident to others. That type of power needs no organisational position or approval to be manifest. It is neither given by an organisation, nor can it be taken away. If someone leaves the organisation the power will still be there. But it is easy to make the assumption that within a 'spiritual organisation' with a 'spiritual leader' at the head, the two types of power are so closely related that they can be merged, or that one can easily be subsumed within the other. It is also assumed – wrongly – that if a man is a capable spiritual leader he will also be a capable manager; or that a good manager within a religious organisation must also be a man of spiritual gifts. Many organisations throughout history have assumed just that, and have lived to regret it.

When I spoke some years ago to a Catholic priest about the subject he was unequivocal: "Oh, we used to merge temporal and spiritual power centuries ago, but we don't do that anymore. It really doesn't work. If someone is a very good, inspirational or charismatic spiritual leader with a popular following then that, of course, is good for the church. He can have his following, and he can even start his own religious order, but he can't have authority or governance of the church over any territory. And if someone is adept at leadership and has management skills, as well as being an emblem of scriptural understanding and pastoral care, he may take up more of an administrative role in a designated geographical region – a bishop, for instance. But he can't have a following. Neither of them can do both; a charismatic figure can't be in the church hierarchy, and a bishop should not have a following. They're two different things."

# Repeating history

Just before he passed away in 1936, Srila Prabhupada's spiritual master dictated his will, explaining that he wanted: "10-12 members to form a governing body, but Kunja Babu can manage as long as he lives." Kunja Babu was a highly competent manager, and Srila Bhaktisiddhanta once described him as 'the co-founder of the Gaudiya Math,' and was indebted to him for his service. Kunja Babu helped to give structure and systems to the growing organisation, while working as a postmaster and giving his household income to help maintain the mission. He would also raise money from others for the mission. But occasionally a portion of that money would be diverted to his family's needs. Some of the other leading members were concerned about this and went to Srila Bhaktisiddhanta Thakur to complain. His response was direct: "For the work he is doing I am willing to throw thousands of rupees in the Ganga." Later he wrote a letter chastising his disciples for their complaints and extolling the virtues of Kunja Babu. But some time after this he became disappointed when he heard that his disciple was conducting a *smarta shraddha* ceremony for his departed relatives rather than a purely Vaishnava ritual.

The main intention of Srila Bhaktisiddhanta Thakur, indicated by his will, was that there be a collegiate governing body comprised of his established spiritual leaders, and a very capable manager to execute the joint decisions of the body. He said nothing about the selection of one disciple above all others as an acharya for the Gaudiya Mission. However, after his departure, the letter he wrote in defence of Kunja Babu and his protective stance towards him seems to have swayed opinions. A section of disciples became convinced that Kunja Babu – who later became

## Part Five | So what went wrong?

Bhakti Vilas Tirtha Swami – had attracted sufficient approval from Srila Bhaktisiddhanta Thakur to merit him being particularly favoured above others. The governing body had their first meeting, and immediately disagreed on how the empty seat of the acharya should be filled, and who that person should be. Managerial expertise – one type of power - and projected spiritual authority - another type of power – became fused into one person, and some time later Kunja Babu became the acharya of one branch of the Gaudiya Math.

What would the Gaudiya Mission have looked like if the last will of its founder had been carried out? Certainly Kunja Babu would have been managing "as long as he lives," (he lived until the 1970s) and there would have been a collegiate governing body. There were eighteen sannyasis and many of them were highly learned, dedicated souls. Certainly ten or twelve of them could have formed such a body. Governance is defined as making sure the organisation does what it was formed to do, and management, taking its instruction from the governing body, then ensures delivery of organisational goals.

But there were other, major problems with the Gaudiya Mission soon after the departure of Srila Bhaktisiddhanta Thakur. Another popular figure, a scholarly leader known for his learning and proficiency in Sanskrit, chose to become affiliated with another Gaudiya group which prided itself on its 'tradition' and 'orthodoxy.' During the lifetime of Srila Bhaktisiddhanta Thakur this group had decried many of his missionary innovations, even to the point of challenging the authenticity of his *parampara* lineage. Surprisingly, there were a good few members of the Gaudiya Mission that were swayed by the arguments of the scholarly leader, and they followed him right out of the organisation.

So there are two types of power. Two different types that, as is evident from history, we should not be tempted to consolidate into one. But had not Srila Prabhupada amalgamated those two types of power in his own life? Had he not been the spiritual leader and the ultimate managing authority – and been both expertly? He was both a genuinely charismatic leader, and managed his movement with good planning and fiscal expertise. And he'd trained his men to do that, too. It's true that at first he'd actually divided the roles: the married men would form the governing body, the GBC, and the sannyasis would travel, preach and inspire the devotees, and do pioneering work in new places, suggesting to the GBC where new temples could be opened. After some time, several householders took to the sannyasa order and kept their GBC positions, and other sannyasis joined the GBC, making the GBC predominantly saffron. Many of the chosen eleven were, in fact, already both GBC members and sannyasis. Their already-existing dual identity probably helped to confuse the situation.

The founder-*acharya* had divided his Society into continental zones for the purposes of administration, and also instructed that this same zoning would make the initiation process easily facilitated. "Whoever is nearest," was his remark when describing who would process candidates through to initiation in the future. So it wasn't entirely a surprise when the new gurus concluded that they were now not only managing a zone as a GBC, but would be responsible for initiating all the new members there, too. They may have had a legitimate sense of territorial ownership due to their managerial responsibilities, but that carried over into a subtle sense of entitlement regarding the local members. While that is a natural consequence of regular interaction between a spiritual leader and others, it is a relationship that can never be presumed.

When someone takes up the work of governance and/or management in an organisation, he takes on a *position* within that organisational structure. When someone acts as a guru, however, he takes on a *role* for specific people – and only those people - who regard him as their teacher. Not everyone will regard him as their teacher, indeed, not everyone will even like him, but everyone must regard him as a regional manager. His position is a matter of organisational pragmatism and his role a matter of personal conviction.

That subtlety was apparently lost in the confusion, grief and general clamour of the movement at that time. The result was that the gurus, sometimes drawing on their considerable organisational power, slowly, gently, asserted their position – or had their position asserted for them by willing followers - so that the 'guru for this zone' became the only person one could even imagine as one's guru. And from there it was only a short time before followers began to insist that *all* new candidates for initiation *must* regard the zonal guru as their personal guru. Not surprisingly, not everyone liked that. The peers of the new guru were not always happy to see such a consolidation of power and an enthusiastic following of impressionable new members regarding the new guru in an idealised way. And the new members sometimes became initiated by the 'zonal guru' against their better judgement.

# Eleven gurus, eleven acharyas

Meanwhile, the third confusion was slowly taking place. Srila Prabhupada had termed himself the 'founder-*acharya*' of ISKCON, a compound title that first appeared in 1933 in an English language Gaudiya Math publication, published to accompany the Indian sannyasis on their preaching expedition to London. The word acharya refers to one whose life is a living example of what he teaches and, in traditional practise, he is the head of the ashram where he and his disciples live. But over the centuries, as the ashrams grew into much larger, multi-branched collectives, the word also became adopted to describe the spiritual head of a much larger institution. Srila Prabhupada was a guru, and he was an acharya. Now ISKCON had eleven gurus. Were they not also acharyas? In their zones they were both the administrative and spiritual heads. *Ipso facto* they were *zonal-acharyas*. In some cases, as the years went by, the new gurus shared in their spiritual master's terminology by styling themselves (with business cards, publications, posters, and headed notepaper) as the *present-acharya* of their zone.

Human beings being what they are, sometimes the *'present-acharyas'* would have disagreements with their fellow acharyas, and sometimes these disputes became common knowledge amongst the disciples of each guru. It wasn't long before some unhelpful feelings of enmity set in between the disciples living in different zones. If their *zonal-acharya* was an absolute authority who disagreed with the other fellow, then the other fellow could surely not be an absolute authority. As the years went by, ISKCON sometimes felt like a loose confederation of eleven distinct movements rather than a single, united mission.

The fourth confusion was very similar to the third, but deserves a separate mention. If Srila Prabhupada was a bona fide guru, and a bona fide guru is a pure devotee of Krishna, then the eleven gurus – particularly because they were 'bona fide', having been chosen by Srila Prabhupada - must also be pure devotees of Krishna. The understanding of pure devotion was not very nuanced at the time. Pure meant completely pure, and utter purity might also include seeing Lord Shri Krishna face-to-face, and probably every day. There was no limit to the disciple's imagination. In their newly-converted zeal, the disciple's saw immense spiritual qualification in their new gurus, and the new gurus felt it was their duty to not deny their disciples faith in them. But both disciple and guru, in their unwitting mutual complicity, were setting themselves up for disappointment.

With hindsight it is easy to find fault with the line of thinking of the day. But it had a lot to do with the clear-cut way the disciples had been trained. Srila Prabhupada had made a clear distinction for them between a 'bona fide guru' and a 'bogus guru.' If a man wasn't a bona fide guru then he was 'simply bogus.' By an extension of this logic, if a man was not bogus then he was bona fide. It was quite simple. A spiritual teacher had to be one thing or the other - there really wasn't anything in between. And if Prabhupada had personally selected eleven of his disciples out of 4,800 – for whatever purpose he'd actually chosen them - how could they be bogus?

Srila Prabhupada had taught his disciples what pure devotion was, how pure devotees behaved, and how to honour a pure devotee. At the time, of course, that described him, and only him. And any honour due to a pure devotee had been given to him. And it had increased over time. He'd gradually become elevated in status and title as his following grew internationally. He began as simple 'Swami-ji' with a few beatniks and bohemians in a depressed neighbourhood of New York, and went on to become 'Srila Prabhupada' of thousands around the world. Along with his status went all the ceremonials and the accoutrements that would engender respect from young followers and consolidate his position into the future.

# Long names, chairs and flowers

Although his movement was centred on Shri Krishna, and although he had objected to other contemporary spiritual masters naming their organizations after themselves, Srila Prabhupada did, in fact, arrange the liturgy and style of his movement so as to make his person the primary focus of the members' attention and devotion. In a departure from his own guru's daily liturgy, he inaugurated the glorification of the guru as the first song in the temple's day. The *Shri Gurvastaka* is a song of eight verses extolling the spiritual credentials of the guru. After the *japa* meditation period came another central ceremony where Srila Prabhupada's framed portrait, installed upon his official seat within the temple, was offered flower petals while the disciples sang another glorification of the guru. Wherever he was personally in the world, Srila Prabhupada would be honoured by this daily guru *puja*, and the singing of the song *Guru Vandana* by Srila Narottama Das Thakura. These two components of the daily liturgy helped to solidify his central position in

Part Five | So what went wrong?

the life of all his disciples, as did the other key elements.

He had a long name, in keeping with Sanskrit tradition, that included his titles and honorific nomenclature such as the English expression 'His Divine Grace.' His title of founder-*acharya* was to be included on any publication, notepaper, poster and sign-board that advertised his ISKCON. His portrait photograph was included in the frontispiece of every book published in his name, and was featured on every altar in every temple and on the large seat – the *vyasasana* – at the rear of every temple. That seat of the guru, often built gorgeously over-sized by enthusiastic disciples, was the focal point of daily worship for all members.

In all this he acted to nurture the developing faith of his followers and so that they could consolidate into a unified and sustainable movement. Disciples needed to worship their guru on a daily basis to achieve *guru-nistha*, the faith in the guru that the Upanishads declare as essential for spiritual revelation. Traditionally this was done in the home, as part of domestic worship, but because all his followers lived communally it was conducted congregationally. So he taught them how to do it. And it was a daily symbol of his headship of the movement that gave unity and strength to a growing, disparate following. For as long as the Hare Krishna movement was identified with him, and the books published were his, it would be his movement, teaching what he'd learned from his guru and coming in line from Shri Chaitanya Mahaprabhu and the acharyas. ISKCON was his service to his guru and he wanted it to last as long as it needed to give all an opportunity to know Krishna. He thought in terms of centuries.

Yet with his passing came a 'transference of charisma' to certain disciples; and with that came an expectation that they would also inherit all the components of status he'd assembled for his legitimate position as the founder-*acharya*. And this was the fifth confusion: to imagine that all gurus, simply because they were gurus - and bona fide gurus at that - should be offered respect at this level, and that too in public, and by all members.

So in came all the accoutrements aforementioned. Large seats, just shy of the height of Srila Prabhupada's *vyasasana* were installed in ISKCON temples; zonal guru photographs were added to the line of acharyas on the temple altar; honorific titles were adopted, and daily guru *puja* offered. This last addition, made compulsory for disciples and strongly recommended even for the zonal guru's peers, was to prove too much for some. It was difficult enough being a member of an organisation that had lost the physical presence of its founder-*acharya*; difficult that the movement had almost become fractured into eleven, competitive divisions; and even more difficult to see the polarization of Srila Prabhupada's disciples into those who were honoured as gurus and those who were not.

What was almost intolerable for the large majority of Prabhupada disciples was that they felt forced to have to adjust to the daily honouring of their peer, or to otherwise become ostracized by the fast-growing section of new members. Although there was no scriptural obligation to do so, there were growing social pressures to comply in the name of unity. The new guru – their erstwhile brother - was also in charge of where funds were directed, leaving his peers' domestic maintenance dependent on his goodwill. To be ostracized by the new disciples for being insufficiently enthusiastic could have stark financial repercussions for a disciple of Srila Prabhupada and his young family.

It was the push that some needed to leave their spiritual master's movement. Many had already left as natural attrition took place in the mid-seventies and early eighties. Some left to restart their education, and some to develop careers to support their young families. Others felt that monastic or community life was no longer for them; some simply lost their faith, while others felt that ISKCON without the presence of Srila Prabhupada was no longer what they wanted. But for quite a few – certainly not 'thousands' as the urban myth tells it – the reason they left was because things were changing and they didn't like the changes they saw.

Part Five | Their father's shoes

# 38

# Their father's shoes

*The saintly devotion of the founder-acharya of ISKCON made him 'one out of many millions' as the Bhagavad-gita puts it. His scriptural learning, his proficiency of Sanskrit, lifetime experience and unlimited determination and energy all meant that no-one could possibly do what he'd done. He'd started an entire religious movement, internationally, and at an advanced age. Yet his followers had to somehow carry on and preserve what he'd started.*

**And that was the real issue - eleven young men had stepped into their father's shoes.** They had all done great things under his guidance, and now they had the burden of the entire movement on their young shoulders. Yet some of them had only been practising devotees for eight years, and all of them for less than ten. One or two of them were still in their twenties. Although spiritual maturity is not congruous with physical years, and though youth can be a time of great spiritual revelation and accomplishment, they were all remarkably inexperienced.

Still to come was the temptation of having hundreds of young followers, all of whom would treat them as gods on earth. To come, too, was the lure of having wealth at their disposal, and women who idolised them. And later on, waiting silently for them, was mid-life loneliness, the barren spiritual desert, and the 'dark night of the soul.' With few peers who completely trusted them or who would speak directly to them, and no-one above them, it was no wonder that some later faltered on their path.

I don't believe for a moment that they were insincere in their purpose and dedication to their spiritual master. But it was specifically because he was the only example of guru they had ever known, that when it came their turn, they simply did whatever he had done. They spoke like him, acted like him; they were honoured like him – and accepted that honour in the name of duty, their service to him. They sat on distinctive seats, ate specially-cooked meals, and were driven in nice cars. Theologically, they thought they were doing the right thing, that this was Vaishnava culture. Organisationally, they felt they were helping to preserve their master's legacy. It was naive, it was imitation, but he had shown them everything and it was all they ever knew. It was all anyone knew.

Even by material estimation, it was impossible for a small group of young converts to remotely approach Srila Prabhupada's level of life experience, religious culture and dedication – what to speak of devotion to Krishna. He'd passed away after eighty-one years of life, being born into a Vaishnava family and living the culture throughout all that time. He'd lived through two world wars, mass starvation under the British, the horrors of India-Pakistan partition and three heart attacks. He'd been a devotee of Lord Krishna since his birth, but his devotion had been tested throughout his life. He'd seen his spiritual master's once vigorous India-wide movement break-up into small, pedestrian factions, and so committed himself to deep seclusion and study for eight years, then laboured hard with no financial support to write his own books and have them published. While selling his books in India he'd been gored by a bull, and after an arduous voyage to America he'd had his manuscript of Bhagavad-gita stolen, all the while experiencing a freezing cold winter. He had no money, no warm clothes, and no friends. Then, in the second year, they started to come.

And they never stopped coming. The speed at which his movement grew was remarkable. Young people flocked to hear him and took up an austere life, dedicated to a God their mothers and fathers never knew. It was nothing short of a modern miracle. To transplant an entire religious tradition based upon something as otherworldly and refined as devotion to Krishna, and to take it all over the world, and to do that in a mere twelve years - was completely unprecedented. One scholar commented that it was the first time since the days of the Roman Empire that a complete religion had been transplanted from east to west; and another remarked that only one person out of many millions could have done what Srila Prabhupada did.

# Ignored warnings

It was always going to be difficult to step into his shoes. But with the novice's perspective of "a guru is a guru," that is exactly what was attempted - and expected - by the new generation of members. It could have been very different; we were warned, but failed to listen. In 1978 a sincere, well-reasoned appeal was written by Pradyumna Das, Srila Prabhupada's Sanskrit editor, whom he affectionately called 'Panditji.' He was knowledgeable about Vaishnava tradition in India, and was very concerned about how things were quickly developing. He circulated a letter to the entire Society imploring them to scale down the new guru's positions to something more in line with the culture of traditional Gaudiya circles, particularly the mission of Bhaktisiddhanta Thakur. The large seats were inappropriate, as was the daily public *puja*, and so many other details that served to elevate the new gurus above their peers.

But the letter was not appreciated. In fact it was misunderstood and treated with some disdain. The author of the letter seemed to be suggesting that ISKCON adopt some of the culture of the Gaudiya Math, but was it not members of that organisation who had complained about the adoption of the title 'Srila Prabhupada' and had not co-operated with the Society at all, not even to wish it well? What had ISKCON to learn from such people? Inside ISKCON, there were still others who challenged the status quo. They wrote and distributed thoughtful papers, magazines and personal letters. In their frustration, some less-thoughtful members fell to creating new philosophies to explain the situation and to offer possible remedies. It was to be quite some years before the movement's leadership would take a serious look at how things had developed, and even longer before any alterations were made.

# Two lines of authority

With hindsight, it is very easy to say that we all should at least have waited. Perhaps five years until the first new initiation would have been sufficient a period for things to become adjusted, better considered and prepared. But Srila Prabhupada had set the pace. For him, initiation was something that took place six months or one year after a person joined the movement. There was a sense of urgency; time was limited. Of course, for men in their twenties and thirties, with a considerable amount of time ahead of them, five years would not have been too long to wait. But the idea was simply to do as Srila Prabhupada had done – and to initiate as he had initiated: with a sense of urgency.

So that was how, from 1978 through to 1986, eleven young men initiated hundreds of new devotees. For certain they felt they were doing it on behalf of Srila Prabhupada, but also for certain they succumbed to a sense of proprietorship over those new members. When their troubles started to appear, corrective measures were gradually introduced. The exclusive furniture was removed and their even more exclusive authority challenged. One *zonal-acharya* along with hundreds of followers was excommunicated. Members of ISKCON could now become initiated by any guru they pleased, wherever they lived. More persons were added to the list of initiating gurus. Eventually the long names disappeared from the public eye, and there was a sense that something of a reform had taken place.

But the fusion of the guru role and the management position persisted, as it does until this day. Some gurus still draw temporal power from their management position, or bolster their management capability by drawing on their guru role. In effect, ISKCON is a matrix of two interlocking cultures: one is the relationship-based culture of guru-disciple; the other is the administrative apparatus of a missionary organization. Both are essential aspects, yet they serve different and, yet mutually supportive functions. It may be more helpful to the smooth running of ISKCON if these different functions are carefully identified, then somewhat separated and allowed to flourish independently.

In the time-honoured spiritual culture of the Vedas, the relationship of guru-disciple is regarded as essential. The guru always thinks of the spiritual welfare of the disciple, and the grateful disciple always cares for the physical welfare of the guru. This may include arranging for his food, water, fuel, clothing and shelter, and sometimes his transport. In the modern world, with its sophisticated financial systems, the disciple may simply serve the guru by providing funds directly. ISKCON upholds the guru-disciple tradition but it does so within the framework of an international organisation. Like other organisations, ISKCON has to make provision for its religious teachers. Accommodation, food and clothing, and transport need to be provided in return for a clearly defined set of duties according to the post. Sometimes, and only in sacrificial amounts, discretionary funding is also provided.

So ISKCON provides for those who encourage, guide and inspire its members. It would not survive long if it didn't. Yet those teachers who are also acting as gurus may be provided both essential resources for their personal maintenance and a stipend: once by the ISKCON organisation, and again by their personal students. The funds given by grateful disciples are sometimes very considerable amounts and are often held in private bank accounts or diverted towards the guru's personal projects, buildings, campaigns and so on. Although valuable and spiritually motivated, these projects may not be carried out in the name of ISKCON. In effect, this means that the guru then acts as the head of a competitive organisation. With seventy or so gurus and their disciples numbering tens of thousands, this means that ISKCON is unwittingly creating many such affiliated but alternative organisations, each with a charismatic figure at its head. The disciples may also experience conflicted loyalties; on the one hand to ISKCON, and on the other to their guru's personal endeavours or organisations. The result is a lack of unity and common purpose within the organisation.

Because the organisation has created a role where too much power is consolidated in one person – and remains so until this day - the organisation consequently feels compelled to limit the power of the guru by controls exercised by the Governing Body. Much of this is done only before the person becomes a guru; once that person is a guru the organisation, curiously, provides comparatively little direct supervision. The guru is still too powerful a figure, and too influential in the lives of members, for such control to be welcome. Instead of regarding the guru as a teaching role, the guru is seen as occupying an exclusive leadership position within the organisation. As such, it is more difficult to regulate an institutional leader than it is to moderate a preacher or teacher's behaviour. Indeed, regulation of the guru is often perceived - by both guru and disciple - as destructive of faith, the very personal conviction that motivates so many thousands and inspires them to serve the institution for free.

Controls exercised by the Governing Body would be more effective if the Governing Body were not constituted predominantly of members who also function as gurus. With all the best intentions, the very composition of the Governing Body means that regulation of the gurus is an exercise in self-regulation of the powerful and human history shows that those in power – even with the very best of intentions - often fail to regulate themselves. Thus there is a glaring conflict of interest which remains unaddressed.

# "ISKCON approved"

A collective desire to restrain the perceived excesses attached to the guru role seems to have inhibited ISKCON from expanding the number of gurus. The logic of this may be that the lower the number of gurus, the lower the potential for future problems. However, for an educational movement, where the role of the teacher, counsellor and pastoral worker is essential, this would seem to be counterproductive. There is yet another problem. In ISKCON of today, one does not take up the role of guru without majority approval of the Governing Body. Candidates are first approved by a ten-person body of local peers, and then their name is submitted to the international GBC body for approval. If there are no objections within six months then the GBC acknowledges that the candidate can initiate ISKCON members. This raises a problem, since all gurus approved under this system come with what amounts to an 'ISKCON Approved' status. If and when the guru falters, the criticism is levelled at the GBC for 'approving' such a fallible candidate. The GBC – the governing authority of the entire movement – then suffers a tremendous loss of credibility, and a consequent drop in its perceived trustworthiness. And the ISKCON organisation also suffers if its ultimate authority is deemed to be untrustworthy.

Vaishnava scripture repeatedly asserts that it is the candidate for initiation who 'approves' the guru. Indeed the person is not even a guru unless accepted as one by the candidate. It is a question of personal faith, not an organisational position or official approval. Scripture states that the aspirant disciple must reside with the prospective guru for one year to ascertain his qualities; similarly the guru may assess the aspirant. In present-day ISKCON this, too, is problematic. Because of the dual-function of the guru, and because so many are sannyasis, the guru may be resident thousands of miles from the aspirant disciple, or may be travelling much of the year. So the aspirant never really gets to make the examination critical to an informed choice of guru. This breeds a dependency on the organisation to do it, further compounding the problem.

In practise, the huge geographical distance between guru and disciple – let alone the aspirant disciple and prospective guru – makes for very weak connections between both. The educative component of the guru's role is also not helped by these distances. And since the guru-disciple relationship is one of the essential ingredients for a healthy spiritual life, it means that many ISKCON members may feel spiritually weak, under-educated and vaguely uneasy about their rate of progress. It also means that they become prone to urban myths – especially ones about ISKCON gurus. Which brings us right back to the beginning.

What went wrong is that a series of simple, yet classical, theological and managerial errors were made, which then became compounded, one on the other. The young followers of Srila Prabhupada did not know history – so they repeated it. It took some time for the initial mistakes to be understood and corrected, and ISKCON is still trying to deal with the long-term legacy of those early years. Over time, various ill-conceived myths have been perpetrated in an effort to explain previous mistakes. I hope I have dispelled some of the more colourful ingredients of the mythology that, at times, surrounds ISKCON. There are a few strands of fact, with a lot of fiction added for journalistic colour and the art of storytelling. And for every person in the short history of ISKCON who has responded to the pushing of desires or weakness brought on by temptation, there have been many millions of kind, uplifting and compassionate actions by truly good people. I just hope that someone tells their stories some day.

There is always a tension in the spiritual life, suspended as we are somewhere between this world and the next. And there is even more tension involved in balancing the life-enhancing personal relationship with a guru, with the necessities that come along when we play our part in this great collective effort to offer *Krishna-bhakti* to the world. It is a wonderful life if we can be involved in any way with the great work of His Divine Grace A.C. Bhaktivedanta Swami Prabhupada. We constantly strive for balance between the often oppositional forces of organisational membership and personal freedom, but we do so in the knowledge that we will be blessed by Krishna Himself for our efforts, and that we ourselves, and ISKCON, will ultimately be successful.

# 39

# Diksha Lite:
# Initiation without all the fuss

*Diksha is when a mantra is given to a disciple along with a set of disciplines. Disciplines are the rules that support the practice of chanting the mantra and enable the adept to gain the most benefit. Some unscrupulous gurus sell or give out mantras without explaining any of the rules - with disastrous results. Over the years I have seen rather a lot of it. So I wrote this piece.*

**Did you hear the story of the man who rode his tricycle up to the gates of a temple in Mayapur, West Bengal, to sell ice-cream?** He had one of those tricycles you see a lot in India – the ones with a refrigerated box on the back. There is nothing that sells quite like cold ice-cream on a hot day. But this particular man wasn't selling ice-cream at all.

He opened the lid of the ice-box, pulled out a hand bell and a bunch of papers, and then began ringing the bell calling out: "*Diksha*! *Diksha*!" or "Initiation! Initiation!" He was selling '*Diksha*' and, as it happens, was selling it very cheaply: "*Diksha doh rupya*" or: "Initiation - two rupees!" People gathered around, examined the papers, and handed their money over.

Such *dikshas* are commonplace in India. For a fee, a certificate of initiation is handed over, like a title deed bestowing a certain spiritual status and religious community identity rights. A person receives a blessing and becomes an '*adhikari*' or 'one who has been awarded the right'. For a relatively modest investment of cash, you too can be a more qualified person than you were yesterday. What's slightly more important is that you can tell others about your improved social status too. Your *Diksha* Certificate, signed in ink by the guru, can also get you into certain places and is very handy when you want to go to particular assemblies or

## Part Five | Diksha Lite: Initiation without all the fuss

festivals.

Over here in England, we have a very long history of mankind's basic urge to own such deeds of entitlement. One of the formative episodes in the history of our nation was the Norman Conquest. Although it's hard for us English to talk about any time when we've been beaten by the French, every English schoolchild knows the date of AD 1066 when the northern French invaded Britain, defeated King Harold in the Battle of Hastings, and never really went home.

The victorious William the Conqueror commissioned the 'Domesday Book', a record of every village and field in the land. He then proceeded to apportion those villages and huge tracts of land to all his friends, bestowing upon them ranks and titles according to their respective landholdings. Thus the English aristocracy was born, with all its lords, earls, dukes, barons and viscounts. Even today, nearly a millennium later, a mere 200 English families still own half of the land in Britain. Yet over the centuries, many of the smaller aristocrats sold off their lands, holding on to only their hereditary title. Still later, even the titles were sold, bestowing upon the purchaser the distinction of a powerful, traditional name, but with no land, and no factual wealth or power.

Thus today, for a mere £3,500, you can become known officially as Baron Such-and-Such, the Baron of three villages – but without owning the villages. You'll receive an attractive, elaborately hand written declaration scribed on vellum, sometimes dating back 3-400 years. You'll have the legal right, under British law, to have others refer to you by your new name and to sign yourself as such on all official documents.

Yet as for the land ownership that the title originally conferred on its owner, you'll see none of that. No serfs will doff their caps as you ride your white horse into 'your' village. You won't get any tithes of the harvest either. Indeed, you won't have any power over anybody or anything, save and except the power to look up from your sofa and gaze at your nicely framed certificate proclaiming your membership of the English aristocracy.

Why am I giving you this English history lesson? Because just as powerless peerages are being sold on the internet, conferring nothing on their owner but a new name and smug satisfaction, so *'diksha'* is now being sold for a few pounds – or sometimes nothing at all – conferring only the notion of spiritual or religious attainment.

*Diksha*, or the process of being enlightened with transcendental knowledge and committing oneself to the spiritual path under the guidance of an authentic teacher, is not something that can be purchased out of a cold-box on the back of a tricycle. Its real price is commitment, demonstrated not only by an intellectual adjustment to one's belief system, but some form of voluntary restraint and the acceptance of discipline as an essential part of the efforts required for inner growth. As in all areas of life: no pain, no gain. Such personal austerity, or *tapa*, is said to be the factual spending power of spiritually progressive people. *Tapa* is the 'wealth of the brahmanas.'

When Brahma, the original created being within the universe, was perplexed as to his origin and true identity, he tried by his own efforts to discover the Truth. It was only after he heard the divine syllables TA-PA echoing from beyond the universe that he was able to comprehend that he should engage in meditation.

In classical Vaishnavism, the guru does not award *diksha* unless and until the prospective disciple has demonstrated some personal *tapa*. Rising early, taking cold water bath, eating frugally from a diet regulated by vegetables, fruit and grains, engaging in menial service, abandoning sinful acts, and placing oneself at the beck and call of the spiritual master – all these are prerequisites for *diksha*. Without *tapa* or *tapasya*, actual *diksha* cannot take place. Even if the external formularies are conducted and titles awarded, no substantial inner transformation actually happens.

Writing back in 1885, in *Pancha Samskara*, an essay explaining the five essential components of Vaishnava initiation and in answering the question as to why, after such initiation, some Vaishnavas are seen not to make progress, Srila Bhaktivinode Thakur says:

> "The answer is that Vaishnava *samskara* is the best, but at the present time it is practised in name only. Both the spiritual teacher and the student block their own spiritual advancement by being content with only the external aspects of *samskara*... Today, the deeper significance of *samskara* is not understood. When the student submits himself to the teacher, the teacher

gives *pancha-samskara* and then abandons him. What good can come from *pancha-samskara* of this type? Externally the student looks good, but internally there is nothing."

"The tongue utters the name of Hari …but the student is addicted to endless sinful practises. At night, he takes intoxicants and practises debauchery! Oh good teacher, how have you benefited your student? What is the difference in him before and after diksha? In fact, he is worse. He is a hypocrite. There is no remorse: "I am sinful. It is my fault. How can my sin be given up?" These days no one thinks like this when they take shelter of a spiritual teacher. Sinful activities are performed without the slightest concern. What misfortune!"

"Why is this? The reason is that the wrong kind of relationship exists between teacher and student. The sastras give rules to guide this relationship, but they are not followed. The student who is burning in the fire of material life, who analyses his predicament and concludes, "My relationship with material nature is not permanent, therefore I must take shelter of a spiritual teacher in order to obtain the feet of God," has reached the stage of faith and is qualified to take shelter of a spiritual teacher."

"The teacher should study the student for one year and observe his atonement. This is called tapa… the faithful soul's first samskara. In English we define the word tapa as "repentance, atonement, and the permanent impression of higher sentiment on the soul." Tapa applies not only to the body, but also to the mind and the soul. If it is only physical, in the form of branding or stamping, (here the Thakur refers to the custom of marking the upper body with the symbols of Vishnu) then tapa has not actually taken place and religious practise becomes hypocritical. At the present time this kind of hypocrisy has weakened Vaishnava culture. Without tapa or inner repentance, the soul cannot live as a Vaishnava. Without tapa the whole process becomes useless. Without tapa the heart remains impure. Therefore good friends, seek atonement without delay!"

Such a seemingly alarmist judgement on the bad practises of Vaishnava *diksha* of the 1880s was intended to be a strong criticism of the gurus of his day. Yet it also stands as a permanent caution to any future would-be disciple collectors. Why such stern warnings from an otherwise compassionate and gentle Vaishnava? Because the tendency of many aspiring prophets, philosophers and messiahs – at least those directly desiring to be socially known as such – is to gather as many devoted followers as possible. And the tendency of many of those would-be disciples is to achieve that status with as little pain and commitment as possible.

This creates the strong possibility that insincere gurus and uncommitted followers will find each other, a situation that has repeated itself down through the centuries. And the result is always that true and authentic *diksha* becomes obscured by popular misconceptions.

For many centuries, both the genuine Vedic system of *diksha* and its pale shadow were contained in India. Since the 1950s however, swamis, yogis and gurus have been coming to the Western countries and offering various kinds of *diksha*. Finding their Western followers somewhat averse to *tapa*, they have trimmed their requirements to appeal to their audience, and now the *diksha* tricycles have come west.

For many years, the Gaudiya Vaishnavas, those devotees of Krishna in the line of Shri Chaitanya Mahaprabhu, were free from this. Represented by ISKCON through the personal vigilance of its founder-*acharya*, His Divine Grace A.C. Bhaktivedanta Swami Prabhupada, the western Vaishnavas were held to the standard of *tapa* as prescribed in scripture. Over the last twenty years, however, there has been a marked increase in the level of *diksha* with diminishing levels of requirements. As Gaudiya Vaishnava preachers attempt to emulate Srila Prabhupada and his successes, they have begun to give 'initiations' leaving aside all traditional requirements of personal *tapa*, mutual scrutiny of guru-disciple, and the normal levels of affectionate guardianship offered by the guru to his disciple after *diksha*.

The result is a large increase in the number of those now holding spiritual names with the suffix '*Dasa*' and '*Dasi*'. Unfortunately, like those Barons and Dukes with their framed certificates, those who have bought their '*Diksha-Lite*' may find that all that has changed is their name.

# 40

# Diksha and drugs: Bad combination

*The giving of sacred mantras without the time-honoured rules of Vaishnava life may seem like an act of compassion but it can often result in disaster...*

**Some years ago, when I heard the story of three young men celebrating their Vaishnava *diksha* with a round of cold Guinness, I thought it was the beginning of an Irish joke.** Unfortunately it was true. The guru who'd given them their initiation had omitted to tell them anything at all about the practical disciplines of spiritual life and so they'd assumed that their old life could continue as normal.

Over the years many similar stories have reached me, all concerning the absence of customary instruction on the life of a Vaishnava, especially the parts about giving up intoxication. There are many tales now of aspiring Vaishnavas, perhaps visiting India for the first time, being misled by a spiritual preceptor who allows them to continue with their drinking or smoking in the name of being 'merciful'. But the combination of initiation and intoxication only produces confusion and, in the long term, sadness and depression.

And it doesn't stop at a celebratory Guinness. Mother Nature produces a wide variety of substances that can be ingested by being licked, chewed, drunk, and sucked. Although she provides them for medicinal or other purposes, when misapplied or taken to excess they can result in powerful intoxication, inebriation, and hallucinogenic experiences. And when men take those gifts of nature and decide to refine, ferment, distil, then drink, smoke or inject the products, the result can be total addiction and complete destruction.

It's nothing new, of course. Alcohol has been a destructive part of life since the days of the Vedic sages, and both the poppy and the *ganja* plant have always grown wild in India. All these, and many more, have been used by certain classes of men since time immemorial. And since time immemorial they have been condemned by wise teachers who wanted to help them towards a greater, longer lasting happiness.

So when a candidate comes for initiation into spiritual life, they are expected to have already made a commitment to refrain from taking intoxicating substances. And the guru is expected to help them make that commitment and to then to uphold it through his good instruction.

The fact that some spiritual preceptors are not doing that is, sadly, nothing new. There have always been forgetful or neglectful gurus who omitted important teachings and inadvertently led their disciples astray; and there have been others that deliberately left out teachings on discipline in order to gather a popular following. But that disciplic descendants in the line of Srila Bhaktivinode Thakur and Srila Bhaktisiddhanta Thakur are now doing so is troubling. Both of those great acharyas, and then, in their line, Srila A.C. Bhaktivedanta Swami Prabhupada, strenuously taught about the dangers of intoxication and campaigned against the foolish combination of *diksha* and drugs.

# Tragic

So I was perturbed when, last year, I saw a young man with neckbeads and forehead *tilak* markings walking through the street of an English town with a half-finished can of cider. When I stopped him to ask his name it was obvious that he'd been drinking for some time. I was equally troubled when I saw another devotee smoking. But I was very saddened when another young man, newly initiated, recently collapsed of a drug overdose in one of our preaching centres.

Then, just two weeks ago, I was told the tragic story of a married man with a wife and child. He was initiated and looking forward to his upcoming trip to India when he would receive his *gayatri-diksha*. Unfortunately, being insufficiently guided by his 'most merciful' preceptor, he'd continued his fascination with his drug of choice. But his favourite substance was an hallucinogenic, used by Amazonian shamans for visionary experiences. At a party he consumed far too much, was taken to hospital, but later died.

Srila Prabhupada instituted the recitation of the 'four regulative principles' at every initiation ceremony. Before he gave a disciple their new Vaishnava name, he would ask them to declare vocally in public that from that moment forward they would consume no intoxicating substance, not even tea and coffee. His disciples followed his example and the declaration of the four principles is now a standard component of every such ceremony.

Yet this is not done by others and it may – albeit inadvertently – give those who are coming so fresh to Vaishnava life the mistaken impression that one can chant the Hare Krishna mantra and simultaneously engage in consumption of intoxicants. Such an idea runs counter to everything taught by the previous acharyas. It runs against the current of advice given by the Srimad Bhagavatam; and is patently not producing the desired results.

If we are to prevent western Vaishnavism descending into an immoral culture – a culture so strenuously fought against by our previous acharyas – then initiations such as these must discontinue. Good advice is required, adequate preparation is needed, and certain dangers must be pointed out. The river of Mercy must always flow within the river banks of Dharma.

# 41

# Guru and disciple in therapy

*The contract between a guru and disciple is a personal relationship voluntarily entered into by them in which one acts as a teacher and the other a student. The ideal is that both are free from materialistic motivations and seek only to serve the mutual goal of enhanced spiritual perception. That's the ideal. In our modern culture, the relationship between two people is often subjected to a psychological analysis. This can serve to help them understand what lies beneath the surface of their interaction. Can the guru and disciple relationship be similarly subjected to analysis?*

**Over the last forty years I have met and befriended a good number of psychotherapists.** We seem to cross paths regularly and mostly, it seems, by accident. It happens with such frequency that I'm beginning to suspect that there's some subtle magnetism between us, otherwise how could a man with clay markings on his nose and dressed in an Indian cotton *dhoti*, manage to bump into so many of them. Perhaps we are drawn to each other because of a mutual interest in the mind; or maybe they simply see in me an interesting case in dire need of psychoanalysis. On the other hand, I live on the outskirts of north-west London, and that might explain their profusion. However it happens, I generally find the conversation better than average – and that's not because they let me do all the talking.

Psychotherapists as a group are compassionate. They're sensitive to the frailties of the human condition, and the ongoing pain caused by historic trauma. Like the gurus of the east, they try to alleviate suffering and help others to restore themselves to wholeness. They do their healing work using the western conception of the psyche, the mind, as the person, rather than the eastern concept of *atma*, the conscious self which observes the mind. There's an important difference.

The mind is understood by most psychotherapists to be a sense of individual identity, perception, and memory derived from the aggregate of sensory information, cognitive processing and cumulative experience stored by the brain. It is a function of the cerebral cortex, the beautifully complex assembly of neural pathways formed by an astonishingly vast network of sophisticated electro-chemical links - a thing of wonder made of organic matter.

In contrast, the Vedantic *atma* is a non-organic, non-matter quantum of consciousness. The *atma* is pure identity, temporarily encased in a quadruple-layered, hierarchical complex of ego (*ahamkara*), intelligence (*buddhi*), mind (*manasa*) and brain (*deha*). The *atma* is not the mind, but it observes mental functioning and can choose to identify with it or not. The *atma's* existence is not dependent on the body/mind complex and it exists both before conception and after death.

Using the organic model of selfhood, many psychotherapists might conclude, not surprisingly, that the idea of the *atma* is a hopeful creation of the mind, a notion properly belonging to a less evolved period of human history when life was shorter and some prospect of eternity desperately needed. By extension, religion itself, especially the male-organised, hierarchical kind, though emotionally reassuring at times, is a man-made creation springing from human need and our innate capacity for myth-making. We would therefore do well to treat it with caution – preferably up until the time we ditch it entirely.

The *parampara* or teacher-student lineage of psychologists that has helped to create this dominant view is not that old – little more than a century – but it has become very widespread and disparate since the days of its acharyas, Carl Jung and Sigmund Freud. Jung was a little more interested in Eastern ideas than was Freud. When one of Freud's friends, the poet Romain Rolland, became a student of the popular Indian guru Ramakrishna, he wrote a letter to Freud and told him that he had recently had 'a feeling of something limitless and unbounded' that he felt was the 'physiological basis of much of the wisdom of mysticism.'

Freud labelled the feeling 'oceanic' and, admitting his puzzlement and failure to find the same feeling within himself, went on to fit it into his worldview, labelling it as a 'feeling of infantile helplessness, the very source of all religious feeling'. The implicit assumption that Freud and others helped to codify rendered centuries of mystical experiences a product only of infantile need or derived from purely physiological origins. In 1961 William James wrote that this 'simple-minded' way of thinking was derived from an antipathy toward certain states of consciousness, and labelled it 'medical materialism.' He wrote: "It finishes up Saint Paul by calling his vision a lesion of the occipital cortex, Saint Francis a hereditary degenerate, and George Fox's pining for spiritual veracity a symptom of a disordered colon." In conclusion he wrote that all such states of spiritual consciousness, so say the 'medical materialists,' can be ultimately traced to 'the perverted actions of various glands which physiology will yet discover."

But not all psychologists think like Freud. And not all psychotherapists are so quick to dispense with the idea of the *atma*. Over the last few decades, independent thinkers in the field have also explored Buddhist and Vedantic classification of mental states and have found a centuries-old system of psychology that has intrigued them. Eastern psychology may yet be found useful. Even now, it is not uncommon for therapists to use meditation techniques to help their clients, or to declare themselves 'Buddhist psychotherapists'.

As someone who is utterly convinced of the power of the meditative state to effect deep personal change, I would say that psychotherapy can only be enriched by the addition of such techniques. And I'd also add that using the conception of *atma* as an alternative theoretical model would surely revolutionise therapy. I look forward to a time when eastern and western models and techniques become synthesised into a new framework for understanding personhood.

In the spirit of moving forward to such a fruitful union, I would like to say that there are many helpful terms within psychotherapy that would serve the interest of those whose frame of reference is mainly theological. Because it serves to highlight hidden motivation and irrational fear, and because it has developed an extensive vocabulary for that purpose, knowledge of psychotherapeutic language can be helpful in exposing weaknesses, negative attachments and the repression that is often their cause. And that's helpful in spiritual life. Attachments, repression, and other forms of weakness tend to get in the way of progress. Yet spiritual practitioners, who may be as yet unaware of the large classical Sanskrit vocabulary describing negative emotional states, or *virodhi*, may find it interesting to delve into the psychotherapist's lexicon occasionally.

## Part Five | Guru and disciple in therapy

I say 'occasionally' because such delving can have its drawbacks. I have known many who, finding themselves unable to move past their current blocks in spiritual practice, have sought the therapist's chair – and simply stayed there. Not physically there, of course - that would be expensive - but more or less mentally. They suddenly discover that they took up the practises of spiritual life only to ease the pain of a difficult childhood; that they always regarded their guru as a father substitute and membership of their guru's *sangha* as a family substitute; and then, after many long years of spiritual practise, they decide that they'd never really been genuinely committed. They may even mistakenly conclude that their relationship with their guru is a neurotic one. And that's when they leave, hardly ever to return. The therapist replaces the guru, and the psyche replaces the *atma*.

Now, it doesn't have to be like this. I believe that both disciplines should be able to get along, both learning from each other. A little therapy can help, but should never foster a complete rejection of genuine spirituality. Like all things in life, balance is always good. It's true that we may have mixed reasons for taking up spiritual life. Authentic spiritual motivations do get mixed with emotional reasons, and they're not always easy to discern and separate. But just because you have some – perhaps hidden – emotional motivations, doesn't mean you're not interested mainly in spiritual emancipation. Our spiritual motivation is authentic because the *atma* desires freedom from the incessant cycle of desire and hate, happiness and revulsion. The emotional baggage we bring with us – whether it is from our parents in this life or from trauma in the last - is also real, but ultimately less important. It's an accretion on the *atma*, stuck to it through the *atma's* attachment to ego, and it will fall away with assiduous practise of meditation. Sometimes there will be almost insurmountable obstacles, but that is not the time to jettison both the guru and the *sangha*.

I have known a few people who gravitated to serious spiritual commitment after emotional trauma, rejection or abuse of some kind. But I have also known many more that had happy, carefree childhoods, loving parents, and a trauma-free adolescence and young adulthood – and they've taken to spiritual life with enthusiasm. And they've gone on to have well balanced emotional lives. They weren't running away and neither did they regard their guru as anything other than a spiritual teacher and guide. So it doesn't seem as if everyone who seeks out a guru is a fugitive from childhood trauma. But I have known others who have neglected to examine their true motivation for years, pretending to themselves and to others that all they did was done with the highest level of spiritual motivation. They hid behind ritual, or philosophy, or used religious clothing as their disguise. Later, at some crisis point, they either dumped all their problems on their guru, still ignoring the internal work that 'they' had to do; or angrily blamed the guru for their unhappiness.

Then there have been a few who have taken on the role of guru for others, unaware that their hidden desire to be loved - or to be respected, or powerful, or sexually active - was the unconscious motivator that would be their fatal obstacle. When they admitted to themselves that it was essential they get some extra help, they discovered, much too late, that there was no-one to help them. They'd made themselves too loved, too respected and much too powerful for anyone else to ever imagine they were struggling inside.

The guru-disciple relationship is the meeting place for all spiritual and emotional motivation. It is the perfect relationship for revealing the true self and achieving our ultimate goal; or it can be the greatest mutual deception that can block the paths of both student and preceptor. I do not believe, as some psychotherapists do, that the guru-disciple relationship is necessarily one where an individual becomes disempowered due to psychological submission to another person. And I do not believe that this same effect is extended when one is a member of the guru's *sangha* – hierarchical though it may be. Both the guru-disciple relationship and membership of the guru's ashram or *sangha* - the 'institution' - are valid and essential. They are not simply eastern cultural manifestations, but universal and indispensible components for spiritual growth. However, even with the presence of a guru in our life I do think that a searching introspection is healthy, provided such introspection always remains subjugated to the spiritual process itself.

I'm not an expert in any of the mind sciences, merely someone who thinks that he's had some interesting conversations with people who are. So with gratitude to them, and with caution, I am reproducing here a few helpful observations. I hope these terms may help to create greater awareness of the hidden mental states that can occur between guru and disciple.

## Part Five | Guru and disciple in therapy

I would like to thank, in particular, Dr. Mariana Caplan, who has supplied most of the detailed discernments presented in the section that follows. She has written what I consider to be the best book on the subject of guru-disciple relationship analysis: *The Guru Question, the perils and rewards of choosing a spiritual teacher*. As both a psychotherapist and a disciple of a guru, her excellent observations have proved invaluable. I have merely lightly glossed them for this chapter:

**Ego-syntonic:** 'compatible with the ego.' This refers to how a spiritual seeker might find it easy or hard to relate to the idea of having a spiritual authority. In India – and throughout Asia – it is still part of the culture to have a spiritual figure of some kind for instruction, guidance and on occasion, correction. It is congruent with traditional social structure and the family system. One who does not have a guru may be looked upon as a spiritual orphan. It is considered quite normal for the spiritual authority to give life instruction, and to expect others to obey. Therefore for one in this culture the guru is ego-syntonic. By comparison, the underlying attitude in the West is: "Well, nobody tells me what to do with my life." The guru figure in this culture is non ego-syntonic, not compatible with the ego. In the western guru-disciple relationship it is therefore common that the disciple, although having bought in to the notion of guru, keeps the guru at a safe distance. The disciple may avoid any personal interaction that might threaten his ego. Pursuant to this, the disciple may attempt to keep the guru as a 'friend' rather than a teacher whose duty it is to correct him, and to diminish his pride. The guru may also keep the disciple at a distance for fear of telling him something which will make him uncomfortable. Progress in this kind of mutually cautious relationship is slow.

**Covert psychological agenda:** This refers to the spiritual aspirant not acknowledging the primary reasons for submitting to a guru. It could be that he gets emotional gratification from 'surrendering' to the guru. The disciple may want approval, acceptance, a sense of belonging, or some other kind of emotional reward. If he has low self-esteem he might gain a greater sense of status by being linked to a powerful, charismatic figure. This type of 'surrender' is egotistical. In the long term, genuine surrender is required within the guru-disciple relationship if the candidate is to proceed spiritually. The original motivation must give way to genuinely spiritual motivation. This normally involves the egotistical motivation being revealed at some stage – and that's not always pain-free.

**Mental Projection or Transference:** Common enough terms that seem to have crossed over into ordinary speech, they refer to processes by which the disciple habitually transfers, or 'projects,' onto the guru both positive and negative dynamics, expectations and beliefs that were formed in situations much earlier in life. Although these ideas and feelings are not inherent in the present circumstances, the disciple's projections serve either to re-create the situation in the present circumstances, or to convince him that this is what is happening. Thus a relationship with the father – or in the case of some female disciples, the husband - is projected onto the guru-disciple relationship. In the formative stages when bonding with the guru is essential, the disciple may be helped by projecting ideal qualities of godliness onto the guru, but as time passes the disciple must examine how much of this idealisation is within his own mind, and how much is factually manifest in the person of the guru. If he doesn't do this, there will be a time when disillusionment sets in. The worst problem with transference is that when it is positive, the guru is wonderful; but when something negative happens that is reversed and the disciple feels that the guru was cheating him from the very beginning.

**Counter-Transference:** This occurs when the guru responds to either the positive or negative projections as if they were true of his person, rather than seeing them for what they are. Counter-transference is also used to describe the phenomenon of projections on the part of the guru towards his disciples, such as the need to be loved, honoured, and respected.

**Intersubjectivity:** This refers to a kind of mutual complicity engaged in by both guru and disciple. The disciple praises the guru for qualities he doesn't possess, or for teachings or guidance he hasn't provided, and the guru accepts the praise, not reminding the disciple of the facts. In return, the guru may also flatter the disciple for qualities he doesn't yet possess. Both gain something in the short term, but lose over time.

**Co-dependency:** One person needs to be a teacher and therefore must have students to fulfil that need. Another person needs to belong to a spiritual teacher and therefore seeks one out. One is dependent for meaning in their life upon the other. Co-dependency lowers the level of the genuine guru-disciple relationship because it then becomes based on the emotional needs of the persons involved. Both guru and disciple cannot function properly because there is a quality of 'grasping' in the relationship because it is needs-based. Anything which threatens those fundamental needs is then regarded with apprehension. However, the genuine guru-disciple relationship is not meant to be comfortable or safe. It is based on the guru challenging the ego of the disciple, something which may risk the continued relationship. But without taking that risk, the comfort of co-dependence threatens genuine progress for them both.

**Borrowed Functioning:** Just as it sounds, this term refers to when the disciple 'borrows' the charisma or status of the guru and uses it as his own. The guru may be charismatic, a great scholar, or acknowledged widely as a saint. By becoming the guru's disciple, the student feels that he no longer has to independently work hard to achieve charisma, scholarship or sainthood. The guru – or his intimate connection with the guru – has done it all for him. He has 'borrowed' something yet behaves as if it was his own accomplishment. This is an abnegation of personal responsibility in spiritual life. Left unchecked, this can result in conceptions of premature advancement, and the resulting onset of pride may lead the disciple into laziness and apathy.

**Self-Responsibility:** The opposite of above. Becoming someone's disciple means that one is being given the opportunity to work with a mature, experienced and hopefully realized teacher. That teacher will instruct, encourage, support, guide and correct. But still the hard work of transformation has to be performed with vigour and enthusiasm by the disciple. The doctrine of *guru-kripa*, or 'grace of the guru,' does not free the disciple from the struggle to overcome temptation, engage in assiduous study, practise mental discipline and so on.

**Arrested Development:** There are a number of developmental capacities, and they may each mature independently, and at different rates. They include physical, cognitive, emotional, sexual, and spiritual development. It is possible that a person may be developed in one area but not in others. One area has been 'arrested.' He might be spiritually developed, faithful to a tradition and capable of explaining it systematically, but emotionally immature and unable to fully express his own emotions or detect varieties of emotions in others. When such a person accepts the role of formal teacher – a guru figure - he may not be able to deliver what's required within a functional personal relationship. Subtle cues in the disciple's disposition indicating a particular level of progress, or an unexpressed obstacle, may not be detected, and the guru is unable to teach or guide the disciple effectively. This can be very confusing for the disciples and can leave them feeling that the guru: "Just doesn't understand me."

A teacher who is knowledgeable and spiritually advanced but emotionally shut down can make the relationship with the students weak – and then the spiritual transmission becomes weak. Or the teacher's unacknowledged or repressed sexuality sometimes comes out as aggression, unconscious motivations for power, or sexualised speech. He may not realise this in himself, but it will be obvious to others who do not have a disciple relationship with him. In addition to knowledge of the spiritual tradition and commitment to daily practise, sense control and so on, someone who elects to teach others formally must have a developed capacity for discernment of their own motivations as well as a sensitivity to those of others. In the absence of emotional self-knowledge, the guru must be prepared to show humility by requesting his peers to be compassionately honest with him.

On the other hand, it is often the disciple who is not mature in one developmental aspect. This can render the disciple blocked to certain aspects of the guru's teaching or guidance. With arrested sexual development, the disciples sexual feelings may arise much later on, after the relationship with the guru has developed, and these may then be projected onto the guru if there is no other suitable recipient. This is problematic for both teacher and student, especially if they are both young.

In spite of all the above, the guru-disciple relationship is the most essentially important element in spiritual life – for a multitude of reasons. Conducted with a commitment to regular introspection, peer group support, and an uncompromising vigilance to any egoistic urges or idealism, the results are genuinely transformative and immensely rewarding.

**Power Dynamics:** The relationship between any two people can involve a complex shifting of power as both parties draw on their status, physical strength and appearance, intellectual expertise or wealth to gain recognition or advantage from the other. As time passes the play for power may settle into a hierarchical order. Between teacher and student – or guru and *shishya* – the relationship may be pre-established because of a difference in knowledge and the deference given to the teacher; or it may come because of the roles traditionally prescribed within the host culture, particularly an eastern culture. The power dynamic between guru and *shishya* in a modern, western setting – where both are 'converts,' so to speak, needs to be established on its own merit without merely acquiescing to any expected, traditional models. Western gurus, unaccustomed to the deference traditionally offered to such a teacher, have exploited their disciples emotionally, financially and sexually. And western disciples, unaccustomed to offering a profound level of deference to anyone, have sometimes missed out on an important aspect of the relationship due to fear of disempowerment or exploitation. To establish the 'correct' relationship between guru and *shishya*, both must carefully examine and be aware of their motivations and be honest with one another, without the inhibition that acknowledging the power of the other may cause loss. Periodically they must be prepared for adjustment in order for the relationship to be sustainable.

**Narcissism:** In psychotherapy, the term refers to a personality disorder originating in arrested development in early childhood. There is a craving for love which manifests in selfish and manipulative behaviour in adulthood. Many narcissists are drawn to environments where they can surround themselves with admirers. Unfortunately, the religious environment has often provided circumstances where that is easily achieved. Priests and gurus, representing as they do the ultimate attraction, draw upon the status of the divine and their role as a representative then becomes a fulfilment of their narcissism. Manipulative behaviour by a guru, and an interest in the adoration of followers who serve to keep the focus on him, are common phenomena.

Because this behaviour can seem to be authentic 'eastern' behaviour – and because, when disguised, it can be so destructive – it is important to know the classic signs of the narcissistic person:

1. An obvious self-focus in interpersonal exchanges.
2. Problems in sustaining satisfying relationships.
3. A lack of psychological awareness and a consequent difficulty with empathy.
4. Problems distinguishing the self from others; an inability to establish boundaries.
5. Hypersensitivity to any insults or imagined insults; prone to rages.
6. Haughty body language.

7. Flattery towards people who admire and affirm them.

8. Detesting those who do not admire them.

9. Using other people without considering the cost of doing so.

10. Pretending to be more important than they really are.

11. Bragging (subtly but persistently) and exaggerating their achievements.

12. Claiming to be an "expert" at many things.

13. Inability to view the world from the perspective of other people.

14. Denial of remorse and gratitude.

A general awareness of the emotions involved in the guru-disciple relationship is helpful, as is an understanding of power dynamics. Sometimes, feeling that he should become less self-directive, the disciple may give his power away needlessly. This may feel like 'surrender' but it is a cheap, psychological stance rather than a genuinely spiritual one. Later on, the disciple may realise what he's done, then blame the guru for taking his power away – a situation that arose from his own mistake. Conversely, the guru who has some need for the submission or reverence of others may, by his speech and actions, infantilise his disciples, treating them as helpless children. Such treatment may cause his adult disciples to respect and honour him as a loving father, but this will be short-lived as the disciples will feel inappropriately dealt with.

So an awareness of age-specific and life-stage emotions is also helpful, particularly when the age difference between guru and disciple is relatively small. It is said in some cultures that the best spiritual transmission takes place between grandfather and grandson – and a guru and disciple of the same ages. However, that is often not the case, particularly in the western world. Adjustment and balance are constant requirements in any relationship, and even though it is meant to represent the eternal relationship between the soul and God, the *guru-shishya* connection is dynamic, not static. A relationship with a guru entered into when the disciple is young may not be the same years later in middle age. An individual's needs change through life, and a guru is meant to be able to sensitively perceive these needs, and to adjust and offer relevant help at different times. If he fails to do this, then the disciple may feel that the relationship has run its course, and is no longer needed. Though there may be no formal disconnection, the disciple may simply allow the relationship to drift into irrelevancy.

In contrast with one's outer physical age, the inner life has an entirely separate childhood, puberty and mid-life, too. A person may reach their 'spiritual puberty' and feel like rejecting their guru just as they might have rejected their parents. The relationship may not be fractured, but it may be strained, and the disciple will look on the guru with a new set of critical eyes.

All these possible elements in the guru-disciple relationship, and all developmental stages in the relationship, need to be understood so that if and when they arise, they can be patiently worked through, and adjustments made to keep the relationship fresh and relevant.

# 42

# When the wise become weak

*When I was young I read John Bunyan's* **Pilgrim's Progress**, *a metaphorical journey of the soul towards the celestial city of God. I was intrigued by how many different characters the hero, Christian, meets along the way. Later on in life, after joining Srila Prabhupada and beginning my own journey, I experienced many of those same 'characters' in real life. The Vaishnava path, despite being made easier by the company of pure-hearted companions, is also a struggle at times, and perhaps we should not be too surprised when even wise travellers become weak or succumb to the Giant Despair. Help is at hand, though. The saints who have walked before us have taken care to illuminate the path and point out the rough or dangerous spots. The going will still be hard at times, but all we have to do is follow their compassionate advice.*

**Perhaps we should begin the advice with the words of Lord Brahma, the original brahmana and celestial speaker of the Vedas.** Taking pure devotional service to Lord Shri Krishna as the very goal of existence, Brahma describes how enlightenment comes step by step as we walk the path, and how we can best help ourselves along the way:

> *pramanais tat-sad-acarais*
> *tad-abhyasair nirantaram*
> *bodhayan atmanatmanam*
> *bhaktim apy uttamam labhet*

"The highest devotion is attained by slow degrees by the method of constant endeavour for self-realization with the help of scriptural evidence, theistic conduct and perseverance in practice." *(Brahma Samhita 5.59)*

'Constant endeavour' indicates that although there be strong resistance from his mind and senses, the spiritual traveller keeps on going, even if it appears that he's not covering very much distance. Perseverance is required, which is based on determination – and a certain amount of optimism. The sacred writings of the Vedas are essential, Brahma says, because they tell us the truth, the goal, the path and what we have to deal with. They act as 'evidence' or *pramana* so that even if the truth is hidden from our material senses, we can still know its there. 'Theistic conduct' is the company of genuine *sadhus* who will act as our companions.

The genuine *sadhus* are those who understand they are finite sparks of the infinite fire of the Supreme Godhead, Krishna, and as such have developed humility. They take shelter of Him and constantly talk about Him and sing His divine names. He takes them as part of His divine nature and gives them bliss at all times. This congregational *sankirtan* is explained in the *Bhagavata-purana* and was taught by Shri Chaitanya Mahaprabhu. As a staunch follower of Lord Brahma's advice and the teachings of Lord Chaitanya, Srila Rupa Goswami echoes their words in his *Upadeshamrita*. He outlines six things which are very helpful:

> *"There are six principles favourable to the execution of pure devotional service: (1) being enthusiastic, (2) endeavouring with confidence, (3) being patient, (4) acting according to regulative principles, (5) abandoning the association of non-devotees, and (6) following in the footsteps of the previous acharyas. These six principles undoubtedly assure the complete success of pure devotional service."* (Upadeshamrita 3)

# The struggles

But genuinely committed brahmanas and *sadhus* sometimes become weak. How does that happen? And how can we avoid it ourselves?

There is a very interesting Sanskrit word which means 'boundary of a field' and is the way that many *sadhus* describe their vows: *Maryada*. Just as a field boundary demarcates the crops of your field from those in your neighbour's field, so the *maryada* of a *sadhu* demarcates the 'field' of actions he permits himself from those of others. While others do not see any wrong in eating fish, for instance, the *sadhu* has chosen that no animal will ever be a part of his diet. Because he has voluntarily accepted the principle of non-violence, he finds it easy to make choices when a householder offers him fish to eat. His eating has 'boundaries.'

Genuine *sadhus* will be equally careful to avoid gambling, prostitution, animal-killing, drinking alcohol or imbibing any other forms of intoxication. They also know that wherever there is gold there is 'falsity, intoxication, lust, envy and enmity' so they also avoid coveting personal wealth. In this way a *sadhu* will construct strong boundaries that mark out the limits of his involvement with the world from those of others.

However, even his careful boundaries become confused if the *sadhu* doesn't understand exactly where they are, or forgets why he made them in the first place. Or he may know his chosen boundaries perfectly well, but being ravaged by the pangs of extreme poverty, lust, hunger and thirst, for instance, he falls prey to temptation. The *sadhu* may not actually stoop to eating fish, but if he accepts a meal from a home where fish are eaten his consciousness may become polluted. In his Yoga *Sutras*, Patanjali Muni explains that even a strict *sadhu* will 'waver in his resolve' if he eats food cooked by a person with a mentality contrary to his own. So a *sadhu* normally chooses not to keep intimate friendship with others who don't share his mentality. This means he may choose not to eat with them, laugh with them, or exchange confidential thoughts or feelings with them. He knows the ancient rule of companionship: that we tend to think like those whose company we keep.

We may note that spiritual life is a gradual and progressive adjustment of one's consciousness, which can be very subtly coloured by sensory input or simply by the close proximity of those who are averse to self-awakening. The inner self can fall asleep just as it can be awakened, and that too happens by 'slow degrees.' By negligence of his vows, forgetfulness of scripture, and distance from the company of other *sadhus*, a spiritually progressive person can gradually lose the effects of his previous austerity and knowledge. Like the bright full moon that loses a little crescent of brilliance every night until it is completely dark, so the *sadhu*'s inner brightness becomes gradually eclipsed. In his 'Light of the Bhagavata', Srila Prabhupada gives another natural analogy for the *sadhu* who has lost his spiritual direction:

> "In the rainy season some of the roads are not frequently used and become covered with long grasses, and thus it becomes very difficult to see the road. Similarly, in this age the transcendental scriptures are not properly studied by the brahmanas. Being covered by the effects of time, the scriptures are practically lost, and it becomes very difficult to understand or follow them.

Part Five | When the wise become weak

> A covered road is exactly like a brahmana who is not accustomed to studying and practicing the reformatory practices of Vedic injunctions--he becomes covered with the long grasses of illusion. In that condition, forgetful of his constitutional nature, he forgets his position of eternal servitorship to the Supreme Personality of Godhead. By being deviated by the seasonal overgrowth of long grasses created by maya, a person identifies himself with illusory productions of nature and succumbs to illusion, forgetting his spiritual life."

It isn't only desires for gross sense gratification which can lure the *sadhu* slowly into maya. He can become deviated by any strong emotion; affection, fear, greed, anger, despair, shame. Any dominant mentality which governs his consciousness can eat away at his attachment to the ultimate goal. If the *sadhu* has turned his back on all material enjoyment, because he knows that it only leads to frustration and is inevitably followed by unhappiness, then he may harbour aspirations for liberation. This selfish desire, though spiritual, will cloud his devotion. Srila Rupa Goswami writes: "There is no question of experiencing the pleasure of devotion as long as the twin ghosts of sensuality and liberation haunt us."

Since the soul is by nature pleasure-seeking, it cannot remain for long in a pleasure vacuum; either it enjoys the nectar of devotion, or it will be drawn inexorably to contemplate other pleasurable states. While contemplating the objects of the senses the mind becomes attached to them, thinks of them again and again, and while so thinking, is not focused on the supreme source of pleasure. Losing taste for the name of Krishna, the *sadhu* then slips into inattentive recitation of the Holy Name, whereupon his material desires increase. If this is prolonged, the inattentive practitioner may begin to regard his travelling companions, the fellow *sadhus*, with dull, tainted vision. If he then begins to regard them not as kindred spirits but as threats to his anticipated enjoyment, he will first think ill of them, then neglect them, and even begin to verbally criticise them. The *sadhu* has strayed into dangerous territory.

# The mad elephant in the garden of devotion

A *sadhu* who has made Krishna his goal is a Vaishnava, and is dear to Krishna. This is not a sectarian or sentimental statement, but is revealed time and again by the Lord through the pronouncements of His many avatars. The Vaishnavas are the very heart of the Lord; they are very dear to Him, and just as they give everything to Him, so He gives Himself to them. There are many examples of the Lord coming to protect His devotees, and just as many cases where a mental, verbal or physical offence to one of His devotees ultimately resulted in dire consequences for the offender.

An offence against a worshipful person is termed an *aparadha* and so an offence against a Vaishnava is known as a *Vaishnava-aparadha*. It is considered to be the equivalent of a mad elephant entering the garden of devotion growing within the heart – all the delicate plants and flowers are destroyed. There are many who have gone down in history for their spectacular *Vaishnava-aparadha*. Saubhari Muni verbally offended Garuda, the winged carrier of the Lord, and had to experience the loss of all his hard-earned yogic power, and Prajapati Daksha offended Lord Shiva, to his great regret. But probably the most famous example of all is Durvasa Muni's attack on Maharaja Ambarish. The king had been fasting for the *Ekadasi* day and Durvasa arrived as an unexpected guest. Waiting for Durvasa Muni to return from his morning ablutions, the king was told that the time had come to break his fast. Not wishing to offend his brahmana guest by eating before him, the king simply drank some water.

Durvasa became enraged at what he thought was improper behaviour and created a towering fire demon from his own hair. When the creature approached the king to do him harm, the brilliant, flaming discus of Lord Vishnu arrived on the scene and vanquished the demon. Then it began to chase Durvasa. The sage ran for his life, seeking the protection of Brahma and Shiva, neither of whom could protect him. Eventually, he fell at the lotus feet of Lord Vishnu. He was struck speechless when Lord Vishnu explained that even He could not help him:

> *"I am completely under the control of my devotees. Indeed, I am not independent. I sit within the core of their heart. What to speak of my devotees, even those who are devotees of my devotees are very dear to me. My pure devotees are always in my heart, and I am always in their heart. My devotees know nothing but me, and I know nothing but them." (Srimad Bhagavatam 9.4.63 and 68)*

Eventually, Durvasa Muni returns to the only person in the universe who could help him - the Vaishnava he had offended. He begged forgiveness from Maharaja Ambarish, who forgave him immediately, and the struggle was over. The story lives on as an illustration of the gravity of *Vaishnava-aparadha*.

The Vaishnavas are so dear to Krishna that even a neophyte devotee must be respected. That does not mean that the spiritual master can never rebuke his disciple – that is one of the functions of the guru, and it is how the disciple becomes free from pride. Srila Prabhupada once told a follower that the disciple should have a relationship of 'good friends' with the guru, but that the job of the guru was to occasionally remind his disciple 'who is the disciple and who the guru.'

One of the endearing qualities of Srila Prabhupada was how much affection he had for his disciples, and how he respected them as Vaishnavas in their own right. Even though he was the beginning of their devotion to Krishna; the teacher of everything about Krishna; and his disciples' constant guide, instructor and director, and sometimes their judge and jury; still he respected them as Vaishnavas and honoured the fact that they had their own relationship with Krishna, and that they were becoming dear to the Lord. From the disciples' point of view, their spiritual master was the essential intermediary in their relationship with Krishna; without him they would have no devotion. Srila Prabhupada, however, saw that they had been sent by his guru to help him fulfil his service to his own spiritual master.

This is the mentality of the pure devotee of Krishna – freedom from the tendency to criticise others. The pure devotee is one who is engaged in undeviating devotional service and whose heart is totally devoid of the propensity to criticise others. As a preacher and teacher, he had to set the *maryada* for his disciples, and occasionally bring them back within their boundaries using strong words, but in his relationship with them, generally, he was more affectionate than a grandfather. He saw their tendency for conflict, and always sought to help them make peace. He asked them to bow down at each others' feet, at least once a day, and to address each other as 'Prabhu.' He said that when disciples' serve each other, and help each other, it was the 'mood of Vaikuntha.'

Srila Prabhupada saw that many of his disciples did fall away from the spiritual path he'd given them, and some of them appeared to reject him and everything he'd taught them. Even then he was kind and compassionate, always seeking to bring his wayward students back to the path. He didn't rebuke anyone when they were in despair, and he deliberately chose not to expose the shortcomings of his leaders or sannyasis when they became weak. What he said to them in private was not made public, and when someone made the mistake of publicly revealing the weaknesses of one of his 'big leaders' he became angry, telling the person that it would impede the devotee's return.

For all these reasons, and for the total loss of devotion it induces, the criticism of Vaishnavas is placed at the very top of the schedule of ten *Vaishnava-aparadhas* listed in the *Padma Purana*.

At different stages in life – and particularly if a Vaishnava spends an entire life on the path of *bhakti* – there may be some periods of struggle. These can come after spells of inattention or complacency, apathy or distraction. They may come at times of great life changes, such as change of circumstances, career or home, or in times of prolonged physical illness or after a bereavement. And, as we've seen, there is inevitably a struggle after a bout of *Vaishnava-aparadha*. At these times it is important for the Vaishnava to hold tight. Just as no-one would seek to leave an aircraft during a spell of turbulence, so no-one should leave the path of *bhakti* when it becomes bumpy.

The solution seems to be that the troubled Vaishnava continues as best as possible, seeking out good company, and the attention of an understanding mentor who can spend sufficient time sympathetically listening and offering sound advice according to the Vaishnava's personal circumstances. Drastic measures and sudden changes are not as important as a compassionate attempt to understand the source of the problem, and an effective remedy. And naturally, confidentiality is important. As always, the holy name of Krishna in the form of the maha-mantra is the greatest solace in difficult times. That, and the company of kind fellow travellers.

Part Five | Loyal disciple...or a mouse?

# 43

# Loyal disciple...or a mouse?

*In 1947 a young shepherd boy, looking for a lost goat, stumbled upon a number of ancient scrolls in a cave. They had been hidden many centuries earlier by a religious sect living in Qumran, on the northwest bank of the Dead Sea. Members of the group were fleeing persecution and wanted to preserve their most precious asset, their library.*

**But the Dead Sea Scrolls, as they came to be known, were to cause a storm in the Christian world.** Years later, when their content was finally revealed to the world, it became clear that not everything Jesus Christ told his disciples was original. Some of his prayers and parables, the way he verbally illustrated his gospel message, had been written down long before he was born.

This was upsetting for the church because it meant that Jesus had borrowed some of his words from a desert sect. If Christianity was indeed the way, the truth and the life; and if Christ was uniquely the son of God, why would he not be able to create his own unique parables? So for many years, even decades, secrecy and censorship surrounded the Dead Sea Scrolls.

For a Vaishnava this alarm does not make sense. The word of God is meant to be repeated by the guru – whether the guru is referred to as the Son of God, Prophet, Angel, Messenger or the Messiah. The fact that Jesus chose to repeat stories simply means that he was a good representative of the wisdom tradition that already existed. It need not detract from the divinity ascribed to him that he wasn't entirely original.

Even God himself repeats the words of God when he makes a visit to this world. On the battlefield of Kurukshetra, when Shri Krishna speaks to Arjuna, he repeats verbatim many entire verses from the Upanishads. And then when the same Lord speaks to his friend Uddhava, some years later, he also tells him some old stories that were already in circulation. This fact should not be surprising, since Krishna says that he comes 'millennium after millennium' to restore Dharma. Since Dharma is eternal, remaining the same age after age, it makes sense that Krishna would speak exactly the same words each time he comes – and sometimes even tell the same stories.

So the business of a guru is not to reinvent the wheel of Dharma; his job is simply to repeat what his guru has told him. For a Vaishnava guru there should be no new revelations or unique message that he alone is privileged to broadcast. He repeats what he has heard from an authorised source, his guru, who in his turn was repeating what his guru told him, and so on. And the whole of the message is substantiated by the *shastra*, the Veda, compiled by Srila Vyasadeva, the original guru.

A guru shows his true value as a guru when he doesn't add or subtract from the basic message he has received. Of course, he may connect with his contemporary audiences by creating modes of expression or fresh analogies and metaphors to explain eternal principles. He may even expand on the basic messages by providing illuminating commentary on an existing text; he may tell new stories, open new temples or stage new plays, but the philosophical conclusions must remain the same.

So the first test to see whether a guru is authentic is to ascertain whether he actually knows the message as given to him, and whether he teaches the same. The second test is to see if he is putting those teachings into practise. Although all scripture insists that we stay with our guru, especially through difficult times when the relationship seems to be unrewarding, scripture also allows for the possibility that circumstances may arise when it is no longer profitable for us to follow the guru so closely. The first element in a guru-disciple relationship breakdown may occur for the very same reason we formed the relationship in the first place: that the person was speaking according to Vedic authority and through those messages our doubts were removed and we felt inspiration.

If the guru is no longer repeating the same theology – meaning if he is teaching another doctrine of the soul's relation to God – then his own authority becomes proportionately jeopardised. If the guru declares that he has been blessed by a 'new revelation' which is slightly more 'complete', or more liberal and understanding, more compassionate or 'merciful' than his own guru, this is also a sign that he is no longer being loyal to his guru. For instance, the guru may explain that he has had a lucid dream or daytime visitation by a heavenly messenger; a unique flash of inspiration, or that he feels compelled to 'work in a new direction.' It sounds full of hope, and his followers may feel privileged to be blessed by someone so graced from above, but they become complicit in deception if they continue to follow him.

As his thoughts become words, and his words become actions, the guru who drifts away from the teachings of his guru will very slowly and incrementally begin to manifest his deviation in his actions. He may otherwise be functioning well in all other areas, displaying all the symptoms of being spiritually strong, renounced from material wealth and distraction, and so on, but his authority will be increasingly compromised as long as his message deviates from his guru. Just as the full moon gradually loses its brightness, night by night, so the disloyal disciple loses his capacity to illuminate his own disciples as a guru.

Since the sum total of the guru's actions are meant to promote *bhakti* within himself and his followers, the activities of the deviant guru will begin to promote a form of *bhakti* occluded by a greater or lesser proportion of a materialistic, personal profit mentality, a spiritual, yet self-centred salvation modality, or a *bhakti* mixed with some desire for mystic power. These mixed forms of *bhakti* are known as *karma-mishra-bhakti*; *jnana-mishra-bhakti*, and *yoga-mishra-bhakti*, respectively.

# From tiger to mouse

In other cases, however, the guru's ability to control his senses will diminish proportionate to how far he fails to follow his guru. Although it is rare, it is not beyond imagination or historical precedent for the guru to lose his sense restraint and to again spiral down into base gratification and pursuit of earthly pleasure. He becomes transformed 'from a tiger back into a mouse,' losing his connection with his own guru, and all the commensurate blessings that bestows.

Signs that a guru has lost spiritual potency might include his dwindling inability to follow basic regulations and his lack of emotional control. The latter becomes revealed in his short temper or in the discharge of anger in his conversation, public speeches or in his guidance of his disciples. When anger is vented towards fellow Vaishnavas, the behaviour constitutes *Vaishnava-aparadha*, or an offence to a devotee of the Lord, and further entangles the guru in a web of spiritual forgetfulness, from where his recovery is even harder. While a guru has the license to speak strongly to his disciples, and even be angry with them, the motivation must always be affection and a desire to improve them. The disciple must never be bullied or used as a foil for uncontrolled outbursts.

A strong attachment for personal wealth also arises at these times, as the guru begins to lose his sense of altruism and thinks more of his own security and well-being than that of his disciples. Bouts of secrecy or unusual behaviour may also become evident. Abuses of authority, sexualised speech and jokes, or turning his spiritual position into an imperial presidency are all similar manifestations.

The organisational position of the guru, rather than simply the position of honour given by his disciples, can also be a confusing element in assessing the guru's ongoing authenticity. The guru may have organisational power or privilege and this can serve to disguise the symptoms of his deviation. Similarly the religion and cultural trappings that surround him, the 'stage presence' that accompanies him, and his unique clothing and any honours shown to him; the deference of large numbers of followers – all these can conceal the actual facts.

Of course, it is not that a disciple should be looking for flaws in the guru, and neither can he be regularly examining his guru for theological authenticity. This would be extremely counter-productive in the guru-disciple relationship. The disciple must trust the guru, and failure to do so means that the guru-disciple relationship is already evaporating. Indeed, if the disciple is the one who is spiritually weak, he will readily see flaws in his guru, whether they are actually there or not!

But should all the symptoms manifest themselves, the disciple should not pretend that he cannot see them out of fear of *guru-aparadha*, or a grave offense to the guru. The good disciple is, after all, training to see reality as distinguished from illusion, and if the spiritual teacher begins to compound the illusion through his aberrant teaching then the disciple is called upon to see the reality. There can be no room for a prolonged suspension of judgement.

# 44

# Leaving a guru

*What happens when the guru drifts from the path? Should a disciple continue to follow him? If the disciple becomes weak in spiritual life is it the guru's fault? Should the disciple leave him and find another?*

**A guru who strays from spiritual life seems an oxymoron. Either someone is a guru, or they are not.** Just as there is no such thing as cold fire, or dry water, there is no such person as a 'materialistic spiritual master.' A guru does not 'stray.' A guru knows and exemplifies the spiritual path, then teaches and enlivens others, and if he doesn't then he isn't a guru. Simple.

At least, that's how it should be. However, in the history of the guru-disciple relationship – and that is a long time - there have been numerous cases of disappointment. Gurus have, often unwittingly, disappointed their disciples. It is a phenomenon that has been spoken of in ancient scripture, mediaeval texts, and in modern accounts.

Sometimes it is impossible to find a genuine guru – someone who not only knows the Vedas but has developed self-realisation and love for God. The Srimad Bhagavatam, fifty centuries ago, foretells the current situation, when sincere people would be unable to find adequate and consistent spiritual guidance. Comparing the world to a blazing forest fire from which the soul desperately seeks cool relief, the prophet writes:

> *"Sometimes, to mitigate distresses in this forest of the material world, the conditioned soul receives cheap blessings from atheists. He then loses all intelligence in their association. This is exactly like jumping in a shallow river. As a result one simply breaks his head. He is not able to mitigate his sufferings from the heat, and in both ways he suffers." (Srimad Bhagavatam 5.14.13)*

The Srimad Bhagavatam also describes the symptoms of so-called gurus in the present age:

> *"Uncultured men will accept charity on behalf of the Lord and will earn their livelihood by making a show of austerity and wearing a mendicant's dress (saffron cloth). Those who know nothing about religion will mount a high seat and presume to speak on religious principles." (Srimad Bhagavatam 12.3.38)*

And sometimes, having found a genuine Vaishnava guru with great difficulty and at great personal commitment, the disciple is distraught to discover, after some time has elapsed, that all is no longer as it seemed.

But it would be wrong to think that aberrations such as these are an exclusively modern phenomenon. Freedom of will gives everyone – gurus included – the power to choose to stay on their path or not. And many, over the centuries, have exercised their will to suspend their dedication temporarily, to change to another path, or to leave spiritual practise altogether. When the very basis of the guru-disciple relationship is a shared commitment to move forward together to a mutually agreed goal, how does a disciple deal with the situation?

One classic case is the relationship between the great Shukracharya and his disciple, King Bali. The acharya was the source of Vedic wisdom, religious ceremony and moral direction for the King, but he had only slight affinity for Vishnu. In fact, despite his vast knowledge of the Vedas he remained relatively uninterested in Him. When the sky-blue Lord approached the arena of Vedic fire-sacrifice disguised as a boy brahmana, Sukra became apprehensive. The guru could discern His real identity. King Bali was about to bestow the customary charity upon the brahmanas gathered there for the sacrifice. He would give horses, cows, gold, land and other valuable items. When the young boy simply asked Bali for nothing more than the amount of land he could cover in three of his small steps, the king smiled: "Nothing more than that?"

His guru, however, knew what was about to happen, that Vishnu in disguise would take absolutely everything, and he therefore began to discourage the king from making any gift at all. Shukracharya was a great brahmana coming in the family line of Bhrigu Muni, the son of Brahma, the original speaker of the Vedas. His lineage and training were therefore impeccable. But he was financially dependent upon the king, and if the king lost all his wealth, then so would Sukra, his family and descendants. Yet King Bali was the grandson of the famous Prahlada, the great devotee of Vishnu. When the king heard his guru instructing him not to offer anything to Vishnu he fell momentarily silent. He considered whether he should follow the instructions of his guru or worship his God. Although the two principles should be one, in this case there was a conflict.

King Bali decided to be a disobedient disciple and offer three steps of land to Vishnu. His guru cursed him. Lord Vishnu's two steps covered the world, and His third step was placed on the king's head, which meant that he'd indeed lost everything, just as his guru had told him. Later, after being confronted with a fearful, gigantic form of Vishnu, Shukracharya seems to have a complete change of heart – or at least he takes expedient precautions in the circumstances. He apologises to Vishnu, saying that: "My Lord, you are the person to whom all sacrifices are offered. When your Holy Name is chanted, everything becomes faultless."

In this case, the Vaishnava acharyas have commented that Bali Maharaja took the right option; it was correct to do the right thing and to serve Vishnu, even though directed by his guru to do otherwise. The great mediaeval philosopher, Jiva Goswami, cites the *Padma Purana* in explaining that the central element in being a spiritual master, guru or acharya is to be a Vaishnava:

> *sat-karma-nipuno vipro mantra-tantra-visaradah*
> *avaisnavo gurur na syad vaishnavah svapaco guruh*

> "A scholarly brahmana expert in all subjects of Vedic knowledge is unfit to become a spiritual master without being a Vaishnava, but if a person born in a family of lower caste is a Vaishnava, he can become a spiritual master."

Shukracharya was fully qualified in many ways, but in the most essential feature of a spiritual guide – to help one's student towards the personal Godhead – he was amiss. So Bali took the only reasonable option and chose Vishnu above the instructions of his guru.

# Family priests

In India there have always been family priests, like Shukracharya, who were expert at memorizing Vedic texts and conducting religious ceremonies. As brahmanas, they were accustomed to giving *mantra-diksha* to all male members of the three upper castes, usually between the ages of eight and twenty, and would serve designated families, and sometimes groups of villages. Some preliminary Vedic instruction would be given to the young men, perhaps topped up at times of religious festivals or important family events such as weddings. Such brahmanas would also be invited to speak from the scriptures in specialised public recitals. Since anyone who teaches the Vedas and gives initiation into Vedic mantra is eligible to be known as a guru, it meant that the whole of India was covered with hundreds of thousands of gurus. From time to time, a wandering, saffron-clad sannyasi mendicant would pass through the village, enlivening the inhabitants with his wisdom, made sharp by his life of austerity.

And for the majority of people, this system served them well. It was Vedic culture, it was religion, and everyone who wanted to had access to a brahmana guru. And if anyone wanted to send their children to a traditional *gurukula* where they could learn Sanskrit and immerse themselves in the culture for several years that was available, too.

As the centuries passed, various changes took place in Indian society. Buddhism brought saffron-clad monks into urban centres where they lived together in communities known as *guhas*. Followers of Adi Shankaracharya (788 - 820) similarly lived together in urbanised pilgrimage centres, and gradually the sannyasi monk guru became as prominent as the householder brahmana guru within Indian society. This was followed by the 17,000 monks of Ramanujacharya (1017-1137) and their well-organized network of *diksha-gurus*. In the north of India, for at least 800 years, the Muslim overlords demanded taxes from the brahmanas, and the pressure was passed on to their disciples. Making disciples and hosting pilgrims became regarded as a source of necessary income for brahmanas, and some undertook disciple-making with business-like enthusiasm.

This type of *diksha-guru*, who taught little if anything at all, and who was sometimes steeped in a manufactured theology, repugnant personal habits and irreligious behaviour, became so prominent that a reactionary sub-culture developed wherein sincere candidates for Vaishnavism were encouraged to reject their 'gurus' and become initiated by pure Vaishnavas.

# Modern times

In more modern times, beginning from the 1950s, Eastern spiritual traditions began to arrive in the West. Sometimes the traditions would be streamlined to be made more accessible to westerners, and occasionally moral principles were sacrificed for the sake of rapid popularity. This led to a number of gurus who were teaching only portions of their ancient tradition. At the same time, the American and western European countercultures were experimenting with novel forms of Christian theology and communal living, occasionally borrowing from Indian thought. Into this mixture came popular psychology and experimental psychotherapeutic techniques. With no standardised method of estimating the factual worth of the rash of new spiritual leaders, many religious cults developed, some leading to disastrous results for their wide-eyed followers.

The culture clash between East and West in the latter part of the 20th century brought a unique set of problems. When Tibetan Buddhist gurus began coming to the West several years ago, all seemed fine for a while. They were fresh, young lamas from the mountain monasteries of Tibet – authentic, steeped in the traditional culture, joyful and deeply experienced in meditation – and celibate, too. But they were inexperienced in the feminine allures of the young goddesses of California, and they succumbed, one by one. When, after some years, the Dalai Lama was asked about the situation, and how one could find a spiritual teacher who would not be a disappointment later on he replied: "You must spy on him, in private, for ten years. Only then will you know what he is."

Amongst this heady mixture was the Hare Krishna movement. Srila Prabhupada did not compromise his Vaishnava tradition, and introduced three elements that were traditionally repugnant to freedom-loving western youth from Judaeo-Christian homes. The first was personal discipline, involving the rejection of intoxication and promiscuous sexual behaviour; the second was worship of the sacred image in traditional temple worship, something proscribed by the Bible and alien to western understanding. The third was the guru-disciple relationship, equally alien to Abrahamic traditions.

When his physical presence came to a close in 1977, the 5,000 young converts to Krishna consciousness were left to carry on. It wasn't long before they discovered how difficult it was to perpetuate a traditional, centuries-old Vaishnava culture on western soil. The guru-disciple relationship was particularly challenging. The relationship between Srila Prabhupada, aged 70-82 during his teaching years, and the young disciples, average age 24, was one of reverence due to a host of factors. After 1977, the relationship between the young converts, largely the same age as each other, and some older ones who had adopted the role of guru, was always going to be a challenge.

Despite all their best intentions, some of those who assumed the role of Vaishnava guru drifted from their chosen path, sometimes after many years. Without realising it until it was too late, they grew weak in their practises and failed to be a constant source of spiritual vitality for their disciples. Some encountered profound challenges in their health, or succumbed to temptations of women, money, or position. Some took too many disciples and became overburdened. Some began formal teaching and accepted disciples prematurely; they had insufficient knowledge and determination to properly assume the role. Just a few had distinct character flaws that would prove their undoing as the years went by.

So what is a disciple meant to do in such circumstances? In the classical case of Bali Maharaja, his guru was educated in the Vedas but not a Vaishnava. In the case of the devotees of Krishna, their guru was certainly a Vaishnava by philosophical conviction but circumstantially weakened. ISKCON history shows that many disciples gradually abandoned the process completely, reasoning that since their spiritual preceptor failed, their own chances of success were slight. Many disciples did not follow their former guru's erroneous path however, and remained following Srila Prabhupada's instructions, taking advantage of the many other senior guides available to them.

Our Vaishnava acharyas have counselled that we should not be too quick to judge our seniors, and in the case of our guru, we must exercise extreme caution. There are many warnings found in scripture that prohibit a disciple from rejecting his guru. Indeed, a very dark future is described for one who abandons his guru, or rejects him for no good reason. The reason for this is that the disciple's perception of his guru's spiritual standing can be quite wrong. In the beginning of the guru-disciple relationship, for instance, the new disciple may imagine many spiritual qualities that the guru doesn't actually possess; and in his darker moments, some years later, the disciple may imagine many flaws the guru just doesn't have. Such is the working of the mind dominated by the ego.

Part Five | Leaving a guru

At certain times on his journey, usually at times when a radical inner growth is called for, the disciple struggles with his guru's efforts to help him, mistakenly imagining that the guru has now become strangely disqualified to do so. Why is this? The process of surrender under the guidance of a guru is, in Srila Prabhupada's words, "suicide of the ego," and the guru has to sometimes rebuke his disciple, reducing his amount of pride by exposing his foolishness. This can be painful for the disciple's ego, and some disciples become tempted to sever their relationship out of a mistaken understanding of self-preservation. So at these points, when the temptation to regard the guru unfavourably is strong, when the connection with the guru becomes temporarily weakened, this is the precise time not to give him up but a time to cling on.

On the other hand, there are certainly parts of scripture that describe circumstances where a guru must be rejected, particularly if he can no longer function as a spiritual preceptor. When he has become hopelessly entangled in material life, for instance, or when he has developed a philosophy opposed to devotion, or is found to be inimical to the devotees. In these circumstances the disciple is counselled to wait for his reformation – at least as long as it took to decide to first accept him as guru – and then to continue to respect him from a distance, remaining thankful for all the help he has given previously. If he thinks he may help the situation he may speak to his guru in a private place, asking him to again take up the path as before.

More than 400 years ago, a great devotee named Narahari Thakur wrote that the phenomenon of a disciple having to leave his guru was not a new one and that there were many cases of this in the times of Chaitanya Mahaprabhu.

Here is a selection of verses which provide both aspects of this issue:

> "Even the vultures do not eat the dead bodies of those ungrateful persons who give up their guru. Their intellect is foul, their degradation manifest. One who rejects the guru also rejects Hari." And elsewhere: "That lowest of men who, having attained a guru, gives him up through ignorance will burn in hell during ten million kalpas." *(Hari Bhakti Vilasa 4.363-365)*

> "Whether knowledgeable or ignorant, the guru is Janardana (Krishna). Situated on the path or not, the guru is indeed the

goal." And elsewhere: "When Hari is angry, the guru can save, when the guru is angry, nobody. Therefore, with all efforts the guru should certainly be pleased." In the Brahma Vaivarta Purana it is said: "Even striking or cursing, illusioned or angry, the gurus are worshipable. Having worshiped them, one should lead them home." *(Hari Bhakti Vilasa 4.359-361)*

And in his novel *Jaiva Dharma*, Srila Bhaktivinode Thakur presents a summary of references as part of a discussion on the subject:

**Raghunatha dasa Babaji**: "...The scriptures have also described a preliminary time of mutual testing between the guru and the disciple. The guru should see that the disciple has become eligible to enter the path of suddha-*bhakti* by his sincerity, faith and respect. In addition, the disciple by his examination should develop the faith in his heart that the guru is truly a qualified pure devotee of the Lord. Seeing the faith and respectful behaviour of the sincere disciple, the bona-fide spiritual master then bestows his mercy."

"There are two categories of gurus: the diksha-guru, initiating guru; and the shiksha-guru, instructing guru. The disciple accepts diksha from the diksha-guru and from him learns the process of *arcana*. The diksha-guru is one and one only, but there can be numerous shiksha-gurus. The diksha-guru may also give shiksha to his disciple as a shiksha-guru."

**Vijaya**: "The scriptures forbid giving up the diksha-guru. However, if he is incapable of imparting proper knowledge of devotion and of Vaishnava etiquette, how can he be in a position to teach?"

**Raghunatha dasa Babaji**: "Before a person accepts formal initiation from a guru, he must test the guru as to whether he is well-versed in the Vedas and in the science of the Supreme Absolute Truth. Only such a bona fide guru is indeed able to instruct his disciple in all matters. It is true that the diksha-guru should not be rejected, but there are two bona fide reasons to give him up. First, if for some reason or another at the time of initiation the disciple did not recognize the devotional calibre of the guru and later found out that the guru was neither conversant with the conclusions of sastra, nor a Vaishnava, so that he, the disciple, could not make any spiritual progress, then he, the disciple, should reject the unqualified guru. Many scriptural sources support this course of action, for example, the *Narada Pancharatra*, as cited in *Hari Bhakti Vilasa*, 1.62, states:

> *yo vyakti nyaya rahitam anyayena srnoti yah*
> *tav ubhau narakam ghoram vrajatah kalam aksayam*

"'Any person posing as an acharya, but speaking unauthorized philosophy contrary to the teachings of the shastra and anyone who claims to be his disciple and hears such, thereby lending credibility to such nonsense, both of these are bound for Hell.'

"The *Mahabharata, Udyoga-parva*, 179.25, explains in the story of Amba:

> *guror apy avaliptasya karyakaryam ajanatah*
> *utpatha-pratipannasya parityago vidhiyate*

"'A person who is wallowing in carnal pleasures and material comforts, who is confused about the human goal of life, even if he is a guru, must be rejected.'

"Another quotation from the *Hari Bhakti Vilasa*, 4.144:

> *avaisnavopadistena mantrena nirayam vrajet*
> *punas ca vidhina samyag grahayed vaisnavad guroh*

"'If one receives mantra-diksha from a non-Vaishnava who runs after women and is bereft of devotion to Shri Krishna, one is certainly doomed to Hell. Therefore, one must immediately act according to scriptural injunctions and take initiation again from a real, properly qualified, Vaishnava guru.'

"The second reason is that if a guru who was a Vaishnava and knowledgeable in Krishna consciousness at the time of initiation becomes a mayavadi and a Vaishnava-hater as a result of bad association or otherwise, or he behaves immorally and sinfully, then the disciple must give him up. However, if the guru is neither inimical to Vaishnavas, nor a *mayavadi*, nor addicted to sinful activities, but however lacks knowledge of the scriptures, then his meagre scriptural understanding should not be a cause for rejection. In this case, the disciple may approach his guru with due deference to procure his permission to receive spiritual knowledge and instructions from an advanced, pure Vaishnava, and thus engage in serving and learning from the knowledgeable Vaishnava." *(Conversation taken from Jaiva Dharma Chapter Eight: Abhidheya: Vaidhi Sadhana Bhakti, the Practice of Regulative Devotional Service)*

Whilst it is hoped that Vaishnavas do not take disciples if they are not ready for the task, it does happen that in spite of all precautions and safeguards, some Vaishnavas, no doubt well-meaning, have placed themselves in the role of initiating spiritual master and later found that they are incapable of continuing. It must be remembered that the guru himself is a disciple too, and although charged with the responsibility of helping others forward in spiritual life, has the simultaneous duty to remain as a humble disciple in the service of his own spiritual master. Pride always precedes a fall, and taking disciples can sometimes lead to pride in many forms.

It is therefore important for a devotee who has taken on the role of guru to form the same type of helpful relationships with those he views as his well-wishing seniors, and to disclose his mind. By service to other Vaishnavas, avoiding those things which may lead to pride, lust, greed, or anger and always striving to perfect his *sadhana* and his preaching activities, such a devotee can continue to make spiritual progress himself and also pass on knowledge, realizations, and guidance to his disciples.

It is equally important for the disciple to refrain from criticising the behaviour or instructions of the guru. However, in the event of a very clear deviation from the path, and after consulting other affectionate guardians – those who are not inimical to his guru – as to their opinion, he may be reluctantly forced to consider his guru's actions or speech as either aberrant from, or neglectful of, his duties as a preceptor.

# Part Six

# Becoming a disciple today

# 45

# Steps toward the big step

*The path of spiritual life is a journey of a thousand steps. It begins with our first enquiries and continues until enlightenment. Our relationship with a guru is an essential part of that path – but how convinced must we be before we take that big step? What do we need to know before we do it? What are we supposed to do before we become initiated?*

**Over the past fifty years the world beyond Britain has become a lot less 'foreign.'** We travel internationally, flying long-distance for work and holidays; we meet people our grandparents would have labelled 'foreigners' and bring their good ideas back home with us in our luggage. The internet and social media has given us all friends in countries other than where we live. Concepts previously considered alien and practises regarded as faintly bizarre – simply because they were foreign - are now common here at home.

We don't find it strange to hear a friend enthusiastically sharing an idea that first saw the light of day beyond the white cliffs of Dover. Good ideas don't have to be English anymore – we're willing to learn from other countries. London, for instance, is now a city of an estimated three hundred languages and cultures. If you want to, you can study martial arts from Japan or yoga from India. You can be inspired by agronomics from Cuba, healed by a therapist from Korea, join a choir at an Ethiopian Church, arrange your house using Chinese Feng-shui, eat your dinner in a Peruvian restaurant, chill out to music from Zaire, and no one will bat an English eyelid.

## You are what you ~~eat~~ believe

We live today, it could be said, in a vast 'supermarket of ideas'. And by the looks of it we are happy shoppers. Like attractively packaged food products on shelves, these ideas compete for our attention, interest

Part Six | Steps toward the big step

and our purchasing power. Just as the foods we regularly buy and eat form our body tissue and influence our health, so ideas, when regularly discussed and digested by the intellect, slowly form our perception of the world and our internal value system. From this flow our reactions, our behaviour, our habits, our character development and our circle of friends. And while everyone knows that 'you are what you eat,' thinkers might also add: "You are what ideas you buy."

There comes a time when all of us must decide what we believe in. Out of all the many ideas, philosophies, belief systems and worldviews we've encountered, which has the most relevance for you? Is there something that seems logically consistent and gives you intellectual satisfaction? What about spirituality – is it important to you? What about faith in a higher power? Are religious feelings and expression a comfortable self-deception or is it something authentic and relevant? Is sharing your faith with like-minded friends important? Which expression of faith gives you a sense of inner fulfilment and progress? What about making a lasting contribution to others around you – what ideas could help you do that?

A Vaishnava is one who has stopped shopping in that big ideological supermarket and is on the way to the checkout counter. To stop shopping in the supermarket of ideas means that you've concluded your browsing of the countless works of religious leaders, poets, saints, yogis, and prophets, and the post-modern wisdom of political reformers, psychologists, therapists and self-help gurus, and you've made up your mind that the Bhagavad-gita has the edge on much that you've read. Or at the very least, that if you begin the daily practice of Krishna consciousness on an experimental basis you won't lose out on the spiritual benefits of any other path.

That's a pretty important stage to get to. The Bhagavad-gita says that if you've come to that point, you'll have reaped the rewards of all the spiritual paths you've ever walked in all your previous lives. It doesn't mean that you'll have to swear never to read a book by any other teacher, or that you must now disregard all other teachers whose words have ever helped you. What it does mean is that you've decided that your main illumination – the inner light by which you now 'see' the world - is that which is found in the Vedas, the way of life described in the oldest teachings of all.

When the guidance found in the Vedic scriptures informs the choices you make in life: how you work, what you eat, who you choose as your closest friends, how you meditate and pray, and what you think of as your spiritual goal; you'll know that you've stopped shopping. When you begin to seriously apply yourself to the daily practices of Vaishnavism, and when you consider the devotees of Krishna to be your spiritual community; you'll know you've left the supermarket and you're on your way home.

# The courage of our convictions

Most of us don't believe everything we're told. We protect ourselves by restricting our belief to those things that can be proven, or that can be at least trusted. Our painful disappointments with the material world and a succession of ineffective but well-meaning guides have prepared us for further misdirection. We don't want to get hurt by misplacing our trust.

Vaishnavism consequently allows us to move gradually forward by asking us to agree to just a few initial concepts at first. When we've agreed to those basic ideas we begin daily spiritual practises based on them. The result should be some reassuring feelings of spiritual awakening – an inner happiness that cannot be explained by external circumstances. When such feelings of spiritual progress do come, then we develop more trust in the process of *bhakti-yoga* itself. This trust then attracts us to make friends with others on the same path, which in turn engages us more enthusiastically in spiritual practices. As we deepen our spiritual practise we tend to ask more questions about the experiences we're having, allowing for more answers which help to remove even more doubts. This cycle of concept-practise-experience-trust becomes a spiral that gradually takes us onwards and upwards in spiritual realisation.

Since initiation involves a commitment to a life-long endeavour in Krishna consciousness it marks the point at which we have a reasonably strong conviction in these areas:

1. The philosophy of the Vedic literature, especially the Bhagavad-gita and Srimad Bhagavatam.
2. The teachings of Chaitanya Mahaprabhu as presented by Srila Prabhupada.

3. The practises of *bhakti-yoga* sadhana as the daily connection to Krishna.

4. Your own ability to maintain your conviction and dedication to practise for life.

5. Your sustained determination to avoid those things that will slow down spiritual progress – and to regulate your life according to certain rules.

6. Trust in the Vaishnava community to offer you guidance and support.

7. Faith in the abilities of one senior Vaishnava to act as your teacher.

8. A strong expectation of your ability to maintain your relationship as his disciple.

# Initial precepts

The level of intellectual conviction required in order to be known as a committed Vaishnava is established when you agree with the initial precepts found in the Bhagavad-gita, the Upanishads and other sacred literature. Bhaktivinode Thakur provides a list of such precepts which he models on those of other Vaishnava acharyas.

1. The Vedas are the authority for knowledge of transcendent reality, beyond the realm of sense perception.

2. The transcendent reality is manifest in three aspects: *Brahman*, the all-pervading absolute; *Paramatma*, the indwelling Supersoul; and the Supreme Person, *Bhagavan*.

3. *Bhagavan* is one without a second, eternally the source of infinite power, and an ocean of bliss.

4. The individual soul is His eternal, separated part.

5. Certain souls are engrossed by illusory material energy (maya), and are subject to the endless cycle of birth and death.

6. Certain souls are released from the grasp of this energy.

7. All spiritual and material phenomenon are inconceivably, and simultaneously, both one with, and different from, God.

8. Bhakti-yoga, or unmotivated and uninterrupted devotional service to God, is the only means for the conditioned souls to go beyond this world of repeated birth and death, and of their attaining the final objective of spiritual existence.

9. Krishna prema, the highest stage of love for Krishna, God, is alone the final goal of spiritual existence.

10. We can develop our inherent, dormant consciousness of Krishna by reciting His sacred names, discussing His teachings and activities, offering our food and daily activities to Him, and serving His representative in the form of the guru.

Implicit within these ten points are other key ideas from the Vedas and *Vedanta* such as reincarnation (*samsara*), the binding nature of work (*karma*), the need to cultivate higher knowledge (*jnana*), the path to become free from the illusory energy (*yoga*), the levels of divine reality concluding in the personal nature of God (*Vishnu*), the appearance within the world of the divine descents of God (*avatar*), the importance of the teacher (*guru*), the scriptures (*shastras*), and the benefits of holy company (*sadhu-sanga*), the practise of devotion (*sadhana*), and the calling out of the names of God (*mantra-japa*) concluding in divine love (*prema*).

Belief in these – or at very least suspension of disbelief until your discovery of a superior set of concepts – constitutes the informed and logical conviction of a committed Vaishnava.

# Before breakfast

And what of the practise of *bhakti*, the meditation, prayer and study that form the foundations of the spiritual life of the Vaishnava? In order to experience the realities of both our own spiritual nature and that of God, it is essential to begin the practical process of spiritual awakening. The daily and practical activities of *bhakti-yoga* take us from the plane of intellectual conviction or religious belief to liberated action and direct experience.

Activities of *bhakti-yoga*, known as *sadhana* or 'the means to reach the goal,' must be performed daily and regulated according to one's personal capability. Efforts must be made to avoid mechanical practise or ritualism; rather, the aim is to always think favourably of Krishna and act in devotion towards Him. Such constant remembrance of Krishna must be like a steady stream of oil, pouring from one vessel to another.

The more you engage in the practical acts of *bhakti-yoga*, the more you will directly experience spiritual pleasure. It's that simple. However, there is an operating level below which the necessary and pleasurable results are experienced only fractionally. Unless a new practitioner comes up to the level of 'committed Vaishnava' the *sadhana* is not always rewarding enough to be sustainable in the long term.

# Two elements

*Sadhana* practise is made up of two elements: things you should do as much as you can, and things you should try to avoid. Negative restraints *(yama)* go hand-in-hand with spiritually liberating practises *(niyama)*, just as dietary restrictions go very well with medicine for a sick person. If we accept the primary truth – that we are infected with the spiritual disease of maya – then we'll resign ourselves to get well soon. What are the rules for a practising Vaishnava such that he or she is considered to be committed in faith and practise? How many rules are there? Which are most important? These are common questions.

The same questions were asked of Lord Chaitanya five hundred years ago in the village of Kulinagram. Two devotees, Ramananda Basu and Satyaraja Khan, enquired as to what were the duties for householder Vaishnavas. The Lord gave them three principles: To serve the Deity of Krishna; to chant the Holy Names of Krishna; and to serve the Vaishnavas - those who are dear to Krishna. When the devotees further enquired how they could identify such an advanced Vaishnava who was dear to Krishna, Lord Chaitanya began his explanation. In the years that followed, the Lord told them even more. He gave many more detailed practical instructions on the daily life of a devotee to Sanatana Goswami, asking him to compile a handbook on the daily practise of Vaishnavism and listing exactly what should be included in its contents. Other philosophical principles and instructions for worship of the Deity were compiled by Sanatana's brother, Rupa Goswami.

The life of a Vaishnava today is based upon Lord Chaitanya's essential teachings as taught to the Goswamis, and as brought to us by the *guru-parampara* – the succession of gurus – who all taught the same principles yet made minor adjustments according to time, place and circumstances. Sometimes, modifications were made as climate, geography and society changed; at other times, certain principles were given more importance in order to curb maladies that had developed within the pseudo-Vaishnava community. In essence, the purpose of all practical directions for a Vaishnava is the purpose of human life itself: to always remember Krishna, and to never forget Him. These are the two foremost and interdependent rules of Vaishnava life.

# Sustainable regular practises

The following is a list of daily, weekly, fortnightly, monthly and annual practises that constitute a level of Vaishnava sadhana and culture that is progressive without being too arduous. It is designed to be sustainable, and suitable for an ever-growing number of Vaishnavas householders who wish to be recognised as having made solid vows in their spiritual life.

Years of experience have shown that lifetime vows are possible and sustainable, but that if one makes a succession of regular vows of increasing commitment then this is a sure way to make gradual but constant progress. We have advised, for instance, that a minimum of four rounds of the maha-mantra is a solid commitment that will result in substantial spiritual progress. However, after maintaining this for six months or one year you may feel that you can easily increase that minimum number. Chanting eight rounds daily, then twelve, are milestones along the path of devotion. The minimum number of rounds required to be initiated is sixteen.

Here are the regular practises and personal disciplines that make up a rewarding and sustainable level of commitment just suitable for initiation.

## Daily practice

1. To chant a minimum of sixteen uninterrupted rounds of maha-mantra *japa* on beads per day.
2. To create a household altar with pictures of *Pancha-Tattva* and the Vaishnava acharyas, and to keep that place always clean and sacred.

3. To systematically study the scriptures with the commentaries of Srila Prabhupada, specifically the seven books: *Bhagavad-gita*; *Srimad Bhagavatam*; *The Teachings of Lord Chaitanya*; The Nectar of Devotion; *Shri Isopanishad*; *Krishna, the Supreme Personality of Godhead;* and T*he Nectar of Instruction*. (And of these books, at least the first four)

4. To cultivate humility by offering obeisances to the Vaishnavas, the guru, and to the Lord.

5. To invite the Vaishnavas to one's home and to honour, feed and serve them.

6. To wear Tulasi neck beads.

7. To wear *tilak* whenever possible.

8. To hold Hare Krishna kirtan with musical instruments, and to sing and chant the standard songs and prayers.

9. To cook purely for Krishna, and to offer everything before you eat.

10. To learn for recitation selected verses from the Bhagavad-gita and other scriptures.

11. To offer *arati* with incense, lamp and flowers.

12. To maintain your health and spirits by rising early each morning and bathing.

13. To always try to feel compassion, and to give mercy, to all living beings.

14. To be enthusiastic in your spiritual life; to endeavour with confidence, yet to be patient.

15. To always understand the deeper reasons why you are following these rules of life.

16. To avoid those things that act as obstacles to spiritual progress: eating of meat, fish and eggs, gambling, illicit sex and intoxication.

# Weekly and two-weekly practise

1. To extend yourself to others by giving them Krishna

consciousness in some form.

2. To go to a temple if possible and attend an *arati* ceremony.
3. To meet other devotees socially and to develop your friendship with them.
4. To observe the holy *Ekadasi* day by fasting from grains and beans, and to increase reading and chanting on that day.
5. To take part in a Vaishnava *sangha* group for discussion and kirtan.

## Monthly practise

1. To meet or discuss your successes and challenges with your spiritual guide, a senior Vaishnava who is helping you. To reveal your mind in confidence and to ask questions related to your spiritual progress.
2. To take part in book distribution *sankirtan* or a *Harinama* procession, or both.
3. To offer your wealth and time to helping the mission to spread the holy names of Krishna.

## Yearly practise

1. To observe and celebrate, either at home or in a temple, the main Vaishnava festivals for Lord Chaitanya and Nityananda, Narasimhadeva, Ramachandra, Shri Krishna, Srimati Radharani, and Balarama. To fast on these occasions – at least half the day.
2. To observe the festival for Srila Prabhupada, Vyasa Puja, the day after Janmashthami.
3. To see and celebrate the Rathayatra of Jagannatha.
4. To try to take a holiday with other Vaishnavas.
5. To try to spend a week or two of the year on retreat with the devotees.

## Every three or four years

To go on pilgrimage to India and to reside in the holy places, travelling out to see the places where the pastimes of Krishna and His incarnations took place.

## Throughout your life

To introduce others to an appreciation of Krishna consciousness, guiding them as they too take up the practises of *bhakti-yoga*.

# Foundational principles

The process of awakening your dormant consciousness of Krishna can be speeded up or slowed down to almost nothing according to the choices you make in your life. Just as there are positive principles that will directly increase your spiritual vision, so there are also negative principles: those thoughts and actions that will cause you to become forgetful of Krishna.

It's understandable that some of the following restrictions and disciplines may present quite a challenge for you. Some of them may be things you have always enjoyed, and certainly they will be things that family and friends enjoy doing. However, they are important and either following them – or at least accepting that you're going to begin the struggle – is the mark of a committed Vaishnava.

Besides all the practises listed above, which relate specifically to the life of a committed Vaishnava, there are foundational principles for good living mentioned in the Vedas and followed generally by Vaishnavas too. By following them you can have balance in your life and increase your health, mental peace, wealth, and harmony in the home. You will generate good feelings, prosperity, and higher consciousness in the world around you. You'll also avoid some of the major disturbances to your spiritual life. There are so many principles of good living – the Vedas are dedicated to raising everyone up in life and are therefore full of good instructions – but the essential ones are mentioned here for simplicity. If you notice any repetition, that means its important!

The *Padma Purana* lists twelve principles of Dharma. These help an individual cultivate personal virtues and inter-personal morality. They are necessary as a foundation to the pursuance of progressive spiritual life. Because the positive principles are so essential to spiritual life, there are also corresponding negative restrictions which, when observed, serve to remove the obstacles to spiritual life.

The personal restraints are meant to harness the instinctive nature of the mind and senses whose restlessness keeps us on the material platform of life. The so-called 'negative restrictions' help to govern the impulses of fear, anger, jealousy, selfishness, greed and lust. The ethical observances help to cultivate and bring out the qualities of the soul. By engaging in these dutifully, even without full enthusiasm, we can lift our consciousness to the level of compassion, tolerance, and the giving of ourselves in love to others.

Each principle of Dharma implies two ingredients: a range of internal feelings and subsequent moral judgements, and a corollary range of external actions when you apply those judgements in daily life.

# The Elements of Dharma

### Worship – *Ijya*

To cultivate an unshakeable faith in God (*astikya*) and to avoid doubt and despair and those who try to break faith by argument and accusation. To make a personal surrender to God (*ishvara-pranidhan*), and to give expression to faith through quietening the mind, reciting the sacred mantra (*japa*), offering personal prayer (*vandana*) and singing (*kirtan*). To offer gifts of food, fruits, flowers and incense to God, setting aside a sacred place in one's home, and a sacred time in the day, for doing so.

### Study – *Adhyayana*

To read Vedic scripture every day when you are peaceful and reflective. Discuss with others as often as you can. Hear, study, and listen to the wise. Note your questions that arise and ask them later. Memorize the words of Krishna so that your mind returns to them.

## Charity – *Danam*

To feel compassion for the discomforts or pain of others. To feel sympathy for others and extend oneself to them, even when they give no thanks in return. To be kind to people, animals, plants, and Mother Earth herself. To forgive those who show remorse and who apologise to you. To honour and assist those who are weak, impoverished, aged or in pain. To be generous, giving liberally without thoughts of reward.

## Austerity - *Tapa*

To practise voluntary restraint for the purpose of self-realisation. To perform acts of self-denial, giving up possessions, money or time. To make constant efforts to focus your mind on your spiritual practises. To follow regular and occasional observances such as fasting and pilgrimage faithfully. To take vows with others for strength.

## Truth – *Satyam*

To refrain from lying or breaking promises. To speak the truth without distortion or deviation. To speak only that which is true, kind, helpful and necessary. To be fair, accurate and frank in discussions. To not engage in slander or gossip. To earn money honestly.

## Forgiveness – *Kshama*

To be tolerant with people, their words and actions, and with circumstances you cannot control. To let others behave according to their nature without adjusting to you. To be patient with children and the elderly. To accept the apologies of others and to forgive what they've done or said, but to also be prepared to forgive even in the absence of an apology.

## Self-control – *Damah*

To develop the willpower to control the urges of lust, greed and anger. To overcome fear, indecision, procrastination, and persevere, even in difficult circumstances or with challenging persons. To avoid laziness. To conquer over negative emotions. To moderate the appetite (mitahara).

## Non-stealing – *Asteya*

To practise honesty (*arjavam*) and be straightforward and renounce deception. To not blame others for one's own faults. To act honourably, even in hard times. To not deceive others. To not use or take anything that does not belong to you – except with permission. To not be grasping, possessive, or greedy. To avoid envy of others possessions. To refrain from theft or prolonged debt.

### Purity – *Saucham*

To practise radical cleanliness. To keep your body, mind and speech pure. To eat clean, fresh food. To take a bath or shower every morning. To avoid swearing and impure language. To develop a higher cognition, free from prejudice. To discover the hidden lesson in each experience to develop a deeper understanding of life and yourself. To cultivate intuition.

To experience healthy remorse for misdeeds. To verbalise remorse in prayer. To seek out and correct one's faults and bad habits. To welcome correction as a means of bettering yourself. To shun pride and pretension.

### Non-violence – *Ahimsa*

To not injure anyone in thoughts, words or deeds, or to sponsor the same. To not subject or allow others to experience pain or unnecessary anxiety. To not place anyone else in anxiety.

### Peace – *Shanti*

To cultivate peace within oneself as an active practise.

### Service to teachers – *Guru sevanam*

To offer one's profound respect and gratitude to all those who have contributed to one's development of knowledge. To honour the preceptor who gives us the highest type of teaching. To listen carefully to the guru's instructions, and to ask intelligent and relevant questions, serving him with affection.

# The Regulative Principles

According to traditional Vaishnava authorities, there are sixty-four regulative principles of devotional service. These are all positive items of *bhakti* - things that should be done in order to come closer to Krishna. Collectively they are known as *sad-acara* or 'virtuous conduct.' There are also negative principles – things that are to be avoided. These are

## Part Six | Steps toward the big step

collectively known as *nishiddha-acara* or 'prohibited conduct.' They are also known as *virodhi*, or 'obstacles' on the path. The following are all taken from Vaishnava texts, the first four – the 'four regulative principles' - are found in the Srimad Bhagavatam and the remainder are from Srila Rupa Goswami's *Upadeshamrita*, a short handbook in which he offers the "essence of all advice."

1. To refrain from eating meat, fish or eggs, and other items such as garlic and onions. To avoid mushrooms. To not eat more than necessary. To only eat food that has been offered to Krishna.

2. To refrain from taking any substance that is an intoxicant.

3. To refrain from promiscuity, remaining faithful to one's own partner. To regulate one's sexual activity for the purpose of procreation. To follow the rules of celibacy if one is unmarried.

4. To avoid gambling, speculative enterprises and time-wasting entertainments.

5. To curb laziness, apathy, inattentiveness and feelings of discouragement.

6. To avoid faultfinding, speech that offends, controversy, and talking unnecessarily about mundane subjects.

7. To avoid collecting more funds than required.

8. To avoid close friendship with those who are too absorbed in worldly enjoyment and those who reject the idea of God.

9. To avoid close friendship with those devotees who are lazy, ill tempered, attached to bad habits, and speculative philosophies. To avoid those who criticise others, and those who use abrasive speech.

10. To avoid close friendship with those devotees who are duplicitous in their dealings; who are pretentious; or who are excessively sentimental.

11. To not be greedy for mundane achievement.

12. To be straightforward in one's dealings.

13. To not reject any items of sadhana or personal disciplines whimsically. To always try to follow them even in times of

personal difficulty or social disapproval.

# In conclusion

The above lists may seem daunting at first reading, but it is surprising at just how rapidly your life can be transformed to accommodate them if there is enthusiasm and determination. In the company of strong spiritual guides, and with the encouragement of a compassionate preceptor, spiritual life is almost immediately rewarding, and the rewards help us to reach the level required for initiation. While some extra resolve may be required as one approaches the time of initiation, it is made easy by the understanding of the immense rewards to be gained.

# 46

# Are you ready for a guru?

*The question is not an easy one. We have all heard so much about gurus, and not all of it is good. Even the word guru has become tainted by scandals. But if we are satisfied that to have a guru is helpful, and we've found a genuine Vaishnava who is learned, exemplary and kind, and who has the time to guide us, how do we know when we're ready? What do we look for within? What are the risks of having a guru - and what are the rewards?*

**Many people are afraid of the guru-disciple relationship. They feel they will lose themselves in the personality of another.** Or they are scornful, thinking that it will cause them to lose their self-respect. To become a disciple is neither self-deprecation nor a matter of sentimental adulation. Rather it is fully empowered, intelligent, discriminating student-hood.

Learning from the guru is not merely a matter of knowledge transmission from a teacher to a student. That may work in ordinary education, but the process of learning about the soul is radically different. So different, in fact, that we have to first learn how to learn. It is a transformational process, not merely a transmission of knowledge.

Srila Prabhupada tells the story of the expert piano teacher in Vienna who had two students. He taught them both for the same number of hours in his home, but charged them vastly different rates. When both students compared notes they came to the teacher and asked for an explanation. "When I asked you how much you knew about playing the piano," he said to the first student, "you said that you knew nothing at all. So you were easy to teach, and I charged you accordingly." Then he turned to the second student: "But when I asked you, you played the piano for me – and you played badly. So I had to first un-teach you, then only could I begin to teach you. I charged you accordingly, too."

# Transformation, not just transmission

A good disciple is a good student who is able to listen to the guru with trust. He first knows that he knows nothing, and is fully prepared to set aside any attachments to knowledge already acquired that may act as an obstacle to spiritual learning. He is prepared to submit himself to a process of transformation which entails many challenges to his ego. In order to be able to relate properly to the guru, he must voluntarily enter the relationship as someone who is open to correction, criticism or even rebuke. The relationship is not a modern one of relative equality between teacher and student, but a very ancient one of deference, profound respect, and even servitude.

And that's the difficulty. Even though we may know about the classical guru-disciple roles, we are very reluctant, as western converts, to enter into the master-servant roles in modern times. There are insufficient cultural precedents in western society to start with, indeed we have been told, from a very early age, that being anybody's servant is not a good thing, and that equity between human beings is always the best political status quo to aim for. Neither do we want to find ourselves in a situation where we've succumbed to naivety and become disempowered.

Srila Prabhupada once said that taking the step to becoming initiated is 'suicide of the ego,' since it really does involve the death of whoever we think we are. But the ego that dies is what he described as 'false-ego' or not the real self at all. All our identities of body and mind are transitory and have nothing to do, ultimately, with the true self. Revealing the true self is the culmination of a lot of hard work and constant re-adjustment internally, and it may take some time. So our hesitancy is based on the ego protecting the mind and body from the pain of change.

But our hesitancy is also based on the common knowledge that not all teachers are what they say they are. Over the past fifty years in the western world there has been a steadily growing backlash against charlatan spiritual teachers, abusive priests and mischievous 'masters.' We know that there is a body of wisdom that can help us, but the flimsy representatives of that wisdom are seldom truly wise and sometimes downright pernicious. We recognise that we need spiritual guidance but also that self-proclaimed teachers may disappoint us. So the response is that we keep our guard up as we try to embrace the light. Like going skydiving but holding on to the edge of the plane door at the same time, we become stuck between adventure and safety.

And that's the difficulty. The full effect of having a guru is only experienced by those who place themselves as disciples. Disciple infers discipline, and that's a relationship different from being a student, pupil or friend. You can relate to a guru as a friend or guide, but you can get much more from him if you relate to him as a disciple.

# The remote guru

It is possible, of course, to become initiated as a disciple and to still avoid discipline. By keeping the guru at a geographical and emotional distance, it is possible for the disciple to avoid whatever ego-discomfort comes from physical proximity. You get what you ask for in spiritual life. A remote guru leads to remote teachings and a remote relationship. We fear a relationship with a guru because its not 'safe', but its not meant to be safe. The guru is employed on the basis of his capacity to dismantle and decompose the limited self-perception that keeps us suffering. Therefore we shouldn't think that we need a guru who is 'just like me.' The guru is not meant to be someone in whose presence we always feel comfortable.

It's not easy for us to relate to authority. Eastern culture regards individual interests as subservient to family and group needs. In that culture, devotion to a guru, a principle beyond one's immediate needs, is 'ego-syntonic' or compatible with the ego. Not so in Western culture. We have no tradition of the guru position. In the East they can respect the guru, but they do not always absorb his message. In the West we are slow to accept and respect a guru, but we may grasp the intellectual component of his message readily.

However, a person with a weak ego may want to achieve self-worth from the guru. He or she may closely align with the guru because of his perceived charisma. Students who surrender to prop up their self-esteem see the guru as powerful and get a reflected sense of self from that 'borrowed functioning.' In this case they will remain with the guru as long as those needs are met and dispense with him when their needs are no longer met. This is not a genuine guru-disciple relationship.

So the true effect of having a guru is only really available to the genuine disciple – someone who is serious about escaping the cycle of reincarnation and its concomitant sufferings. Once Srila Prabhupada asked a group of his disciples, "Who needs a guru?" "Everyone!" they replied energetically. Much to everyone's surprise, Srila Prabhupada said, "No! Not everyone needs a guru. Only one who wants to put an end to the miserable conditions of material existence-he needs a guru, not everyone. Guru is not a fashion."

But what about 'bogus gurus' as Srila Prabhupada called them? Isn't it right for us to be careful in the face of so much spiritual scandal? Guru is a bit of a four-letter word in the west because there has been a history of shocking abuses of power. No faith tradition and no organisation has been left untouched by the phenomenon of 'bogus gurus.' But things are getting better; the culture of guru takes time to transplant. We are in the first century of a cultural transplant unseen since the days of the Roman Empire, and one hundred years is not very long.

Still, there is need for everyone even remotely considering becoming a disciple to evaluate fully the character, ability, and authenticity of their prospective guru, and for as long as it takes for them to be satisfied. Traditionally that period lasts for at least one year. When the Dalai Lama, confronted with accounts of young Tibetan lamas that had strayed from the path, was asked how long one should inspect one's prospective teacher he replied, shaking his head, "You must spy on him, in private, for ten years."

# 'Not teachers, but cheaters'

When Srila Prabhupada's guru, Srila Bhaktisiddhanta Thakur, was asked about the deplorable state of affairs regarding gurus in India he made it clear to his disciples that many so-called teachers were, in fact, 'not teachers but cheaters,' and he said that, as some people were prone to be cheated, the situation was one of 'the cheaters and the cheated.' He told the story of Kumbha Mela, the enormous religious gathering that fell once every twelve years. Some ordinary men dressed themselves in the saffron robes of a sannyasi and went there to attract feminine attention. Meanwhile, some women went there dressed in the white *saree* of a widow and sought out masculine attention. Both groups thought that the other was the genuine article, and yet both exploited the other for sexual favours. "In this way," he said, "The world is filled with the cheaters and the cheated."

But it is rarely the case that a teacher consciously instigates such a spiritual scandal. More often the scandal comes about as a result of unattended subconscious hankering. The teacher may have lingering desires, but they are regularly excused, ignored or philosophised away. Under the scrutiny of others these desires may be disguised by a veneer of intellectual, institutional or apparently spiritual strength.

When this kind of self-deception does occur, and particularly when others less discerning become implicated in it, it can propel dishonest teachers to try to gain some advantage in the arenas of power, money, or sex by playing on the weakness of others. Sometimes badly wounded in childhood, they feel they have been cheated so much in life they have every right to now take advantage of others. They can even consider their abuse as virtuous. They can have an exaggerated vision of their own greatness.

It is more common than acknowledged that a spiritual leader or religious teacher who has some genuine advancement may – surprisingly – have a correspondingly lower level of emotional intelligence. Sometimes they may not be psychologically aware enough to notice erotic transference as what it is, happening between the disciple and them. And if they have an undeveloped sense of ethical behaviour, particularly the behaviour that is appropriate to their station in life, their age or ashram, an emotional deviation may easily become a physical one.

A very common scenario for this emotional confusion and subsequent erotic transference is an 'east-west' setting, such as a celibate Tibetan *lama* and a western female yoga student. Yet almost the same scenario can be re-created when a western person adopts the position of a spiritual teacher as a consequence of having converted to an eastern tradition. In all cases, a lack of awareness of subtle exchanges, masked by religious terminology and naive trust, can produce complications.

Problems can also occur when the guru, whether from east or west, has had periods of genuine enlightenment in youth or early maturity only to have it fade for some reason after having taken disciples. His reputation, based upon his attainment earlier in life, now serves to confuse prospective followers as to his current level of realisation. His established position of respect, and the hierarchical position that may accompany it, can all but obliterate the actual facts. A psychologist, examining the relationship that develops between the guru and a chosen follower, might describe it as an example of 'inter-subjectivity' – two people helping to create a scandal, both dependent on each other, but both oblivious – until it is too late – of the effect they are having on each other. So for all these good reasons, the guru should be carefully analysed by the prospective disciple for as long as it takes to ascertain his credentials.

# The 'Rabbi test'

The aspiring disciple may like to take a hint from the Jewish tradition, and place the questions that a synagogue congregation ask when they interview a prospective rabbi: "Where did you study?" "Under whom did you study?" "Up to what level have you studied?" "What teaching experience do you have?" and finally, "Who sent you to teach others?" A rabbi who fails to answer these questions satisfactorily cannot become a spiritual leader of a community. Similarly, one searching for a Vaishnava guru would want to establish the capability of a prospective teacher by asking what particular branch of which *sampradaya* he was in, who his guru was, what experience he has of teaching and guiding others and so on. A guru must have received his mantras and training in *parampara*, and he must be able to mention the names of reputable teachers that contributed to his spiritual formation and character development. He should be able to provide examples of his successful teaching of others before he presumes to take disciples.

Entering into a lifelong relationship with anyone is a considerable risk, particularly when the boundaries of the relationship are created by a traditional religious code and sustained by a mutual philosophical conviction. The guru may be as much a convert to this code and conviction as the disciple, and just as someone may change their mind to become a Vaishnava at one stage of their intellectual and spiritual journey, so they often exercise their freedom of choice and retreat back to their mother culture and previous convictions. So it is a risk for the disciple – and for the guru, too.

The prospective disciple may be concerned about the authenticity of the guru, but the guru is also taking a risk by investing his time and making a commitment to the student. Disciples can, and do, also drift from the path, even after making their lifetime vows in good faith. They can become ungrateful for the guru's guidance, and grow resentful at his presence in their life. Both being a disciple and being a guru are thus fraught with the potential for disappointment. But if nothing is ventured then nothing is gained. Too much analysis will lead to paralysis and no-one will move forward.

Basing their approach on extreme caution, or having been disappointed, some newcomers to Vaishnavism have created new philosophies over recent decades. Initiation without a guru is one of them. But the guru and initiation come as a package, because it is the guru who gives initiation. Since a mantra read from a book is simply syllables, the novel idea of 'guru-less initiation' is nothing more than a hopeful invention.

Another notion is that: "I will wait until the guru manifests before me." This is much better than an impetuous decision to become initiated, followed some time later by an equally hasty rejection of the guru, and the prospective disciple is right to wait. But if the waiting continues for decades, life passes by without a guru at all. It may be, for instance, that the guru has already been sent by Krishna, but the seeker did not recognise the guru. As Srila Prabhupada said, it is not that the guru must have four hands.

Others believe that Krishna sends gurus along at frequent intervals. They become initiated by one, then take advice from another without referring to the first, then leave both their gurus for a third who is a 'genuine *mahatma.*' In this way they effectively become initiated by a pseudo-guru each time because their actual guru is their own mind. They mentally project their own novel conceptions upon successive figures and initiate themselves. As their mind changes, so does their choice of guru.

It is essential that the guru is the person who, in addition to having all the other qualifications, has the ability to cut through the imaginations of the candidate, argue convincingly against lower conceptions, and establish the candidate in spiritual strength. What does that feel like? Most say that when it happens it is a relief. Indeed, without that sense of having found someone who can inspire, inform, remove doubt, and give hope, it is impossible to put oneself forward for initiation.

# Blowing on a cold lassi

But it would be wrong to assume, even in the face of so many 'bogus gurus,' that were was no-one genuine who could ever be trusted. And it would be completely incorrect to draw the conclusion that the much safer path was to not have a guru at all. In India there is a saying:

> *"Once, years ago, you burned your mouth on a cup of hot milk. Now, even when you hold a cup of cold yogurt you blow on it."*

The great Sufi sage Rumi said: "Fool's gold exists because there is real gold" and Srila Prabhupada explained: "Just because there is counterfeit money, it does not mean there is no real money."

The guru-disciple relationship is an essential component of all spiritual paths derived from the Vedas, and it exists in different forms throughout all religious traditions. For the Vaishnava aspirant, the guru is an expression of Krishna's compassion; a teacher of sacred lore, ethics and ritual; a living exemplar of the tradition; a confidential friend, guide, mentor and intercessor. He petitions Krishna on behalf of his disciples, inspires them to take the various processes of devotion, and gives them courage at moments when they stall. The guru inspires them, corrects them, trains them and congratulates them. The guru is thus the best friend anyone could ever have, and there is always a genuine guru to be sought out – although it may take some effort on the part of the aspirant.

And that may be part of our problem as would-be disciples. We are sometimes singularly lacking in effort, or even blind to the very conception that spiritual progress may involve making a physical effort to find a teacher. We have notions that spiritual life should come almost effortlessly as a series of internal, and highly personal, flashes of enlightenment – with or without the external agency of a guru. As westerners we are raised as individualists, and sometimes a sense of our own individuality and singular thought process is our most prized human virtue. It is consequently difficult for us to assume a role as a spiritual student – a role that comes to us, it seems, from a foreign cultural context and tradition. We may become a student at a local adult education centre for a course of lessons in exchange for money, but we'll be reluctant to perpetuate the student-teacher relationship much beyond the end of the course. We wouldn't hang a picture of the teacher in a prominent place in our home, and we would be aghast if the teacher pointed out our weaknesses, or offered us advice on our choices of conduct beyond the classroom.

Of course, with other teachers and trainers we may adopt a different approach. If we seek out a personal physical trainer then we expect him to do whatever it takes to get us into top condition. If he asks us to exercise strenuously in front of him – so hard that we perspire profusely and even shed a tear at the muscular pain – we think we have found a 'very good trainer' and we'll pay handsomely and tell all our friends. If our psychotherapist asks us to explore our most painful moments of rejection and trauma, so much that we break down and weep, we feel that we have encountered a 'very good therapist' who really knows her stuff.

Curiously, we do not always imagine that a guru should similarly occupy such a privileged place in our life, and we feel uncomfortable about giving them a similar level of access to our vulnerability. We are reluctant to become a disciple of anyone, at any time. We fear the loss of our own discrimination, our intelligence, and the precious prerogative to argue with ideas we do not accept. Even if we do manage to place the guru in our life we remain cautious. At the first sign of the guru's imperfection – either actual or imagined - we abandon the relationship, never to explore it again. Should the guru even think of correcting us with strong words, our connection is jettisoned without a further thought. Regarding the occasionally sharp words of the guru, a positive contribution to the life of the disciple, Srila Gaura Kishor Das Babaji said:

> "Those sadhus who speak sharp words to drive away the witch of the illusory energy are actually the only real devotees of Krishna and friends of the living entities. The conditioned living being experiences the distressful quarrelling of his wife and close relatives and is rudely treated by them until death, yet he never desires to leave their association. On the other hand, he absorbs himself in trying to appease and serve them. But when a devotee of the Lord, who is always desirous of the living entity's ultimate welfare, chides him just once with instructions meant to drive away Maya, then that conditioned entity immediately makes plans to leave the saintly person for his entire life."

Therefore the prospective disciple, once having satisfied himself as to the qualifications of the guru, should think of his own suitability as a prospective disciple. He can change places with the guru for a few moments. Instead of considering whether the guru will meet his expectations, and subjecting the guru to his exacting scrutiny, he can instead think of himself from the guru's own perspective: "Am I good enough to become his disciple? Will I be able to do justice to the teaching and help that my guru will offer me? Am I ready to learn, and be corrected? Can I keep the commitments of initiation?"

When all these questions have been answered positively, and when all measures have been put in place to sustain and develop one's spiritual practise – even in the face of all life's challenges – it is time to say to oneself: "Yes, I am ready for a guru."

*Please turn to Appendix 1 Becoming a Disciple: A self-test, and Appendix 2 Becoming a Disciple: A Checklist*

# 47

# Serious to find a guru

*In chapter seven of his book,* Raja Vidya, *His Divine Grace A. C. Bhaktivedanta Swami Prabhupada explains how our inclination towards Krishna is reciprocated by the Lord's favourable instructions within our heart. When we become more serious we are enjoined to seek out a holy person who can teach us further. But we had better exercise caution, explains Srila Bhaktisiddhanta Saraswati - if we have some residual pride then Krishna may send us, through His illusory energy, someone who matches our mentality.*

**Krishna is a friend to everyone, but he is a special friend to his devotees.** As soon as we become a little inclined toward him, he begins to give favourable instructions from within our hearts so that we can gradually make progress. Krishna is the first spiritual master, and when we become more interested in him, we have to go to a *sadhu*, holy man, who serves as spiritual master from without. This is enjoined by Shri Krishna himself in the following verse:

*tad viddhi pranipatena pariprasnena sevaya*
*upadeksyanti te jnanam jnanitas tattva-darsinah*

"Just try to learn the truth by approaching a spiritual master. Inquire from him submissively and render service unto him. The self-realized soul can impart knowledge unto you because he has seen the truth". *(Bhagavad-gita 4.34)*

"It is necessary to select a person to whom we can surrender ourselves. Of course, no one likes to surrender to anyone. We are puffed up with whatever knowledge we have, and our attitude is, "Oh, who can give me knowledge?" Some people say that for spiritual realization there is no need for a spiritual master, but so far as Vedic literature is concerned, and as far as Bhagavad-gita, Srimad Bhagavatam, and the Upanishads are concerned, there is need of a spiritual master. Even in the material world if one wants to learn to be a musician, he has to search out a musician to teach him, or if one wants to be an engineer, he has to go to a technological college and learn from those who know the technology.

Nor can anyone become a doctor by simply purchasing a book from the market and reading it at home. One has to be admitted to a medical college and undergo training under licensed doctors. It is not possible to learn any major subject simply by purchasing books and reading them at home. Someone is needed to show us how to apply that knowledge which is found in the books. As far as the science of God is concerned, Shri Krishna, the Supreme Personality of Godhead himself, advises us to go to a person to whom we can surrender. This means that we have to check to see if a person is capable of giving instructions in Bhagavad-gita and other literatures of God realization. It is not that we are to search out a spiritual master whimsically. We should be very serious to find a person who is actually in knowledge of the subject. In the beginning of Bhagavad-gita, Arjuna was talking to Krishna just like a friend, and Krishna was questioning how he, as a military man, could give up fighting. But when Arjuna saw that friendly talks would not make a solution to his problems, he surrendered unto Krishna, saying:

*sisyas te 'ham sadhi mam tvam prapannam*

"Now I am your disciple and a soul surrendered unto you. Please instruct me." *(Bhagavad-gita 2.7)*

This is the process. It is not that we should blindly surrender, but we should be able to inquire with intelligence. Without inquiry, we cannot make advancement. In school, a student who makes inquiries from the teacher is usually an intelligent student. It is generally a sign of intelligence when a small child inquires from his father, "Oh, what is this? What is that?" We may have a very good spiritual master, but if we have no power to inquire, we cannot make progress.

Nor should the inquiry be of the nature of a challenge. One should not think, "Now I will see what kind of spiritual master he is. I will challenge him." Our inquiries *(pariprasnena)* should be on the subject of service *(sevaya)*. Without service, our inquiries will be futile. But even before making inquiries, we should have some qualification. If we go to a store to purchase some gold or jewellery and we know nothing about jewels or gold, we are likely to be cheated. If we go to a jeweller and say, "Can you give me a diamond?" he will understand that this is a fool. He could charge us any price for anything. That kind of searching will not do at all. We first have to become a little intelligent, for it is not possible to make spiritual progress otherwise." — *Raja Vidya, chapter 7.*

## Types of guru

"Only the person Lord Krishna sends us as spiritual master will manifest before us as our guru. We are given a spiritual master according to our fortune. Different people have different mentalities, and the omniscient Lord sends each an appropriate spiritual master. There are those who desire the Lord's non-duplicitous mercy and who completely depend on Him for their success. These souls please the Lord with their simple sincerity. To bestow His mercy upon them, He appears before them personally.

To those who want something else from the Lord, who are not actually aspiring for His complete mercy, the Lord sends through His illusory energy a spiritual master appropriate to the mentality. A sincere person never faces difficulty but quickly finds a bona fide guru."

*(From the book of lectures 'Amrita Vani' as spoken by Srila Bhaktisiddhanta Saraswati Thakur and written down by his secretary Sundarananda Vidyavinode.*

# 48

# Testing the guru

*How do you test a guru? How can you assess a person whom you already acknowledge as a spiritually advanced teacher? How much does he have to know? What are the indicators of spiritual realisation, or inspiration? How do you test authenticity, or sincerity? And how can anyone measure humility – or compassion? Is it all arbitrary and subjective – or is there a standard against which a guru must be tested?*

**It is not easy to evaluate another's enlightenment from the unenlightened state.** Even having criteria for identifying an authentic teacher may prove difficult. Yet as difficult as it may be, it is the duty of the prospective disciple to test the guru – for as long as required – in order to establish his credentials. Only by the process of testing can a guru be selected with confidence. Without such testing it is possible to accept an unqualified person as a guru, thus becoming a gullible, blind follower as Srila Prabhupada describes it:

> "Blind following and absurd inquiries - these things are condemned in this verse. Blind following means: "Oh, there is a swami. So many thousands of people are following. Let me become his disciple." This is called blind following. You do not know what is that swami, whether he is a swami or a rascal. You do not know. But because everyone is going, 'Oh, let me become his disciple.' This is blind following, without any knowledge, blind following." *(Srila Prabhupada, Bhagavad-gita 4.34-39 lecture, 12th January 1969, Los Angeles)*

Srila Prabhupada always explained that having a guru was not merely having a teacher, but a spiritual preceptor to whom one could 'surrender' as the human representative of God. This implied a high degree of trust in his words. Referring to the same verse, the famous Bhagavad-gita 4.34 where Lord Krishna advises Arjuna to find a guru, he comments:

"First of all, you must find out a person, who, if you can surrender there...*tad viddhi pranipatena* [Bg. 4.34]. *Pranipata*, surrender, that is required first. If you think somebody, that he's not worth surrendering, then don't make him guru. Don't make a fashion. First of all you test that 'Whether I can surrender?' *Pranipata*. Then try to understand." *(Srila Prabhupada, Srimad Bhagavatam 7.6.2 lecture, 18th June 1976, Toronto)*

If you have located a person who seems to be more spiritually advanced than yourself, and seems capable and willing to teach you, how long should you take to test him so that you can prove that he is everything he seems? Srila Prabhupada suggests it might take longer than you think:

"First of all you find out the person, that one who is better than you. Then you submit. Therefore the rules and regulation are that nobody should accept blindly any guru, and nobody should blindly accept any disciple. They must behave, one another, at least for one year so that the prospective disciple can also understand, 'Whether I can accept this person as my guru.' And the prospective guru also can understand, 'Whether this person can become my disciple.' This is the instruction by Sanatana Goswami in his *Hari Bhakti Vilasa.*" *(Srila Prabhupada, Bhagavad-gita 13.1-2 lecture, 25 February 1975, Miami)*

Where does this testing period of one year originate? Was it an arbitrary period set purely as a cautionary measure for his western followers, or was it based on something from tradition? Srila Prabhupada, as he usually did, had faithfully reproduced an instruction given by Sanatana Goswami:

"By living together for one year they can ascertain from seeing each other's nature whether they can act as guru and disciple. Indeed, there is no other way to determine this." *(Hari Bhakti Vilasa 1.74)*

During the period of one year the disciple, preferably living with the prospective guru, has to establish whether he is indeed better than him, whether he speaks what has been spoken before by the Lord and other holy persons; and whether the holy man is actually a living example of what he's teaching. The guru cannot be a hypocrite; he must speak and act according to the gurus who have lived before him.

> "But if you want to know who is a spiritual master, then you have to test him whether he is speaking exactly like the bona fide spiritual master. Shri Narottama Das Thakura has explained about this, who is spiritual master. What is that? He says, *sadhu sastra guru vakya, citete kariya aikya*. If you want to advance yourself in spiritual science, then you have to test these three things. What is that? Sadhu, saintly person. Sadhu, sastra, scriptures, and spiritual master. Now suppose you want to know who is a spiritual master. Then you have to test whether he's speaking just like other saintly persons and whether he's following scriptures. Sadhu sastra. So you have to test a spiritual master by corroborating whether he is speaking according to the scriptural injunction, whether he's speaking (according) to other saintly persons." *(Srila Prabhupada, Teachings of Lord Chaitanya lecture, 25th September 1968, Seattle)*

The aspirant disciple must reach the point where he feels that the person he's been scrutinizing has passed all his tests and is fit to become his guru. He has to accept everything the guru says as the truth. At the same time, the guru scrutinizes the prospective disciple for one year, to see whether he can accept him as a spiritual student:

> "Unless one is prepared that 'I am accepting somebody as my spiritual master. I must accept whatever he says,' if there is any doubt, that 'I cannot accept his words verbatim,' then one should not accept him as spiritual master. That is hypocrisy. One must be first of all convinced. Therefore it is the duty of the spiritual master and the disciple to associate—that is the injunction of Sanatana Goswami—for some time, and both of them should study. The disciple should study "whether I can accept this saintly person as my spiritual master." And spiritual master also will see "whether I can accept this boy, this person, as my disciple." That is the way. But sometimes the time is reduced. That doesn't matter. But the principle is this, that before accepting a spiritual master you can examine him, you can scrutinize him, but not after accepting him." *(Srila Prabhupada Initiation lecture, 13th July 1971, Los Angeles)*

Sometimes, the guru may delegate someone else to ascertain the qualifications of the disciple. The guru must, of course, trust that his delegate has a good sense of character and can spot a good disciple when he sees one. The delegate may then supervise the candidate for the entire year, reporting back to the guru. Equally, the aspiring disciple may choose to delegate responsibility to others to ascertain the authenticity of the guru. This sometimes happens if the disciple has no physical access to the guru or meets him only occasionally. It may also happen if the guru's credentials have already been established by a group of his peers and seniors and if he has a long track record of excellent behaviour and teaching. The prospective disciple is often tempted to take the easy option and accept the Vaishnava as his prospective guru simply because he is celebrated by his community or honoured by many others. However, just because someone is a guru for many disciples doesn't mean that he is the right guru for the aspirant. The idea is to match the disciple's personal requirements with the right guru for him – not simply the most popular one.

Deputising one's personal prerogative of testing the guru to a committee – even when that committee is a group of esteemed elders - tends to reduce the power of the disciple. It removes the personal element in the guru-disciple dynamic by placing full responsibility for the guru's credentials onto a third party. Although this may be a quite understandable measure given the prevailing circumstances, having a committee approve or disapprove the guruship of an individual indirectly helps to turn the figure of the guru into an organisational post, rather than a personal role – and that can have unhelpful repercussions over time.

That is because a group of inspired peers living and working in spiritual community can gradually, over several generations, become devitalised into a religious body that is sapped of its original vitality. The sacred blessing of a person to act as a guru can similarly degenerate over time into the mere certification of a priest. In this way the dynamic figure of the guru becomes lost and an institutional functionary takes his place. So the scripture states that the guru and disciple are never obviated from the personal responsibility of scrutinizing and approving each other. This insistence on keeping it personal (even when circumstances seem to prevent it) is yet another method to ensure the purity of the guru-disciple relationship and, through it, the healthy continuity of the *parampara*. Srila Prabhupada writes:

> "It is imperative that a serious person accept a bona fide spiritual master in terms of the sastric injunctions. Shri Jiva Goswami advises that one not accept a spiritual master in terms of hereditary

or customary social and ecclesiastical conventions. One should simply try to find a genuinely qualified spiritual master for actual advancement in spiritual understanding." *(Srila Prabhupada, Chaitanya Charitamrita, Adi 1.35 purport)*

In ISKCON many of the most spiritually advanced members travel and preach, taking the Krishna consciousness movement to new countries. Because of this they are often faced with the prospect of initiating disciples they have not personally scrutinized. It is also the case that aspirant disciples select their gurus from a number of those senior members simply because they are already known as gurus, and they have been approved by both their peers and other disciples like themselves. This is obviously at odds with the ideal situation as described above. But it has proven difficult to preserve personal scrutiny within a rapidly expanding international movement, especially when the culture of testing the guru *in absentia* has been in place since the extensive travelling of Srila Prabhupada himself and his deputising of the task. Yet when he was asked, Srila Prabhupada insisted that the disciple must somehow test the prospective guru himself. Not only that, but the one acting as guru must have been commissioned and approved by his own spiritual master, not by a committee:

> **Svarupa Damodara:** [The professor asked me] how do you know that guru is qualified, spiritual master is qualified? Then I said [answered] everything is written in the sastras, so we have to follow according to the injunctions written in the sastras. So all the qualifications of a pure devotee, of a bona fide guru, is written there. Just like you are a professor of physics in the university. Before you came, you had some qualification, degree of doctors. And then there is a committee to decide you whether you are qualified for the post. So it is selected by a committee of members and then they interview and then they find out your qualifications. If they find that you are qualified for the post, so you are selected as a professor. It's like that in the spiritual field also. There are revealed scriptures and there everything is written what will be the qualification of a guru and then how to choose a bona fide one. So everything is written, you should follow the injunctions of the revealed scriptures accordingly.
>
> **Srila Prabhupada:** Committee is his spiritual master, he orders that you do this.

Part Six | Testing the guru

*(Morning Walk, 1-3 October 1972 LA)*

All the necessary qualifications of the guru can be summed up in just one qualification: he is a devotee of God. And all the tests can be shrunk into one: that he has raised himself up to the level where he is capable of carrying out the order of Shri Chaitanya Mahaprabhu – to 'become guru' and take the names of Krishna to every town and village:

**Atreya Rsi:** How many qualifications does a spiritual master have in terms of being a spiritual master?

**Prabhupada:** One qualification: he is a devotee of God. That's all.

**Atreya Rsi:** Does he have to be designated by the former spiritual master? He has to be devotee...

**Prabhupada:** Oh, yes, oh yes.

**Atreya Rsi:** ...surrendered and designated. That is...identifies disciplic succession: both surrender and designation.

**Prabhupada:** And by the result.

**Atreya Rsi:** And the result of activity.

**Prabhupada:** So far designation is concerned, the spiritual master authorizes every one of his disciples. But it is up to the disciple to carry out the order, able to carry out or not. It is not that spiritual master is partial, he designates one and rejects other. He may do that. If the other is not qualified, he can do that. But actually his intention is not like that. He wants that each and every one of his disciple become as powerful as he is or more than that. That is his desire. Just like father wants every son to be as qualified or more qualified than the father. But it is up to the student or the son to raise himself to that standard.

**Atreya Rsi:** Yes, I understand.

**Prabhupada:** If you are incapable of raising yourself to the standard of becoming spiritual master that is not your spiritual master's fault; that is your fault. He wants, just like Chaitanya Mahaprabhu said, amara ajnaya guru hana[Cc. Madhya 7.128], 'By My order, every one of you become a guru'. If one cannot carry out the order of Chaitanya Mahaprabhu, then how he can become a guru? The first qualification is that he must be able to carry out the order of Chaitanya Mahaprabhu. Then he becomes guru. So that carrying out the order of Chaitanya Mahaprabhu depends on one's personal capacity. Amara ajnaya guru hana. *(Room Conversation, 29 June 1972, San Diego)*

The following year, Srila Prabhupada explained that his personal order to 'become a spiritual master' came when he was ordered to 'preach this gospel' in the English language by his superior authority, his own spiritual master.

"One does not become spiritual master by his own whims. That is not spiritual master. He must be ordered by superior authority. Then he's spiritual master. Amara ajnaya. Just like in our case. Our superior authority, our spiritual master, he ordered me that: 'You just try to preach this gospel, whatever you have learned from me, in English.' So we have tried it. That's all. It is not that I am very much qualified. The only qualification is that I have tried to execute the order of superior authority. *(Bhagavad-gita 2.2 Lecture, 3rd August 1973, London)*

So the fact that a senior Vaishnava has disciples, or that he has been 'approved' by the GBC of ISKCON, does not in itself make him qualified to be your spiritual master. The GBC does not 'certify' anyone as guru, it simply says that it has 'no objections' to the person giving initiations to novices in *bhakti*. Ultimately, you are the one who is to approve the Vaishnava as a guru - and no organisational arrangements can obviate your responsibilities in doing this. Only you can confer that status on someone. 'Guru' is a description of how you regard that senior Vaishnava; it is not a certification of a devotee's level of spiritual attainment. It may take some time for you to ascertain the worthiness of the particular devotee you are interested in, but any time invested will be well spent.

Your first duty is to carefully read what Srila Prabhupada describes as the qualities of a guru and the duties of a disciple. These can be found throughout his books and recorded lectures. There are additional useful passages in the *Uddhava-gita* and the *Hari Bhakti Vilasa*. There are also some sections in this book which can be reviewed. The second element of testing is to see whether a particular Vaishnava seems to be speaking and acting in a way that would allow you to select him as your guru.

Once you have reached that point, you can also test his efficacy as a guru by looking at the disciples he has produced. Ask yourself this question: what are his students like? If you choose this guru you may develop at least some of the peculiarities of his long-term students. Some questions might be: are they bright, energetic and aware? Do they have a good understanding of the philosophy and some expertise in its practical application? Have you experienced that they're considerate of your needs? Are they generally helpful, polite in speech and clean-living?

Or are they excessively intellectual, sentimental, touchy-feely, provocative, passive or impersonal in their dealings? Do they have a tendency to work or live separately from others? Are they under-educated, a bit on the lazy side, prone to superstition, or given to messianic notions? Do they become involved in side issues, excessive fund-raising, or campaigning on single issues? Just as a tree can be judged by the fruits it produces, so you can also test a guru by the disciples.

You can write down a list of your personal requirements of a guru and then test the guru by comparing his capabilities to your list.

*Please turn to Appendix 3 The Guru: A Checklist*

# 49

# The practical path of initiation

*In this chapter I present the steps towards initiation in ISKCON. Although requirements are slightly different according to locality, most of the stages described here are common throughout the Society. Details are available from your local ISKCON centre.*

**Initiation means the beginning of something.** In spiritual life, it refers to the beginning of a new stage of spiritual practice, normally when you begin some new discipline, begin a course of study of an ancient text, start performing a particular ritual, or enter into a student-teacher relationship with a guru – or all of the above. Srila Prabhupada offered two initiations to his disciples; the first was given when they had reached a level of stability in their daily meditation on the maha-mantra and a personal commitment to ethical and moral principles which he styled 'the four regulative principles.' The second initiation, although not offered to everyone, came when the disciple had become 'spiritually purified.'

Both of these initiations are based upon the disciple's understanding of the Vaishnava philosophy and theology and their free and voluntary acceptance of the personal discipline and regular practise involved. There are no forced initiations and no-one is obliged or pressured to become a commited follower or disciple of anyone else. The candidate for initiation is meant to understand that the vows he or she will be making are for life. Although no-one can predict their future, the candidate is meant to take into consideration their current circumstances, and to examine whether those look set to endure for the foreseeable future.

To receive the first, or '*Harinama*', initiation within ISKCON means to formally hear the Hare Krishna mantra from an experienced Vaishnava and to promise to recite it a fixed number of times daily. It also means to rigorously avoid committing any offenses to the Hare Krishna mantra which, as you will have been instructed, is non-different from Krishna

## Part Six | The practical path of initiation

Himself. It also means to refrain from bad habits that compromise your spiritual focus, your determination, or your morality. It also means that from now on you promise to live as a Vaishnava for the rest of your life, dedicating your days to His devotional service from early morning, to offer everything you eat first to Krishna, to study Krishna's words, and to serve Him and His representative, the guru.

The long road to initiation begins from the moment you find you're becoming serious about the teachings of Krishna because of the difference they've made to your life. In keeping with most people who experiment with the teachings and practices of *bhakti-yoga*, you've probably found that you can only move forward in spiritual life when you begin to enjoy it. That's as it should be.

Many newcomers to Krishna consciousness, for instance, discover they can move relatively easily from chanting one round of the Hare Krishna mantra to two, then four and so on, until they reach a level that's comfortable for them. They also find that being a vegetarian is not too difficult, and the other dietary rules don't pose too much of a problem. As they experience the pleasurable results of a new way of life, it becomes easier for them to trust that any other efforts they make towards Krishna will also be more than amply rewarded, and so they adjust their life, their circle of close friends, and their daily routine to reflect their new goals.

At this time, as you begin to think seriously of making further commitment to spiritual practises and personal disciplines, it will also be essential to consider how the upcoming changes in your life may affect your intimate circle of family and closer friends. While it may be easy for you to choose some new friends who will be more sympathetic to your spiritual development, you cannot choose a new family. Becoming a vegetarian, for instance, even in these more enlightened times, can still present difficulties for family members and it will require thorough discussion until, by mutual agreement, you can move forward together in a shared understanding.

The minimum qualifications for becoming initiated are that you have been chanting sixteen rounds of *japa* and following the four regulative principles for a significant period of time. You must be able to say that you accept the teachings of Krishna as taught by Srila Prabhupada, and that you have a supportive network of devotee friends who will assist you to maintain the promises you make at initiation. You should also understand the meanings of the 'Ten Offenses' as listed in the *Padma Purana* (see Appendix 4). These are to be avoided by the initiated disciple. With all that in mind we can now have a look at the stages involved in the process of your becoming initiated.

# Spiritual friends

If you have gradually made progress in your commitment up to chanting sixteen rounds each day, studying Srila Prabhupada's books regularly, and you've successfully given up your unwanted habits, there's a good chance that you managed to do it with help from other devotees. Perhaps you have some good friends who have always encouraged you; maybe you belong to a group that meets regularly for kirtan and discussion, or perhaps you have the help of a senior devotee who guides you.

Whoever helped you this far in your spiritual life is going to be even more important to you after you become initiated. At the time of initiation you will be making lifetime vows that you will be expected to keep. You'll also be promising to continue to make spiritual advancement just as seriously as you've been doing up until now. In order to be successful in all this, you will need various types of help. Taking help from others is not a sign of weakness; it is one of the cardinal elements of the life of a Vaishnava. In addition to being helped by your guru, there are others who will form a traditional framework of spiritual community that will be essential in your spiritual development.

Firstly, you will need solid, supportive friendships with other devotees who can offer you moral and sometimes practical help. They should be encouraging of your efforts in spiritual life, and be ready to discuss the philosophy and how it applies practically. They should also be able to discuss any challenges or obstacles you may have in a sympathetic and understanding manner. Preferably they should be ready to offer you constructive criticism, and you should also be ready to hear that from them.

Initiation is a stage on your journey of spiritual life. Although it is a time of change for you, the change should not include moving away from those who have helped you and supported you so far. Good friends, especially spiritually strong friends, should not be relegated to your past.

Rather, initiation is a time for deepening existing friendships as well as making new ones, because those good friends will be an important part of your future as well.

# Creating community

A very good practise is to meet together with your friends separate from any temple functions you attend. You can chant *japa* and sing kirtan together, read the Bhagavad-gita and discuss your spiritual goals. You can also share any doubts or obstacles you might have. By meeting together as a group of friends you will gain strength and inspiration; by discussing common challenges or question you will maintain a sense of realistic perspective in your life as you balance your spiritual practice with your study, work and family commitments. It is for this reason that small, local groups were created. These are not for newcomers only, but are meant to provide the foundation for sustainable spiritual practise. The dynamics of such a group – the sum total of the relationships that comprise it – work best when everyone is a close friend. In many towns and cities there are, in fact, two groups: a monthly open meeting for newcomers to Krishna consciousness, and a weekly or fortnightly group just for committed devotees and the initiated.

In the early days of the Hare Krishna movement, devotees would all live together at the temple, often a large, converted house in the suburbs of a large city. It would be their place of worship, their place of work, and their home. They would sing together, work together, and eat together – all in the same place. Today, that communal way of life comprises only a small fraction of the Vaishnava community, but the principle of coming together with other Vaishnavas remains a time-tested method of gaining spiritual inspiration and knowledge. If devotees cannot live together in the same building – and most cannot - then the next best thing is to speak with each other regularly, to enjoy each other's company – and to eat together. The success of Krishna consciousness has meant that there are now many thousands of places where devotees come together to sing, study and enjoy *Krishna prasadam*, so spiritual friendship and community-building remains an essential component in the life of the devotee. The local group is thus the basic building block of the Hare Krishna movement today.

Without being a member of a group, it is not guaranteed that you will have regular access to kirtan, study and devotee fellowship. For these and many other reasons, it is highly recommended - and is now obligatory in many places - that as a candidate for initiation, you join a group near to you and enjoy the benefits offered. If there is no group within easy reach, the devotees will help you to start one. Groups may be styled and formatted variously according to the local preferences, with titles such as *Sanga*, *Bhakti-Sanga*, *Nama-Hatta* or *Bhakti-Vriksha*, but the central purpose is to gather together at least monthly for kirtan, readings and discussions. Some groups may opt for meetings that are simply kirtan all the way through, and some groups gather simply for reading. The extra component of these meetings is that, through them, the combined effort of the group can be channelled toward outreach and attracting new members to the message of Krishna.

# Spiritual Guidance

It is also essential to have at least one friend who you regard as your spiritual guide. Although you may have many friends, all of whom enthusiastically support you and wish you well in your spiritual progress; your spiritual guide has something extra. He or she has more practical experience of the application of the Vaishnava life, substantially more knowledge, is a bit further along the path and is someone you can depend on. They also have time to meet with you one-to-one when required. They are there to listen to you, to help you discern your response to personal doubts and challenges, and to help you grow to maturity. Initially, they will help you work out your personal application of the various principles and practises of Vaishnava life, reviewing it with you regularly. They will be interested to hear about what has happened since the last time you met and will help you set your personal goals.

In practise, there are many types of spiritual guide in a wide spectrum of Vaishnavas. Some are purely friends with whom the relationship is very informal, some are more like coaches or personal trainers, some like counsellors or therapists, and some resemble spiritual directors or philosophers. All of them, to one degree or another, are gurus in the sense that anyone who teaches you spiritual knowledge, embodies spiritual wisdom, and offers spiritual guidance is a guru. But the difference between the guide and the guru is one of level of *bhakti*, the degree of formal commitment, and the nature of respect that flows from you to him. The spiritual guide can be changed, another taking his place if and when circumstances or the relationship demands; but the guru-disciple relationship is lifelong in all but the most extreme circumstances.

It is the nature of language that, internationally, several terms have evolved for such a spiritual guide. Sanskrit terms have not proved universally popular – they probably have too many syllables – but traditionally the terms *deshaka*, *upadeshaka*, *vidvan* and so on would be employed. The term *shiksha-guru* has been mooted occasionally, but since the earliest Vedic texts have a very specific meaning for this term, and mediaeval texts use the term to indicate the highest level of guru, the term has not been taken up to indicate an intermediate spiritual guide. The English terms 'Mentor' or 'Counsellor', or simply 'Senior Devotee' and sometimes 'Siksha Guru' now appear to be increasingly popular.

Whatever the term employed locally, the function of the spiritual guide is the most important thing. He or she – or perhaps you will be lucky enough to be guided by a couple - will be able to provide you with regular instruction and guidance. Your guide should be acquainted with the scriptures and Srila Prabhupada's commentary, style and presentation. The spiritual guide should be well acquainted with a range of philosophical notions antagonistic to Vaishnavism and expert in arguing against them. He should be well experienced in the devious nature of the mind under the influence of the ego, and aware of the many emotional pitfalls along the spiritual path, such as apathy, impatience, lethargy and despondency. He should be balanced in his spiritual life, should have consideration for your particular needs and goals, and have sufficient time and concern to help you. Your guide must demonstrate a good example of a positive, confident approach to devotional life and must, of course, be practising Vaishnava *sadhana* at a serious level.

Meetings should take place regularly, preferably in person. In some locations such meetings are obligatory every three months and in some other locations only twice a year. In cases where distance is a factor, the meetings may be over the telephone or some other electronic media. During meetings any questions on the philosophy can be discussed and challenges revealed. Since revelation of one's doubts and challenges will arise during these meetings, confidentiality is an absolute requirement, naturally. Some devotees like to keep a record or chart of their progress in chanting their daily *japa*, their reading and so on and they may choose to share these records with their guide as part of their regular discussions.

# Understanding the subject

Prior to initiation, it is advised that you learn about Krishna consciousness – the philosophy, theology, the values, the history and culture – by reading the legacy of words left to us by Srila Prabhupada. He wrote his books not simply for his disciples of yesterday, but for the disciples of today and tomorrow. He is not only the founder of the Hare Krishna movement, but the acharya, the spiritual master upon whom all other teachers base their life and teaching. Regarding Srila Prabhupada as your guru, and carefully studying his books, you can discuss any questions that may arise with your guide. By understanding the standard characteristics of an initiating spiritual master from the scriptures and the founder-*acharya's* commentaries, you will know what qualities to look for in your own prospective guru.

Although you will hear from many senior and advanced devotees, it is not recommended for you to regard anyone in particular as your future guru until you have had time to become fully acquainted with the life of a devotee. Sometimes at least one year is recommended for this foundational stage; others advise around six months. There are some adherents that are certainly ready for initiation within a relatively short time, while others take longer to come to their decision. There is no maximum duration of such a formation period, and care should be taken that a lifelong decision is not rushed. On the other hand, if the decades are passing by with the prospect of initiation always kept at a distance, it may be time to seriously consider the exact nature of one's reluctance. Of course, the difficulty may be that one is unable to follow the requirements for initiation. In that case one's personal goals may be in need of adjustment. Better not to be initiated than to take that step in denial of one's actual conviction and ability.

Upon maintaining the standard of sixteen rounds and four regulative principles for the required amount of time – in some places one year, in others eighteen months or two years - may you then seriously begin to develop a relationship with a senior Vaishnava with a view to taking initiation.

Part Six | The practical path of initiation

# The Disciple Course

In order to ensure that you and others get comprehensive information on the many different aspects of initiation you may be requested to attend a course of classes on the subject. This course includes subjects that you may have not heard about before and will help to prepare you to take the next step. You will learn more about the qualifications of a guru, the significance of initiation, how to relate to your guru and what to expect from him, the characteristics of a disciple and some episodes from Vaishnava history. The course also touches on the particulars of what acceptance of a guru practically means in a modern context within an international society such as ISKCON. The course also touches on what may go wrong in the guru-disciple relationship and therefore what pitfalls to avoid.

The course usually runs at least once every year and is well advertised beforehand. In some regions of the ISKCON world it is a compulsory part of the procedure for becoming an initiated disciple. Although such courses have been offered locally for some years, there have been recent efforts to standardise the teachings throughout the ISKCON world, and an online course is now available.

At some stage you will be given a 'Pre-Initiation Exam' to complete. It consists of some questions that Srila Prabhupada himself wanted initiation candidates to answer, and they are quite easy. You are allowed to answer the questions at home, in your own time, and by referring to Bhagavad-gita, a copy of which you may have open beside you as you answer the questions. There is no time limit for the exam. The exam paper will also ask you for confirmation that you have read one statement and one essay that describe Srila Prabhupada's unique position within our Vaishnava community. These have been prepared by ISKCON's GBC. The GBC statement can be found as an appendix to the pre-initiation exam and the essay, entitled 'Harmonizing ISKCON's Lines of Authority', can be found by searching the internet. Printed copies may also be available from your local centre.

Once you have completed the exam, you can hand it to your local temple authority. Around this time, you may also wish to declare your interest in becoming initiated and let the relevant persons in your local temple know. It doesn't mean that you have definitely decided to become initiated, nor that if you do, who you have chosen as your guru, but it does mean that the relevant person has understood your intentions. Perhaps this step will also involve you being registered formally, with your name and details being taken by the local temple president or his representative. Having your details and understanding your intentions will mean that your local authority will be fully informed when you do make a decision.

# Testing and being tested

Your guide will continue to encourage you to listen to Srila Prabhupada's recorded lectures, carefully read his books, and in general discover for yourself the teachings of Krishna consciousness directly as taught by the founder-*acharya*. This hearing from Srila Prabhupada is crucial, since he is our perfect example of a guru, both in words and living example. Initiation means to be initiated by someone who is a follower of Srila Prabhupada in his teachings and behaviour, so study of Srila Prabhupada will enable you to understand what exemplary teaching and behaviour is. You will be able to make a comparison of any other Vaishnava with the perfect example of Srila Prabhupada.

You will probably know some advanced senior Vaishnavas in whose company you feel particularly inspired and encouraged. You will have listened to them carefully, studied their lives, and felt uplifted by their words and example. Although you will continue to receive the blessings of such teachings and inspiration from these and many other Vaishnavas, for the purposes of initiation, you will be required to choose only one as your initiating guru.

There are a number of senior Vaishnavas who act as gurus within ISKCON, each of whom has been approved for the role both by a local committee and ISKCON's international governing body. Although a range of opinions exist on the validity of such an approval process, the procedure has endured, albeit with certain modifications. While it is customary for an aspirant to select a guru from those already functioning as such, it is by no means mandatory. In the ultimate sense, a guru becomes regarded as such by the aspirations and estimation of the disciple. It is therefore fitting that the disciple chooses the guru and institutional approval applied retrospectively. At the time of writing, this is not an entirely uncommon course of events.

# An 'Aspiring disciple'

Once you have settled that question, and upon your satisfactory completion of the pre-initiation exam, and in consultation with your guide, you can begin the next period as an 'aspiring disciple'. You should not become an aspiring disciple without informing your guide. You must inform your guide when you feel the time is right for you to cultivate a relationship with someone you wish to regard as your guru. Generally speaking, your guide will be positive about your decision. He or she will be encouraging you to begin this next stage, but also helping you to reflect on the inner resolution involved, as well as the life-long responsibilities you will be taking on.

At this time, it would also be wise to discuss your aspirations with anyone in your life who might be affected by your impending spiritual commitment. Although your immediate family may be aware of certain changes that have been taking place in your life, they may not fully understand the implications for them. It's important that you talk about it with them. If your diet changes drastically, for instance, that will affect the family meals and the emotional exchanges that take place. The same is true of family visits and invitations to the home of friends. Similarly, in the following of other regulative principles, those who might be affected should be sensitively informed. Some branches of ISKCON may request a written letter of consent from a spouse, or parents. You will need to check on this beforehand.

At the time when you formally become an aspiring disciple, a period of testing the guru and being tested by him will begin. In some parts of ISKCON this may last for quite some time. During this period of testing, your aspirations to become a disciple, your understanding of yourself as a spiritual practitioner, and the prospective guru's acceptance of you, all continue to grow. Since it is also a time when many realisations develop within you, previous conceptions are challenged, and sometimes adherence to basic practises increase or decrease in strength it will, on average, require a longer period for you to adequately prepare. Previous experiences have shown a decrease in preparation time to be inadequate, so most ISKCON centres are now asking for a period of more than a year be allowed before initiation takes place.

You should now write to the senior Vaishnava asking if you can begin ongoing correspondence with a view to developing a relationship of teacher-student and possibly guru-disciple. When permission is given a 'testing period' begins.

# Mutual scrutiny

Your duty as a prospective initiate is to carefully scrutinise the instructions and personal behaviour of the senior Vaishnava in order to ascertain how faithfully he represents Srila Prabhupada in word and deed. You are looking for the many devotional qualities you've learned about up to this point as well as commitment to Srila Prabhupada's mission and care for others. In addition to your own observation and discussions with the Vaishnava's senior disciples, you will also need to talk to other senior devotees. All scriptures recommend this period of examination; it should not be dispensed with due to any reason. Only when you have adequately tested your prospective guru, and he has tested you, or asked others to test you, will the relationship become strong.

Testing questions to put to your own prospective guru should also include enquiries on how often he regularly corresponds with his disciples, and offers them relevant and helpful instruction. You need to ascertain how often he visits your country (or your part of the country) and how he tends to deal with principal life questions such as marriage, studies, employment, family life, child-rearing and so on. You should satisfy yourself that your prospective guru has factually been successful in helping his other disciples move forward in spiritual life and that he will have adequate time and inclination to teach and assist you if you become his disciple. If he already has many disciples whom he does not instruct personally, then you must look for his concern to either establish or endorse a system to care for his disciples. Somehow he must make some kind of regular assessment of his disciples' progress within an existing system.

You should also look to see whether he has formed healthy relationships with his own peers, and that he is responsive to the GBC, the governing body of ISKCON. You should also check to see whether he has tried hard to push forward the *sankirtan* movement and that he has attracted new members through his efforts.

During this period he will also test you in order to understand your suitability for discipleship. This may be done through correspondence, personal interview or referring to others. After an indefinite period of time, your faith may have developed to the point where you decide that you would like to formalise your relationship and take initiation as a disciple of the person you now fully regard as your guru.

# Acting in the relationship

There now begins a period of acting in the relationship of aspiring disciple and prospective guru. During this period you are continuing to allow yourself to be tested by the guru and should be prepared for anything this might entail. In consultation with your guide you may begin reciting your prospective guru's *pranam* verse in addition to Srila Prabhupada's *pranam* verse, offering flowers or incense to his picture in your home, (somewhere separate from the main altar on which you offer your food), and assisting him with various services as and when possible. This period should last a minimum of six months. Please note that the offering of food to the guru's picture should properly begin only after formal initiation has taken place. Until then, you can continue to offer your food to Srila Prabhupada. At any stage prior to the day of initiation you may change your mind about accepting a guru. You may also change your choice of guru.

# Recommendation

Your guide will naturally check to see if you've taken all relevant issues into consideration and whether you seem ready for the initiation. When he or she is satisfied, he will ask the temple president, the initiation committee, or the congregation director, whoever is appropriate in your local area, to write a letter of recommendation to your prospective guru. No initiation may take place without such a letter from your local authorities. Once the recommendation has been sent, the decision to offer initiation, as well as the time and place, is in the hands of your prospective guru.

Your local authority needs to be satisfied that you have met all the requirements pertaining to all of the above stages before giving you a recommendation. In addition to this, they will have concerns about:

1. Your maturity and ability to seriously fulfil responsibility which ensue from initiation
2. The quality of your relationship with other devotees generally
3. Steadiness in the main activities of *bhakti-yoga*
4. Attendance whenever possible of group meetings, temple festivals, kirtans and classes
5. Involvement in some form of devotional service to the mission of Srila Prabhupada.

At the time of writing, it is the temple president of a registered ISKCON temple or centre that formally processes your application for initiation. The regional ISKCON congregational director can also do this in the absence of a local temple president. In some locations there may be an additional registered ISKCON entity that has been authorised to do this. ISKCON law does not permit that a guru initiate in the absence of a Letter of Recommendation from the local temple president or similar authority. This has been the case since the movement's earliest days.

# Support

You should consider that whatever standards you meet before initiation will need to be maintained afterwards, too. You will require help to remain steady in your spiritual life. There are varying standards of practise amongst the initiated congregation. In fact it is sometimes observed that initiated devotees have strayed from their previously good practise and slipped into bad habits without anyone asking them how they were doing. So different ISKCON centres have felt the need to clarify and reiterate the essentials of maintaining a healthy spiritual balance and delivering support where needed.

Although upon taking initiation you will be required to promise publicly to chant sixteen rounds and follow the four regulative principles, you will not be asked to promise to rise early in the morning or to go for preaching service, or to raise funds for the mission. Neither will you be asked to contribute funds in order to become initiated. However, items like these are all corollary functions that serve your main promises. They are helpful for strong spiritual life and were certainly important enough for Srila Prabhupada to ask devotees to do them. In fact, there was no question of not doing these things in Srila Prabhupada's time. It was unheard of for an initiated devotee to rise after six in the morning, or to not attempt some form of *sankirtan*, or, if they were working householders, to fail to make a financial contribution.

In order to ensure those essential elements are not lost to the Vaishnava community; to protect the spiritual life of all initiates, and to ensure our strong and continued growth as a movement, your local temple or equivalent authority may remind you, occasionally, of the duties and responsibilities incumbent upon you as an initiated member of the Society.

# The Day of initiation

On the day of initiation you will be promising to follow the regulative principles and to chant sixteen rounds every day. You may also be promising to read Srila Prabhupada's books and to remain faithful to his society. Your guru will give a talk either on the significance of initiation or on the ten offences to the Holy Name. Three strands of tulasi beads will be placed on your neck. You will be asked to perform acaman – a purifying ritual involving sipping water and saying a mantra. You will then be called forward to make your obeisances to Srila Prabhupada and to your guru. Then you will be asked to recite the vows. You'll be handed your chanting beads, and then given a name ending in dasa or dasi, indicating that you are now initiated. A fire sacrifice follows during which you'll join in the chanting of prayers to the members of the Vaishnava parampara and the Deities. During the fire sacrifice you will be directed to offer grains into the flames. It is traditional for the new disciple to beg for some alms to give to the spiritual master immediately after the fire sacrifice.

Some months before the initiation takes place, you can ask your mentor to show you how to perform acaman and to check your pronunciation of the prayers to the parampara.

# Second initiation

Being offered the Gayatri mantra and other Pancharatrika mantras constitute Second Initiation within ISKCON. Known colloquially as

Brahmana Initiation, it is normally offered at some time after the first initiation, sometimes one or two years afterwards. Second initiation is not compulsory nor is it universally given to all who have received first initiation.

While requirements differ regionally, and even from one guru to another, there are a commonly agreed range of qualifications. A greater level of maturity and scriptural knowledge is required, together with stability in spiritual practice, personal and ritual cleanliness, and an aspiration to further dedication. Other qualities looked for may be a clear demonstration humility in daily behaviour, respect in dealings with fellow Vaishnavas and an attitude of service.

Srila Prabhupada requested that candidates for second initiation sit an exam based on several of his main books: Bhagavad-gita As It Is, *Shri Isopanishad*, The Nectar of Instruction and The Nectar of Devotion (Rupa Goswami's *Upadeshamrita* and *Bhakti Rasamrita Sindhu*, respectively). He also required that they be conversant with his 'small books' such as The Perfection of Yoga and Krishna Consciousness, the Topmost Yoga System.

While this requirement has not been instituted internationally, there may be regional tests for knowledge of the standard books. You may need to enquire from your guide.

At the time of initiation you will be promising to recite additional mantras three times a day, at sunrise, noon and sunset. There are no 'hard and fast rules' for the chanting of the maha-mantra, but there a number of rules for the chanting of the *Gayatri*. For details of these you may consult your most knowledgeable local brahmana.

# Appendix 1
# Becoming a disciple: A self-test

**Use this together with chapters 13, 46 & 49**

1. What attracts me to this person? Am I attracted to the philosophy, the tradition, or him?
2. Am I star-struck by his personal charisma and showmanship, his singing and speaking, his cleverness? His robes?
3. He is a guru for other people – but what particularly makes him right for me?
4. Will he make efforts to help me make spiritual progress?
5. Is my opinion of him swayed by others?
6. Do I know him well enough?
7. Am I motivated deep down by fear or love?
8. Is my response to this person primarily emotional, intellectual, or an intuitive resonance?
9. What would persuade me to trust him more than I trust myself?
10. Am I looking for a parent figure to relieve me of the responsibility of my life?
11. Am I looking for a group where I feel I can belong, and be taken care of in return for doing what I'm told?
12. Am I moving towards something I'm drawn to, or running away from my life as it is?
13. What am I giving up in order to become a disciple? How do I feel about that?
14. Am I willing to commit to the requirements of the guru-disciple

relationship? Do I have the necessary determination?

15. Am I responsible and reliable? Can I be trusted with any other commitments I make?

16. Am I willing to alter the habits of a lifetime in order to be a disciple?

17. Do I idealise this person? Or am I moved to reduce him to my own level? What is my approach to him?

18. When I'm with him, do I feel I'm with a saviour figure, a friend, a parent?

19. Am I ready to learn from him? Can I place questions before him that may make me appear foolish?

20. Can I allow myself to be vulnerable with him?

21. Am I ready to be guided and, if necessary, corrected?

22. How would I feel if he pointed out my weaknesses? Would I become resentful?

23. Do I feel that this person is someone who can occupy the place of guru in my life?

24. Is this a relationship that I can maintain for life?

25. Am I convinced of the philosophy, theology, morals and ethics such that I can follow them indefinitely?

26. If I have philosophical misconceptions or deep-seated attachments, am I prepared to have them challenged?

27. Do I have any lingering doubts that need attention? Am I prepared to expose them?

28. Will I be a disappointment to my guru or a cause for his unhappiness?

29. Can I be a credit to him and assist him in his service to his guru?"

# Appendix 2

# Becoming a disciple: A Checklist

1. Please read through the chapter *Steps towards the Big Step* and see how far you have managed to incorporate the regular Vaishnava activities into your life. Don't become despondent if there appears to be gaps, much progress can be achieved with even minor adjustments.

2. Read through chapter 48, *Testing the Guru,* and *Appendix 3: The Guru – A Checklist* and make sure you have understood the contents.

3. Answer the following questions. You don't have to submit this to anyone, it is your self-test as an aspirant disciple:

    a. How are your daily, weekly and monthly practises? Which would you rate as 'strong' and which are 'weak?'

    b. Are you generally steady in your practise?

    c. Are you completing your sixteen rounds?

    d. Are the four regulative principles easy to follow or do you struggle?

    e. How would you say you're doing with the additional items on the list of The Regulative Principles? (chapter 45)

    f. To what extent have you incorporated the Elements of Dharma in your life? (chapter 45)

    g. Do you understand what the Ten Offenses against the Holy Name are and do you avoid them? (Appendix 4)

    h. Do you attend temple festivals?

i.  Do you listen to classes by Srila Prabhupada?

j.  Do you have a regular service to Srila Prabhupada's ISKCON mission?

k.  How are your relationships with others in your local group?

l.  How many devotees are you in regular connection with apart from your local group members?

m.  Do you have a 'spiritual guide' with whom you meet regularly?

n.  Have you attended the Guru and Disciple course?

o.  Have you completed the Pre-initiation Exam and handed it in?

p.  Do you have written permission from your next of kin?

q.  Have you read the essay *Harmonizing ISKCON's Lines of Authority*?

r.  Have you carefully tested your prospective guru using the guidance you've been given?

s.  Have you reflected on your own worthiness as a prospective disciple?

t.  Have you carefully considered your ability to uphold the vows you'll be making at initiation?

u.  Do you have written confirmation from your prospective guru that you can begin your relationship as teacher-student? (with a view to formalising this as guru-disciple in the future)

# Appendix 3
# The Guru: A Checklist

Here is a brief checklist to help you with your testing of the guru. Use in conjunction with chapters 13-17 and 48.

## Education

1. Has he studied Vedic literature sufficiently to become a teacher?
2. Has he become an expert in any particular literature?
3. Has he passed any examinations?
4. Can he recite verses from memory?
5. Does he demonstrate his learning by references when he gives classes?
6. Is he faithful to Srila Prabhupada's translations and commentaries in his presentations?
7. Are you sure that he does not unduly emphasize any particular portion of the philosophy but provides a balanced presentation?
8. Is he knowledgeable of Deity worship?
9. Does he perform Deity worship himself?
10. Can he conduct ceremonies and teach others how to celebrate festivals?
11. Does he know how to cook for Krishna?
12. Does he know the standard Vaishnava songs and prayers?

## Personal example

1. Is he faithfully following Srila Prabhupada's instructions regarding *sadhana-bhakti*, the daily practise of chanting sixteen rounds on beads, studying the Vaishnava literature and discussing it with others, engaging in worship and kirtan and so on?
2. Does he exhibit the devotional qualities you have read and heard about?
3. Is he controlled and moderated in his speech, eating and sleeping?
4. Is he free from attachment to money, power or sexualised speech?
5. Would you describe him as having the 'spirit of service?'
6. Does he personally exemplify the qualities you'd like to have?
7. His personal example should make you aware of your own obstacles – is this happening?

## Association

1. Does he have strong friendships with his peers?
2. Are there any devotees he considers to be his superiors?
3. Does he meet with them for guidance?
4. Does he deal affectionately with other Vaishnavas?
5. Is he helpful to those who are not his disciples?

## Teaching

1. Does he personally teach you, or can you regularly access his teaching?
2. Does he encourage learning, and does he make it enjoyable?
3. When he answers your questions do you feel as if your doubts have been removed?
4. After a class or talk from him you feel inspired and determined?
5. Does his teaching leave you enthusiastic? Hopeful?

6. Apart from his guru, who were his teachers?
7. Has he been blessed by his seniors to teach officially and accept disciples?
8. What are his other disciples like?

## Mission

1. Is he committed to advancing the mission of his own guru?
2. Does he personally exert himself in establishing Krishna consciousness in new places?
3. Does he advocate standard preaching activity such as street chanting, book distribution, *prasadam* distribution, hall festivals and home gatherings?
4. Does he answer the questions of new enquirers, correspond with them, or host a website for introducing visitors to Krishna consciousness?
5. Is he successful at attracting new people to Krishna?

## Guidance

1. Does he have time to offer you guidance and encouragement in addition to teaching?
2. Is he somewhat experienced in offering help at important points in life such as times of transition, bereavement, adversity or spiritual challenge?
3. Does he have the ability to care for you in addition to his existing disciples?
4. Does he reply to correspondence or offer some other way of regular connection?
5. Does he schedule personal visits to your country, at least annually?
6. Has he successfully helped others in their spiritual lives and does he have a good number of balanced, happy and successful disciples?

7. How many of his disciples do you personally know?
8. Will you be able to take instructions from him if you choose him as your guru?
9. Can you trust his guidance?
10. Would he be pleased if you surpassed his knowledge or service?

## Personal qualities

1. Is he generally happy?
2. Is he free from the tendency to criticise others?
3. In conversations and actions, does he direct attention to himself or to others?
4. Is he free from distracting eccentricities of behaviour, speech, eating or dress?
5. Is he emotionally balanced or is he prone to spells of negativity, anger or depression?
6. Does he request large sums of money as '*dakshina*'?
7. What is his personal history? How much do you know?

## Team player

1. Does your prospective guru function well as a member of a team?
2. Does he become involved in joint projects with his peers?
3. Does he generally work in a spirit of cooperation with local leaders?
4. Is he respectful of, and responsible to, a governing body that supervises him?

# Appendix 4

# The Ten Offences to the Holy Name

**The offenses against chanting the holy name are as follows:**

1. To blaspheme the devotees who have dedicated their lives for propagating the holy name of the Lord.
2. To consider the names of the demigods like Lord Siva or Lord Brahma to be equal to, or independent of, the name Lord Visnu.
3. To disobey the orders of the spiritual master.
4. To blaspheme the Vedic literature or literature in pursuance of the Vedic version.
5. To consider the glories of chanting Hare Krsna to be imagination.
6. To give some interpretation on the holy name of the Lord.
7. To commit sinful activities on the strength of chanting the holy name of the Lord.
8. To consider chanting of Hare Krsna one of the auspicious ritualistic activities offered in the Vedas as fruitive activities (karma-kanda).
9. To instruct a faithless person about the glories of the holy name.
10. To not have complete faith in the chanting of the holy names and to maintain material attachments, even after understanding so many instructions on this matter.

Every devotee who claims to be a Vaisnava must guard against these offenses in order to quickly achieve the desired success.

# *Bibliography*

**After the Ecstasy the Laundry, how the heart grows wise on the spiritual path,** Jack Kornfield. Bantam Books, 2000.

**Apasampradayas, Deviant Vaishnava Sects, The,** Suhotra Swami.

**Art of Sadhana, a Guide to Daily Devotion,** Swami B.P. Puri Maharaja. Mandala Publishing.

**As Good as God, the guru in Gaudiya Vaishnavism,** Dr. Mans Broo. ABO – Akademi University Press, 2003.

**Feet of Clay, A Study of Gurus,** Anthony Storr. Harper and Collins, 1997.

**Follow the Angels, the Path of Dedication,** Swami B.R.Sridhara. Mandala Publishing Group.

**Governance and Authority in the Roman Catholic Church, beginning a conversation.** Edited by Noel Timms and Kenneth Wilson.SPCK, 2000.

**Halfway up the Mountain, the Error of Premature Claims to Enlightenment,** Mariana Caplan PhD. HOHM Press, 1999.

**Heart of Krishna, Vaishnava Aparadha and the Path of Spiritual Caution,** Bhakti Promode Puri Goswami Maharaja.Mandala Media.

**History and Literature of the Gaudiya Vaishnavas and their relation to other mediaeval Vaishnava Schools, The.** Dr. Sambidananda Das Bhaktishastri. Sree Gaudiya Math 1991.

**How to close your church in a decade,** David Cohen and Stephen Gaukroger. Scripture Union, London, 1992.

**Impact of Shri Ramanujacharya on Temple Worship,** Smt. S. Jagannathan. Nag Publishers, Delhi, 1994.

# Bibliography

**Introduction to the Pancaratra and the Ahirbudhnya Samhita,** F. Otto Schrader. The Adyar Library and Research Centre, 1995.

**Is Religion Dangerous?** Keith Ward. Lion, 2006.

**Jaiva Dharma** by Srila Bhaktivinode Thakur, translated Kesidamana Das. Brihat Mridanga Press, 2004.

**Living Still in Sound,** various authors. New Jaipur Press, 1985

**Longing for God, Seven Paths of Christian Devotion,** Richard Foster and Gayle Beebe. Hodder and Stoughton, 2009.

**Madhurya Kadambini,** translation Sarvabhavana Das.

**Modern Hindu Personalism, the history, life and thought of Bhaktisiddhanta Saraswati.** Ferdinando Sardella. Oxford University Press, 2013.

**Prakrita Rasa Aranya Chedini, Cutting the Jungle of Misconception,** Swami B.G. Narasinga. Gosai Publishers, 2004.

**Rise and Fall of the Nine o' Clock Service: A Cult within the Church?** Roland Howard. Continuum-3PL, 1996.

**Sat Kriya Sar Dipika,** Gopala Bhatta Goswami. Translation Bhanu Swami, 1999.

**Shattered Vows, Exodus from the Priesthood,** David Rice. The Black Staff Press, Belfast, 1990.

**Shoes outside the Door: Desire, Devotion and Excess at the San Fransisco Zen Center,** Michael Downing. Counterpoint Books, 2002.

**Singing the Body of God: The Hymns of Vedanta Deshika in their South Indian Tradition,** Steven Paul Hopkins. Oxford University Press, New York, 2002.

**Soul Friendship, Celtic insights into spiritual mentoring,** Ray Simpson. Hodder and Stoughton, 1999.

**Shri Brahma Samhita,** Srila Bhaktisiddhanta Saraswati Thakur.

**Shri Chaitanya Vaisnavism and its sources,** Dr. K.P.Sinha. Punthi Pustak, Kolkata, 2001.

**Shri Gaura-Govindarcana Smarana Paddhati,** Dhyanachandra Goswami. Translation Haridham Das, 1993.

**Shri Guru and his Grace, a guide to the genuine spiritual master,** Swami B.R.Sridhara. Guardian of Devotion Press, 1983.

**Shri Hari Bhakti Vilasa, Vilasas I and II, and Pancha Samskara,** Kesidamana Das. Brihat Mrdanga Press, 2005.

**Srimad Bhagavatam, eleventh canto,** translated by disciples of His Divine Grace A.C. Bhaktivedanta Swami Prabhupada. Bhaktivedanta Book Trust, 1988.

**Tattva Sandarbha** by Srila Jiva Goswami. Translated by Gopiparanadhana Daṣ. Giriraja Publishing, 2013.

**The Authorised Shri Chaitanya Saraswata** *Parampara*, Swami B.G.Narasinga. Gosai Publishers, 1998.

**The Cult at the end of the world, the incredible story of Aum,** David E. Kaplan & Andrew Marshall. Hutchinson, London, 1996.

**The Dignity of Difference, how to avoid the clash of civilizations,** Rabbi Jonathan Sacks. Continuum, 2004.

**The Guru and what Prabhupada Said,** Virabahu Das, second edition, 2012.

**The Guru Papers, Masks of Authoritarian Power,** Joel Kramer and Diana Alstad. Frog Books, 1993

**The Guru Question, the perils and rewards of choosing a spiritual teacher,** Mariana Caplan PhD. Sounds True, 2011.

**The Philosophy and Religion of Shri Chaitanya,** O.B.L. Kapoor. Munshiram Manoharlal Pvt, Delhi, 1977.

**The Principle of Shri Guru and Service to Shri Guru, an examination of the role of the spiritual guide and the disciple in Gaudiya Vaishnava theology,** Svami B.V.Madhava PhD.

**The Purpose Driven Church, Growth without compromising your message and mission,** Rick Warren. Zondervan, 1996.

**The Spiritual Master and the Disciple,** quotations of His Divine Grace A.C. Bhaktivedanta Swami Prabhupada, compiled and edited by Subhananda Das Brahmachari. Bhaktivedanta Book Trust, 1995.

**The Vedas,** Shri Candrasekharendra Saraswati. Bharatiya Vidya Bhavan, 2000.

**When Religion Becomes Evil, Five Warning Signs,** Charles Kimball. Harper-Collins, 2002.

**Who is Prabhupada? The first complete delineation on** *Guru-tattva*, *R. Sadhu.*

# About the author

Kripamoya Das teaches courses and classes on the *Bhagavad-gita* and *Practical Bhakti* around the UK and Europe. He is a regular speaker at the numerous kirtan groups that have sprung up in many cities. He provides encouragement and support as a mentor; conducts celebrations such as weddings, and occasionally guides groups of pilgrims to holy places in India. He lives close to the Bhaktivedanta Manor in Hertfordshire with his wife Guru Charana Padma, and has three grown children, Jahnavi, Tulasi and Mali. He was born in 1956 and has been a disciple of His Divine Grace A.C. Bhaktivedanta Swami Prabhupada since 1975.